RELATED KAPLAN BOOKS

College Admissions and Financial Aid
Access America's Guide to Studying in the U.S.A.
Guide to College Selection
Kaplan/Newsweek College Catalog
Parent's Guide to College Admissions
Scholarships
What to Study: 101 Fields in a Flash
You Can Afford College
The Yale Daily News Guide to Succeeding in College

Test Preparation
ACT
ACT Essential Review
SAT & PSAT
SAT & PSAT Essential Review
SAT Math Workbook
SAT or ACT? Test Your Best
SAT II: Biology
SAT II: Chemistry
SAT II: Mathematics
SAT II: Writing

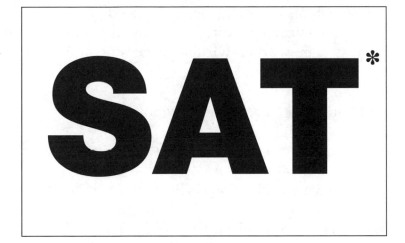

VERBAL WORKBOOK

By the Staff of
Kaplan Educational Centers

Simon & Schuster

Kaplan Books
Published by Kaplan Educational Centers and Simon & Schuster
1230 Avenue of the Americas
New York, NY 10020

"Brightening the City," by Juan Carlos Langlois, *The Unesco Courier*, April 1992.

"Earth's Ozone Shield under Threat," by Francis Bequette, *The Unesco Courier,* June 1992.

From *Life Itself* by Francis Crick. Copyright © Francis Crick 1981. Reproduced with permission of Felicity Bryan Literary Agency.

Editor: Donna Ratajczak
Cover Design: Cheung Tai
Desktop Publishing Manager: Michael Shevlin
Managing Editor: Brent Gallenberger
Executive Editor: Del Franz
Executive Director, Pre-College Programs: Seppy Basili

Special thanks to: Laura Barnes, Maureen Blair, Michael Cader, Gerard Capistrano, Gordon Drummond, Kate Foster, Amparo Graf, Jay Johnson, Liza Kleinman, Annaliza Martinez, Kiernan McGuire, Marie Mockett, Krista Pfeiffer, and John Polstein.

Manufactured in the United States of America
Published simultaneously in Canada

July 1998
10 9 8 7 6 5 4 3 2

ISBN 0-684-84984-4
ISSN 1081-0897

CONTENTS

How to Use This Book vii

A Special Note for International Students.........................ix

SAT Analogies

Introduction to SAT Analogies 3

Practice Set 1 7

Practice Set 2 11

Practice Set 3 15

Practice Set 4 19

Practice Set 5 23

Practice Set 6 27

Practice Set 7 31

Practice Set 8 35

Practice Set 9 39

Practice Set 10 43

SAT Sentence Completions

Introduction to SAT Sentence Completions 49

Practice Set 1 53

Practice Set 2 57

Practice Set 3 61

Practice Set 4 65

Practice Set 5 69

Practice Set 6 75

Practice Set 7 79

Practice Set 8 83

Practice Set 9 87

Practice Set 10 91

Continued

SAT Critical Reading

Introduction to SAT Critical Reading 97

Practice Set 1 99

Practice Set 2 103

Practice Set 3 107

Practice Set 4 111

Practice Set 5 117

Practice Set 6 123

Practice Set 7 127

Practice Set 8 131

SAT Vocabulary

How to Use the SAT Word and Root Lists 139

SAT Word Lists 140

SAT Root Lists 170

Practice Tests

Practice Test A 179

Practice Test A Answers and Explanations 197

Practice Test B 211

Practice Test B Answers and Explanations 229

Compute Your Score 241

HOW TO USE THIS BOOK

Since a great way to prepare yourself for the SAT is to practice answering testlike questions, this workbook gives you hundreds of sample verbal problems to work on.

Practice Sets

Most of this workbook is divided into practice sets corresponding to the three verbal question types you'll get on the SAT: Analogies, Sentence Completions, and Critical Reading. There's an introduction for each of these question types that briefly goes over the key strategies you need to effectively answer each question type. Write your answers directly in the book on the answer ovals provided.

Order of Difficulty

With the exception of Critical Reading, questions within each practice set are arranged by order of difficulty—just like on the real SAT. You should practice with all three question types, paying attention to the recommended time for each practice test. Score cards are provided to help you track your progress.

Explanations

We've included explanations for every question in this workbook. Use these explanations to figure out why you got questions wrong and how to avoid making the same mistakes in the future. You should also look at the explanations for questions that you got right—especially if you weren't sure and guessed—to find out the best way to answer questions. You'll also notice intervals where we give you words and their definitions—use these helpful sidebars to learn new words and flex your vocabulary muscles on the SAT.

Sample Tests

This workbook contains verbal sections of two sample SAT tests—for a total of six verbal sections. You should take these under timed, test-like conditions.

Kaplan's Word List and Root List

Finally, there's a reference section at the end of the book that gives you a Word and Root List to help you build your SAT-level vocabulary for Test Day.

> Note: For more tips on the verbal portion of the new SAT, pick up Kaplan's *SAT & PSAT 1999*. For a last-minute, well-organized practice, look for Kaplan's *SAT & PSAT Essential Review*. If you have any questions about the SAT, or want more information about Kaplan, call us at 1–800–KAP–TEST.

A Special Note for
International
Students

If you are not from the United States, but are considering attending a U.S. college or university, here's what you'll need to get started:

- If English is not your first language, start there. You'll probably need to take the Test of English as a Foreign Language (TOEFL) and the Test of Written English (TWE), or show some other evidence that you are fully proficient in English in order to complete an academic degree program. Colleges and universities in the United States will differ on what they consider to be an acceptable TOEFL score. A minimum TOEFL score of 550 or better is often expected by the more prestigious and competitive institutions. Because American undergraduate programs require all students to take a certain number of general education courses, all students, even math and computer science students, need to be able to communicate well in spoken and written English.

- You might also need to take the SAT or the ACT. Many undergraduate institutions in the United States require both the SAT and TOEFL of international students.

- There are over 2,700 accredited colleges and universities in the United States, so selecting the correct undergraduate school can be a confusing task for anyone. You will need to get help from a good advisor or at least a good college guide that explains the different types of programs and gives you some information on how to choose wisely. Since admission to many undergraduate programs is quite competitive, you might also want to select three or four colleges and complete applications for each school.

- You should begin the application process at least a year in advance. An increasing number of schools accept applications year-round. In any case, find out the application deadlines, and plan accordingly. Although September (the fall semester) is the traditional time to begin university study in the United States, at most schools you can also enter in January (the spring semester).

- Finally, you will need to obtain an I-20 Certificate of Eligibility in order to obtain an F-1 Student Visa to study in the United States. This you will request from the university. The school will send you the I-20 document once you have been accepted.

For details about admissions requirements, curriculum, and other vital information on top colleges and universities, see Kaplan's *Guide to College Selection*.

ACCESS AMERICA ENGLISH LANGUAGE PROGRAMS

If you need more help with English language learning, TOEFL preparation, or the complex process of university admissions, you may be interested in Kaplan's Access America® program.

Kaplan created Access America to assist international students and professionals who want enter the United States university system. The program was designed for students who hav received the bulk of their primary and secondary education outside the United States in a languag other than English. Access America also has programs for obtaining professional certification in th United States. A brief description of some of the help available through Access America follows.

The Access America Certificate Program in English for University Admission
The Access America Certificate Program in English for University Admission is a comprehensiv English launguage training program that prepares serious students for admission to an accredite American university. Using a content-based approach to studying English, this course trains studen in three main areas:

- Academic English for university admission
- TOEFL test-taking skills and strategies
- University admissions counseling and placement

This course is designed for international students at the high intermediate, advanced, and supe advanced levels of English proficiency who have as their end goal admission into a university degre program. Some American universities will accept Kaplan's Certificate of High Achievement ir English for University Admissions in lieu of a TOEFL score. This means that they trust the Kaplar Certificate as a reliable evaluation of a student's readiness for university work. A list of schools pro viding TOEFL waivers for Kaplan's certificate will be provided upon request.

In this course, students use actual material written for native speakers of English and work or improving the following critical skills:

(1) Listening and lecture note-taking skills

(2) Extended and rapid textbook reading skills

(3) Vocabulary enhancement for developing nativelike intuition about words

(4) Understanding and applying English grammar in a real context

(5) Effective use of a monolingual dictionary

(6) Time management skills for academic study

(7) Computer literacy and computer keyboarding skills

(8) Successfully taking the TOEFL (on paper and on computer) and other standardized test skills

(9) Functional conversation perfromance skills

(10) Learning strategies

Applying to Access America
To get more information, or to apply for admission to any of Kaplan's programs for international stu- dents or professionals, you can write to us at:

> Kaplan Educational Centers
> International Admissions Department
> 888 Seventh Avenue
> New York, NY 10106

You can call us at 1-800-527-8378 from within the United States, or at 1-212-262-4980 outside the United States. Our fax number is 1-212-957-1654. Our e-mail address is world@kaplan.com. You can also get more information or even apply through the Internet at http://www.kaplan.com/intl.

SAT Analogies

Analogies test your ability to define relationships between words. Analogies also test your knowledge of college-level vocabulary.

The Structure

You'll probably see thirteen Analogies in one of the two 30-minute Verbal sections and six Analogies in the other. Both sections also include Sentence Completions and Critical Reading.

Analogies are arranged in order of difficulty. The hardest questions are at the end of each set.

The Format

The directions for Analogies appear at the top of the questions. They look something like this:

> **Directions—Choose the lettered pair of words that is related in the same way as the pair in capital letters.**
> **Example:**
> FLAKE : SNOW ::
> (A) storm : hail
> (B) drop : rain
> (C) field : wheat
> (D) stack : hay
> (E) sky : cloud   Ⓐ ● Ⓒ Ⓓ Ⓔ

Kaplan's Method

Here's our simple 3-Step Method for doing Analogies.
- Build a bridge.
- Plug the bridge into the answer choices.
- Adjust the bridge if you need to.

1. Build a bridge. First, build a bridge between the two words in capital letters, the *stem words*. In the example above, your bridge might be: Snow is made of flake(s).

> Hint: A good bridge is a sentence that makes a strong, definite connection, such as "Snow is always made of flakes."

2. Plug the answer choices into the bridge. Take your bridge and plug in answer choices (A) through (E). The two words in the correct answer relate in the same way as the stem words.
- (A) Hail is made of storm(s). No.
- (B) Rain is made of drop(s). Yes.
- (C) Wheat is made of field(s). No.
- (D) Hay is made of stack(s). No.
- (E) Cloud is made of sky. No.

3. Adjust the bridge if you need to. If more than one answer fits your bridge, try building a different bridge. Here the only correct answer is (B), so there's no need for adjustments.

Hint: If more than one answer choice works, make your bridge more specific.

Pacing

You need to leave plenty of time for Critical Reading, so work systematically.
- Do the early, more basic Analogies quickly.
- Take no more than 40 seconds on any Analogy.

Hint: Stumped? Circle the question in your test book and skip it on your answer sheet. Come back if there's time after you've finished the whole section.

What If a Stem Word Could Be Two Parts of Speech?

If a stem word could be either a noun or a verb, how can you build a bridge? Look down the column below the word, and see what all the other words are.

Hint: In the same column, every word will be the same part of speech.

In the Analogy below, how do you know whether *peel* is a noun (a banana peel) or a verb (to peel a banana)?

BANANA : PEEL ::
(A) egg : crack
(B) carrot : uproot
(C) apple : core
(D) bread : slice
(E) corn : husk

Hint: Look at the answer choice words under *peel*. Four words—*crack, core, slice,* and *husk*—can be nouns or verbs. But answer choice (B) **uproot** must be a verb. Since all the words in the same column must be the same part of speech, you know *peel* is being used as a verb. So your bridge could be: When you peel a banana, you take off the skin.

What If You Don't Know a Stem Word?

In addition to testing your thinking skills, Analogies test your vocabulary. That's why it's important to study Kaplan's Word List and Root List, found at the back of this book.

Regardless of how hard you study, sometimes you won't know one or both stem words. If that happens, don't give up. Instead, focus on the answer choices and use the following strategies.

Analogy Strategy 1: Eliminate Answer Choices With Weak Bridges

Even without understanding the stem pair on an Analogy question, you can often tell which answer choices are likely to be right and which are probably wrong. Think of it this way: The stem pair in an SAT Analogy almost always has a strong bridge. The correct answer must have the same bridge, so it will have a strong bridge, too. By a "strong bridge" we mean a specific, definite connection. For example, the pair **STABLE : HORSE** has a strong bridge: "a **stable** is where you keep a **horse**." On the other hand, **STABLE : OATS** has a weak bridge. You may or may not find **oats** in a **stable**. As you do Analogy questions, you can safely eliminate such pairs with weak bridges because they can't be correct. Don't waste time thinking about them. Cross them out. Then focus on the answer choices that are more likely to be correct.

Analogy Strategy 2: Eliminate Pairs With Identical Bridges

There's another way of eliminating some wrong choices that's so obvious you might not think of it. If two choices have the same bridge, it follows that neither one can be more right than the other. And since they can't both be right, they must both be wrong.

Analogy Strategy 3: Look For a Strong Bridge

Since the correct answer has to have the same strong bridge as the stem pair, after you've eliminated choices with distinctly weak bridges, and after you've eliminated choices with identical bridges, it's a good guessing strategy to pick the choice with the strongest bridge.

Analogy Strategy 4: Work Backwards From the Answer Choices

Even if you're not sure what one of the stem words means, you always know that the two stem words are related to each other in some way. The five answer choices provide you with five ways in which the stem words **might** be related to each other. Work out bridges for the answer choices, then compare these with the stem pair. Some of the answer choices will seem unlikely given the stem word that you already know —these can be rejected.

   Keep in mind that you may not always be able to eliminate *all* the wrong answer choices. However, if you can eliminate any choices at all, it is worth your while to guess.

Analogies Checklist

✔ Use Kaplan's 3-Step Method: Build a bridge, plug it in, and adjust it if you need to.

✔ Spend no more than 40 seconds on even the hardest Analogy.

✔ If you don't know a stem word, try Analogy Strategies:
   • Eliminate answer choices with weak bridges.
   • Eliminate pairs with identical bridges.
   • Look for a strong bridge.
   • Work backwards from the answer choices.

✔ If all else fails, guess—as long as you can eliminate at least one wrong answer choice.

ANALOGIES—PRACTICE SET 1

Suggested Time: 7 minutes

Directions—Choose the lettered pair of words that is related in the same way as the pair in capital letters.

Example:
FLAKE : SNOW ::
(A)   storm : hail
(B)   drop : rain
(C)   field : wheat
(D)   stack : hay
(E)   sky : cloud   Ⓐ ● Ⓒ Ⓓ Ⓔ

1   TREE : FOREST ::
(A) bird : sky
(B) fish : sea
(C) star : galaxy
(D) mammal : land
(E) lake : river   Ⓐ Ⓑ Ⓒ Ⓓ Ⓔ

2   MARE : HORSE ::
(A) cat : dog
(B) shark : fish
(C) worm : snake
(D) lion : tiger
(E) ewe : sheep   Ⓐ Ⓑ Ⓒ Ⓓ Ⓔ

3   CEASE-FIRE : HOSTILITIES ::
(A) reckoning : probabilities
(B) truce : belligerents
(C) artillery : tanks
(D) campaign : strategies
(E) adjournment : proceedings   Ⓐ Ⓑ Ⓒ Ⓓ Ⓔ

4   FLORAL : FLOWERS ::
(A) perennial : plants
(B) morbid : cemeteries
(C) emotional : feelings
(D) moral : stories
(E) maniacal : men   Ⓐ Ⓑ Ⓒ Ⓓ Ⓔ

5   SEQUESTER : JUROR ::
(A) quarantine : patient
(B) cloister : convent
(C) parole : prisoner
(D) graduate : pupil
(E) elect : mayor   Ⓐ Ⓑ Ⓒ Ⓓ Ⓔ

6   VOID : EMPTY ::
(A) glut : prosperous
(B) system : organized
(C) answer : questioning
(D) ration : scarce
(E) intent : clear   Ⓐ Ⓑ Ⓒ Ⓓ Ⓔ

7   EVADE : STRAIGHTFORWARD ::
(A) leave : inviting
(B) enliven : animated
(C) flatten : smooth
(D) boast : modest
(E) assist : helpful   Ⓐ Ⓑ Ⓒ Ⓓ Ⓔ

8   FICKLE : INCONSISTENCY ::
(A) cloudy : warmth
(B) innate : capability
(C) worthy : heroism
(D) placid : calmness
(E) solid : order   Ⓐ Ⓑ Ⓒ Ⓓ Ⓔ

9   IMMATURE : DEVELOP ::
(A) tempestuous : explode
(B) unready : prepare
(C) superstitious : believe
(D) unfeasible : originate
(E) fortuitous : plan   Ⓐ Ⓑ Ⓒ Ⓓ Ⓔ

10   INDOLENT : SLOTH ::
(A) fertile : fecundity
(B) presumptuous : deviation
(C) miserable : tragedy
(D) appealing : delineation
(E) destructive : progress   Ⓐ Ⓑ Ⓒ Ⓓ Ⓔ

SCORECARD	
Number of Questions Right:	
Number of Questions Wrong:	
Number of Questions Omitted:	
Number of Correct Guesses:	
Number of Wrong Guesses:	
Time Used:	

Answers and Explanations

1 **C**—A strong bridge here might be: A **FOREST** *is made up of many* **TREES**.

When you plug it in to the answer choices, only (C) makes sense. A **galaxy** is made up of many **stars**.

There may be **birds** in the **sky**, **fish** in the **sea**, and **mammals** on **land**, but the sky, seas, and land aren't *made up of* these creatures. Finally, a **lake** and a **river** are two different kinds of bodies of water.

2 **E**—Bridge: *A* **MARE** *is a female* **HORSE**. The only answer choice that makes sense is (E)—A **ewe** is a female **sheep**.

If you knew that a **MARE** is a female **HORSE**, but you didn't know that a **ewe** is a female sheep, you could still have picked (E) by process of elimination. No other answer choice has the bridge "X is a female Y."

If you knew that a **MARE** is some type of **HORSE**, but you didn't know that it was a female horse, you could still have eliminated (A), (C), and (D), where the word pairs don't refer to the same kind of animal. Then you would guess between (B) and (E).

3 **E**—Bridge: *A* **CEASE-FIRE** *marks the end of* **HOSTILITIES**.

(B) is tempting, but the bridge doesn't fit. A **truce** marks the end of **belligerents**—no. A **truce** marks the end of fighting, but **belligerents** are the warring parties, and they don't disappear when you make a truce.

(E) An **adjournment** marks the end of **proceedings**. The answer choice fits.

---

cease-fire: temporary end to fighting
hostilities: warlike activities
adjournment: a temporary suspension
proceedings: activities or events
belligerents: warring parties or sides
reckoning: estimation or calculation
artillery: large-caliber firearms

---

4 **C**—Bridge: **FLORAL** *means "having to do with* **FLOWERS."**

In (A), **perennial** means having to do with special kinds of **plants**, but not with plants as a whole. In (B), **morbid** has to do with death, but not specifically with **cemeteries**. In (C), **emotional** means having to do with **feelings**. A good definition, but continue

to plug the bridge into the other choices.

(D) **Moral** means ethical, relating to principles of right and wrong, not having to do with **stories**. This connection is weak.

(E) **Maniacal** means having to do with **men**—no. Although the words look similar, "maniacal" has no relation to men. It's related to "mania."

---

perennial: coming back every year, as with perennial plants
morbid: referring to death or disease
maniacal: frantic or characterized by madness

---

5 **A**—The first bridge you thought of might have been: **JURORS** *get* **SEQUESTERED**. But that's a weak bridge because it's so general. So think again.

A strong bridge might be: *To* **SEQUESTER JURORS** *means to isolate them*. When you plug the bridge into the answer choices, (A) fits. To **quarantine patients** is to isolate them. This could be the answer, but check the other choices.

(B) **Cloister** might be tempting, but to cloister isn't to isolate a **convent**.

---

sequester: to set apart or segregate
quarantine: to isolate
cloister: to cut off from the world
convent: a place where nuns live
parole: to release a prisoner conditionally, before a sentence is fully served

---

6 **B**—To make your bridge you need to know that **void** is a noun and **empty** is an adjective. Remember the rule: All the words in the same column must be the same part of speech (see Introduction to Analogies, p. 1).

Since **system** and **intent** in column one can only be nouns, all words in the first column must be nouns. Since **prosperous** and **scarce** in column two can only be adjectives, all the words in the second column are adjectives.

Bridge: *Something* EMPTY *is a* VOID. Plug it into the answer choices:

(A) Something **prosperous** is a **glut**—doesn't make sense.

(B) Something **organized** is a **system**—yes.

(C) Something **questioning** is an **answer**—no.

KAPLAN

(D) Something **scarce** is a **ration**—no.
(E) Something **clear** is an **intent**—no.
(B) is the only possible answer.

> *prosperous: flourishing or wealthy*
> *glut: oversupply*
> *ration: allotment or share*

7 **D**—Bridge: *Someone who* **EVADES** *is not* **STRAIGHTFORWARD.**
When you plug it into all the answer choices, the only one that makes sense is (D): Someone who boasts is not modest.

> *evade: to avoid or go around something*
> *animated: lively*

8 **D**—Bridge: *To be* **FICKLE** *is to show* **INCONSISTENCY.**
Now plug the bridge into the answer choices.
(A) To be **cloudy** is to show **warmth**—no.
(B) To be **innate** is to show **capability**—no.
(C) To be **worthy** is to show **heroism.** Not necessarily. You can be worthy without displaying heroism.
(D) To be **placid** is to show **calmness**—definitely.
(E) To be **solid** is to show **order**—no.
So (C) is a possibility, but (D) is the stronger choice. Pick (D).

> *innate: essential or inborn*
> *placid: calm*

9 **B**—This bridge is: *Someone (or something)* **IMMATURE** *hasn't* **DEVELOPED.**
When you plug it in:
(A) Someone **tempestuous** hasn't **exploded.** Maybe or maybe not.
(B) Someone **unready** hasn't **prepared**—a possibility.
(C) Someone **superstitious** hasn't **believed**—no. Superstitious people *do* believe.
(D) Something **unfeasible** hasn't **originated**—no.
(E) Something **fortuitous** hasn't been **planned**—true. Here's another possibility.
To choose between (B) and (E), define the stem bridge a little more carefully. Someone who's **IMMATURE** hasn't **DEVELOPED** *yet*, but should.
(B) fits that bridge; someone who's **unready**—for the SAT, for example—hasn't **prepared** yet, but should.

But (E) doesn't work. It doesn't make sense to say: Something **fortuitous** hasn't **planned** yet.
So (B) is correct.

> *immature: not mature or developed*
> *tempestuous: stormy*
> *superstitious: believing in magic or chance*
> *unfeasible: impossible*
> *fortuitous: fortunate, lucky, occurring by chance*

10 **A**—The bridge is a definition: **SLOTH** *is the quality of being* **INDOLENT.**
Now plug the bridge into the answer choices.
(A) **Fecundity** is the quality of being **fertile.** True, so (A) has the same relationship as the stem pair.
(B) **Deviation** is the quality of being **presumptuous**—no. They have nothing to do with each other.
(C) **Tragedy** is the quality of being **miserable**—not quite. *Misery* is the quality of being miserable. Still, you might think (C) is a possibility.
(D) **Delineation** is the quality of being **appealing**—not so.
(E) **Progress** is the quality of being **destructive**—nonsense.
Even if you thought (C) was a possible answer, (A) is the stronger, clearer match.

> Hint: Sometimes a stem word has two meanings.

In this case, a **SLOTH** is also a lazy, slow-moving mammal. If your original stem bridge doesn't fit any answer choice, build a new bridge using the second meaning.

> *indolent: lazy*
> *sloth: laziness; also a type of tree-dwelling, slow-moving animal*
> *fecundity: the ability to reproduce or be fruitful*
> *fertile: fruitful*
> *tragedy: a disastrous event, a calamity*
> *presumptuous: taking liberties or overstepping boundaries*
> *deviation: departure from the norm*
> *delineation: outline or sketch*

Suggested Time: 7 minutes

Directions—Choose the lettered pair of words that is related in the same way as the pair in capital letters.

Example:
FLAKE : SNOW ::
(A)   storm : hail
(B)   drop : rain
(C)   field : wheat
(D)   stack : hay
(E)   sky : cloud   Ⓐ ● Ⓒ Ⓓ Ⓔ

1 **PILOT : AIRPLANE ::**
(A) team : players
(B) helmsman : ship
(C) horse : cart
(D) passenger : train
(E) army : country   Ⓐ Ⓑ Ⓒ Ⓓ Ⓔ

2 **BANANA : PEEL ::**
(A) egg : crack
(B) carrot : uproot
(C) apple : core
(D) bread : slice
(E) corn : husk   Ⓐ Ⓑ Ⓒ Ⓓ Ⓔ

3 **BONE : BODY ::**
(A) floor : house
(B) motor : boat
(C) driver : car
(D) knob : door
(E) beam : building   Ⓐ Ⓑ Ⓒ Ⓓ Ⓔ

4 **WHIP : LASH ::**
(A) mitt : throw
(B) shoe : walk
(C) baton : defy
(D) paddle : play
(E) club : beat   Ⓐ Ⓑ Ⓒ Ⓓ Ⓔ

5 **MIGRATION : SWALLOW ::**
(A) hibernation : groundhog
(B) dissection : frog
(C) predation : elk
(D) diversity : finch
(E) mimicry : ape   Ⓐ Ⓑ Ⓒ Ⓓ Ⓔ

6 **TOUCH : TACTILE ::**
(A) sound : noisy
(B) smell : olfactory
(C) mouth : verbal
(D) vision : beautiful
(E) taste : critical   Ⓐ Ⓑ Ⓒ Ⓓ Ⓔ

7 **CURIOSITY : KNOW ::**
(A) chattiness : listen
(B) talent : develop
(C) greediness : possess
(D) deception : disclose
(E) boredom : entertain   Ⓐ Ⓑ Ⓒ Ⓓ Ⓔ

8 **ARTICULATENESS : SPEECH ::**
(A) behavior : society
(B) music : note
(C) ballet : form
(D) legibility : handwriting
(E) painting : palette   Ⓐ Ⓑ Ⓒ Ⓓ Ⓔ

9 **ATTENTIVENESS : RAPT ::**
(A) loyalty : unscrupulous
(B) diatribe : derisive
(C) creativity : innovative
(D) jealousy : indolent
(E) impudence : polite   Ⓐ Ⓑ Ⓒ Ⓓ Ⓔ

10 **DISPUTANT : ALTERCATION ::**
(A) interlocutor : conversation
(B) lecturer : dialogue
(C) deliverer : message
(D) chatterbox : refutation
(E) orator : language   Ⓐ Ⓑ Ⓒ Ⓓ Ⓔ

SCORECARD	
Number of Questions Right:	
Number of Questions Wrong:	
Number of Questions Omitted:	
Number of Correct Guesses:	
Number of Wrong Guesses:	
Time Used:	

Answers and Explanations

1 **B**—The first bridge you think of might be: A **PILOT** flies an **AIRPLANE**. But a quick trip through the answer choices will tell you that bridge doesn't fit. So try another: A **PILOT** *is someone who operates or steers an* **AIRPLANE**.

A **team** is not the person who operates **players**. But a **helmsman** does operate or steer a **ship**. If you don't know a **helmsman** from a helmet, see if you can rule out any more wrong answers. **Horses** pull **carts**, but they don't operate or steer them; drivers do. And **passengers** ride in **trains**, but they don't run them. Finally, although the **army** runs some **countries**, operating or steering a **country** is not part of the definition of an **army**. So even if you didn't know what **helmsman** means, you could have chosen (B) by the process of elimination.

2 **E**—To build this bridge you have to know whether **PEEL** is a noun (the skin of a banana) or a verb (to peel a banana). Remember our rule: All words in the same column are the same part of speech. In the answer choices below **PEEL**, four words (**crack, core, slice, husk**) can be either verbs or nouns. But **uproot** can be used only as a verb. That means **PEEL** and all words beneath **PEEL** are verbs. So the bridge is: *To* **PEEL** *a* **BANANA** *means to remove its outer covering*.

(C) means almost the opposite: To **core** an **apple** means to remove the center portion. **Uprooting** a **carrot** means to dig it up. The only two choices that involve removing an outer covering are (A) and (E). **Cracking** an **egg** doesn't necessarily remove the eggshell. But **husking** means removing the covering from an ear of **corn**, so (E) fits the stem bridge.

3 **E**—The obvious stem bridge here is: *A* **BONE** *is part of a* **BODY**, but that would fit too many answer choices. So try working backwards. Define bridges for each answer choice, and see which one also fits the stem pair.

The **floor** of a **house** is a horizontal surface. That doesn't work for the stem pair. A **motor** provides power to make a **boat** move, but a **BONE** doesn't make a **BODY** move. Nor does a **BONE** steer a **BODY** as a **driver** steers a **car**. And you don't use a **BONE** to open a **BODY**, as you would use a **knob** to open a **door**. So it looks like (E) is correct, by process of elimination. A **beam** is part of the structural support of a **building**. Sure enough, a **BONE** is part of the structural support of a **BODY**.

4 **E**—To make your bridge, you need to know whether **WHIP** and **LASH** are verbs or nouns. Again, apply our rule: The answer choices below each column are all the same part of speech. In the first column, **mitt** can only be a noun (you can't **mitt** someone), so **WHIP** is also a noun. In column two, **defy** can't be a noun, so all the words must be verbs, including **LASH**.

Now you can build your stem bridge: *You* **LASH** *someone with a* **WHIP**.

The only tempting choices are (D) and (E). You can't **paddle** someone with a **play**—a paddle is used to **play** a game. But you can **beat** someone with a **club**.

5 **A**—Your bridge might be: **MIGRATION** *is something* **SWALLOWS** *do every year*. **Hibernation** is something **groundhogs** do every year, so (A) looks like a winner. Check out the other choices, though.

Choices (B) through (E), **dissection, predation, diversity,** and **mimicry** have nothing to do with seasonal activities of the animals or birds paired with these words, so stay with (A).

---

migration: movement from one area to
    another; seasonal change of location
hibernation: sleeplike state many animals go
    through each winter
dissection: process of surgical cutting to
    expose parts for scientific examination
predation: the act of preying on
diversity: variety
mimicry: the practice or art of imitation

---

6 **B**—Here you really have to know what the stem words mean to create the bridge: **TACTILE** *means pertaining to the sense of* **TOUCH**. In the same way, **olfactory** *means pertaining to the sense of* **smell**.

Check the other answers; in (A), **noisy** doesn't mean pertaining to the sense of **sound**. **Noisy** means loud. In (C) **verbal** doesn't mean pertaining to the sense of **mouth**. In (D) **beautiful** doesn't mean pertaining to the sense of **vision**. In (E) **critical** doesn't mean pertaining to the sense of **taste**.

7 C—A strong bridge would be: **CURIOSITY** *is the urge to* **KNOW** *things*. In the same way, **greediness** is the urge to **possess** things.

In (A), **chattiness** is not an urge to **listen**. In (D), **deception** has more to do with an urge to hide something than with an urge to **disclose**. In (B), **talent** does not imply an urge to **develop**. Now look at answer choice (E). **Boredom** and **entertain** relate, but not in the same way as the stem words. **Boredom** is not the urge to **entertain**. It might prompt an urge to be entertained (by others), but that's another story.

> disclose: to reveal
> deception: fraud, double-dealing, trickery

8 D—If you know what **ARTICULATENESS** means, finding the answer is easy. Your bridge is: **ARTICULATENESS** *is clarity of* **SPEECH**. Since **legibility** is clarity of **handwriting,** (D) is the right answer.

If you're not sure how **ARTICULATENESS** relates to **SPEECH,** you can still find the answer by working backwards from the answer choices. There's no obvious bridge between **behavior** and **society,** so rule out (A). In (B), you could say **music** is made up of **notes,** but it's unlikely that **ARTICULATENESS** is made up of **SPEECH,** so (B) is probably wrong.

In (C), **form** has no direct relationship to **ballet,** so it's probably wrong. In (D), **legibility** means clarity of **handwriting. ARTICULATENESS** could be clarity of **SPEECH,** so (D) could be right. Checking out (E), a **palette** for mixing colors when **painting** has nothing in common with the stem words.

(D) sounds the best, and in fact, is right.

> articulateness: the quality of clear and
>   effective speech
> legibility: the quality of being readable
>   or decipherable
> palette: small, hand-held board for mixing
>   paint colors; range of colors

9 C—Your bridge: *Someone who's* **RAPT** *is* **super**ATTENTIVE. Similarly, an **innovative** person is **super**creative, choice (C).

Pairs (A) and (E) are both almost opposites: If you're **unscrupulous,** you're certainly not **loyal.** If you're **polite,** you're not **impudent.** Keep in mind that when two pairs have the same bridge, they must both be wrong. After all, they can't both be right! As for (B), a **diatribe** may or may not be **derisive.** And in (D), **indolent** has no connection whatsoever with **jealousy.**

> rapt: fascinated, wholly absorbed
> unscrupulous: having no morals or ethics
> diatribe: a long, bitter speech
> derisive: mocking
> innovative: highly original, novel
> indolent: lazy
> impudence: insolence, cockiness

10 A—The stem bridge is: *A* **DISPUTANT** *takes part in an* **ALTERCATION.** An **interlocutor** takes part in a **conversation,** so the relationship in (A) is the same.

> Hint: Our Root List (near the back of the book) clues you in to the meanings of words like **interlocutor.** It comes from **INTER-** (between) and **LOC** (speech, talk).

Checking out the other answers, a **lecturer** (B) doesn't participate in a **dialogue** with others; he gives a speech. In (C), a **deliverer** doesn't exactly take part in a **message.** In (D), **chatterbox** has no clear relationship to **refutation.** And in (E), an **orator** uses **language** masterfully, but a **DISPUTANT** doesn't use an **ALTERCATION.**

> disputant: someone who disputes or argues
> altercation: noisy, angry argument
> interlocutor: someone who takes part in
>   a conversation
> deliverer: savior, rescuer, someone who
>   delivers others from danger or hardship
> refutation: act of proving something wrong
> orator: public speaker

Suggested Time: 7 minutes

Directions—Choose the lettered pair of words that is related in the same way as the pair in capital letters.

Example:
FLAKE : SNOW ::
(A)   storm : hail
(B)   drop : rain
(C)   field : wheat
(D)   stack : hay
(E)   sky : cloud

(A) ● (C) (D) (E)

1   RINK : SKATE ::
(A) escalator : turn
(B) track : run
(C) boat : swim
(D) airplane : fly
(E) office : drive

(A) (B) (C) (D) (E)

2   GENERAL : ARMY ::
(A) officer : uniform
(B) rifle : bullet
(C) soldier : barracks
(D) quarterback : team
(E) manager : profit

(A) (B) (C) (D) (E)

3   SODA : BEVERAGE ::
(A) hat : coat
(B) sand : desert
(C) coffee : milk
(D) cat : animal
(E) cup : handle

(A) (B) (C) (D) (E)

4   DENOUNCE : DISAPPROVAL ::
(A) enfeeble : weakness
(B) pass : legislation
(C) rant : anger
(D) condemn : building
(E) award : gift

(A) (B) (C) (D) (E)

5   FLURRY : BLIZZARD ::
(A) dew : meadow
(B) warmth : coolness
(C) moisture : sponge
(D) coat : protection
(E) glance : stare

(A) (B) (C) (D) (E)

6   COLLABORATE : WORK ::
(A) question : borrow
(B) clot : bleed
(C) cohabit : live
(D) synchronize : watch
(E) cooperate : please

(A) (B) (C) (D) (E)

7   CHRONICLE : EVENTS ::
(A) transcribe : statements
(B) heal : medicine
(C) remove : predicaments
(D) flatter : compliments
(E) review : documents

8   CONTENTMENT : PURR ::
(A) irrationality : growl
(B) terror : scream
(C) hatred : yelp
(D) distress : whisper
(E) entanglement : snarl

(A) (B) (C) (D) (E)

9   ERADICATE : DISEASE ::
(A) complicate : tangle
(B) elaborate : theme
(C) lengthen : dimension
(D) symbolize : model
(E) exterminate : species

(A) (B) (C) (D) (E)

10   PUTREFACTION : FRESH ::
(A) cohesion : disjointed
(B) delectation : pungent
(C) contraction : complex
(D) excoriation : proud
(E) emendation : flawed

(A) (B) (C) (D) (E)

SCORECARD	
Number of Questions Right:	
Number of Questions Wrong:	
Number of Questions Omitted:	
Number of Correct Guesses:	
Number of Wrong Guesses:	
Time Used:	

Answers and Explanations

1 **B**—A simple bridge is: *You* **SKATE** *on a structure called a* **RINK.** The only answer choice that fits is (B): *You* **run** *on a structure called a* **track.**

The only other answer choice that might tempt you is (D): You can **fly** in an **airplane,** but the airplane does the flying, not you. However, you do **run** on a **track** or **SKATE** on a **RINK,** so pick (B).

2 **D**—Your bridge is: *A* **GENERAL** *commands an* **ARMY.** An **officer** doesn't command a **uniform,** so (A) is wrong, and a **rifle** doesn't command a **bullet,** so (B) is wrong. And a **soldier** command a **barracks.** That leaves (D) and (E).

When you can't decide between two or three answer choices, do one of two things: Rephrase your stem bridge, or define a bridge for each remaining answer choice and see which one also fits the stem pair. Let's try the the latter.

In (D), a **quarterback** leads a **team,** the same way a **GENERAL** leads an **ARMY.** In (E), **profit** is the goal for a **manager,** but an **ARMY** isn't a goal for a **GENERAL.** So (D) is correct.

barracks: living quarters for soldiers

3 **D**—The test makers try to distract you with **coffee, milk,** and **cup**—words that remind you of **BEVERAGE.** But your bridge is: *A* **SODA** *is a type of* **BEVERAGE.** The only answer choice whose first word is a type of its second word is (D): A **cat** is a type of **animal.**

4 **C**—Bridge: *You show strong* **DISAPPROVAL** *when you* **DENOUNCE** *someone.* Similarly, you show strong anger when you **rant** at someone.

At first glance (A) looks possible, but check out the bridge: You don't show **weakness** when you **enfeeble** someone.

enfeeble: to weaken
rant: to be in a rage, to talk noisily
*   and excitedly*

5 **E**—The stem pair refers to different types of snow activity. A good bridge would be: *A* **FLURRY** *is much less intense than a* **BLIZZARD.** Similarly, a **glance** is much less intense than a **stare.** A **glance** is a quick, surface look; a **stare** is a prolonged, intense look.

> Hint: Don't pick answer choices just because they refer to the same topic as the stem words. Look for the one that the stem bridge fits.

flurry: quick, surface sprinkling of snow
blizzard: prolonged, intense snowstorm
glance: quick, casual look
stare: prolonged, intense look

6 **C**—The bridge is: *To* **collaborate** *is to* **WORK** *together.* In the same way, to **COHABIT** is to **LIVE** *together,* so (C) is correct.

If you didn't know what **COLLABORATE** meant, you might have figured it out: the prefix **CO-** means "with" or "together," and the root **LABOR** means "work."

Plugging your bridge into the other choices, (A) and (B) make no sense. In (D), you might think: When watches are **synchronized,** they work together. But **watch** in choice (D) isn't a noun, it's a verb—to watch.

> Hint: Remember, the parts of speech in corresponding words of an analogy question are always consistent. You'll never find a verb : noun combination in the stem and a noun : verb combination in the correct answer.

collaborate: to work together
clot: to become semisolid; to coagulate
cohabit: to live or reside together
synchronize: to cause to operate at the
*   same time or rate*

7 **A**—A quick glance at the first words in the answer choices tells you **CHRONICLE** is being used as a verb. So build a bridge: *To* **CHRONICLE** **EVENTS** *means to record them, usually in writing.* When you **transcribe** you also write down or record. A court stenographer **transcribes** the proceedings of a trial, including all **statements** made by the witnesses. To **transcribe** statements is to record them, so (A) is correct.

Choice (E) might have attracted you because of associations called up by the words **CHRONICLE,**

EVENTS, review, and **documents.** But when you review documents, you don't write them down—you just reread them.

> *predicaments: difficult or perplexing situations, dilemmas*

8 **B**—All the second words here can act as either nouns or verbs. So the stem bridge could be phrased one of two ways. If **PURR** is a verb: *To* **PURR** *means to utter sounds of* **CONTENTMENT.** If **PURR** is a noun: *A* **PURR** *is a sound of* **CONTENTMENT.** Either way, the only answer that matches is choice (B).

In (C), a **yelp** is more often associated with pain than with **hatred.** In (E), a **snarl** is a growl or tangle. A snarl is not a sound of **entanglement.**

> *irrationality: the quality of being illogical*
> *yelp: a quick, high-pitched sound*
> *distress: discomfort or trouble*

9 **E**—The bridge: *To* **ERADICATE** *a* **DISEASE** *is to wipe it out*, as smallpox was **ERADICATED** earlier in the twentieth century. Similarly, to **exterminate** a **species** is to wipe it out.

In choice (B), **elaborate,** like all the other first words here, is a verb; a composer **elaborates** on a **theme** by ornamenting and varying the original motif.

> *exterminate: to destroy completely*

10 **A**—**PUTREFACTION** is related to the simpler words *putrid* and *putrefy*. The stem bridge is: *Something characterized by* **PUTREFACTION** *is not* **FRESH.**

> Hint: **PUTREFACTION** comes from the roots **PUTER** (rotten), and **FAC** (to make or do). See our Word Root List.

Here you need to know the hard words in the answer choices. In (A), something—a speech, for example—characterized by **cohesion** displays unity and is *not* **disjointed.** That's true. But check out the other choices.

The stem bridge doesn't make sense in (B). In (C), something that contains no **contraction** is not necessarily **complex.** In (D), the stem bridge doesn't fit. You wouldn't say: Something that contains no **excoriation** is considered **proud.**

In (E), it's not necessarily true that something—like a document—characterized by **emendations** is not **flawed.**

> *putrefaction: state of decay, process of rotting*
> *cohesion: sticking together, displaying physical, logical, or political unity*
> *disjointed: separate and unconnected*
> *delectation: delight or enjoyment*
> *pungent: having a sharp smell or taste, like vinegar*
> *contraction: shortening, as of a muscle or word (won't is a contraction for will not)*
> *excoriation: a bitter denunciation*
> *emendation: a correction*

Suggested Time: 7 minutes

Directions—Choose the lettered pair of words that is related in the same way as the pair in capital letters.

Example:
FLAKE : SNOW ::
(A)   storm : hail
(B)   drop : rain
(C)   field : wheat
(D)   stack : hay
(E)   sky : cloud   Ⓐ ● Ⓒ Ⓓ Ⓔ

1   **FEATHER : BIRD ::**
(A) scale : fish
(B) hair : braid
(C) wing : flight
(D) fang : snake
(E) antenna : insect   Ⓐ Ⓑ Ⓒ Ⓓ Ⓔ

2   **CHALK : BLACKBOARD ::**
(A) eraser : mistake
(B) needle : thread
(C) brush : paint
(D) pen : paper
(E) crayon : drawing   Ⓐ Ⓑ Ⓒ Ⓓ Ⓔ

3   **FOOT : LENGTH ::**
(A) hour : watch
(B) height : growth
(C) teaspoon : recipe
(D) canyon : depth
(E) acre : area   Ⓐ Ⓑ Ⓒ Ⓓ Ⓔ

4   **DEAFENING : LOUD ::**
(A) believable : dramatic
(B) penurious : sad
(C) mysterious : quiet
(D) hilarious : amusing
(E) desirous : pathetic   Ⓐ Ⓑ Ⓒ Ⓓ Ⓔ

5   **BOTANIST : PLANTS ::**
(A) zoologist : animals
(B) linguist : verbs
(C) philologist : stamps
(D) physicist : experiments
(E) chemist : laboratories   Ⓐ Ⓑ Ⓒ Ⓓ Ⓔ

6   **STETHOSCOPE : LISTEN ::**
(A) microscope : record
(B) needle : inject
(C) bandage : cut
(D) scale : reduce
(E) cough : breathe   Ⓐ Ⓑ Ⓒ Ⓓ Ⓔ

7   **INCITE : ACTION ::**
(A) control : crowd
(B) conserve : fuel
(C) kindle : fire
(D) start : end
(E) become : thing   Ⓐ Ⓑ Ⓒ Ⓓ Ⓔ

8   **WATERLOGGED : MOISTURE ::**
(A) buoyant : balloon
(B) extroverted : personality
(C) overinflated : air
(D) windblown : pollen
(E) coarse : steam   Ⓐ Ⓑ Ⓒ Ⓓ Ⓔ

9   **REPREHENSIBLE : BLAME ::**
(A) incomprehensible : knowledge
(B) treasonable : invasion
(C) relevant : information
(D) difficult : evasion
(E) admirable : praise   Ⓐ Ⓑ Ⓒ Ⓓ Ⓔ

10   **DISCIPLINARIAN : STRICTNESS ::**
(A) curmudgeon : sadness
(B) miser : stinginess
(C) boor : heartiness
(D) innovator : forgetfulness
(E) soldier : wariness   Ⓐ Ⓑ Ⓒ Ⓓ Ⓔ

SCORECARD	
Number of Questions Right:	
Number of Questions Wrong:	
Number of Questions Omitted:	
Number of Correct Guesses:	
Number of Wrong Guesses:	
Time Used:	

Answers and Explanations

1 **A**—If you simply say: *A* **BIRD** *has* **FEATHERS,** you won't know whether to pick (A), (D), or (E). You'll have to restate the stem bridge more specifically: *A* **BIRD** *is covered with* **FEATHERS;** a **fish,** with **scales.**

2 **D**—With years of school behind you, this stem bridge should come easily: *You use* **CHALK** *to write on a* **BLACKBOARD,** just as you use a **pen** to write on **paper.**

Again, don't be misled by associations that the stem words and answer choices evoke for you. Many of the other answer choices may make you think about grade school, but the only pair that fits the stem bridge is (D).

3 **E**—Your bridge is: *A* **FOOT** *is a measurement of* **LENGTH.**

(E) is the only answer choice that fits: An **acre** is a measurement of **area.** Some of the wrong answers have strong bridges, but they're not the same as the stem bridge. A watch can be used to measure an **hour,** but an **hour** isn't a measurement of **watch.** **Growth** is a change in dimension, most commonly in **height.**

4 **D**—A strong bridge would be: *Something that's* **DEAFENING** *is extremely* **LOUD.** In (D), something that's **hilarious** is extremely **amusing,** but check the other choices.

In (B), **penurious** has no direct relationship to **sad.** Choice (E) is a good example of a word pair with a weak bridge. Someone who is **desirous,** that is, whose actions are ruled by desire, may or may not be **pathetic.** There's no definite connection between the two words.

penurious: stingy; poor
pathetic: worthy of pity

5 **A**—The bridge is: *A* **BOTANIST** *is someone who studies* **PLANTS.** A **zoologist** is someone who studies **animals.** In (B), a **linguist** studies language in general, not **verbs** in particular.

Incidentally, a **philologist** is someone who loves words and studies their history, not to be confused with a philatelist, who collects or studies **stamps.**

6 **B**—Try this bridge: *A* **STETHOSCOPE** *is a medical device that's used to* **LISTEN.** Look for a first word that's a device, preferably medical. That rules out (E) immediately, because a **cough** isn't a device, medical or otherwise. The second word of the correct answer should tell us what the device is used for. Only choice (B) does that: A **needle** is a medical device that's used to **inject.**

7 **C**—You can incite a riot, or an action, so a good bridge would be: *To* **INCITE** *is to provoke or start an* **ACTION.** That's certainly not the same bridge as (A), (B), (D), or (E). But it's close to the connection between **kindle** and **fire.** To kindle means to light or start a **fire.**

> Hint: Don't reject an answer choice just because it's not a perfect match for your bridge. Pick the *one* choice that is the best fit.

Since none of the other answer choices fits the stem bridge at all, (C) must be correct.

incite: provoke to action; stir up

8 **C**—Your bridge is: *Something that contains way too much* **MOISTURE** *is* **WATERLOGGED.** In (A), something **buoyant** doesn't contain way too much **balloon.** And (E) makes no sense at all. (B) and (C) seem like good possibilities. But **extroverted** doesn't mean having too much **personality.** On the other hand, something that contains way too much **air** is **overinflated,** so (C) is correct.

buoyant: floating or capable of floating
extroverted: having an outgoing personality

9 **E**—The bridge is: *A person or action that is* **REPREHENSIBLE** *is deserving of* **BLAME.** The only answer choice that fits the bridge is (E): Something **admirable** is worthy of **praise.**

If you didn't know what **REPREHENSIBLE** meant, you could have tried working backwards from the answer choices. It's hard to build a strong bridge between the words of most of the answer choices. For instance, **treasonable** means "relating to or involving treason." There's no strong link with **invasion,** so (B) is out. **Information** that's relevant is pertinent or significant; it doesn't seem likely that **BLAME** that is **REPREHENSIBLE** is pertinent or significant. But something that's **admirable** is worthy of **praise,** and **REPREHENSIBLE** could (and does) mean "worthy of **BLAME**"; therefore, (E) is correct.

> reprehensible: deserving of blame
> incomprehensible: impossible to understand
> treasonable: relating to or involving betrayal, especially of one's country
> relevant: pertinent or significant
> admirable: worthy of praise

10 **B**—Your bridge: *A* **DISCIPLINARIAN** *is characterized by* **STRICTNESS.**

In (A), a **curmudgeon** isn't necessarily characterized by **sadness.** In (B), a miser is indeed characterized by stinginess. But check out the other answer choices, just to make sure.

Look for an answer choice whose first word is a person or thing, and whose second word characterizes the first word.

In (C), a **boor** doesn't have to be **hearty.** In (D), an **innovator** has nothing to do with **forgetfulness.** The root **NOV** means "new." Finally, in (E), **wariness** is not necessarily a characteristic of **soldiers.** It has nothing to do with the word **war.**

> disciplinarian: someone who enforces order
> miser: someone who lives miserably in order to hoard his wealth; extremely stingy person
> boor: rude or insensitive person
> innovator: someone who produces new ideas or inventions
> wariness: caution or carefulness
> curmudgeon: grouch, ill-tempered person

Suggested Time: 7 minutes

Directions—Choose the lettered pair of words that is related in the same way as the pair in capital letters.

Example:
FLAKE : SNOW ::
(A)   storm : hail
(B)   drop : rain
(C)   field : wheat
(D)   stack : hay
(E)   sky : cloud   (A) ● (C) (D) (E)

1   **SKUNK : SCENT ::**
(A) fur : cat
(B) porcupine : quill
(C) prey : animal
(D) gland : odor
(E) leaf : shrub   (A) (B) (C) (D) (E)

2   **RECESS : SCHOOL ::**
(A) intermission : play
(B) pause : reflection
(C) vacation : time
(D) score : game
(E) dining : restaurant   (A) (B) (C) (D) (E)

3   **DISMANTLE : APPARATUS ::**
(A) dismay : emotion
(B) distend : stomach
(C) distort : static
(D) disband : group
(E) display : window   (A) (B) (C) (D) (E)

4   **BIPED : HUMAN ::**
(A) tentacle : octopus
(B) quadruped : horse
(C) foot : centipede
(D) kingdom : animal
(E) pouch : kangaroo   (A) (B) (C) (D) (E)

5   **CALM : COMPOSURE ::**
(A) scared : trouble
(B) cold : sickness
(C) congested : traffic
(D) sad : melancholy
(E) bored : gladness   (A) (B) (C) (D) (E)

6   **ILLICIT : LEGALITY ::**
(A) grateful : thanklessness
(B) innocent : punishment
(C) hardy : graciousness
(D) guilty : uncertainty
(E) wicked : evil   (A) (B) (C) (D) (E)

7   **ANNOYED : RAGE ::**
(A) glad : euphoria
(B) useless : necessity
(C) humorous : attentiveness
(D) aggressive : hopefulness
(E) nasty : amusement   (A) (B) (C) (D) (E)

8   **ABDICATE : THRONE ::**
(A) rule : nation
(B) revolt : government
(C) defeat : candidate
(D) impeach : official
(E) resign : job   (A) (B) (C) (D) (E)

9   **LUCRATIVE : PROFIT ::**
(A) valuable : price
(B) fictitious : hero
(C) fertile : offspring
(D) commanding : chaos
(E) episodic : publicity   (A) (B) (C) (D) (E)

10   **MISANTHROPE : HUMANKIND ::**
(A) cynic : kindness
(B) martyr : punishment
(C) xenophobe : foreigners
(D) optimist : hope
(E) derelict : officers   (A) (B) (C) (D) (E)

SCORECARD	
Number of Questions Right:	
Number of Questions Wrong:	
Number of Questions Omitted:	
Number of Correct Guesses:	
Number of Wrong Guesses:	
Time Used:	

Answers and Explanations

1 **B**—Your bridge could be: *A* **SKUNK** *uses a* **SCENT** *to repel its enemies.* You'll probably see right away that a **porcupine** uses **quills** to repel its enemies.

2 **A**—Your bridge is: *A* **RECESS** *is a short break in the middle of* **SCHOOL,** *just as an* **intermission** *is a short break in the middle of* a **play.**

In (B), a **pause** is also a short break, but not in the middle of a **reflection.** Similarly, in (C) a **vacation** is a break, but not in the middle of **time.**

3 **D**—A good bridge might be: *To* **DISMANTLE** *an* **APPARATUS** *is to take it apart.* Similarly, to **disband** a **group** is to break it up or dissolve it. No other answer choice involves the idea of taking some collective unit apart.

In choice (B), if you eat too much, your **stomach** becomes **distended.** In (C), if you **distort** an audio signal by turning up the volume past what your speakers can handle, you may get what sounds like radio **static.**

---

dismantle: to take apart piece by piece
apparatus: a piece of equipment made of different parts and used for some particular function
distend: to swell or extend
distort: to deform or twist out of shape

---

4 **B**—A clear bridge would be: **HUMANS** *are* **BIPEDS,** *i.e., they have two legs.*

In (A) and (E), a **tentacle** or **pouch** is something an **octopus** or **kangaroo** has, not something it is. You can use the same logic to eliminate (C). The bridge doesn't fit (D) at all. But a **horse** is a **quadruped,** a four-legged animal, so (B) is correct.

> Hint: **BIPED** comes from the prefix **BI-** meaning "two" (as in bicycle), and the root **PED** meaning "foot" or "leg" (as in pedal). Quadruped has the prefix **QUAD-,** meaning "four."

5 **D**—A good bridge would be: *When you're* **CALM,** *you are in a state of* **COMPOSURE.** In the same way, *When you're* **sad,** *you are in a state of* **melancholy.** No other answer choice fits.

composure: self-possession or calmness of mind
melancholy: depression, gloominess
congested: clogged

---

6 **A**—There's a suggestion of opposites in the stem pair, so your bridge could be: *Something* **ILLICIT** *is not characterized by* **LEGALITY.**

Now look for a similar contrast in the answer pairs. (A) comes closest: *Someone* **grateful** *is not characterized by* **thanklessness.** In (B), it doesn't make sense to say: *Someone* **innocent** *is not characterized by* **punishment.**

---

legality: the quality of being legal
illicit: illegal
hardy: strong, robust, capable of withstanding hardships

---

7 **A**—These two stem words represent different degrees of the same emotion. Bridge: *Someone who becomes extremely* **ANNOYED** *feels* **RAGE.**

Since (B), (C), (D), and (E) don't fit that bridge, you might have been able to choose (A) without even knowing what **euphoria** meant. *Someone extremely* **glad** *feels* **euphoria,** so (A)'s right.

---

euphoria: an overwhelming feeling of elation or happiness

---

8 **E**—A strong bridge is: *When you* **ABDICATE** *a* **THRONE,** *you give it up.* The only choice that fits this bridge is (E): *When you* **resign** *from a* **job,** *you give it up.*

---

abdicate: to withdraw from or give up a high office or function

---

9 **C**—A strong bridge would be: *Something,* like a business, *that's* **LUCRATIVE** *produces* **PROFIT.** The only answer choice that fits the bridge is (C): *Something* **fertile,** like an animal, *produces* **offspring,** or children.

lucrative: profitable
fictitious: made-up
fertile: capable of producing offspring,
    fruitful
episodic: temporary, occasional, made up
    of separate episodes

10 **C**—Your stem bridge is: *A* **MISANTHROPE** *is a person who hates all* **HUMANKIND.** In (C), *A* **xenophobe** *is a person who hates* **foreigners,** so that's probably the right answer, but check the other choices.

> Hint: if you didn't know what a **MISAN-THROPE** was, our Root List could help you. The prefix **MIS-** is negative, and the root **ANTHROP** (also found in *anthropology* and *philanthropy*) means "human beings."

In (A), a **cynic** sees ulterior motives behind all good deeds, but doesn't necessarily hate all **kindness.** In (B), a **martyr** doesn't hate **punishment**; he or she willingly suffers **punishment** for his or her beliefs. In (D), an **optimist** certainly doesn't hate **hope.** Finally, in (E), **derelict** is being used as a noun to mean "a vagrant," and there's no direct connection between **derelict** and **officers.**

misanthrope: someone who hates other people
cynic: one who believes only selfishness
    motivates human actions
martyr: someone willing to suffer or die for
    a cause or religion
optimist: one who looks on the bright side
    of things
xenophobe: someone who hates and fears
    foreigners
derelict (noun): a vagrant
derelict (adjective): negligent or neglectful

Suggested Time: 7 minutes

Directions—Choose the lettered pair of words that is related in the same way as the pair in capital letters.

Example:
FLAKE : SNOW ::
(A)   storm : hail
(B)   drop : rain
(C)   field : wheat
(D)   stack : hay
(E)   sky : cloud   Ⓐ ● ⓒ ⓓ ⓔ

1   IRON : WRINKLE ::
(A) bleach : color
(B) mow : lawn
(C) sweep : broom
(D) cook : food
(E) build : model   Ⓐ Ⓑ Ⓒ Ⓓ Ⓔ

2   WRITER : NOVELIST ::
(A) scientist : astronomer
(B) teacher : student
(C) physician : patient
(D) poet : researcher
(E) worker : exertion   Ⓐ Ⓑ Ⓒ Ⓓ Ⓔ

3   COW : CALF ::
(A) hog : pork
(B) horse : mule
(C) sheep : lamb
(D) tiger : stripe
(E) ram : ewe   Ⓐ Ⓑ Ⓒ Ⓓ Ⓔ

4   STAR : STELLAR ::
(A) space : spherical
(B) comet : planetary
(C) vapor : solid
(D) earth : terrestrial
(E) ship : orbital   Ⓐ Ⓑ Ⓒ Ⓓ Ⓔ

5   BAY : WOLVES ::
(A) canter : horses
(B) parley : people
(C) low : cattle
(D) molt : lizards
(E) root : swine   Ⓐ Ⓑ Ⓒ Ⓓ Ⓔ

6   MOVEMENT : SYMPHONY ::
(A) note : piano
(B) frame : film
(C) canvas : painting
(D) rhythm : poem
(E) act : play   Ⓐ Ⓑ Ⓒ Ⓓ Ⓔ

7   SLAKE : THIRST ::
(A) stoke : fire
(B) starve : hunger
(C) assuage : pain
(D) endure : discomfort
(E) induce : sleep   Ⓐ Ⓑ Ⓒ Ⓓ Ⓔ

8   REBEL : AUTHORITY ::
(A) solver : problem
(B) anarchist : change
(C) farmer : urbanity
(D) pacifist : serenity
(E) nonconformist : convention   Ⓐ Ⓑ Ⓒ Ⓓ Ⓔ

9   PHILANTHROPIST : GENEROSITY ::
(A) teacher : pedantry
(B) swindler : deceitfulness
(C) novice : intelligence
(D) editor : validation
(E) coward : tenacity   Ⓐ Ⓑ Ⓒ Ⓓ Ⓔ

10   RUTHLESS : MERCY ::
(A) judgmental : theory
(B) unmarred : blemish
(C) arresting : evidence
(D) vicious : circle
(E) avaricious : selfishness   Ⓐ Ⓑ Ⓒ Ⓓ Ⓔ

SCORECARD	
Number of Questions Right:	
Number of Questions Wrong:	
Number of Questions Omitted:	
Number of Correct Guesses:	
Number of Wrong Guesses:	
Time Used:	

Answers and Explanations

1 **A**—In case you had doubts, a quick look at the answer choices will tell you that **IRON** is being used as a verb (**mow** can't be either a noun or adjective) and **WRINKLE** as a noun (**lawn, broom,** and **food** can't be used as verbs).

So make your bridge: *You* **IRON** *to remove a* **WRINKLE.**

At first glance, you might think two answer choices fit that bridge: You **bleach** to remove **color,** and you **mow** to remove a **lawn.** But when you **mow** the grass, you don't remove a **lawn;** you simply cut it back. **IRON**ing and **bleaching,** on the other hand, take out **WRINKLES** and **color,** respectively.

2 **A**—This bridge should come easily: *A* **NOVELIST** *is a type of* **WRITER.** Look for the answer choice pair with the same relationship.

Don't pick an answer just because the two words are closely related, as in choices (B) and (C). A **student** is not a type of **teacher.** And a **patient** is not a type of **physician.** But an **astronomer** is a type of **scientist,** so (A) is correct.

---

exertion: effort or labor

---

3 **C**—You know this bridge: *A* **CALF** *is a young* **COW.** Look for an answer choice whose second word is a young animal. The only one is (C): *A* **lamb** *is a young* **sheep.** In choice (E), **rams** and **ewes** are male and female sheep, respectively.

4 **D**—The bridge is: **STELLAR** *means coming from or having to do with* **STARS.**

In (D), **terrestrial** means coming from or having to do with the **earth.** In science fiction, alien creatures from other planets are often called **extraterrestrials,** indicating that they come from beyond (**EXTRA-**) the earth (**TERR**).

5 **C**—Here, all the words in the first column are verbs, so you need to know what **BAY** means as a verb. **WOLVES,** coyotes, and dogs are all said to **BAY** at the moon.

Your bridge might be: **WOLVES** *make a sound called* **BAYING.**

The only answer choice that fits the bridge is: **CATTLE** make a sound called **LOWING,** so (C) is correct.

---

bay (verb): to bark or howl
canter: of horses, an easy gallop
parley: to speak with, consult with
low (verb): to moo
molt: to shed feathers, fur, or scales
root (verb): of pigs, to dig in the dirt looking
  for food

---

6 **E**—If you phrased your stem bridge as: *A* **MOVEMENT** *is a piece of a* **SYMPHONY,** you probably had trouble choosing between (A), (B), (E), and maybe even (D). The problem was that your bridge wasn't specific enough.

A better bridge would be *A* **SYMPHONY** *is divided into three or four long sections, called* **MOVEMENTS.** Only in (E) is the first word *a long section or division of the second word.*

7 **C**—Try this bridge: *To* **SLAKE** *is to relieve your* **THIRST.**

Look for a first word in the answer choices that also means "relieve." The only one is **assuage.** You **assuage,** or relieve, **pain,** so the bridge fits, and (C) is correct.

---

slake: to quench or satisfy
assuage: to relieve, ease
stoke: to feed a fire
induce: to cause something to occur

---

8 **E**—The stem bridge could be: *A* **REBEL** *defies* **AUTHORITY.** The only answer choice that fits the bridge is (E): *A* **nonconformist** *defies* **convention.**

---

anarchist: one who believes that the best
  government is no government at all
urbanity: smoothness or sophistication
pacifist: someone who embraces peace and
  seeks to avoid physical conflict
nonconformist: someone who doesn't abide
  by society's expectations or conventions

KAPLAN

9 B—Bridge: *A* **PHILANTHROPIST** *always shows* **GENEROSITY.** In (A), a **teacher** doesn't always show **pedantry.** But **deceitfulness** is a fundamental, defining characteristic of a **swindler.** None of the other choices has the same relationship as the stem words, so (B) is right.

---

philanthropist: *someone who donates money to socially useful purposes*

pedantry: *narrow-minded or overly detailed teaching*

novice: *someone who is new to a given position or activity*

validation: *the act or process of confirming something*

tenacity: *dogged persistence, stubbornness*

---

10 B—Bridge: *Someone who's* **RUTHLESS** *has or shows no* **MERCY.** Something that's **unmarred** has or shows no **blemish.**

Hint: Answers like choice (D), in which the two words combine to form a common phrase, can be very attractive but are rarely correct. If the relationship between the two words doesn't match the relationship between the stem words, eliminate the choice.

---

marred: *spoiled by a flaw*

arresting *(adjective): striking, impressive*

avaricious: *greedy*

Suggested Time: 7 minutes

Directions—Choose the lettered pair of words that is related in the same way as the pair in capital letters.

Example:
FLAKE : SNOW ::
(A)   storm : hail
(B)   drop : rain
(C)   field : wheat
(D)   stack : hay
(E)   sky : cloud   Ⓐ ● Ⓒ Ⓓ Ⓔ

1   ILLNESS : MEASLES ::
(A) beverage : meal
(B) insect : creature
(C) reptile : mammal
(D) flower : tree
(E) bird : sparrow   Ⓐ Ⓑ Ⓒ Ⓓ Ⓔ

2   GLASSBLOWER : VASE ::
(A) stonecutter : monument
(B) lumberjack : tree
(C) gentleman : manners
(D) landlord : building
(E) storekeeper : merchandise   Ⓐ Ⓑ Ⓒ Ⓓ Ⓔ

3   GROCER : FOOD ::
(A) bureaucrat : paper
(B) locksmith : jewels
(C) librarian : books
(D) writer : pens
(E) apothecary : medicine   Ⓐ Ⓑ Ⓒ Ⓓ Ⓔ

4   BRIGAND : BAND ::
(A) gourmand : crew
(B) despot : retinue
(C) performer : troupe
(D) musician : instrument
(E) organizer : union   Ⓐ Ⓑ Ⓒ Ⓓ Ⓔ

5   GLOBAL : WORLD ::
(A) national : security
(B) tropical : jungle
(C) municipal : city
(D) internal : medicine
(E) regional : state   Ⓐ Ⓑ Ⓒ Ⓓ Ⓔ

6   VAGUE : DEFINE ::
(A) sterile : produce
(B) disguised : recognize
(C) tough : strengthen
(D) precious : save
(E) modest : hide   Ⓐ Ⓑ Ⓒ Ⓓ Ⓔ

7   LITIGATION : COURT ::
(A) population : room
(B) experimentation : laboratory
(C) gesture : motion
(D) accusation : jury
(E) competition : promotion   Ⓐ Ⓑ Ⓒ Ⓓ Ⓔ

8   ABUNDANT : ADEQUATE ::
(A) arid : moist
(B) peaceful : boisterous
(C) timid : illegitimate
(D) overflowing : full
(E) bold : fearless   Ⓐ Ⓑ Ⓒ Ⓓ Ⓔ

9   PERTURBED : TRANQUILITY ::
(A) joyous : pleasure
(B) impudent : dissension
(C) consoled : weeping
(D) reassured : anxiety
(E) admiring : awe   Ⓐ Ⓑ Ⓒ Ⓓ Ⓔ

10 PLATITUDE : TRITE ::
(A) riddle : cryptic
(B) axiom : geometric
(C) attitude : sinister
(D) syllogism : wise
(E) circumlocution : concise   Ⓐ Ⓑ Ⓒ Ⓓ Ⓔ

SCORECARD	
Number of Questions Right:	
Number of Questions Wrong:	
Number of Questions Omitted:	
Number of Correct Guesses:	
Number of Wrong Guesses:	
Time Used:	

Answers and Explanations

1 E—The stem bridge is: **MEASLES** *is a type of* **ILLNESS.**

As you scan the answer choices, look for one whose second word is a type of its first word. A **meal** isn't a type of **beverage;** a **creature** isn't a type of **insect;** a **mammal** isn't a type of **reptile;** and a **tree** isn't a type of **flower.** But a **sparrow** is a type of **bird,** so (E) is correct.

2 A—A **GLASSBLOWER** is a person who makes objects from molten glass by blowing air through a hollow rod.

Your bridge is: *A* **VASE** *would be created by a* **GLASSBLOWER.**

Similarly, a **monument** would be created by a **stonecutter.** None of the other answer choices has as its first word a person who creates its second word. A **lumberjack** doesn't create **trees;** she or he cuts them down. A **gentleman** displays or is known for having good **manners;** a **landlord** owns a **building;** and a **storekeeper** sells **merchandise.**

3 E—Bridge: *A* **GROCER** *is someone who sells* **FOOD.**

Bureaucrats are often called **paper** shufflers, but a **bureaucrat** doesn't *sell* **paper.** A **locksmith** has no direct connection with **jewels.** A **librarian** catalogues, sorts, and lends **books,** but doesn't sell them. And, of course, **writers** don't sell **pens.** But an **apothecary** *is someone who sells* drugs or **medicine.**

> Hint: If you didn't know what *apothecary* meant, you could still have found the answer by eliminating the choices that did *not* make sense.

---

bureaucrat: *government or corporate*
employee who works within narrow
channels of authority and follows a rigid
routine
locksmith: *someone who makes and installs*
locks and keys
apothecary: *a pharmacist*

---

4 C—Your bridge is: *A group of* **BRIGANDS** *is called a* **BAND.** Looking quickly through the choices, the only two that have a similar relationship are (C) and (E).

The words in choice (A) have nothing to do with each other. A group of **gourmands** is not a **crew.** In (B), a **despot** may or may not *have* a **retinue,** but he would not be *part* of a **retinue.** In (C) a group of **performers** is called a **troupe.** In (D), a group of **musicians** is not an **instrument.** In (E) an **organizer** tries to start a union, but a group of organizers is not a **union,** so (C) is the best available answer.

---

brigand: *someone who robs people, usually*
as part of a group or band
gourmand: *a glutton, someone who eats a lot*
of fine food
despot: *tyrant*
retinue: *a group of attendants serving an*
important person
troupe: *a group of theatrical performers*

---

5 C—Your bridge is: *Something* **GLOBAL** *pertains to the* **WORLD.** In the same way *something* **municipal** *pertains to a* **city.**

In (A), **national** doesn't necessarily pertain to **security,** though it can. In (B), **tropical** doesn't necessarily pertain just to a **jungle;** it relates to the tropics in general, i.e., the latitudes around the equator. In (D), **internal** just means "inner"; it doesn't necessarily have anything to do with **medicine.** And something that's **regional** pertains to an area that may be smaller, or broader, than one **state.**

---

global: *characteristic of or pertaining to the*
world
municipal: *characteristic of or pertaining to*
the city

---

6 B—At least two bridges seem to fit this stem pair. *Something that's* **VAGUE** *can be* either *hard to* **DEFINE** *or poorly* **DEFINED.**

(B) seems the best bet. Something that's **disguised** can be hard to **recognize.** That's certainly true. (B) is probably right, but check the other choices, just to make sure.

In (A), something that's **sterile** isn't hard to **produce** or poorly **produced;** it can't **produce** offspring, but that's something else. The other choices don't fit either, so (B) is correct.

KAPLAN

7 **B**—If you know what litigation means, you can build your bridge: **LITIGATION** *is a process that takes place in* **COURT.**

Look for an answer choice whose first word describes a process, and whose second describes the place where the process goes on. In (B), **experimentation** is a process that takes place in a **laboratory**. **Room** in choice (A) also describes a place, but **population** doesn't take place in a **room,** so choice (B) is correct.

---

litigation: a lawsuit

---

8 **D**—Here the two words reflect different amounts. So you can build a bridge: *Something* **ABUNDANT** *is much more than* **ADEQUATE.**

Look for an answer choice whose the first word means *more than* the second word.

The bridge doesn't fit in (A), where **arid** and **moist** are almost opposites. **Peaceful** and **boisterous** are also opposites, so (B) is also wrong. The stem words in (C) have no clear connection. In (E), **bold** and **fearless** are almost synonyms; **bold** doesn't mean "more than **fearless.**" The only choice in which the first word means *more than* the second word is (D): **overflowing** means "more than **full.**"

---

abundant: extremely plentiful
adequate: enough to fulfill requirements
arid: very dry
boisterous: rough and noisy
illegitimate: unlawful, illegal, born out of
    wedlock
overflowing: more than full

---

9 **D**—Again, the stem words feel like opposites. Your bridge might be: *Someone who feels* **PERTURBED** *does not feel* **TRANQUILITY.**

Look for an answer whose two words describe opposite states.

You can reject (A) and (E), in which both pairs are positive. In (B), the words have a weak connection, and they're both negative. In both (C) and (D), the relationships between the words seem to involve opposites. To choose between them, plug the word pairs into the stem bridge. Which sounds right: Someone who feels **consoled** does not feel **weeping?** Or: Someone who feels **reassured** does not feel **anxiety?** Since both **TRANQUILITY** and **anxiety** are states of mind, while **weeping** is an action, (D) is a better fit.

---

perturbed: upset
tranquility: calmness
impudent: cocky or insolent
dissension: disagreement or quarreling with
    in a group

---

10 **A**—To do well on this one, you need to know the meaning of some hard words. A strong bridge is: *A* **PLATITUDE** *is a* **TRITE** *saying.* The second word describes the first.

(A) fits the stem bridge and is probably right: *A* **riddle** *is a* **cryptic** *saying.* But check the other choices. Although you probably memorized **axioms** in geometry class, **axioms** are not **geometric** sayings, so (B) doesn't fit. In (C), an **attitude** is not a saying, though it sounds like **PLATITUDE.** In (D), a **syllogism** is a form of deductive logic (e.g., all dogs are mammals; this animal is a dog; therefore, this animal is a mammal), not a **wise** saying. Finally, in (E), both meanings of **circumlocution** imply beating around the bush rather than coming to the point, so a **circumlocution** is definitely not a concise saying.

---

platitude: a cliché, usually with a moral
trite: stale, ordinary, commonplace
cryptic: obscure or secret
axiom: statement that is self-evident or
    doesn't require proof
syllogism: a form of deductive logic
circumlocution: using more words than
    necessary, or speaking evasively

Suggested Time: 7 minutes

Directions—Choose the lettered pair of words that is related in the same way as the pair in capital letters.

Example:
FLAKE : SNOW ::
(A)　　storm : hail
(B)　　drop : rain
(C)　　field : wheat
(D)　　stack : hay
(E)　　sky : cloud
　　　　Ⓐ ● Ⓒ Ⓓ Ⓔ

1 **BAKER : BREAD ::**
(A) artist : studio
(B) weaver : cloth
(C) factory : clearance
(D) florist : flowers
(E) druggist : illness
　　　Ⓐ Ⓑ Ⓒ Ⓓ Ⓔ

2 **SHIP : FLEET ::**
(A) grass : field
(B) container : milk
(C) cow : herd
(D) beak : bird
(E) swamp : glade
　　　Ⓐ Ⓑ Ⓒ Ⓓ Ⓔ

3 **HYPOCRITE : INSINCERITY ::**
(A) braggart : modesty
(B) criminal : sympathy
(C) liar : dishonesty
(D) patriot : disloyalty
(E) witness : truthfulness
　　　Ⓐ Ⓑ Ⓒ Ⓓ Ⓔ

4 **ANCHOR : BOAT ::**
(A) sink : ship
(B) launch : pier
(C) propel : rocket
(D) tether : horse
(E) waddle : duck
　　　Ⓐ Ⓑ Ⓒ Ⓓ Ⓔ

5 **CRUTCH : SUPPORT ::**
(A) needle : measurement
(B) thermometer : fever
(C) drill : numbness
(D) bandage : protection
(E) hospital : gravity
　　　Ⓐ Ⓑ Ⓒ Ⓓ Ⓔ

6 **FUNNEL : CONICAL ::**
(A) pipe : cylindrical
(B) solid : spherical
(C) hose : spiral
(D) line : parallel
(E) hive : hexagonal
　　　Ⓐ Ⓑ Ⓒ Ⓓ Ⓔ

7 **REND : TATTERS ::**
(A) fry : onions
(B) burn : ashes
(C) donate : beggars
(D) irrigate : clods
(E) water : plants
　　　Ⓐ Ⓑ Ⓒ Ⓓ Ⓔ

8 **DOUBLE-CROSSER : BETRAY ::**
(A) slowpoke : lag
(B) watchdog : dread
(C) trendsetter : pace
(D) sweetheart : hug
(E) pessimist : cooperate
　　　Ⓐ Ⓑ Ⓒ Ⓓ Ⓔ

9 **SUBMISSION : KNEEL ::**
(A) equilibrium : stand
(B) leisure : sit
(C) mutiny : lie
(D) disrespect : bow
(E) assent : nod
　　　Ⓐ Ⓑ Ⓒ Ⓓ Ⓔ

10 **CONCORD : AGREEMENT ::**
(A) insurrection : calm
(B) chaos : order
(C) promise : peace
(D) revolution : army
(E) flux : change
　　　Ⓐ Ⓑ Ⓒ Ⓓ Ⓔ

SCORECARD	
Number of Questions Right:	
Number of Questions Wrong:	
Number of Questions Omitted:	
Number of Correct Guesses:	
Number of Wrong Guesses:	
Time Used:	

Answers and Explanations

1 **B**—Your bridge links the person with the product he or she makes: *A* **BAKER** *makes* **BREAD.**

A **weaver** makes **cloth,** so (B) is probably correct. But check out the other answers.

(C) is clearly wrong. A **factory** doesn't make a **clearance.** In (A), a **studio** is a place where an **artist** works; an **artist** doesn't make a **studio.** In (D), **flowers** are sold, but not made, by **florists.** In (E), a **druggist** doesn't make **illness;** he or she sells products that treat and cure **illnesses.**

2 **C**—A strong bridge is: *A group of* **SHIPS** *is called a* **FLEET.**

The only answer choice in which the second word obviously describes a group is (C). So check whether it fits the stem bridge. It does: *A group of* **cows** *is called a* **herd.**

> *glade: an open space surrounded by woods.*

3 **C**—If you know how a hypocrite behaves, you have your bridge: *A* **HYPOCRITE** *is someone who displays* **INSINCERITY.**

In (E), a **witness** doesn't necessarily display **truthfulness,** so (E) is a weak possibility at best. But a **liar** displays **dishonesty,** so (C) is the best answer.

If you make your bridge more specific, the choice between (C) and (E) becomes clearer. Try the bridge: *A* **HYPOCRITE** *is someone who is guilty of* **INSINCERITY.** A **witness** is not guilty of **truthfulness,** but a **liar** is certainly guilty of **dishonesty.**

> *braggart: someone who boasts*
> *hypocrite: a deceiver, a dissembler, someone who pretends to be what he or she is not*

4 **D**—If you tried to build a bridge that linked an **ANCHOR** and a **BOAT,** you were slightly off track. A quick look at the answer choices indicates that all the first words are verbs, including **ANCHOR.**

Your bridge could be: *To* **ANCHOR** *a* **BOAT** *means to secure it so that it doesn't drift away.* Similarly, to **tether** a **horse** means to tie it to some fixed point so it doesn't wander off. No other answer choice fits the stem bridge.

5 **D**—Bridge: *A* **CRUTCH** *provides* **SUPPORT.**

The answer choices all contain words associated with injuries or medicine. Don't be tempted by these associations. You'll have to plug each word pair into the stem bridge and see which fits best. The only one that fits at all is (D): *A* **bandage** *provides* **protection.**

> *gravity: the attractive force that makes objects fall towards the earth; also seriousness, e.g., the gravity of the situation.*

6 **A**—Bridge: *A* **FUNNEL** *looks like a cone; it's* **CONICAL** *in shape.* A **pipe** looks like a cylinder; it's **cylindrical** in shape.

Checking out the other choices, in (B), something **spherical** can be either **solid** or hollow. In (C), a **hose** isn't necessarily a **spiral** in shape, only when it's wound up. In (D), two **lines** may be **parallel,** but a **line** is not **parallel** in shape. (E) is tricky. The cells of a honeycomb are **hexagonal** in shape, but the **hive** that contains them is generally not.

> *spherical: globular, shaped like a sphere or ball*
> *hive: colony of bees; place swarming with occupants*

7 **B**—A good bridge is: **RENDING** *fabric thoroughly will reduce it to* **TATTERS,** or rags.

So look for an answer choice whose first word describes an action that reduces something to an unusable state. Only **burn** in answer choice (B) fits that description, so plug in your stem bridge: **Burning** *something thoroughly will reduce it to* **ashes.** That's true, so (B) is correct.

> *rend: to tear*
> *irrigate: to supply with water*
> *clods: lumps of earth*

8 **A**—Your bridge is: *A* **DOUBLE-CROSSER** *is someone who* **BETRAYS.**

(A) works quite well. A **slowpoke** *is someone who* **lags,** or falls behind.

(D) doesn't quite fit the stem bridge. By definition, **DOUBLE-CROSSERS BETRAY** and **slowpokes lag;** but while it's very common for **sweet-**

hearts to **hug,** the definition of a **sweetheart** isn't someone who **hugs.**

9 E—**SUBMISSION** has several meanings, but the one most closely connected with **KNEEL** has to do with being humble. With that in mind, you can phrase this stem bridge as: *One* **KNEELS** *to express* **SUBMISSION.**

In (A), your sense of **equilibrium** allows you to stand, but you don't **stand** to express **equilibrium.** If you have **leisure,** or free time, you may choose to sit for a while, but you don't **sit** in order to express **leisure.** In fact, none of the answer choices fits the stem bridge until you get to the last one: You **nod** to *express* **assent,** or agreement.

---

submission: condition of being humble;
  something submitted, like an application
equilibrium: balance

---

10 E—To build a stem bridge you need to know what **CONCORD** means: **CONCORD** *is a state of* **AGREEMENT.** The two words are almost synonymous. The only answer choice whose words mean almost the same thing is (E), **flux** and **change.** So plug in your bridge: **Flux** *is a state of* **change.** It fits.

In (A) and (B), the word pairs are almost opposites. In (C), a **promise** is not *a state of* **peace.** In (D), a **revolution** is fought by an **army,** but **revolution** is not a state of **army.**

---

insurrection: rebellion
chaos: total disorder

Suggested Time: 7 minutes

Directions—Choose the lettered pair of words that is related in the same way as the pair in capital letters.

Example:
FLAKE : SNOW ::
(A)   storm : hail
(B)   drop : rain
(C)   field : wheat
(D)   stack : hay
(E)   sky : cloud   Ⓐ ● Ⓒ Ⓓ Ⓔ

1 WATCH : TIME ::
(A) tape : measurement
(B) ruler : length
(C) meter : measurement
(D) barometer : gauge
(E) hour : minute   Ⓐ Ⓑ Ⓒ Ⓓ Ⓔ

2 ARBOREAL : TREES ::
(A) national : government
(B) chemical : solution
(C) urban : city
(D) botanical : garden
(E) lunar : eclipse   Ⓐ Ⓑ Ⓒ Ⓓ Ⓔ

3 ARCHIPELAGO : ISLANDS ::
(A) ocean : fish
(B) constellation : stars
(C) universe : comets
(D) zoo : bears
(E) delta : rivers   Ⓐ Ⓑ Ⓒ Ⓓ Ⓔ

4 PREAMBLE : DOCUMENT ::
(A) overture : opera
(B) exit : door
(C) paragraph : line
(D) stanza : poem
(E) score : music   Ⓐ Ⓑ Ⓒ Ⓓ Ⓔ

5 ENTICING : ATTRACT ::
(A) welcome : warm
(B) elusive : allure
(C) withering : shock
(D) glittery : engross
(E) repugnant : repulse   Ⓐ Ⓑ Ⓒ Ⓓ Ⓔ

6 PUERILE : IMMATURITY ::
(A) hardworking : dexterity
(B) sly : craftiness
(C) unscrupulous : honesty
(D) boorish : politeness
(E) loquacious : oratory   Ⓐ Ⓑ Ⓒ Ⓓ Ⓔ

7 KINETIC : MOTION ::
(A) insipid : taste
(B) extinct : species
(C) frenetic : speed
(D) fictional : literature
(E) scholastic : education   Ⓐ Ⓑ Ⓒ Ⓓ Ⓔ

8 PUTRID : DECAY ::
(A) compelling : fear
(B) tortuous : pain
(C) old : rusty
(D) decrepit : age
(E) superficial : depth   Ⓐ Ⓑ Ⓒ Ⓓ Ⓔ

9 CONFLAGRATION : FIRE ::
(A) match : tinder
(B) sanctuary : church
(C) ice : storm
(D) bees : swarm
(E) deluge : flood   Ⓐ Ⓑ Ⓒ Ⓓ Ⓔ

10 SACROSANCT : CRITICISM ::
(A) quiescent : calm
(B) precise : time
(C) therapeutic : relaxation
(D) unmanageable : control
(E) subversive : law   Ⓐ Ⓑ Ⓒ Ⓓ Ⓔ

SCORECARD	
Number of Questions Right:	
Number of Questions Wrong:	
Number of Questions Omitted:	
Number of Correct Guesses:	
Number of Wrong Guesses:	
Time Used:	

Answers and Explanations

1 **B**—The bridge is clear: *the function of a* **WATCH** *is to measure* **TIME**. The correct answer is (B)—*the function of a* **ruler** *is to measure* **length**.

> *gauge: standard measure, an instrument for measuring*

2 **C**—**ARBOREAL** means having to do with **TREES**. In (C), the word **urban** means "having to do with the **city**."

The other answer choices are wrong; either the words within each pair are connected only loosely, or their relationship doesn't have anything to do with the relationship between the stem words. For example, in (A), a **national government** is the **government** of a particular nation. **ARBOREAL TREES** aren't the **TREES** of a particular arbor, or shelter of vines and branches, so (A) can't work. In (B), a **chemical** substance may or may not be a **solution**— this word pair has a weak bridge. A **botanical garden,** (D), is a place where plants and trees are grown for scientific study. Again, that bridge does not sound right when used with the stem words.

> *arboreal: having to do with trees*
> *urban: having to do with the city*

3 **B**—An **ARCHIPELAGO** *is a group of* **ISLANDS**; a **constellation** is a group of **stars**.

The **universe** consists of all matter known to exist; it's not a group of **comets**.

4 **A**—The prefix *pre-* in the word **PREAMBLE** should suggest to you that it has something to do with "going before." In fact, *a* **PREAMBLE** *is a preliminary statement, or introduction to a* **DOCU-MENT**.

Now let's check through the answer choices and see which one fits this bridge. In (A), an **overture** is, by definition, an orchestral composition that forms the prelude or introduction to an **opera,** or ballet. So (A) is correct.

You should always run through the other choices just to be sure. In (B), an **exit** does not come before a door. In (C), a paragraph contains **lines**, but a **paragraph** isn't the introduction to a **line**. In choice (D), a **stanza** is a subdivision of a **poem,** not the introduction to a **poem**. In (E), the **score** is the written copy of a piece of **music**.

> *preamble: a preliminary statement, or introduction to a document*
> *overture: an orchestral composition that forms the prelude to an opera or ballet*

5 **E**—Bridge: *Things that are* **ENTICING** *tend to* **ATTRACT**. Things that are repugnant tend to **repulse,** or repel.

6 **B**—**PUERILE** means childish, so the bridge is: *Someone* **PUERILE** *shows* **IMMATURITY**. (B) is right—someone **sly** shows **craftiness**.

Choices (A) and (E) can be eliminated because they have weak bridges; someone **hardworking** is not necessarily gifted with **dexterity,** or nimbleness. Similarly, someone **loquacious** does not necessarily practice **oratory**. Because choices (C) and (D) have the same bridge, they can both be eliminated. Someone **unscrupulous** lacks **honesty,** as someone **boorish** lacks **politeness**. So (B) is the correct answer, by process of elimination.

> *unscrupulous: lacking principles; unethical*
> *puerile: childish*
> *loquacious: talkative*
> *boorish: ill-mannered and rude*
> *oratory: the art of public speaking*

7 **E**—**KINETIC** *means having to do with* **MOTION**. In (E), **scholastic** means having to do with **education**.

> *kinetic: having to do with motion*
> *scholastic: having to do with education*
> *insipid: tasteless, dull, lacking in flavor*
> *extinct: no longer active or existing*
> *frenetic: frantic, wildly exciting*
> *fictional: invented, imagined*

8 **D**—*Something* **PUTRID** *shows signs of* **DECAY**, just as something **decrepit** shows signs of **age**.

If you did not understand the meaning of **PUTRID**, how could you proceed? Well, you know **PUTRID** is an adjective, since the first word in each of the answer choices is an adjective. Also, **PUTRID** sounds negative. You could reason that the words in the correct answer choice will also be similar in meaning to each other. Choices (A), (B), and (C) can be ruled out, because they all have weak bridges.

(E) has a strong bridge: Something that is **superficial,** or shallow, lacks **depth.** However, since we've already decided that we are looking for two words that have the same "charge," this bridge does not fit. Either way, (D) must be the correct answer.

---

putrid: decomposed, rotting, foul-smelling
decrepit: made weak by hard use, or old age
tortuous: twisted, crooked, or winding

---

9 E—*A* **CONFLAGRATION** *is an enormous* **FIRE.** *A* **deluge** *is an enormous* **flood.**

---

sanctuary: a place of refuge or protection; or
the most sacred part of a religious
building

---

10 D—Bridge: **SACROSANCT** *means beyond* **CRITICISM.** (D) is correct, because something **unmanageable** *is beyond* **control.**

Could you arrive at the right answer without understanding the meaning of **SACROSANCT?** Yes, if you work backwards. (A), (B), (C), and (E) have bridges that are either weak, or unworkable with the stem words, so they can all be ruled out. (C) has a weak bridge—the purpose of something **therapeutic** is not necessarily to induce **relaxation,** but to remedy an ailment. In (E), a **subversive** act—one that is designed to weaken authority—may or may not be against the **law;** (E) is also weak.

---

sacrosanct: accorded the highest reverence
and respect, beyond criticism
quiescent: calm

Suggested Time: 7 minutes

Directions—Choose the lettered pair of words that is related in the same way as the pair in capital letters.

Example:
FLAKE : SNOW ::
(A)   storm : hail
(B)   drop : rain
(C)   field : wheat
(D)   stack : hay
(E)   sky : cloud   Ⓐ ● Ⓒ Ⓓ Ⓔ

1   PLAYWRIGHT : PLAY ::
(A) painter : canvas
(B) critic : literature
(C) composer : score
(D) announcer : radio
(E) musician : instrument   Ⓐ Ⓑ Ⓒ Ⓓ Ⓔ

2   CLOG : SHOE ::
(A) boot : mud
(B) drain : liquid
(C) sombrero : hat
(D) gold : jewelry
(E) wig : head   Ⓐ Ⓑ Ⓒ Ⓓ Ⓔ

3   SWILL : DRINK ::
(A) consume : digest
(B) gossip : talk
(C) risk : gamble
(D) gorge : eat
(E) swallow : sip   Ⓐ Ⓑ Ⓒ Ⓓ Ⓔ

4   THRIFTY : PARSIMONIOUS ::
(A) inquisitive : prying
(B) brave : timid
(C) aggressive : alert
(D) timorous : gentle
(E) stern : yielding   Ⓐ Ⓑ Ⓒ Ⓓ Ⓔ

5   PLANE : SMOOTH ::
(A) embellish : expensive
(B) burnish : shiny
(C) merge : complex
(D) pulverize : dusty
(E) flatten : small   Ⓐ Ⓑ Ⓒ Ⓓ Ⓔ

6   WHIFF : SMELL ::
(A) pain : sensation
(B) food : taste
(C) tinge : color
(D) fall : accident
(E) answer : solution   Ⓐ Ⓑ Ⓒ Ⓓ Ⓔ

7   PHARMACY : DRUGS ::
(A) nursery : florists
(B) terrarium : sod
(C) seminary : textbooks
(D) auditorium : plays
(E) haberdashery : clothing   Ⓐ Ⓑ Ⓒ Ⓓ Ⓔ

8   IMPROVIDENT : FORESIGHT ::
(A) fortunate : opportunity
(B) ill-tempered : prudence
(C) incapacitated : wisdom
(D) ambitious : success
(E) skeptical : belief   Ⓐ Ⓑ Ⓒ Ⓓ Ⓔ

9   BOMBASTIC : GRANDILOQUENCE ::
(A) unyielding : resolution
(B) finicky : variety
(C) timid : confidence
(D) retiring : age
(E) calm : excitement   Ⓐ Ⓑ Ⓒ Ⓓ Ⓔ

10   APOSTATE : RELIGION ::
(A) pedant : erudition
(B) benefactor : largess
(C) politician : sovereignty
(D) defector : cause
(E) reprobate : crime   Ⓐ Ⓑ Ⓒ Ⓓ Ⓔ

SCORECARD	
Number of Questions Right:	
Number of Questions Wrong:	
Number of Questions Omitted:	
Number of Correct Guesses:	
Number of Wrong Guesses:	
Time Used:	

Answers and Explanations

1 C—A **PLAYWRIGHT** *is the author of a* **PLAY** just as a **composer** is the author of a **score.**

A **painter** is not really the author of a **canvas,** since a **canvas** is a piece of cloth framed and backed so as to be a surface for painting.

2 C—A **CLOG** *is a type of* **SHOE,** just as a **sombrero** is a type of **hat.**

(A) might have tempted you, since **boot** and **SHOE** are similar. But a **boot** isn't a type of **mud.** In (B), a **drain** is a means by which **liquid** is drawn off or emptied; a **drain** isn't a type of **liquid.**

3 D—Bridge: *To* **SWILL** *is to* **DRINK** *in a greedy manner or to excess. To* **gorge** *is to* **eat** *in a greedy manner or to excess.*

(A) **consume: digest** may remind you of the stem pair, but that's not enough to make it the right answer. If you plug (A) into the bridge, you get: To **consume** is to **digest** in a greedy manner. That makes no sense, so (A) can't be right.

4 A—The bridge is: *Someone who is overly* **THRIFTY** *is* **PARSIMONIOUS.** *Someone overly* **inquisitive** *is* **prying.**

In (D), someone **timorous** is probably also **gentle,** but you wouldn't say that someone overly **timorous** is **gentle.**

timorous: meek

5 B—The challenge here is to think of the right meaning of **PLANE.** **PLANE** is being used as a verb here, so your bridge is: *To* **PLANE** *is to make something* **SMOOTH.** *In the same way, to* **burnish** *is to make something* **shiny.**

plane: to make smooth or level
burnish: to polish until shiny
pulverize: to crush into powder

6 C—Bridge: a **WHIFF** *is a slight trace of* **SMELL.** A **tinge** *is a slight trace of* **color.**

7 E—The bridge is: *You buy* **DRUGS** *at a* **PHARMACY,** *just as you buy* **clothing** *at a* **haberdashery.** In (A), a **nursery** is where plants are grown or sold. **Florists** might go to a **nursery,** but **florists** aren't bought there.

terrarium: a glass container for raising plants or animals indoors
seminary: an institution of higher education, especially one that trains people to be priests, ministers, or rabbis
haberdashery: clothing store

8 E—The bridge is: *someone* **IMPROVIDENT** *lacks* **FORESIGHT** the same way *someone* **skeptical** *lacks* **belief.**

improvident: thoughtless, unwary, neglecting to provide for future needs

9 A—**BOMBASTIC** *means characterized by* **GRANDILOQUENCE. Unyielding** *means characterized by* **resolution,** or firmness.

If you were not able to define these words, the only effective strategy open to you was elimination of wrong answers. Let's see how it works here. As we've already seen, (A) has a strong bridge: **Unyielding** means characterized by **resolution.** In (B), someone **finicky** may or may not like **variety.** The two words in (B) have a weak relationship, so (B) can be eliminated. (C) is pretty strong: Someone who is **timid** does not exhibit **confidence.** It's a possible right answer, so keep it in mind for the moment. (D) **retiring,** has nothing to with **age.** (E) has a strong bridge: Someone who is **calm** does not exhibit **excitement.** However, since (C) and (E) have the same bridge, they must both be wrong. After all, there can be only one answer choice that has the same bridge as the stem words. By process of elimination, (A) is the correct answer.

grandiloquence: extravagant, pompous language
bombastic: using pompous language
unyielding: characterized by resolution
retiring: reserved or shy

10 D—Bridge: An **APOSTATE** *is someone who has renounced a particular* **RELIGION.** In (D), a **defector** *is someone who has renounced a particular* **cause.**

apostate: someone who has renounced a
   particular religion
pedant: someone overly concerned with small,
   insignificant details of knowledge
erudition: learning
benefactor: a donor, one who makes
   a large gift
largess: generosity
sovereignty: supreme power or freedom from
   external controls
reprobate: a scoundrel, an immoral or
   wicked person

SAT Sentence Completions

INTRODUCTION TO SAT SENTENCE COMPLETIONS

Sentence Completions test your ability to read carefully and think logically. Sentence Completions also test your knowledge of college-level vocabulary.

The Structure

You'll probably see nine Sentence Completions at the beginning of one 30-minute Verbal section, and ten at the beginning of the other. The rest of those sections will consist of Analogies and Critical Reading.

The Format

The directions for Sentence Completions appear at the top of the questions. They look something like this:

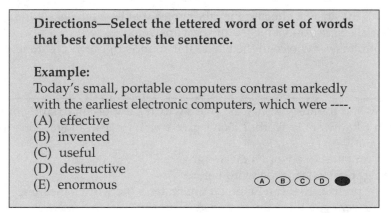

Directions—Select the lettered word or set of words that best completes the sentence.

Example:
Today's small, portable computers contrast markedly with the earliest electronic computers, which were ----.
(A) effective
(B) invented
(C) useful
(D) destructive
(E) enormous

In the example, the new computers, which are small and portable, are contrasted with old computers. You can infer that the old computers must be the opposite of small and portable, so (E) **enormous** is right.

Though the real SAT directions and sample question will look slightly different, they'll mean the same thing. Now you know what to do when you open your booklet to Sentence Completions. So don't waste time reading the directions on Test Day.

Sentence Completions are arranged in order of difficulty. The hardest questions are at the end of each set, so pace yourself accordingly. Take no more than 40 seconds on each Sentence Completion. Save the bulk of your 30 minutes for Critical Reading questions.

If a question stumps you, mark it in your test booklet, skip it on your answer sheet, and come back to it later if you have time. But first finish all the other questions in Sentence Completions, Analogies, and Critical Reading.

> Hint: Don't get hung up on any one question. Your goal is to answer correctly as many questions as possible.

Like everything else on the SAT, Sentence Completions come in a standard format. Once you get used to solving them, they can be quite easy. So if you're having trouble, practice.

Kaplan's Method

Kaplan has a tested method for solving Sentence Completions. It works whether your sentence deals with tarantulas, stained glass windows, or Native American dance forms. Here's what to do.
- Read the sentence carefully, searching for clue words or phrases.

> Hint: Words or phrases like *and, but, although,* and *such as* are clues because they indicate contrast or similarity. Clues like these can tell you where a sentence is headed and what kind of word goes in the blank or blanks.

- Predict what should go into the blank or blanks. Do this before you glance at the answer choices.

> Hint: Your prediction doesn't have to be exact. A rough idea of what goes in the blanks will do.

- Compare your prediction to the answer choices. Pick the choice that best matches your prediction.
- Scan the other choices to make sure you've picked the best answer.
- Read the sentence with your answer choice in the blank. If it sounds right, you're done.

Dealing With Hard Words

You'll find hard words in the sentences and the answer choices. That's why it's important to study our Word and Root Lists. But what if you still don't know some words? Don't give up. Try these suggestions for working around unknown words:

- Look in the sentence itself for clues to a word's meaning.
- Think about where you might have heard the word before.
- Try to spot familiar roots or prefixes that can help you understand the word's meaning.
- If all else fails, eliminate answers you think are wrong and guess.

Dealing With Hard Sentences

It's important to read the sentences and answer choices carefully, especially near the end of the set. Follow the twists and turns of the sentence, and be sure you understand what it says. Then you won't get caught by tricky answers that the test makers like to include.

- Don't pick an answer just because it sounds hard. Be sure the answer you choose makes sense.
- Don't choose an answer choice that is the opposite of the correct answer. Read the sentence carefully.

Dealing With Two-Blank Sentences

Two-blank sentences can be easier than one-blankers. In two-blankers you can:

- Scan the sentence and start with the easier blank.
- Eliminate all answer choices that won't work for that blank.
- Try only the remaining choices in the second blank.

> HINT: In two-blankers, don't pick a choice that fits one blank but not the other.

Sentence Completion Checklist

✔ Use Kaplan's Method: Read carefully, predict an answer, find a match for your prediction, and check your answer.

✔ Work systematically, but quickly.

✔ Spend no more than 40 seconds on each question.

✔ Search the sentence for clue words and phrases.

✔ To figure out what a hard word means, figure out how it's used in the sentence, think where you may have heard it before, and look for familiar prefixes and roots. If all else fails, eliminate wrong answers and guess.

✔ On two-blankers, do the easier blank first. Then make sure the answer choice you pick fits both blanks.

✔ On the last few questions, don't pick answers just because they sound hard. Watch out for wrong answer choices that are opposites of right answers.

Suggested Time: 7 minutes

Directions—Select the lettered word or set of words that best completes the sentence.

Example:
Today's small, portable computers contrast markedly with the earliest electronic computers, which were ----.
(A) effective
(B) invented
(C) useful
(D) destructive
(E) enormous   Ⓐ Ⓑ Ⓒ Ⓓ ●

1. Joseph's employees were ---- by the ---- manner in which he dealt with them.
(A) repulsed . . placid
(B) irritated . . curt
(C) incensed . . droll
(D) perturbed . . amiable
(E) weakened . . sullen   Ⓐ Ⓑ Ⓒ Ⓓ Ⓔ

2. It is sometimes customary to view rain as ---- sign; many believe that if it rains on the day of your wedding, you will enjoy financial prosperity.
(A) an inopportune
(B) a meager
(C) an auspicious
(D) an untimely
(E) a modest   Ⓐ Ⓑ Ⓒ Ⓓ Ⓔ

3. Once a ---- population center, the city gradually lost residents to the factory towns of the North.
(A) bustling
(B) manufactured
(C) rural
(D) seedy
(E) deserted   Ⓐ Ⓑ Ⓒ Ⓓ Ⓔ

4. The scene was even ---- than Rebecca had ----; dead trees and patchy brown grass seemed to stretch on forever under a leaden sky.
(A) uglier . . feigned
(B) drearier . . envisioned
(C) lazier . . divulged
(D) scantier . . desired
(E) keener . . perceived   Ⓐ Ⓑ Ⓒ Ⓓ Ⓔ

5. Proponents of a bill requiring each home to keep a firearm and ammunition sought to placate their opponents by including ---- for those who did not ---- gun possession.
(A) a penalty . . frown upon
(B) an exemption . . support
(C) a theory . . relish
(D) an addendum . . continue
(E) a waiver . . abolish   Ⓐ Ⓑ Ⓒ Ⓓ Ⓔ

6. Otis ---- agreed to ---- his partner's decision, misguided though he thought it was.
(A) gracefully . . rail at
(B) maliciously . . compromise on
(C) wistfully . . bargain with
(D) grudgingly . . abide by
(E) cynically . . reign over   Ⓐ Ⓑ Ⓒ Ⓓ Ⓔ

7. The name of the housing development is a ----; although it is called "Forest Hills," it is located in a ---- valley.
(A) dilution . . river
(B) fallacy . . neglected
(C) misnomer . . treeless
(D) retelling . . contented
(E) fault . . barren   Ⓐ Ⓑ Ⓒ Ⓓ Ⓔ

8. Far from being ----, today's television advertising, with its constant barrage of last-minute sales and new-and-improved products, practically ---- the viewer.
(A) subtle . . assaults
(B) engaging . . titillates
(C) utilitarian . . assists
(D) obtuse . . ridicules
(E) informative . . ignores   Ⓐ Ⓑ Ⓒ Ⓓ Ⓔ

9. Unfortunately, the treasurer's plan to get the company out of debt ---- gaining access to certain funds that may never become available.
(A) speaks to
(B) treats with
(C) delves into
(D) metes out
(E) hinges on   Ⓐ Ⓑ Ⓒ Ⓓ Ⓔ

10 A true ascetic, Jorge ---- luxuries and other worldly pleasures in an effort to ---- his spiritual side.

(A) spurns . . fortify
(B) embraces . . emulate
(C) relishes . . assist
(D) condones . . reclaim
(E) lambastes . . interpret

Ⓐ Ⓑ Ⓒ Ⓓ Ⓔ

SCORECARD	
Number of Questions Right:	
Number of Questions Wrong:	
Number of Questions Omitted:	
Number of Correct Guesses:	
Number of Wrong Guesses:	
Time Used:	

Answers and Explanations

1 **B**—In this sentence, you can figure out the relation between the two words. Either the employees were "pleased" by the "nice" manner in which he dealt with them, or they were "displeased" by the "not nice" manner in which he dealt with them. In other words, the two words must reinforce each other.

In (A), **placid** and **repulsed** have nothing to do with each other. In (B), it makes sense that employees would be **irritated** by their employer's **curt** manner, so (B) is probably right. But check out the other answers.

In (C) and (D), the words are almost opposites. In (E), they have little connection. So go with (B).

> *repulsed: repelled*
> *placid: calm*
> *curt: rudely brief in speech*

2 **C**—*Financial prosperity* is a strong clue. Since it's a good thing, rain must be a sign of good fortune. Scanning the answer choices, the closest match is **auspicious**.

> *inopportune: inconvenient*
> *auspicious: foretelling good fortune*

3 **A**—Clue words here are *once* and *lost residents.* Since it *lost residents*, the city once must have been a large *population center.* That sense is conveyed by (A) **bustling**. It certainly is not conveyed by **deserted, seedy, manufactured,** or **rural.**

> *bustling: crowded and busy*
> *seedy: rundown*

4 **B**—The semicolon offers a clue. The words that go in the blanks must fit the gloomy description after the semicolon. Your phrase might be: the scene was even "worse" than Rebecca had "imagined." In the first blank, **lazier, keener,** and **scantier** aren't close to "worse," and they don't fit, so you are left with (A) and (B). Since either **uglier** or **drearier** would fit the first blank, you have to decide between (A) and (B) based on their second words. **Feigned** doesn't make sense in this context. But **envisioned** works fine.

> *feigned: pretended*
> *envisioned: imagined*
> *scantier: scarcer*

5 **B**—This one's tough if you don't know the vocabulary (see box). The **proponents** were trying to get the bill passed by the legislature. They wanted firearm possession to be mandatory. Presumably **their opponents** didn't favor keeping guns, so the second blank should be filled by something that means "supported."

The first blank might be filled by something like *a loophole,* a way for people who don't want to obey the law to avoid its requirements.

(A) is out because **penalty** doesn't fit the first blank, and **frown upon** is the opposite of what we want for the second blank. In (C), it doesn't make sense for **a theory** to be included in *a bill.* Moreover, **relish** is totally at odds with our description for the second blank. **An addendum** is usually "attached to" something, rather than *included* in it. And since **continue** doesn't make any sense in the second blank, (D) must be wrong. In (E), **a waiver** precisely matches our word *loophole* for the first blank, but it doesn't make sense to talk about exempting those who do not **abolish** *gun possession.* (B), the only remaining choice, fits both blanks.

> *proponents: supporters*
> *placate: soothe or appease*
> *exemption: waiver or exception from a*
>   *requirement*
> *relish: enjoy greatly*
> *addendum: addition*

6 **D**—Your clue here is *misguided.* Since *Otis* thought his partner's decision was *misguided,* he obviously "reluctantly" agreed to "go along with it." (D) fits both descriptions. *Otis* **grudgingly** *agreed to* **abide by** *his partner's decision.*

Checking the other choices, (A) **gracefully,** (B) **maliciously,** and (C) **wistfully** don't make sense. In (E), **cynically** could possibly fit, but **reign over** is clearly wrong.

maliciously: spitefully
grudgingly: unwillingly or reluctantly
abide by: act according to
cynically: pessimistically, distrustfully

7 **C**—The sentence suggests that the housing development's name is misleading. It may have been called *Forest Hills*, but it was actually constructed *in a ---- valley*, not in the *Hills*. So you need a word like *mistake*, or even *fraud*, for the first blank. And for the second blank, you're looking for something that contrasts with *Forest*.

Start with the first blank. (B) **fallacy** and (C) **misnomer** are the only two possible choices. So rule out the others and check the second words for (B) and (C). In (B), **neglected** doesn't fit. In (C), **treeless** does fit the second blank. Since both the words in choice (C) match the predicted meanings, (C) is correct.

fallacy: logical error
misnomer: a wrong name

8 **A**—The clue here is *far from being*. It tells you that you are dealing with two contrasting sentence parts. *Far from being ----, today's television ---- the viewer.* We're also told that *today's television advertising* consists of a *constant barrage* of information. The implication is that today's television advertising "attacks" the viewer. So you need to look for a second word that's similar to *attacks*, and a first word that contrasts with it.

The only second word that means "attacks" is **assaults**, in (A). The *advertising practically* **assaults** *the viewer* in a heavy-handed way. **Subtle** is a good opposite, so this fits.

In (B), **engaging** and **titillates** are not opposites; **engaging** commercials might very well **titillate** the viewer. (C) **utilitarian** makes no sense. (D) **obtuse** has little to do with **ridicules**. In (E), **informative** might be right, but the *barrage* of television advertising certainly doesn't **ignore** the viewer.

barrage: rapid, concentrated outpouring
subtle: indirect, delicate
engaging: attractive
titillates: arouses or stimulates
utilitarian: functional
obtuse: dull or stupid

9 **E**—Your clue is *unfortunately. The treasurer's plan unfortunately* may not work because it ---- gaining access to certain funds that may never become available. To fill the blank, look for a phrase like *relies on* or *is based on*. The closest choice is (E), **hinges on.** The other four familiar phrases don't make sense in this sentence.

speaks to: addresses (an issue or a point)
treats with: negotiates with
delves into: digs or searches deeply
*   and carefully*
metes out: gives out small rations
*   or allotments*
hinges on: depends on

10 **A**—Since *Jorge* is a *true ascetic*, the word in the first blank must support that description. You could say: A true ascetic "gives up" luxuries. To make sense, the second blank has to reinforce that. He "gives up" *luxuries* in order to "strengthen" his spiritual side.

Checking the first words in the answer choices, you'll see **spurns** works best. Now check out the second word. A true ascetic **spurns** luxuries in an effort to **fortify** his spiritual side. That makes sense.

Later on in a set, answer choices often contain some difficult words. If you don't know them all, eliminate choices when one word doesn't make sense. In this case, you probably knew that **embraces** and **relishes** mean almost the opposite of "gives up," so you could eliminate (B) and (C). You might also have guessed that **interpret** has nothing to do with "strengthen," so you could eliminate (E). Then you could guess between (A) and (D).

ascetic: one who practices self-denial
spurns: rejects
fortify: strengthen
embraces: clasps in one's arms, accepts
*   wholeheartedly*
emulate: imitate or strive to equal
relishes: enjoys
condones: pardons
reclaim: rescue
lambaste: whip verbally or censure
interpret: explain or give the meaning of

SENTENCE COMPLETIONS—PRACTICE SET 2

 Suggested Time: 7 minutes

Directions—Select the lettered word or set of words that best completes the sentence.

Example:
Today's small, portable computers contrast markedly with the earliest electronic computers, which were ----.
(A) effective
(B) invented
(C) useful
(D) destructive
(E) enormous ⒶⒷⒸⒹ●

1 Barbara Walters distinguished herself as a journalist by asking famous people the kinds of ---- questions that other reporters shied away from.
(A) discreet
(B) intriguing
(C) pointed
(D) gentle
(E) indirect ⒶⒷⒸⒹⒺ

2 Ozone in the upper layers of Earth's atmosphere is beneficial, ---- animal and plant life from dangerous ultraviolet radiation.
(A) reflecting
(B) withdrawing
(C) displacing
(D) thwarting
(E) protecting ⒶⒷⒸⒹⒺ

3 All of today's navel oranges are ---- of a single mutant tree that began producing seedless fruit nearly 200 years ago.
(A) progenitors
(B) hybrids
(C) descendants
(D) conglomerations
(E) spores ⒶⒷⒸⒹⒺ

4 So ---- was the saleswoman's pitch about the value of the used car that Hallie nearly missed the ---- in its logic.
(A) convincing . . fallacy
(B) inept . . liability
(C) relieving . . reason
(D) tired . . persuasiveness
(E) sarcastic . . rejoinder ⒶⒷⒸⒹⒺ

5 Certain members of the pack viciously ---- others, ---- the hierarchical structure of the group.
(A) venerate . . destroying
(B) bully . . reinforcing
(C) coax . . subsidizing
(D) terrorize . . memorizing
(E) pass . . reacting ⒶⒷⒸⒹⒺ

6 After inventing a sign language for the deaf in the mid-1700s, Giacobbo Rodriguez Pereira ---- his business activities in order to ---- all his energies to humanitarian work.
(A) shouldered . . donate
(B) elicited . . transmit
(C) abandoned . . devote
(D) ceased . . attach
(E) ceded . . sell ⒶⒷⒸⒹⒺ

7 Investigators are trying to determine whether the recent rash of fires is the work of ---- or simply a ---- of unfortunate accidents.
(A) a pyromaniac . . source
(B) an accomplice . . consequence
(C) a criminal . . premonition
(D) an arsonist . . series
(E) an assortment . . string ⒶⒷⒸⒹⒺ

8 Despite his physical disability, the soccer player was ---- in helping his country's team capture the World Cup.
(A) ungainly
(B) accessible
(C) rampant
(D) instrumental
(E) unvarying ⒶⒷⒸⒹⒺ

9   Doing much more than was expected of her, Henrietta ---- the responsibilities of a department supervisor's position for eight months before she finally received the title.
(A) undertook
(B) procured
(C) entreated
(D) bestowed
(E) precipitated   Ⓐ Ⓑ Ⓒ Ⓓ Ⓔ

10 The poet received room, board, and ---- from the university in return for leading two seminars.
(A) an impetus
(B) an amulet
(C) a writ
(D) a niche
(E) a stipend   Ⓐ Ⓑ Ⓒ Ⓓ Ⓔ

SCORECARD	
Number of Questions Right:	
Number of Questions Wrong:	
Number of Questions Omitted:	
Number of Correct Guesses:	
Number of Wrong Guesses:	
Time Used:	

KAPLAN

Answers and Explanations

1 **C**—The sentence says that *Barbara Walters* earned a reputation for *herself as a journalist by* doing what *other reporters shied away from* or "avoided." The clue lies in *the kinds of questions* she asked—the kind *others shied away from.* You can predict that Ms. Walters asked personal, probing questions about controversial subjects. The only answer that describes such questions is (C), **pointed.**

A journalist wouldn't *shy away from* (D) **gentle** and (E) **indirect** questions. So (D) and (E) are thus eliminated. As for (B), all reporters try to make their questions intriguing.

> *discreet: prudently quiet or circumspect*
> *intriguing: exciting interest or curiosity*

2 **E**—In the upper layers of the Earth's atmosphere, ozone is said to be beneficial or "helpful," so it must do something good for animal and plant life.

> *thwart: to hinder, obstruct, or frustrate*

3 **C**—You have to predict a relationship between *all of today's navel oranges* and *a single mutant tree that* produced *seedless fruit* a long time ago. *Today's navel oranges* are (C) **descendants** or offspring of that first tree.

Mutant may confuse the hasty reader into selecting (B) **hybrids,** but the sentence does not suggest that *today's navel oranges* are offspring of two different species. (A) **Progenitors** describe a *mutant tree,* but not *today's navel oranges.* Likewise, in (D), **conglomeration** does not describe *navel oranges.* Finally, **spores** have to do with reproductive methods that are not discussed here, so (E) is not a good choice.

> *progenitors: ancestors, forebears*
> *conglomeration: mixture of various things*
> *spores: reproductive bodies released by*
> *certain primitive plants*

4 **A**—*The saleswoman's pitch* is her sales talk. We need a word like *persuasive* for the first blank and something like *flaw* for the second. Choice (A) is the only one that matches either prediction.

> *fallacy: error in logic*
> *inept: incompetent*
> *rejoinder: reply or "comeback"*

5 **B**—Suppose you didn't know some of the difficult words in this question. You could still eliminate wrong choices and guess. The only two choices whose first words can reasonably be modified by *viciously* are (B) **bully** and (D) **terrorize.** Choices (A) **venerate,** (C) **coax,** and (E) **pass** don't fit at all.

Checking the second blank, (B) makes sense and (D) doesn't. The aggressive behavior of these pack animals was **reinforcing** the *structure of the group* rather than **memorizing** it. So you could arrive at (B) by process of elimination.

Had you known the vocabulary words, you could have reached the same conclusion more quickly and with more certainty. The first part of the sentence indicates that some *members of the pack* get away with *viciously* attacking *others.* The second part implies that these attacks have something to do with the group's *hierarchical structure.* (B) best fits the meaning of the sentence, since the aggressive members of the pack control the weaker members.

> *hierarchical: having grades or ranks of*
> *authority or status*
> *venerate: worship, esteem highly*
> *coax: persuade gently*

6 **C**—You can find the correct answer by examining the main clause alone: *Pereira ---- his business activities in order to ---- all his energies to humanitarian work.* In other words, he wanted to spend less time on *business activities* and more on *humanitarian work.* In the second blank, (A) **donate** and (C) **devote** are the only choices that fit. You can't **transmit, attach,** or **sell** your *energies* to a project.

So the only options you need to consider for the first blank are (A) **shouldered** and (C) **abandoned.** Since he wanted to spend less time on business activities, he probably abandoned them, so (C) is the right answer. He **abandoned** *his business activities in order to* **devote** *all his energies to humanitarian work.*

shoulder: to take on a burden or
responsibility
abandoned: gave up, relinquished
elicited: evoked or produced
ceded: gave over or granted

7 **D**—In this context, a *rash* is not a skin irritation but a large number of instances within a short period of time. Here we're talking about a recent series of fires. For the first blank, we'll need a person or thing that might have caused the *fires*. The best options for the first blank are (A) **a pyromaniac** and (D) **an arsonist**. Although (C) **a criminal** might have started the fires, **a criminal** does not have as specific a connection with *fires.* And (B) **an accomplice** would by definition have helped set the *fires*, rather than setting them himself or herself.

Now look at the words that (A) and (D) offer for the second blank. *The recent rash of fires* could not have been *a* **source** *of unfortunate accidents* unless it caused accidents, which we are not told. But **series** *of accidents* fits well with the idea of a *rash of fires.*

pyromaniac: someone who has an irresistible
impulse to set fires
arsonist: someone who burns property
for spite or profit
premonition: a hunch or feeling of foreboding

8 **D**—*Despite* is the clue word. It allows you to predict that in spite of his *physical disability*, the soccer player was important to his team. The only answer choice that comes close to that prediction is **instrumental,** or helpful. In other words, the *team* won *the World Cup* because of the disabled player's efforts.

instrumental: serving as a means,
agent, or tool
ungainly: awkward
accessible: open, capable of being reached
rampant: widespread
unvarying: unchanging

9 **A**—A long time elapsed between when *Henrietta ---- the responsibilities of a department supervisor's position* and when *she finally received the title.* You might predict a word like *assumed* or *shouldered* for the blank. The closest choice is (A) **undertook.** As for (B), Henrietta eventually **procured** *the*

title, but first she **undertook** *the responsibilities.*

procured: obtained or achieved by some effort
entreated: pleaded with, begged
bestowed: presented as a gift
precipitated: brought about suddenly

10 **E**—What might the university have given *the poet* as compensation *for leading two seminars?* We know that *the poet received room* and *board,* or living quarters and meals. The other obvious form of compensation would be money. The only answer choice that has anything to do with monetary compensation is (E) **a stipend.**

stipend: wage or other form of compensation
to defray expenses
impetus: stimulus or driving force
amulet: good luck charm
writ: formal legal document
niche: small opening or space

Suggested Time: 7 minutes

Directions—Select the lettered word or set of words that best completes the sentence.

Example:
Today's small, portable computers contrast markedly with the earliest electronic computers, which were ----.
(A) effective
(B) invented
(C) useful
(D) destructive
(E) enormous   Ⓐ Ⓑ Ⓒ Ⓓ ●

1 The first primitive fish had lungs; in most of their descendants, these ---- have ----- into swim bladders.
(A) animals . . merged
(B) organs . . evolved
(C) ancients . . combined
(D) organisms . . stretched
(E) functions . . barged

2 Martha's wardrobe looked as though it had been ---- from a rag bin; her expensive boots were her sole ---- fashion.
(A) swiped . . agreement with
(B) compartmentalized . . return to
(C) beguiled . . contribution to
(D) salvaged . . concession to
(E) bought . . interruption from   Ⓐ Ⓑ Ⓒ Ⓓ Ⓔ

3 John Price was ---- from the slave-hunters who had abducted him by the citizens of Oberlin and the neighboring towns; 37 of these citizens were then ---- under the Fugitive Slave Act.
(A) kidnapped . . legislated
(B) recovered . . deemed
(C) rescued . . indicted
(D) serenaded . . jailed
(E) pressured . . penalized   Ⓐ Ⓑ Ⓒ Ⓓ Ⓔ

4 The 150-year-old church had been ---- for demolition until architects and neighborhood residents ---- to have it declared an historic landmark.
(A) scheduled . . declined
(B) excommunicated . . prayed
(C) slated . . rallied
(D) exchanged . . paid
(E) repaired . . sought

5 In 1883, ---- eruption of Mount Krakatoa killed many thousands of people and ---- havoc on the coasts of Java and Sumatra.
(A) a fateful . . diminished
(B) an inoffensive . . spawned
(C) an immoral . . reigned
(D) a blistering . . authorized
(E) a disastrous . . wreaked   Ⓐ Ⓑ Ⓒ Ⓓ Ⓔ

6 The contractor first quoted an outrageous figure to repair the roof but appeared willing to ---- when Ben ---- at the price.
(A) negotiate . . balked
(B) bargain . . floundered
(C) participate . . recoiled
(D) reconsider . . waived
(E) intensify . . fainted   Ⓐ Ⓑ Ⓒ Ⓓ Ⓔ

7 Because the ancient Egyptians ---- the hour as one-twelfth of the time from dawn to dusk, its length varied during the ---- of the year.
(A) measured . . remainder
(B) revered . . occurrence
(C) imagined . . dates
(D) defined . . course
(E) idealized . . seasons   Ⓐ Ⓑ Ⓒ Ⓓ Ⓔ

8 The candidate answered tough questions with ---- candor, winning over many viewers who had previously supported her rival.
(A) presumptuous
(B) impatient
(C) unintentional
(D) dogmatic
(E) disarming   Ⓐ Ⓑ Ⓒ Ⓓ Ⓔ

9 Henry Louis Gates Jr. believes that Frederick
   Douglass ---- patterned his 1845 autobiography
   after the ---- of former slave Olaudah Equiano,
   whose life story was published in 1789.
   (A) patronizingly . . reminder
   (B) consciously . . narrative
   (C) anxiously . . capture
   (D) expectantly . . epitaph
   (E) belatedly . . antiquity   Ⓐ Ⓑ Ⓒ Ⓓ Ⓔ

10 It was difficult to imagine George, ---- man, as a
   psychiatrist; listening while others talked was
   not his style.
   (A) a voluble
   (B) an insensitive
   (C) a pessimistic
   (D) a truculent
   (E) a depressed   Ⓐ Ⓑ Ⓒ Ⓓ Ⓔ

SCORECARD	
Number of Questions Right:	
Number of Questions Wrong:	
Number of Questions Omitted:	
Number of Correct Guesses:	
Number of Wrong Guesses:	
Time Used:	

Answers and Explanations

1 **B**—You don't need a science background to complete this sentence correctly. You just need to understand the logic of the sentence. For the first blank, the phrase *these* ---- must refer to lungs. Apparently the lungs have developed into *swim bladders* in most of today's fish. So you might predict a word like *structures* for the first blank, and something like *developed* for the second blank. The choice that comes closest to those predictions is (B): the **organs** *have* **evolved** *into swim bladders.*

> *organs: parts of an organism (e.g., brain, heart, eye) that perform a specific function*
> *organisms: individual life forms, such as plants or animals*
> *merged: combined or joined into one unit*
> *barge: to intrude or move clumsily*

2 **D**—The word that goes in the first blank has to mean something like "taken." (B) **compartmentalized** and (C) **beguiled** don't make sense. You might **beguile,** or try to win over, someone in order to take something from him or her, but **beguiled** doesn't mean "taken." The remaining three choices have first words that mean "taken," but only one of them matches up with *a bin* that contains worthless rags and clothes. (A) and (E) won't work, because no one would have **swiped** or **bought** anything from a rag bin. But **salvaged** makes perfect sense. It also makes sense to say that *her expensive boots were her sole* **concession** *to fashion.* The only acknowledgment to fashion in Martha's wardrobe were her *expensive boots.*

> *compartmentalized: separated into compartments or categories*
> *beguiled: cheated, charmed*
> *salvaged: rescued from scrap or demolition*
> *concession: acknowledgment or admission*

3 **C**—Since the citizens must have "taken" *John Price* away from *the slave-hunters,* choices (A), (B), and (C) might fit the first blank. (D) and (E) are out, because **serenaded** and **pressured** have no meaning in this context.

Now check the second blanks of (A), (B), and (C). You have to decide between three relatively tough second words. In (A), one can **legislate** behavior, but not people, so it doesn't make sense to say that

the *citizens were then* **legislated.** (B) **deemed** doesn't work either, since the word has to be followed by an adjective or noun. *These citizens* might have been "judged" or "tried" *under the Fugitive Slave Act;* they might even have been **deemed** "guilty," but they could not simply have been **deemed.** However, they could have been **indicted** for helping a runaway slave, so (C) is correct.

> *serenaded: sang love songs to*
> *legislated: governed by passing and enforcing laws*
> *deemed: judged or believed*
> *indicted: charged with or accused of a crime*

4 **C**—Your clue is the conjunction *until,* which divides this sentence into two time periods. In the first period, you can predict that the *church* was scheduled *for demolition;* in the second, people banded together to *have it declared an historic landmark.* You can rule out (B) immediately. People can be **excommunicated;** an old *church* cannot. (D) and (E) are also wrong, since the *church* couldn't have been **exchanged** or **repaired** *for demolition.*

On the other hand, **scheduled** matches our prediction, and so does **slated,** so (A) and (C) would both fit the first blank. But in (A), **declined** doesn't fit the second blank. If people had **declined** or refused *to have it declared an historic landmark,* the *church* would presumably still have been demolished. Instead, they must have **rallied** on its behalf.

> *demolition: tearing down or destroying by explosion*
> *excommunicated: excluded from the church or from a group*
> *slated: put on the schedule*
> *rallied: banded together for action*

5 **E**—An eruption that kills *many thousands of people* must be "bad" or "severe." (E) **disastrous** is the obvious choice for the first blank, although **fateful** and **blistering** are possible. (B) **inoffensive** is clearly wrong, and it doesn't make sense to describe a natural disaster as (C) **immoral.**

For the second blank, check out (A), (D), and (E). It makes no sense to say the *eruption* **diminished** or **authorized** *havoc.* Clearly, (E) **wreaked** is our best answer.

> spawned: sired, gave birth to, or (figuratively)
>   caused
> diminished: reduced
> authorized: granted authority, gave permission
> wreaked: inflicted

6 **A**—The clue word *but* suggests that the contractor was willing to lower his price because of Ben's response, so the word that goes in the first blank should mean something like "lower his price" or "bargain." The second blank probably has to do with Ben's refusing to pay or being shocked.

(A) **Negotiate**, (B) **bargain**, and (D) **reconsider** would all work in the first blank, but (C) and (E) don't fit the prediction at all.

Now try the second blanks for (A), (B), and (D). The second words in most of the answer choices are relatively difficult. (B) doesn't work well. Why would Ben have **floundered** *at the price*? In (D), **waived** makes no sense because it should be *the contractor* who **waived** *the price*, not *Ben*. But (A) **balked** makes sense here: The *outrageous figure* stopped *Ben* cold, and he refused to complete the transaction unless *the contractor* was *willing to* **negotiate**.

> balked: stopped short, failed to complete a
>   motion or activity
> floundered: struggled to move, proceeded clumsily
> recoiled: pulled back in horror or fear
> waived: voluntarily gave up a claim or right

7 **D**—This one's hard to predict, but we need a word that describes an hour. Looking at the first word in each answer choice, **measured** and **defined** seem more likely than **revered, imagined,** or **idealized.** So ignore (B), (C), and (E), and examine the second words in (A) and (D).

The only one that makes sense in this context is **course.** If you plug (D) into the blanks, the logic of the sentence becomes clear. A summer's day is longer than a winter's day; therefore, *one-twelfth of the time from dawn to dusk* is not constant through the year. So the *length* of an ancient Egyptian hour *varied during the* **course** *of the year because* it was **defined** in terms of the total length of a day.

> revered: honored or worshipped

8 **E**—To figure out which answer choice best modifies *candor* in this sentence, you don't even have to know the meaning of *candor.* The fact that *the candidate's candor earned her many new* supporters suggests that it was a good trait, so the word that fills the blank should be positive.

Presumptuous, impatient, and **dogmatic** are all negative. **Unintentional** isn't inherently negative, but it certainly isn't positive. The only positive word here is (E) **disarming.** *The candidate's candor* **disarmed** or won over voters *who had previously supported her rival.*

> candor: frankness, honesty, and openness
> presumptuous: taking liberties, overstepping
>   the bounds of one's position
> dogmatic: dictatorial, insisting on one's
>   own beliefs
> disarming: easing or neutralizing
>   criticism or hostility

9 **B**—If *Frederick Douglass ... patterned his ... auto-biography after* something, he must have modeled it on another literary work. The type of work should go in the second blank. Of the second words in the answer choices, only **narrative** and **epitaph** are in any sense literary works. It would be hard to model an entire *autobiography* on a simple **epitaph,** so you can pick (B) as the correct answer on the basis of the second blank alone. But in any two-blank sentence, you should check to make sure that both words fit the respective blanks. **Consciously** fits fine in the first blank, so (B) is indeed correct.

> narrative: story or account of events
> epitaph: tombstone inscription, brief
>   saying that commemorates the dead
> patronizingly: with a smug or superior air
> expectantly: with anticipation
> consciously: with full awareness

10 **A**—Ignore the phrase *as a psychiatrist.* The main hint lies in the contrast between the two halves of the sentence: *George was* ----; **listening** *while others talked* was not his style. Look for a word that means "noisy" or "talkative." The only choice that has anything to do with talking or not talking is (A) **voluble.**

> voluble: talkative
> truculent: cruel, fierce

Suggested Time: 7 minutes

Directions—Select the lettered word or set of words that best completes the sentence.

Example:
Today's small, portable computers contrast markedly with the earliest electronic computers, which were ----.
(A) effective
(B) invented
(C) useful
(D) destructive
(E) enormous   Ⓐ Ⓑ Ⓒ Ⓓ ●

1   Happy ---- have replaced the ---- outcomes of some stories in the updated English translations of Hans Christian Andersen's fairy tales.
(A) plots . . silly
(B) endings . . gloomy
(C) characters . . mythical
(D) results . . lanky
(E) moods . . historic   Ⓐ Ⓑ Ⓒ Ⓓ Ⓔ

2   A report that the corporation was precariously close to the ---- of bankruptcy caused panic among its creditors and stockholders.
(A) cessation
(B) deficit
(C) brink
(D) absorption
(E) absence   Ⓐ Ⓑ Ⓒ Ⓓ Ⓔ

3   Gary was ---- about the ---- of his family heirlooms and personal mementos in the fire.
(A) depressed . . meaning
(B) noncommittal . . eradication
(C) incensed . . recovery
(D) mournful . . insurance
(E) distraught . . destruction   Ⓐ Ⓑ Ⓒ Ⓓ Ⓔ

4   Julio's good mood was ----; within minutes, his normally ---- partners were grinning and choking back laughter.
(A) promiscuous . . glum
(B) genial . . famished
(C) ghastly . . intolerable
(D) pretentious . . forlorn
(E) infectious . . stolid   Ⓐ Ⓑ Ⓒ Ⓓ Ⓔ

5   Many novels by the Brontë sisters and other nineteenth-century female authors were initially published under masculine ---- in the belief that works by ---- authors would meet more favorable reception.
(A) monikers . . patriarchal
(B) aliases . . established
(C) rubrics . . famous
(D) pseudonyms . . male
(E) criteria . . talented   Ⓐ Ⓑ Ⓒ Ⓓ Ⓔ

6   Moira forced herself to eat every morsel on her plate; although she found the food practically ----, she wanted to avoid offending her kind hosts.
(A) egregious
(B) nourishing
(C) inedible
(D) overheated
(E) sodden   Ⓐ Ⓑ Ⓒ Ⓓ Ⓔ

7   Architect Tadao Ando's penchant for placing ---- concerns above technical practicalities sometimes ---- unsettling, even precarious, structures.
(A) artistic . . results in
(B) monetary . . clashes with
(C) mundane . . replaces
(D) lofty . . cuts down
(E) social . . supports   Ⓐ Ⓑ Ⓒ Ⓓ Ⓔ

8   With his army already ---- in the snow, Napoleon's retreat from the outskirts of Moscow turned into a rout after Russian troops began to ---- his soldiers.
(A) vacillating . . ravage
(B) jangling . . harass
(C) plummeting . . insinuate
(D) foundering . . assault
(E) tottering . . upbraid   Ⓐ Ⓑ Ⓒ Ⓓ Ⓔ

9   Traditionally, any citizen is entitled to be tried by a jury of her peers; however, the law does not ---- how or to what extent the jurors must ---- the defendant.
(A) monitor . . assess
(B) specify . . resemble
(C) indicate . . charge
(D) necessitate . . enable
(E) predict . . mirror   Ⓐ Ⓑ Ⓒ Ⓓ Ⓔ

10 The features of Noh, the oldest form of Japanese drama, are highly ----; verse sections must be sung, and the vocal style in the prose passages has to be based on the chanting of specific Buddhist prayers.
(A) prescribed
(B) undertaken
(C) ineffectual
(D) frugal
(E) absolute

Ⓐ Ⓑ Ⓒ Ⓓ Ⓔ

SCORECARD	
Number of Questions Right:	
Number of Questions Wrong:	
Number of Questions Omitted:	
Number of Correct Guesses:	
Number of Wrong Guesses:	
Time Used:	

KAPLAN

Answers and Explanations

1 **B**—The first blank must have something to do with *outcomes*, because you can't replace *outcomes* with a word that serves an entirely different function. The second blank seems to refer to mood: If happy *outcomes* replaced the original *outcomes* the original *outcomes* were probably sad.

Either (B) **endings** or (D) **results** would match the prediction for the first blank, but only **gloomy** matches the prediction for the second.

lanky: tall and thin, ungraceful

2 **C**—You don't really need to know what *precariously* means to find the right answer here. The word that fills the blank must be something like *point* or *edge*. A **brink** is the edge of a steep place such as a cliff or a river bank, so it's the best answer.

precariously: characterized by
*   instability or uncertainty*
cessation: stopping
deficit: shortage or shortfall

3 **E**—*Gary* must have been upset because *his family heirlooms and personal mementos* had been lost or destroyed *in the fire.* So look for a first word that means "upset" and a second word that means "loss." (A) **depressed,** (E) **distraught,** and (D) **mournful** work best for the first blank. Since **destruction** fits the second blank best, (E) is correct.

In (B), **eradication** is related to **destruction** but isn't usually applied to objects, such as *personal mementos.* Besides, Gary certainly wasn't **noncommittal** about the loss, so the first blank for (B) does not fit.

distraught: extremely upset or agitated
mournful: sorrowful
noncommittal: giving no clear
*   sign of how one feels*
eradication: extermination
incensed: outraged, extremely angry

4 **E**—It sounds as though *Julio's* colleagues don't usually go around *grinning and choking back laughter,* so we can predict that the second blank might be filled by something like *stern* or *glum.* To explain why they suddenly found them-

selves in such a *good mood,* we can predict a word like *catching* or *contagious* to fill the first blank. **Infectious** is a good synonym for *contagious,* and **stolid** means "unemotional," so (E) matches the predictions well.

infectious: contagious
stolid: unemotional
genial: kindly
famished: starving
ghastly: frightening, horrible
forlorn: alone, isolated, miserable

5 **D**—The major contrast in this sentence is one of gender: *female authors* versus *masculine* pen names. The second blank will almost certainly be filled by something like *masculine.* The only answer choices whose second words have anything to do with *masculine* are (A) and (D). **Patriarchal** seems a bit over-specialized in this context, but check the first words to make sure that (D) **male** is the better choice.

Pseudonyms are used by people who don't want their work published under their real names. When you plug (A) and (D) into the sentence, (D) makes the internal logic tighter: The *novels* written by *female authors were initially published under masculine* **pseudonyms** because *works by* **male** *authors* generally received more favorable reviews.

patriarchal: ruled by men
rubrics: category headings
monikers: nicknames
pseudonyms: fictitious names, pen names

6 **C**—*Moira* didn't want to eat *the food,* but she also didn't want to offend her *hosts.* The word *practically* tells us she must have disliked the food very much, so the correct answer will be a very negative word like *revolting.* (B) **Nourishing** is positive, and (D) **overheated** doesn't seem negative enough. **Egregious** describes bad mistakes but not bad *food.* In (E), **sodden** *food* isn't necessarily bad; a rum cake, for example, tastes good when saturated with rum. So the best answer is (C) **inedible,** which means "uneatable."

egregious: conspicuously bad
sodden: soaked, saturated

7 **A**—If Ando places **artistic,** or **monetary,** or any other interests *above technical practicalities*, the building he designs could be *precarious*. So most choices would fit in the first blank. But only choice (A) provides a suitable answer for the second blank: If Ando places **artistic** interests above *technical practicalities*, it **results in** *precarious structures*.

penchant: tendency
mundane: ordinary, everyday
monetary: relating to money
precarious: unstable

8 **D**—We can predict that *Napoleon's army* was stuck *in the snow* and "doing badly" as they tried to *retreat* from Moscow. As a result, the retreat became a *rout*. (D) **foundering** and (E) **tottering** are the best options. **Vacillating** means the army was wavering, which doesn't fit the context. For the second blank, it makes sense to say the *Russian troops began to* **assault** the *soldiers*, so (D) is the logical choice.

rout: hasty, humiliating retreat
foundering: stumbling
vacillating: failing to make up one's mind
assault: to attack physically
upbraid: to criticize verbally

9 **B**—The *citizen* who is *tried*, or brought to court on criminal charges, is the *defendant*. A jury of your *peers* is a jury of your equals. So it sounds as though *the law does not* dictate the exact way in which *the jurors* should be the equals of *the defendant*.

In (A), **monitor** is not quite what we had predicted, but it might still fit. However, **assess** doesn't match the predicted meaning at all. If we plug it into the second blank, the two halves of the sentence no longer connect to each other. An SAT Sentence Completion generally has tight internal logic, but choice (A) doesn't. Choice (C) has the same problem. (D) just doesn't make sense when you plug it into the blanks. That leaves (B) and (E).

(B) works better; the function of *the law* is to (B) **specify**, not to (E) **predict.** (B) explains that, although tradition dictates that a *defendant* be judged by *a jury of her peers*, the law doesn't **specify**

in what way *the jurors* should **resemble,** or be *peers* of *the defendant*.

peer: equal
monitor: watch closely
assess: evaluate or estimate

10 **A**—At first glance, you might think that the blank should be filled by a word like "musical" or "vocal." But no such word appears in the answer choices. The only choice that tightens up the internal logic of the sentence when you plug it in is (A) **prescribed**. The words *must be* and *has to be* indicate that aspects of *Noh* are strictly dictated or **prescribed.**

prescribed: ordered or dictated
ineffectual: not effective, futile
frugal: thrifty

Suggested Time: 7 minutes

Directions—Select the lettered word or set of words that best completes the sentence.

Example:
Today's small, portable computers contrast markedly with the earliest electronic computers, which were ----.
(A) effective
(B) invented
(C) useful
(D) destructive
(E) enormous   Ⓐ Ⓑ Ⓒ Ⓓ ●

1 Because of the ---- and prolonged nature of the ----, water must be carefully conserved and rationed.
(A) arid . . reservoir
(B) dire . . forecast
(C) severe . . drought
(D) negligible . . emergency
(E) miserly . . supply   Ⓐ Ⓑ Ⓒ Ⓓ Ⓔ

2 The spectacular ---- of the Grand Canyon cannot be fully captured by a two-dimensional ---- such as a photograph.
(A) periphery . . benchmark
(B) vista . . opportunity
(C) foliage . . screening
(D) topography . . representation
(E) graphics . . likeness   Ⓐ Ⓑ Ⓒ Ⓓ Ⓔ

3 Until his defeat by the newcomer, the veteran boxer won most of his bouts by knockouts and had achieved an ---- series of wins.
(A) inconsequential
(B) exaggerated
(C) able-bodied
(D) unbroken
(E) observable   Ⓐ Ⓑ Ⓒ Ⓓ Ⓔ

4 Although the whale shark is found in equatorial waters around the world, it is ---- encountered by divers because of its low numbers and ---- nature.
(A) persistently . . reluctant
(B) successfully . . aggressive
(C) anxiously . . unfortunate
(D) constantly . . indifferent
(E) rarely . . solitary   Ⓐ Ⓑ Ⓒ Ⓓ Ⓔ

5 Some of the paintings formerly ---- the Italian Renaissance artist are now thought to have been created by one of his students.
(A) exhibited with
(B) submitted to
(C) adapted from
(D) attributed to
(E) denied by   Ⓐ Ⓑ Ⓒ Ⓓ Ⓔ

6 Although both plants control soil erosion, kudzu disrupts the local ecology by displacing native fauna, while vetiver has no ---- effects.
(A) foreseeable
(B) adverse
(C) domestic
(D) permanent
(E) advantageous   Ⓐ Ⓑ Ⓒ Ⓓ Ⓔ

7 Because its bookkeepers altered some figures and completely fabricated others, the company's financial records were entirely ----.
(A) spurious
(B) disseminated
(C) singular
(D) concealed
(E) cursory   Ⓐ Ⓑ Ⓒ Ⓓ Ⓔ

8 The journalist's ---- to accurately describe events in the region was not attributable to a lack of effort, but to a dearth of ---- and unbiased information.
(A) willingness . . prevalent
(B) failure . . reliable
(C) training . . universal
(C) hesitation . . dominant
(E) incentive . . clear   Ⓐ Ⓑ Ⓒ Ⓓ Ⓔ

9 As ---- as she is original, choreographer Twyla
   Tharp has created dances for mainstream ballet,
   Hollywood films, and commercial theater, as
   well as more offbeat venues.
   (A) charming
   (B) redundant
   (C) versatile
   (D) polished
   (E) rarefied   Ⓐ Ⓑ Ⓒ Ⓓ Ⓔ

10 Peach pits, which contain small amounts of the
   poisonous compound cyanide, are not usually
   harmful, but, if consumed in sufficient quanti-
   ties, can be ----.
   (A) acerbic
   (B) superfluous
   (C) virulent
   (D) unpalatable
   (E) multifarious   Ⓐ Ⓑ Ⓒ Ⓓ Ⓔ

SCORECARD	
Number of Questions Right:	
Number of Questions Wrong:	
Number of Questions Omitted:	
Number of Correct Guesses:	
Number of Wrong Guesses:	
Time Used:	

Answers and Explanations

1 C—You're told that *water must be carefully conserved and rationed because of the prolonged nature of the ----*, so you can predict that the word in the second blank will be something like *water shortage*. Choice (C) **drought** seems like a perfect match. Choice (D) **emergency** would also be a possibility, so check out the first blank for (C) and (D).

The word in the first blank is connected by *and* to the phrase *prolonged nature*. So the word for this blank should be consistent with *prolonged*. You need a word like *serious*. The first word in choice (C), **severe,** means the same thing as *serious*. Our other contender, choice (D), has **negligible** in the first blank. **Negligible** means "not serious," so (C) is correct.

If you checked out the first blanks in the other choices, you might have been tempted by (A) and (B), **arid** and **dire.** But these two choices don't make sense when you plug the second blank into the sentence. (A) is not logical because if a **reservoir** were **arid,** or completely dry, there would be no water to ration. (B) doesn't explain why water must be rationed. A **dire forecast** isn't necessarily a **forecast** of **drought**—a **forecast** of a violent thunderstorm would also be **dire.** Always look for the choice that fits best.

---

negligible: unimportant, not serious
dire: terrible
miserly: stingy

---

2 D—What could be *spectacular* about the Grand Canyon? Three choices seem possible for the first blank: the **vista** in (B), the **foliage** in (C), the **topography** in (D). You can eliminate two unlikely choices: (A) **periphery** and (E) **graphics.**

In the second blank, you want a word that could apply to photography, which the sentence calls *a two-dimensional ----*. **Opportunity** and **screening** clearly don't fit, so eliminate (B) and (C). That leaves (D) **representation,** which means "a presentation or depiction." You can say that a two-dimensional **representation** can't capture the spectacular **topography.**

vista: view
foliage: the leaves of a tree, or plant life
topography: physical contours and features
periphery: outer boundary
representation: presentation, depiction

---

3 D—Since *the veteran boxer* had *won most of his bouts by knockouts,* you can assume that he was pretty successful. **Unbroken** is the only choice that describes his *series of wins* in a way that suggests success; an **unbroken** series of victories would be a winning streak with no losses.

(A) **inconsequential** and (B) **exaggerated** are contradicted by information in the sentence itself. Choice (C) **able-bodied** may seem to fit in a sentence about a boxer, but what's *an* **able-bodied** *series of wins?* (E) **Observable** makes some sense, since you could watch someone win lots of fights, but we have to reject it because the sentence is about a boxer who, after winning many fights, finally loses to a newcomer. In Sentence Completions, the correct answer is the one that makes the whole sentence cohere, and that would be choice (D).

---

inconsequential: of slight importance
observable: visible

---

4 E—The clue word *Although* sets up a contrast between the whale shark's appearance all over the world and the way that it's *encountered by divers.* A word like *seldom* would set up the needed contrast. (E) **rarely** is the best fit.

For the second blank, look for a word that explains why the shark's *nature* makes it hard for humans to spot. *Shy* or *tending to avoid people* would work well. (E) **solitary** fits the bill. **Reluctant,** in (A), could be a longshot to fill the second blank, but we don't need to spend time thinking about the other choices, since only (E) fits the first blank.

---

equatorial: relating to the region of the earth halfway between the north and south poles

---

5 D—This sentence tests your understanding of the word **attributed,** a word often followed by *to.* A painting that's **attributed to** a Renaissance painter is one "credited to" him, or generally thought to have been painted by him.

The sentence contains a virtual definition of **attributed** in the phrase *thought to have been created by*. The clue words *formerly* and *now* in the sentence signal a contrast between the past and present: The paintings were *formerly* **attributed to** the artist, but *now* they're thought to have been painted by one of his students.

---

attributed: assigned or credited to

---

6 **B**—*Although* sets up a contrast between *kudzu*, which *disrupts the local ecology*, and *vetiver*, which *has no ---- effects*. The sentence is comparing the consequences of the two plants. The missing word refers to kudzu's disruptive ecological effects. Look for a word like *bad* or *negative*. (B) **adverse** most closely matches this prediction.

(E) **advantageous** is the opposite of what's needed. **Foreseeable** and **permanent,** choices (A) and (D), don't make sense because nothing else in the sentence refers to the predictability or lasting effect of the two plants. (C) is wrong because nothing in the sentence refers to either foreign or **domestic** origins.

> Hint: You don't have to know the meaning of every exotic word in the sentence to pick the right answer. To see what fits in the blank(s), figure out how the parts of the sentence relate.

---

vetiver: a grass with long roots
kudzu: a kind of vine
adverse: unfavorable

---

7 **A**—A good vocabulary will help you figure out this one. The bookkeepers *altered some financial records and completely fabricated others*, so you need a word like *altered, falsified,* or *fictitious* for the blank. (A) **spurious** is the only choice that matches.

It makes no sense to say the financial records were entirely **disseminated** or entirely **singular,** so rule out (B) and (C). (D) can be eliminated because the sentence doesn't say the records have been **concealed.** (E) **cursory** doesn't fit either. The sentence doesn't say the records were hastily thrown together; it says they were faked.

---

fabricated: made up
spurious: false, lacking authenticity
concealed: hidden
cursory: hastily done
disseminated: distributed widely
singular: unique

---

8 **B**—The second blank may be easier to fill here, so start with that. The clue word *and* tells you that the missing word in the phrase *---- and unbiased information* will be consistent with *unbiased*. So you can predict that the missing word will have a meaning similar to *unbiased*, like *impartial*. (B) **reliable** and (E) **clear** are both pretty close to *unbiased*, so let's try them in the first blank.

For the first blank, *the journalists' ---- to accurately describe events* results from a *dearth* or "lack" of good information. A lack of good information might prevent someone from describing a situation accurately. We can predict a word like *inability* for this blank. The first word in (E), **incentive,** means *motivation*, which doesn't match. The first word in (B), **failure,** matches perfectly.

---

unbiased: impartial, unprejudiced
dearth: lack

---

9 **C**—Since *Twyla Tharp has created* a wide range of *dances* ranging from movies and *mainstream ballet* to *more offbeat* forms, she's a **versatile** *choreographer*. Though her work may also be **polished,** the sentence concerns the range of her activities, not their quality, so (D) is wrong. Someone who works in several *mainstream* areas wouldn't be termed **rarefied,** so (E) is out. Even though several kinds of dance production are mentioned, nothing suggests that they are **redundant,** so (B) is wrong, too; moreover, **redundant** is a negative term, but the sentence is positive—it praises Tharp's work. Choice (A)'s **charming** sounds okay with the word *original*, but the sentence talks about Tharp's accomplishments as a choreographer, not about her personality.

---

rarefied: understood only by a select group;
*   rarer and more refined*
redundant: repetitive

---

10 **C**—The sentence hinges on knowing what **virulent** means. You're told that certain *poisonous compounds* in *peach pits* are *usually not harmful.*

KAPLAN

But, the sentence continues, if you eat enough of them, they are ----. So you need a word that means *poisonous* or *harmful* for the blank. **Virulent** fits that definition.

If you couldn't figure that out, you could have tried eliminating answer choices. (A) **acerbic** and (D) **unpalatable** relate to things that taste bad, but neither word means *poisonous*. Neither (B) nor (E) makes sense in the blank.

> Hint: Knowing related words can help here. If you didn't know **virulent,** you might have known the related word *virus,* a disease-causing agent. Then you could have figured out **virulent** has something to do with disease and harm.

acerbic: sour, harsh
unpalatable: distasteful, unpleasant
superfluous: unnecessary
multifarious: diverse
virulent: intensely poisonous

Suggested Time: 7 minutes

Directions—Select the lettered word or set of words that best completes the sentence.

Example:
Today's small, portable computers contrast markedly with the earliest electronic computers, which were ----.
(A) effective
(B) invented
(C) useful
(D) destructive
(E) enormous

Ⓐ Ⓑ Ⓒ Ⓓ ●

1 Once ----, wolves have been hunted almost to extinction.
(A) nonexistent
(B) numerous
(C) garrulous
(D) captive
(E) natural

Ⓐ Ⓑ Ⓒ Ⓓ Ⓔ

2 The benefits of the exchange program are ----, with both countries acquiring new technical insights and manufacturing techniques.
(A) promised
(B) inclusive
(C) blatant
(D) mutual
(E) applicable

Ⓐ Ⓑ Ⓒ Ⓓ Ⓔ

3 The author monotonously catalogues the ---- points of fashion history, while omitting the details that might ---- the reader's interest.
(A) vital . . acquire
(B) trivial . . enhance
(C) salient . . offend
(D) undisputed . . limit
(E) essential . . rescind

Ⓐ Ⓑ Ⓒ Ⓓ Ⓔ

4 The Morgan Library in New York provides a ---- environment in which scholars work amidst tapestries, paintings, stained-glass windows, and handcrafted furniture.
(A) realistic
(B) frugal
(C) sumptuous
(D) friendly
(E) practical

Ⓐ Ⓑ Ⓒ Ⓓ Ⓔ

5 The eruption ---- tons of mineral-rich volcanic ash, restoring to the soil nutrients long since ---- by decades of farming.
(A) deposited . . depleted
(B) clumped . . harvested
(C) removed . . secreted
(D) displaced . . entrenched
(E) regained . . fertilized

Ⓐ Ⓑ Ⓒ Ⓓ Ⓔ

6 The fullest edition of the letters of H. P. Lovecraft consists of five volumes; however, only a small fraction of Lovecraft's ---- correspondence has ever been published.
(A) laconic
(B) unknown
(C) voluminous
(D) verbal
(E) popular

Ⓐ Ⓑ Ⓒ Ⓓ Ⓔ

7 The candidate denounced as ---- his rival's solution to the problem of unemployment, but offered no ---- alternative.
(A) arbitrary . . altruistic
(B) elitist . . virulent
(C) salutary . . absolute
(D) convoluted . . provincial
(E) unworkable . . viable

Ⓐ Ⓑ Ⓒ Ⓓ Ⓔ

8 The government decided against ---- assemblies and strikes organized by the opposition, fearing that such a measure might ---- armed conflict.
(A) continuing . . multiply
(B) intimidating . . interrupt
(C) banning . . precipitate
(D) granting . . reapportion
(E) welcoming . . voice

Ⓐ Ⓑ Ⓒ Ⓓ Ⓔ

9 Prime Minister Neville Chamberlain of Great Britain adopted a ---- approach to Hitler, even accepting Germany's annexation of Austria.
(A) hasty
(B) precarious
(C) haughty
(D) conciliatory
(E) dependent

Ⓐ Ⓑ Ⓒ Ⓓ Ⓔ

10 Medieval kings customarily gave away valuables and property, expecting that their ---- would ensure the ---- of their vassals.
(A) imprudence . . probity
(B) largess . . fidelity
(C) adaptation . . integrity
(D) formality . . sophistry
(E) haste . . mirth

Ⓐ Ⓑ Ⓒ Ⓓ Ⓔ

SCORECARD	
Number of Questions Right:	
Number of Questions Wrong:	
Number of Questions Omitted:	
Number of Correct Guesses:	
Number of Wrong Guesses:	
Time Used:	

KAPLAN

Answers and Explanations

1 **B**—*Once,* the first word in the sentence, is an important structural clue. It signals that there's a contrast between the status of wolves at an earlier time (before excessive hunting) and the status of wolves now (almost extinct). To set up the contrast, the word in the blank has to mean something like "abundant." Choice (B) **numerous** is the most logical option.

2 **D**—Since *both* countries are *acquiring new technical insights and manufacturing techniques* in their exchange program, they are benefiting from each other. We can predict that the word in the blank will mean something like "shared" or "reciprocal," since the benefits go both ways. Choice (D) **mutual** matches this prediction perfectly.

Don't be fooled by choice (E) **applicable**. The *technical insights and techniques* may very well be **applicable** somewhere, but we're being asked to describe the success of *the exchange program,* not the status of the *manufacturing techniques.*

3 **B**—The important clue word here is *monotonously.* If the author is *monotonously cataloguing the ---- points of fashion history,* we can safely predict that those points are going to be *boring* or another such negative word. Choice (B), **trivial,** best fits the description.

In the second part of the sentence, *while,* which follows the comma, is another clue. It signals a contrast between the boring *cataloguing* and the omitted details that *might have ---- the reader's interest.* Look for a second-blank word that means something like "increased." Choice (B) again makes the most sense: *The author monotonously catalogues the* **trivial** *points while omitting the details that might* **enhance** *the reader's interest.*

---

monotonously: without variety or variation
enhance: to increase
salient: striking, prominent
rescind: to disavow, take back

---

4 **C**—What word would you use to describe an environment that's full of *tapestries, paintings, stained-glass windows, and hand-crafted furniture?* Probably something like *fancy* or *elegant.* The closest choice to this prediction is (C) **sumptuous.**

It doesn't make sense to describe such an environ-

ment as (A) **realistic** or (B) **frugal.** And, while the library's atmosphere may very well be (D) **friendly** or (E) **practical,** those choices don't make sense in the context, which mentions only the elegant surroundings.

---

sumptuous: luxurious, elegant, stately
frugal: thrifty, not wasteful

---

5 **A**—When a volcano erupts, it ejects lava, ash, and other material. Therefore, it's unlikely that the volcano (B) **clumped** or (C) **removed** tons of volcanic ash. Choice (E) **regained** means the volcano was sucking ash into itself instead of spewing it out—a very unlikely situation. This leaves choices (A) and (D).

Choice (A) sounds good—*the eruption* **deposited** *mineral-rich ash, restoring to the soil nutrients long since* **depleted** *by decades of farming.* In (D), the eruption could conceivably **displace** ash, but the second-blank word doesn't make sense in the sentence. If nutrients were long since **entrenched** in the ground, there would be no need to restore them to the soil. Choice (A) is the best answer.

---

clumped: assembled, bundled
depleted: exhausted, used up
displaced: pushed out
entrenched: established, settled

---

6 **C**—The clue word *however* sets up a contrast between *the fullest edition* and the *small fraction of correspondence* that's *been published.* This tells us that a great deal of *Lovecraft's ---- correspondence* remains unpublished, so fill the blank with a word like *abundant.* Choice (C) **voluminous** best completes the sentence's meaning. Choice (E) **popular** is a weak second best.

---

voluminous: abundant
laconic: restrained, uncommunicative

---

7 **E**—If *the candidate denounced his rival's solution as ----,* the word in the first blank will be negative. Since four of the five answer choices have negative first words, you'll find it hard to eliminate possibilities. So start with the second blank.

> Hint: In a sentence with two blanks, you can choose which blank to do first. Start with the blank that's easier to fill.

If the candidate *offered no ---- alternative,* we can infer that the candidate offered no good or workable alternative. Choice (E)'s **viable** best matches this prediction.

Plugging the first word of (E) into the sentence, we see that it makes sense too—*the candidate denounced as* **unworkable** *his rival's solution, but offered no* **viable** *alternative himself.* None of the other choices makes as much sense.

---

denounced: condemned
viable: workable, achievable
virulent: severe, poisonous
salutary: healthful
convoluted: complicated, involved

---

8 **C**—The second half of this sentence follows directly from the first: *The government decided against* doing something *to assemblies and strikes* because they *feared armed conflict.* Choice (C) best completes the logic of the sentence—*The government decided against* **banning** *assemblies and strikes* because they feared such a move would **precipitate** *armed conflict.*

---

intimidating: threatening
banning: prohibiting, especially by official decree
precipitate: instigate, bring about
reapportion: distribute anew

---

9 **D**—Since *Chamberlain even accepted Germany's annexation of Austria,* his approach to German aggression was certainly not tough or militant. He probably adopted a nonaggressive, accepting approach to Hitler. The choice that comes closest to this prediction is (D) **conciliatory.**

---

conciliatory: tending to pacify or accommodate
precarious: uncertain, dangerous
haughty: arrogant, snobby

---

10 **B**—The *kings gave away valuables and property, expecting* something back from their subjects. The first blank relates to the action of giving away all these nice things, so we can predict a word like

generosity. As for what they expected in return, we might predict something like *respect, happiness,* or *loyalty.* Therefore, the two blanks have to be filled by two positive words.

Looking through the answer choices, we see that choice (B) has two distinctly positive words—**largess** and **fidelity.** Plugging (B) into the sentence, we see it makes perfect sense—*The kings gave away property, expecting that their* **largess** *would ensure the* **fidelity** *of their subjects.*

You may have been tempted by (D) **formality,** since the kings' generosity could be seen as a formal exercise. But this kind of thinking is stretching the sentence's meaning. Besides, if you check out the second blank, **sophistry** doesn't make sense.

---

largess: generosity
fidelity: faithfulness, loyalty
sophistry: misleading argumentative style

SENTENCE COMPLETIONS—PRACTICE SET 7

Suggested Time: 7 minutes

Directions—Select the lettered word or set of words that best completes the sentence.

Example:
Today's small, portable computers contrast markedly with the earliest electronic computers, which were ----.
(A) effective
(B) invented
(C) useful
(D) destructive
(E) enormous   Ⓐ Ⓑ Ⓒ Ⓓ ●

1. Unlike her first novel, which received kudos for its ----, her second effort was widely criticized as uninventive and predictable.
(A) monotony
(B) originality
(C) conventionality
(D) prudence
(E) literacy   

2. Medieval alchemists tried to attain wealth by ---- lead and other base metals into gold.
(A) transforming
(B) encouraging
(C) replicating
(D) displacing
(E) copying   

3. The dance critic was ---- in her praise of the company, describing the choreography in glowing terms and ---- the poise and elegance of every dancer.
(A) agreeable . . insulting
(B) vague . . demonstrating
(C) conciliatory . . relating
(D) timorous . . describing
(E) effusive . . extolling   

4. The British social philosopher Thomas Malthus predicted that population growth would eventually ---- world food production, resulting in massive famine and political unrest.
(A) pressure
(B) forbid
(C) resist
(D) surpass
(E) confront   

5. Bird species ---- to this island were exterminated by feral cats, ---- of pets abandoned here decades ago by sailors.
(A) provincial . . competitors
(B) harmless . . liberators
(C) indigenous . . descendants
(D) unusual . . signals
(E) benign . . ancestors   Ⓐ Ⓑ Ⓒ Ⓓ Ⓔ

6. Soon after adopting a syllabic system of writing, the Greeks made the final step to a phonetic alphabet, dividing the consonants from the vowels and writing each ----.
(A) formally
(B) abstractly
(C) separately
(D) mysteriously
(E) accurately   Ⓐ Ⓑ Ⓒ Ⓓ Ⓔ

7. In the early nineteenth century, some British agricultural workers felt that newly invented farm machinery threatened their jobs, and they ---- their fear of ---- by smashing machines.
(A) lessened . . injustice
(B) aggravated . . landlords
(C) displayed . . technology
(D) accommodated . . equipment
(E) magnified . . exploitation   Ⓐ Ⓑ Ⓒ Ⓓ Ⓔ

8 The restaurant manager, who had ---- provided crayons and paper tablecloths for the amusement of small children, found that adult patrons were equally ---- the opportunity to express themselves.
(A) aggressively . . delighted by
(B) impulsively . . anxious about
(C) warily . . shrewd about
(D) initially . . enthralled with
(E) imaginatively . . alarmed by

Ⓐ Ⓑ Ⓒ Ⓓ Ⓔ

9 Before it became involved in the Second World War, the United States held to a policy of neutrality, setting up legislation explicitly ---- the sale of weapons to ---- nations.
(A) repealing . . expatriate
(B) forbidding . . belligerent
(C) enacting . . dependent
(D) prompting . . arbitrary
(E) defending . . isolated

Ⓐ Ⓑ Ⓒ Ⓓ Ⓔ

10 By 1918, the painter André Derain had ---- both Cubism and the new abstract art in favor of a more ---- approach based on the example of the old masters.
(A) compiled . . reticent
(B) vexed . . indulgent
(C) thwarted . . expressive
(D) discarded . . tentative
(E) repudiated . . traditional

Ⓐ Ⓑ Ⓒ Ⓓ Ⓔ

SCORECARD	
Number of Questions Right:	
Number of Questions Wrong:	
Number of Questions Omitted:	
Number of Correct Guesses:	
Number of Wrong Guesses:	
Time Used:	

KAPLAN

Answers and Explanations

1 **B**—This sentence contains the word *kudos,* which might have thrown you off. But, as in most Sentence Completions, you can get the answer if you focus on the logic of the sentence. Notice the clue word *unlike; unlike* signals a contrast. If her first novel is *unlike* her *uninventive and predictable* second novel, her first novel must be the opposite. It must have had (B) **originality.**

kudos: praise, honor

2 **A**—Again you've got a difficult word in the sentence. And again, you can work around it. If you don't know what *alchemists* are, keep reading. The *alchemists tried to attain wealth by ---- lead into gold.* (C) and (E) won't work because you don't **copy** *lead into gold,* you transform it. The only logical answer is (A) **transforming.**

replicating: duplicating, copying
alchemists: in the Middle Ages, practitioners
of a study combining chemistry and
philosophy who tried to turn base metals
into gold

3 **E**—The important clue here is the word *glowing.* Since *the critic described the choreography in glowing terms,* she was ---- in her praise. Look for a positive word in the first blank that means "enthusiastic." You can quickly eliminate (B) **vague,** (C) **conciliatory,** and (D) **timorous.** That leaves (A) **agreeable** and (E) **effusive,** so let's try (A) and (E) in the second blank.

In the second part of the sentence, the connecting word *and* indicates consistency, so the second blank must also be positive. Look for an answer choice that means she praised the poise and elegance of the dancers. Remember, we've already eliminated (B), (C) and (D). (A) **Insulting** is obviously wrong. A critic wouldn't *describe the choreography in glowing terms,* and then **insult** *the poise of the dancers.* But **extolling** is a positive word, so (E) is correct.

glowing: enthusiastic; shining
conciliatory: appeasing
timorous: meek
effusive: excessively demonstrative, gushing
extolling: praising highly

4 **D**—Don't be intimidated by the serious subject matter. Just take the sentence apart and look for clues. The biggest clue is the word *famine.* The sentence says: When the relationship between *population growth* and *world food production* changes in some way, the result is *famine.* You know that *famine* happens when there's not enough food for a large number of people to live on. Or, as the sentence puts it, *population growth would eventually exceed food production, resulting in massive famine.* The answer choice that best matches this prediction is (D) **surpass.**

surpass: exceed

5 **C**—Don't give up if you don't know the word *feral.* Instead, read this two-blank sentence looking for one blank that leaps out as predictable. Start working with that one, and use it to rule out choices for the second blank.

If the second blank looks easier, start with that. You're told that *bird species were exterminated by cats.* These cats had something to do with *pets abandoned here decades ago by sailors.* That probably means the cats were (C) **descendants** of pets. But check out the other choices.

Since the pets were abandoned on the island decades ago, the cats couldn't logically be (B) **liberators** of pets, (D) **signals** of pets, or (E) **ancestors** of pets. And it's unlikely they'd be (A) **competitors** of pets, either. (C) makes the most sense in the second blank.

Now try the first blank. Bird species **indigenous** to the island were exterminated by the descendants of abandoned pets—that seems to make sense. A quick glance at the other choices confirms that (C) is right.

exterminated: killed off
feral: wild
provincial: unsophisticated, narrow-minded
benign: harmless
indigenous: native

6 **C**—This fairly easy sentence contains the clue word *and.* Since the phrase *dividing the consonants from the vowels* is joined to *writing each* with the word *and,* the two phrases must agree with each other. So whatever goes in the blank must go along with the idea of dividing consonants and vowels. The choice that makes sense is (C) **separately:** *The Greeks divided consonants from vowels and wrote each separately.* The rest of the choices don't fit the context. For instance, (E) **accurately,** might have seemed sensible, but the whole point is that the Greeks divided up their letters, not that they wrote precisely.

7 C—Again the clue word *and* indicates consistency throughout the sentence: The workers felt threatened, *and* their fear led them to smash machines. Their fear of what? Probably a fear of (C) **technology.** (C)'s first blank works well, too—the farm *workers* **displayed** *their fear of* **technology** *by smashing machines.* So (C) looks correct. Check the other answers just to make sure they don't work.

(A) **injustice** and (E) **exploitation** might seem to go along with the subject. But there's nothing in the sentence to indicate the workers *fear* those things. Besides, in both cases the first blanks don't fit. (C) works best.

8 D—Since this is a two-blank sentence, pick one blank to work on—whichever strikes you as more predictable—and use that blank to rule out possibilities for the other blank. In the first half, you read that *the crayons and paper tablecloths had been provided for the amusement of small children.* In the last half, you read that adults were *equally ---- about the opportunity to express themselves.* The clue word *equally* tells you the adults felt the same way as the kids. So the adults must have been equally (A) **delighted by** the opportunity, or (D) **enthralled with** the opportunity.

Now all you have to do is try (A) and (D)'s first words in the first blank. In (A), **aggressively** doesn't fit with the rest of the sentence. Why would a restaurant **aggressively** provide crayons and paper to kids? But (D) **initially** works fine. The restaurant, which had **initially** *provided crayons and paper just for kids, found that adults were equally* **enthralled with** *the opportunity to express themselves.*

---

enthralled: enchanted, captivated, held
  spellbound
initially: at first

---

9 B—If the United States is practicing *neutrality,* you can predict it will forbid *the sale of weapons* to *nations* taking part in the war. The answer choice that matches that prediction is (B): *Holding to its policy of neutrality,* the United States *set up legislation* **forbidding** *the sale of weapons to* **belligerent** *nations.*

(C) **enacting,** (D) **prompting,** and (E) **defending** suggest that the United States was encouraging the sale of weapons. (A) **Repealing** implies that legislation already existed and was being overturned.

---

neutrality: the policy of not favoring either
  side in a dispute or a war; impartiality
belligerent: waging war, hostile
expatriate: exiled

---

10 E—Two important phrases clue you in to the sentence's meaning: *in favor of* and *based on the example of the old masters.* The second blank looks easier, so let's deal with it first.

If Derain's new approach is *based on the example of the old masters,* you can predict it must be old-fashioned. The answer choice that fits this prediction is (E) **traditional.** (C) **expressive** might also seem like a good word to describe a painting style. But you're not told that the old masters were expressive—you just know they were old. Let's try (C) and (E) in the first blank just to make sure.

(C) **thwarted** clearly doesn't fit. It's not clear how Derain was hindering or obstructing Cubism and abstract art, and it's not correct English to say he hindered one style of art *in favor of* another. Looking at (E), **repudiated** makes much more sense. Derain rejected abstract art *in favor of* a more traditional approach. (E) fits well in both blanks, so it's our answer.

---

thwarted: hindered or obstructed
repudiated: rejected
vexed: annoyed, aggravated

Suggested Time: 7 minutes

Directions—Select the lettered word or set of words that best completes the sentence.

Example:
Today's small, portable computers contrast markedly with the earliest electronic computers, which were ----.
(A) effective
(B) invented
(C) useful
(D) destructive
(E) enormous   Ⓐ Ⓑ Ⓒ Ⓓ ●

1. Rosa embarked on a ---- of strenuous exercise to build up the ---- to complete a marathon.
(A) program . . lethargy
(B) regimen . . endurance
(C) pursuit . . stamina
(D) commitment . . strength
(E) complex . . rhythm   Ⓐ Ⓑ Ⓒ Ⓓ Ⓔ

2. An editorial praised the generosity of an anonymous ----, who had donated over a million dollars and several priceless paintings to the college.
(A) mercenary
(B) agnostic
(C) curmudgeon
(D) benefactor
(E) harbinger   Ⓐ Ⓑ Ⓒ Ⓓ Ⓔ

3. Some historians claim that the concept of courtly love is a ---- that dates from the age of chivalry, while others believe it has more ---- origins.
(A) relic . . simultaneous
(B) notion . . ancient
(C) memento . . discovered
(D) period . . documented
(E) suitor . . amorous   Ⓐ Ⓑ Ⓒ Ⓓ Ⓔ

4. The general was ---- of low morale among his troops, but still refused to ---- his command.
(A) informed . . bequeath
(B) appreciative . . subvert
(C) fearful . . proscribe
(D) wary . . deprecate
(E) cognizant . . relinquish   Ⓐ Ⓑ Ⓒ Ⓓ Ⓔ

5. In the wake of several tragic accidents caused by wind shear, major airports installed new radar systems ---- enough to ---- this complex atmospheric phenomenon.
(A) generalized . . track
(B) lamentable . . honor
(C) flimsy . . withstand
(D) sophisticated . . detect
(E) sturdy . . demolish   Ⓐ Ⓑ Ⓒ Ⓓ Ⓔ

6. Although marine engineers claimed that its hull was ----, the Titanic sank after hitting an iceberg.
(A) amorphous
(B) equivocal
(C) preeminent
(D) impenetrable
(E) viscous   Ⓐ Ⓑ Ⓒ Ⓓ Ⓔ

7. Based on factual ---- rather than conjecture, Dr. Singh's report will ---- previously held views about the nesting habits of the rare species.
(A) conjecture . . ignore
(B) evidence . . refute
(C) theory . . negate
(D) projections . . corroborate
(E) documentation . . inspire   Ⓐ Ⓑ Ⓒ Ⓓ Ⓔ

8. As they helped the community recover from the storm's devastation, the apparently ---- relief workers worked around the clock with an energy that never seemed to wane.
(A) dexterous
(B) indefatigable
(C) obsequious
(D) syncopated
(E) transcendent   Ⓐ Ⓑ Ⓒ Ⓓ Ⓔ

9. Although others found them impressive, Lewis found Senator Gantry's speeches ---- and believed that they ---- the real issues with elaborate but meaningless rhetoric.
(A) bombastic . . obscured
(B) verbose . . clarified
(C) captivating . . defined
(D) exuberant . . misconstrued
(E) persuasive . . illuminated   Ⓐ Ⓑ Ⓒ Ⓓ Ⓔ

10 The characters in Jane Austen's novels never argue; rather, they employ more subtle verbal weapons: irony and ----.
(A) candor
(B) humility
(C) innuendo
(D) farce
(E) pantomime   Ⓐ Ⓑ Ⓒ Ⓓ Ⓔ

SCORECARD	
Number of Questions Right:	
Number of Questions Wrong:	
Number of Questions Omitted:	
Number of Correct Guesses:	
Number of Wrong Guesses:	
Time Used:	

Answers and Explanations

1 **B**—Let's concentrate on the second blank first. What do you need to complete a *marathon*, a very long race? You need **endurance, stamina,** or **strength,** so (B), (C), and (D) are all possibilities. **Lethargy** would slow you down in a race, so you can definitely eliminate (A). **Rhythm** might be of some value in running a marathon, but it's not the most important thing, so eliminate (E). As for the first blank, you embark on a **regimen** of exercise, but you don't embark on a **pursuit** or a **commitment** of exercise. So (B) is the best answer.

lethargy: extreme sleepiness or sluggishness

2 **D**—You're looking for a very positive word, since this anonymous person is being praised for his or her very generous donations. The most positive answer choice is (D) **benefactor.** None of the other answer choices make sense.

> Hint: Benefactor contains the roots **BENE,** "good," and **FAC,** "make or do." A benefactor is someone who does good things for someone else's sake.

*mercenary: professional soldier who serves
    a foreign army*
*agnostic: doubter, one who doubts the
    existence of God*
curmudgeon: cranky or grumpy person
harbinger: herald or omen

3 **B**—The word *while* signals contrast. If *some historians claim that the concept of courtly love dates* from a specific period—*the age of chivalry*—the others must be saying that it has either earlier origins or more recent origins. Only **ancient** in choice (B) relates to time and provides the necessary contrast. As for the first blank, *the concept of courtly love* can't be a **relic,** or a **memento,** or a **period,** or a **suitor;** it can only be a **notion.** (B) is the answer.

4 **E**—*But* is a signal of contrast. If *morale was low among his troops,* what should the general have done about *his command?* He might have **relinquished** it, as choice (E) suggests; none of the alternatives makes sense. Checking out the first blank, if *the general was* **cognizant** *of low morale among his*

troops, that would have been reason to do something about it. (E) is the answer.

cognizant: aware
relinquish: to give up

5 **D**—Since *wind shear* is a *complex atmospheric phenomenon,* which caused *several tragic accidents,* the radar systems installed by the airports need to be technologically advanced. They're certainly not (B) **lamentable,** (C) **flimsy,** or (A) **generalized.** They're probably (D) **sophisticated.** But they could also be (E) **sturdy.**
So check out the second word for these two choices. (E)'s second word doesn't work; a radar system can't **demolish** *wind shear.* Rather, you'd expect it to **detect** *wind shear,* so the correct answer is (D).

6 **D**—*Although* signals contrast; we want a word that suggests why marine engineers would not have expected the *Titanic* to *sink.* The best answer is (D) **impenetrable.**

impenetrable: incapable of being penetrated
amorphous: shapeless
equivocal: ambiguous, doubtful
preeminent: outstanding
viscous: thick, as applied to a liquid

7 **B**—In the first blank, something *factual* is contrasted with *conjecture;* (B) **evidence** and (E) **documentation** are both possible answers. In the second blank, it doesn't make sense to say that something could **inspire** *previously held views,* but something could certainly **refute** *previously held views,* so choice (B) is the correct answer.

*conjecture: speculation, opinion based on
    incomplete evidence*
refute: to prove to be false or erroneous
negate: to nullify or invalidate
corroborate: confirm

8 **B**—The definition of the missing word is implicit in the sentence; we're looking for a word that means able to *work around the clock with an energy that never seems to wane.* That's the meaning of (B) **indefatigable.** (E) **transcendent** is too vague here. So (B) is the answer.

indefatigable: tireless
dexterous: nimble, adroit
obsequious: submissive
syncopated: in music, stressing normally
unaccented beats
transcendent: supreme

9 **A**—*Although* indicates a contrast with *impressive*. We want negative words for both blanks. For the first blank, (A) **bombastic** and (B) **verbose** are negative. For the second, (A) **obscured** and (D) **misconstrued** are negative. Only choice (A) provides suitable negative answers for both blanks, so it's correct.

bombastic: inflated, pretentious
obscured: hid
verbose: overly wordy
clarified: made clear or intelligible
exuberant: lavish, overflowing, full of
unrestrained enthusiasm
misconstrued: misunderstood, misinterpreted

10 **C**—The key word is *subtle*. (D) **farce** is not *subtle*, it's a form of obvious humor. (A) **candor**, or complete honesty, isn't *subtle* either. (B) **humility** isn't a verbal weapon, and it's not a subtle alternative to arguing. And (E) **pantomime** isn't verbal at all, it's an art form consisting of silent gestures and movements. The answer is choice (C) **innuendo.**

candor: complete honesty
innuendo: hinting, indirect statement

SENTENCE COMPLETIONS—PRACTICE SET 9

Suggested Time: 7 minutes

Directions—Select the lettered word or set of words that best completes the sentence.

Example:
Today's small, portable computers contrast markedly with the earliest electronic computers, which were ----.
(A) effective
(B) invented
(C) useful
(D) destructive
(E) enormous
Ⓐ Ⓑ Ⓒ Ⓓ ●

1 The famous movie star regarded her mountain cabin as ----; she felt safe there from the annoying ---- of reporters and photographers.
(A) a retreat . . writings
(B) a liability . . prying
(C) an excuse . . adulation
(D) a haven . . intrusions
(E) an occupation . . attentions

2 The congressman promised that he would consider all viewpoints and that he was willing, not only to discuss his proposal, but to ---- it.
(A) amend
(B) state
(C) silence
(D) accept
(E) approve

3 The ombudsman was critical of the city's law enforcement agencies for the ---- of their efforts to stem the increase in criminal activity.
(A) renewal
(B) inadequacy
(C) rejection
(D) ratification
(E) model

4 The review board ruled that the intern's behavior had been ----; he had violated the high standards required of members of the profession.
(A) usual
(B) exemplary
(C) laudatory
(D) unethical
(E) ineffective

5 Critics ---- the play and described the playwright as prolific, brilliant, and ----.
(A) acclaimed . . incisive
(B) berated . . entertaining
(C) praised . . prosaic
(D) welcomed . . derivative
(E) censured . . imaginative
Ⓐ Ⓑ Ⓒ Ⓓ Ⓔ

6 Because of her ---- views, the professor frequently found herself defending traditional values and the status quo in arguments with her more radical students.
(A) liberal
(B) extreme
(C) conservative
(D) unorthodox
(E) economic
Ⓐ Ⓑ Ⓒ Ⓓ Ⓔ

7 The dramatist lived ---- life and his fame was achieved ----; few people had ever heard of him, or his works, until several years after his death.
(A) a hapless . . effortlessly
(B) an obscure . . posthumously
(C) an infamous . . gradually
(D) a monastic . . publicly
(E) an eventful . . prematurely
Ⓐ Ⓑ Ⓒ Ⓓ Ⓔ

8 Despite his usual sensitivity to criticism, the commissioner did not ---- his position on the issue, even after he was ---- in the press.
(A) develop . . approached
(B) abandon . . ridiculed
(C) alter . . acclaimed
(D) explain . . covered
(E) relinquish . . substituted
Ⓐ Ⓑ Ⓒ Ⓓ Ⓔ

9 In his later work, the artist finally attained a maturity of style utterly ---- his early, amateurish pieces.

(A) descriptive of
(B) superseded by
(C) absent from
(D) celebrated in
(E) featured in

Ⓐ Ⓑ Ⓒ Ⓓ Ⓔ

10 The ambitions of tyrants are not ----, but excited, by partial concessions; that is why we must be ---- in opposing their demands.

(A) realized . . clement
(B) stimulated . . adamant
(C) satisfied . . yielding
(D) appeased . . resolute
(E) inhibited . . generous

Ⓐ Ⓑ Ⓒ Ⓓ Ⓔ

SCORECARD	
Number of Questions Right:	
Number of Questions Wrong:	
Number of Questions Omitted:	
Number of Correct Guesses:	
Number of Wrong Guesses:	
Time Used:	

Answers and Explanations

1 **D**—The semicolon is important in this sentence. The part of the sentence that follows the semicolon will elaborate on, and possibly help define, what has gone before. The real clue to filling both blanks lies in the phrase *she felt safe there.* It is clear that the first blank means a "safe place," while the second will refer to something negative that the movie star wishes to avoid. (D) should have jumped out as the correct answer. The cabin is a **haven** from the **intrusions** of reporters and photographers. In (A), **retreat** is good, but the second blank doesn't make sense. Choice (B) is wrong because **liability** does not fit the meaning of the sentence. Both words in choice (C) are way off. (E)'s second word, **attentions,** is fine, but **an occupation** is wrong in this context. So (D) is the correct answer.

> *haven: safe place*
> *retreat: a place for withdrawal*
> *liability: a disadvantage or handicap*
> *adulation: excessive flattery*

2 **A**—The structural clue in this sentence is the expression *not only . . . but.* The congressman was willing, *not only* to discuss his proposal, *but* to do something else consistent with his promise to consider all viewpoints. Choice (A) **amend** is right. Choice (B) is incorrect; **state** is too close in meaning to *discuss.*

> *amend: to correct or change*

3 **B**—You don't need to know what an *ombudsman* is to answer this one. What would *law enforcement* officials be criticized for? Probably their failure to do enough to fight crime. Or, as (B) puts it, *the* **inadequacy** *of their efforts to stem the increase in criminal activity.* (A) **renewal** contradicts the meaning of the sentence. Choices (C), (D), and (E) do not make sense when plugged into the sentence, so you can eliminate them.

> *ombudsman: someone who settles people's*
> *complaints against a government,*
> *agency, or public institution*
> *ratification: formal approval*

4 **D**—The semicolon is the clue here. Again, what follows the semicolon will elaborate on what comes before. Clearly, the intern's behavior was very bad; the word *violated* tells you that. You can eliminate (A) because **usual** behavior is not in violation of standards. Eliminate (B) and (C) also. Being **ineffective** is bad, but it's not necessarily violating any standards, so (E) is wrong. Choice (D) is correct.

> *exemplary: deserving imitation*
> *laudatory: praiseworthy*
> *ineffective: not achieving any results*
> *unethical: not conforming to accepted*
> *or professional standards of behavior*

5 **A**—If you noticed the clue word *and,* you might have found it easier to work with the second blank first. *And* tells you that the word in the second blank has to be positive, to go along with *prolific* and *brilliant.* Once you've established that, you can eliminate (C) **prosaic** and (D) **derivative**. The second words in (A), (B), and (E) will work, so let's try their first-blank words. Clearly, the critics liked the play, so we need a positive word here. **Acclaimed,** in (A), is the only positive first-blank choice, and the only one that works when plugged in, so it's correct.

> *prosaic: dull and unimaginative, ordinary*
> *derivative: taken from some original source*
> *incisive: perceptive*
> *acclaimed: enthusiastically applauded*
> *berated: harshly criticized*

6 **C**—*Radical* in the political sense means "desiring radical reforms." If the *professor defended tradition* in arguments with *radical* students, her views must be the opposite of radical. They must be **conservative.** So (C) is the correct answer. (A) **liberal** is not sufficiently different from *radical* to be the answer. (B) and (D) don't make logical sense either; a person with **extreme** or **unorthodox** (unconventional) views may or may not defend tradition. Finally, saying that the professor's views were **economic** in (E) does not explain why she would defend the status quo.

> *conservative: traditional or opposing change*
> *liberal: tolerant, open-minded*

7 **B**—In sentences whose clauses are separated by a semicolon, you should always very carefully read the part that does not contain the blanks. Often the clue to filling the blanks lies there. Since *few had heard* of the dramatist, you can predict that he lived a quiet or secluded life. The word in the second blank describes how his fame was achieved, so it will mean something like "after his death." (B) is the correct answer. *The dramatist lived* **an obscure** *life and his fame was achieved* **posthumously**. (A) makes no sense. You wouldn't say that *the dramatist lived a* **hapless** *life and that his fame was achieved* **effortlessly**. When you plug the other choices in, you'll find them equally unworkable.

> *obscure: not well known*
> *posthumously: after one's death*
> *hapless: unlucky*
> *infamous: having a bad reputation*
> *monastic: secluded*

8 **B**—The word *despite* jumps right out here as a clue to the direction that the sentence will take. You can predict that this time the commissioner wasn't so sensitive to criticism. He did not change his position on the issue just because of the censure it brought him. For the first blank, we need a word like **change.** Choices (B), (C), and (E) look good: **abandon**, **alter**, and **relinquish** might all work.

Now that we've narrowed the choices to three, let's try to fill the second blank. We're looking here for something like *criticized.* (C) **acclaimed** means "praised," so eliminate it. (E) **substituted** doesn't mean "criticized." By process of elimination, (B) is right. It makes sense to say, *he would not* **abandon** *his position, even after he was* **ridiculed** *in the press.* So (B) is the correct answer.

> *acclaimed: praised*
> *ridiculed: scorned, criticized*

9 **C**—The opening phrase of the sentence—*in his later work*—and the concluding words—*his early, amateurish pieces*—tell us that a comparison is being drawn between the two stages of the artist's career. We are told that he attained a *maturity of style*—something that we might expect to come with age and therefore not to have been present in his early work. Choice (C), **absent from**, is consistent with this idea. (A) is wrong because it contradicts

the sense of the sentence: A mature style wouldn't be **descriptive of** early, amateurish works. In (B), **superseded by** is clearly wrong. You'd expect more mature art to supersede amateur art, not the other way around. (D) is similarly illogical; so is (E).

> *superseded: replaced*

10 **D**—The word *not* is an important clue in filling the first blank. It suggests that the missing word will be the opposite of *excited.* So you can predict a word like *calmed* for the blank. That eliminates answer choice (B) at once. (A) and (E) can also be ruled out since their first words aren't anywhere near *calmed.* That leaves (C) **satisfied** and (D) **appeased** as possible right answers.

Now let's try (C) and (D)'s second-blank choices. **Yielding** is wrong. The idea is that since partial concessions encourage tyrants to push for more, we must be strong in opposing their demands. (D)'s **resolute** is the only answer that makes sense in this context.

> *clement: merciful*
> *adamant: uncompromising, unyielding*
> *inhibited: repressed or restrained*

SENTENCE COMPLETIONS—PRACTICE SET 10

 Suggested Time: 7 minutes

Directions—Select the lettered word or set of words that best completes the sentence.

Example:
Today's small, portable computers contrast markedly with the earliest electronic computers, which were ----.
(A) effective
(B) invented
(C) useful
(D) destructive
(E) enormous Ⓐ Ⓑ Ⓒ Ⓓ ●

1 Generally, fund-raising parties are quite labor-intensive and not very cost-effective; in other words, putting in a great deal of ---- doesn't mean you'll ---- a great deal of income.
(A) restraint . . obtain
(B) effort . . generate
(C) management . . spend
(D) reception . . limit
(E) materials . . lose Ⓐ Ⓑ Ⓒ Ⓓ Ⓔ

2 The leader of the task force on food quality deplored the fact that her efforts at investigation were ----, largely because of a lack of ---- between task force members and the health departments under investigation.
(A) final . . disagreement
(B) persistent . . energy
(C) successful . . resistance
(D) challenged . . discussion
(E) futile . . cooperation Ⓐ Ⓑ Ⓒ Ⓓ Ⓔ

3 Scientists had incorrectly assumed that parasites were primitive and ---- life forms; further research has revealed that parasites are actually quite ----.
(A) uncomplicated . . complex
(B) viable . . unproven
(C) mobile . . remote
(D) vigorous . . unscientific
(E) humorous . . inaccurate Ⓐ Ⓑ Ⓒ Ⓓ Ⓔ

4 Though people often think of them as ---- carnivores, many species of piranha are vegetarian.
(A) nomadic
(B) lugubrious
(C) voracious
(D) covetous
(E) exotic Ⓐ Ⓑ Ⓒ Ⓓ Ⓔ

5 On the Serengeti Plain, gazelles ---- from place to place in search of food until forced to run from hungry ---- like lions.
(A) migrate . . reprobates
(B) saunter . . predators
(C) ramble . . insurgents
(D) falter . . carnivores
(E) meander . . tyrants Ⓐ Ⓑ Ⓒ Ⓓ Ⓔ

6 Inflation has made the cost of consumer goods so ---- that most people can barely afford to buy basic food items.
(A) insignificant
(B) dubious
(C) coercive
(D) exorbitant
(E) repugnant Ⓐ Ⓑ Ⓒ Ⓓ Ⓔ

7 In the 19th century, a number of ---- farming communities were founded in the United States by groups of people who sought to create ideal societies.
(A) utopian
(B) mawkish
(C) decorous
(D) venerable
(E) surreptitious Ⓐ Ⓑ Ⓒ Ⓓ Ⓔ

8 Although the applicant was well qualified, she wasn't even considered for the job because the ---- way in which she boasted of her past accomplishments seemed ---- to the interviewer.
(A) awkward . . haughty
(B) candid . . optimistic
(C) exemplary . . antagonistic
(D) pompous . . excessive
(E) effusive . . frugal Ⓐ Ⓑ Ⓒ Ⓓ Ⓔ

9 Yeats's poetry became steadily more elaborate and more ---- during the 1890s; his audience found his poems increasingly difficult to interpret.
(A) laconic
(B) inscrutable
(C) effusive
(D) lyrical
(E) euphonious   Ⓐ Ⓑ Ⓒ Ⓓ Ⓔ

10 Even if ---- life exists elsewhere in the universe, we humans may never know it, since it may be impossible for us to ---- with these alien beings.
(A) avaricious . . confer
(B) prodigal . . reside
(C) sentient . . communicate
(D) lachrymose . . traipse
(E) extraneous . . exit   Ⓐ Ⓑ Ⓒ Ⓓ Ⓔ

SCORECARD	
Number of Questions Right:	
Number of Questions Wrong:	
Number of Questions Omitted:	
Number of Correct Guesses:	
Number of Wrong Guesses:	
Time Used:	

Answers and Explanations

1 **B**—The suggestion made in this sentence is quite straightforward: The energy expended on fund-raising parties does not always match the income that results from them. If you have trouble, simply plug in the answer choices one at a time and listen to the logic of the sentence. Try choice (A): Putting in **restraint** doesn't mean you'll **obtain** income. That doesn't make any sense. Move on to (B): *Putting in* **effort** *doesn't mean you'll* **generate** *income.* That sounds perfectly sensible, and it follows through on the idea expressed in the first part of the sentence. (B) is the correct answer.

Continue to check the others just to make sure. In (C), "putting in **management** and **spend**ing income" sounds funny and doesn't make sense. In (D), **reception** has nothing to do with **limit**ing income. And in (E), why would you put in **materials** in order to **lose** income?

2 **E**—In the first part of the sentence the verb *deplored* lets us know that the first blank will be a "negative" word. So, we can predict that the task force leader must have regretted that her efforts were *disregarded, useless,* or some other negative quality. Looking at the answer choices, we can rule out (A), (B), and (C).

That leaves us with (D) and (E), so let's try out (D) and (E)'s second words. (D) is too vague: Why would the leader's efforts be **challenged** because of a lack of **discussion?** (E) makes more sense. *Efforts at investigation were* **futile** *because of a lack of* **cooperation** *between task force members and the people being investigated.*

> *deplored: regretted deeply or disapproved of*
> *futile: useless*

3 **A**—You know that the parasites were assumed to be primitive and ---- life forms. So whatever goes in the first blank must go along with the word *primitive.* The first word will be something like *simple.* In the second blank, the parasites are *actually quite* ----. So we are looking for a word like **complex** for the second blank. That means (A) is right. Life forms first thought to be primitive and **uncomplicated** have been revealed to be quite **complex**.

4 **C**—The clue is the word *although.* We need a word that is consistent with the piranha's image as a carnivore, yet contrasts with the reality that many piranhas eat only plants. (C) **voracious** works best. None of the other choices makes sense. If you knew that piranhas were tropical fish, you might have fallen for (E), but piranhas' exotic nature has nothing to do with their diet.

> *voracious: greedy, having a huge appetite*
> *nomadic: wandering from place to place*
> *lugubrious: mournful*
> *covetous: eagerly desiring something*
>   *belonging to someone else*
> *exotic: foreign*

5 **B**—A number of the first-blank words look possible here, so it's easiest to start on the second blank. Of the second words, only two are real possibilities. The lions are either (B) **predators** or (D) **carnivores**. Checking (B) and (D)'s first words, we see that only (B) works for the first blank, since gazelles wouldn't **falter** from place to place.

6 **D**—Since *most people can barely afford to buy basic food items,* we can predict that inflation has made the cost of consumer goods extremely expensive. The best choice is (D).

> *exorbitant: excessive or costly*
> *dubious: doubtful*
> *coercive: forceful, threatening, bullying*
> *repugnant: offensive, repulsive*

7 **A**—A virtual definition of the word in the blank is found in the sentence. *People who sought to create ideal societies* would set up **utopian** *farming communities.*

> *utopian: idealistic or visionary*
> *mawkish: sickeningly sentimental*
> *decorous: dignified or proper*
> *venerable: deserving of respect because of*
>   *great age or character*
> *surreptitious: secret or clandestine*

8 **D**—*Although* implies contrast. Even though *the applicant was well qualified,* there was definitely something wrong with the way she *boasted* about her *accomplishments*. So the first blank must be filled by a negative word, and looking at the first-position answer choices, the only ones we have are (A) **awkward** and (D) **pompous**.

Trying (A) and (D) in the second blank, we see that only (D) makes sense. If she had boasted **awkward**ly, that probably wouldn't have seemed **haughty** to the interviewer. But if she had boasted **pompously**, that could indeed seem **excessive**.

9 **B**—There are two significant clues in this sentence. The first is the word *and*, which tells us that the word in the blank will continue the idea expressed by the adjective elaborate, that Yeats's poetry became more complex. Secondly, the semicolon suggests that an explanation of the missing word will follow in the second part of the sentence—which goes on to tell us that people had difficulty interpreting his poems. We should look, therefore, for a word that means "difficult to understand." (B), **inscrutable**, is the correct answer. None of the three words in (A), (C), and (E) would make Yeats's poetry difficult to understand, so they are wrong.

---

inscrutable: difficult or impossible to understand or interpret
laconic: using few words
effusive: expressing emotions in an unrestrained way
euphonious: pleasant-sounding
lyrical: having the quality of a song

---

10 **C**—Assuming some alien intelligence exists, why might humans never know it? Logically, it must be because we can't (C) **communicate** with the alien life forms. (C) works: If conscious life exists, we humans might never know because we could be unable to communicate with that life. In (A), **confer** might be possible, but **avaricious** won't fit.

---

sentient: conscious, characterized by sensation
avaricious: greedy
prodigal: extravagant
lachrymose: tearful, mournful
traipse: walk aimlessly
extraneous: external; not relevant

KAPLAN

SAT Critical Reading

INTRODUCTION TO SAT CRITICAL READING

The Critical Reading section tests your ability to read long passages quickly and perceptively. It also tests your understanding of how words are used in context. You'll be asked questions about the overall point of the passage, the author's point of view, the details, and what's implied. You'll also need to compare and contrast related passages.

The Structure

Critical Reading passages and questions appear in all the Verbal sections of the SAT. Each section contains either one long passage (or a paired passage) with 12–13 questions or two separate, shorter passages with a total of 15–16 questions.

The Format

Although the Critical Reading directions you'll see on the actual test will be worded slightly differently than the following sentence, they'll be basically the same. Get familiar with the directions now, so you won't waste precious time on Test Day:

Answer the questions below based on the information in the accompanying passages.

After the directions, you'll see four long (400–850 word) reading passages. One "paired passage" requires you to read and compare two related passages whose views oppose, support, or otherwise complement each other.

Critical Reading passages cover a wide variety of subjects, including the humanities, the arts, the social sciences, and the natural sciences. One reading selection will be narrative or fiction.

> Hint: A brief introduction precedes each passage. It often contains valuable information about the author and the passage that will help you earn points. Never skip it.

Each passage is followed by five to thirteen questions. The questions are ordered: The first few ask about the beginning of the passage, the last few about the end of the passage. With paired passages, some questions will ask you about individual passages; some questions will ask you to compare and contrast the pair.

> Hint: Most unfamiliar words will be defined. You don't need any outside knowledge to answer the Critical Reading questions.

Reading Tips

One Verbal section has two reading selections. You can start with either one. Scan both introductions, and do the passage you find easier first.

Don't read the passage thoroughly—that's a waste of time.

Do *skim* the passage to get the drift. If you miss the details, don't worry. The questions will direct you back to important points in the passage.

> Hint: The less time you spend reading the passages, the more time you'll have to answer questions, and that's where you score points.

Answering the Questions

There are three kinds of Critical Reading questions: Big Picture, Little Picture, and Vocabulary-in-Context. All three are worth the same number of points. So don't get hung up on any one question.

Big Picture questions ask about the overall focus of the passage and the main points. To answer them accurately, you need to read *actively*, asking yourself, "Why did the author write this?" "What's the point of this?"

Little Picture questions are usually keyed: They give you a line reference, or refer you to a particular paragraph—a strong clue to where in the passage you'll find your answer. If you're given a line reference, don't read only that line. Read a few lines before and after to get an idea of the *context* in which that line appears.

Vocabulary-in-Context questions don't test your ability to define hard words. Instead, they ask how a word is used in the passage. The most common meaning of the word is probably not the correct answer. *Always* look back to the passage to see how the word is used in context.

Paired Passages

With paired passages, the first few questions relate to the first passage, the next few to the second passage, and the final questions ask about the passages as a pair. The best way to do paired passages is:

- Skim the first passage, and do the questions about it.
- Skim the second passage, thinking about how it relates to the first.
- Do the questions about the second passage.
- Do the questions about the relationship between the two passages.

Critical Reading Checklist

✔ Learn the instructions now.

✔ Always read the brief introductions.

✔ In the section with two passages, do the passage you find easier first.

✔ Read actively, searching for important points.

✔ Don't sweat the details.

✔ Read the lines before and after a line reference.

✔ Don't spend too much time on any one question. If you come across a hard one, move on and come back to it later.

✔ Avoid the "obvious" choice in Vocabulary-in-Context questions.

✔ In a paired passage, do all the questions about the first passage before you read the second passage.

Suggested Time: 7 minutes

Directions—Answer the questions below based on the information in the accompanying passage.

Practice Passage 1: Willa Cather

The following passage analyzes one of Willa Cather's (1873–1947) novels.

Sapphira and the Slave Girl was the last novel of Willa Cather's illustrious literary career. Begun in the late summer of 1937 and finally completed in
Line 1941, it is often regarded by critics as one of her
(5) most personal works. Although the story takes place in 1856, well before her own birth, she drew heavily on both vivid childhood memories and tales handed down by older relatives to describe life in rural northern Virginia in the middle of the 19th
(10) century. She even went on an extended journey to the area to give the story a further ring of authenticity.

Of all of Cather's many novels, *Sapphira and the Slave Girl* is the one most concerned with providing
(15) an overall picture of day-to-day life in a specific era. A number of the novel's characters, it would seem, are included in the story only because they are representative of the types of people to be found in 19th-century rural Virginia; indeed, a few of them
(20) play no part whatsoever in the unfolding of the plot. For instance, we are introduced to a poor white woman, Mandy Ringer, who is portrayed as intelligent and content, despite the fact that she has no formal education and must toil constantly in the
(25) fields. And we meet Dr. Clevenger, a country doctor who, with his patrician manners, evokes a strong image of the pre-Civil War South.

The title, however, accurately suggests that the novel is mainly about slavery. Cather's attitude
(30) toward this institution may best be summed up as somewhat ambiguous. On the one hand, she displays almost total indifference to the legal and political aspects of slavery when she misidentifies certain crucial dates in its growth and development.
(35) Nor does she ever really offer a direct condemnation of slavery. Yet, on the other hand, the evil that was slavery gets through to us, albeit in typically subtle ways. Those characters, like Mrs. Blake, who oppose the institution are portrayed in a sympa-
(40) thetic light. Furthermore, the suffering of the slaves themselves and the petty, nasty, often cruel, behavior of the slaveowners are painted in stark terms.

Although *Sapphira and the Slave Girl* was certainly not meant to be a political tract, the novel is some-
(45) times considered to be a denunciation of bygone days. Nothing could be further from the truth. In spite of her willingness to acknowledge that particular aspects of the past were far from ideal, Willa Cather was, if anything, a bit of a romantic.
(50) Especially in the final years of her life, an increasing note of anger about the emptiness of the present crept into her writings. Earlier generations, she concluded, had been the real heroes, the real creators of all that was good in America.

1 The word *extended* in line 10 most nearly means
(A) enlarged
(B) increased
(C) postponed
(D) stretched
(E) prolonged

2 In the discussion of Willa Cather's *Sapphira and the Slave Girl*, the author refers to the book primarily as a
(A) heroic tale of the Civil War
(B) sweeping epic of the old South
(C) story based on personal material
(D) political treatise on slavery
(E) veiled condemnation of 1930s America

Ⓐ Ⓑ Ⓒ Ⓓ Ⓔ

3 In the second paragraph, the author mentions Mandy Ringer and Dr. Clevenger in order to emphasize which point about *Sapphira and the Slave Girl*?

(A) A number of the characters in the novel are based on people Cather knew in her childhood.

(B) The novel displays Cather's mixed feelings about slavery.

(C) Cather took four years to complete the novel because she carefully researched her characters.

(D) One of Cather's purposes in writing the novel was to paint a full portrait of life in rural Virginia in the years before the Civil War.

(E) The characters in the novel are portrayed in a positive light since Cather was a great admirer of the old South.

Ⓐ Ⓑ Ⓒ Ⓓ Ⓔ

4 According to the author, why is Willa Cather's attitude toward slavery "somewhat ambiguous" (line 31)?

(A) She was ignorant of the legal and political aspects of slavery even though she was a keen observer of history.

(B) She did not denounce slavery directly but criticized it in more roundabout ways.

(C) She sympathized equally with both slaves and slaveowners.

(D) She was an enemy of slavery but refrained from getting involved in political issues.

(E) She disliked the treatment of slaves yet never tried to help improve their lot in life.

Ⓐ Ⓑ Ⓒ Ⓓ Ⓔ

5 In context, "a bit of a romantic" (line 49) suggests that Willa Cather

(A) condemned the evils of slavery

(B) favored the past over the present

(C) disliked writing about life in the 1930s

(D) denounced certain aspects of 19th-century life

(E) exaggerated the evils of earlier generations

Ⓐ Ⓑ Ⓒ Ⓓ Ⓔ

SCORECARD	
Number of Questions Right:	
Number of Questions Wrong:	
Number of Questions Omitted:	
Number of Correct Guesses:	
Number of Wrong Guesses:	
Time Used:	

KAPLAN

Answers and Explanations

Passage 1: Willa Cather

After your first reading, you should know roughly what the passage as a whole is about, and what each paragraph is about. The first paragraph tells us *Sapphira and the Slave Girl* is one of Cather's most authentic and personal works. The second paragraph tells us that *Sapphira and the Slave Girl* sets out to provide a picture of everyday life in the pre–Civil War South. Paragraph three tells us that while the novel is mainly about slavery, Cather's attitude toward slavery is ambiguous. The final paragraph says that although some consider *Sapphira* a denunciation of the past, the author feels the opposite is true. You'd be wasting time to go into further depth before looking at the questions. The only points you need to spend time with are the ones you're asked about.

1 E—This is a Vocabulary-in-Context question. If an answer choice has already grabbed your eye, try it in context. If not, check out each choice. (A) **enlarged** might seem related to a long trip, but it doesn't sound right. Definitely check the rest of the choices. (B) **increased** doesn't make sense; increased from what? (C) **postponed** is easy to eliminate; Cather's trip was not put off till a future time. (D) **stretched** is a definition of *extended*, but not one that works here. Finally, (E) **prolonged** makes sense. The line, "She went on an extended journey," keeps its meaning if you substituted **prolonged** for *extended*. Both words give the idea of an extensive trip, one where Cather could get a real feel for the places she would later describe in her novel.

> Hint: Always turn to the cited line to see how the word is used before you pick an answer.

2 C—Look in the first paragraph for the answer to this question. The first paragraph tells us that *Sapphira* is one of Cather's most personal works and drew heavily on her childhood memories. The answer is almost certainly (C).

If you doubt it, check out the other choices. In paragraph two we learn that the novel is largely a portrait of the pre–Civil War South, and in paragraph three that *Sapphira* is mainly about slavery—so choice (A) is out. There's nothing in the passage

to suggest that *Sapphira* is a **sweeping epic**—choice (B). If anything, it's the opposite, a very personal novel. (D) can't be right, because the first line in paragraph four says *Sapphira* is "not meant to be a political tract." Choice (E) is less obviously wrong, but is still wrong. Also in paragraph four, the author tells us Cather was dissatisfied with the present, but this is not the focus of her novel.

3 D—Go back to paragraph two and see what's going on. The author mentions two characters who are included mainly to help complete Cather's portrait of rural Virginia. Choice (D) states this nicely and is the right answer.

Other answer choices might agree with points the author makes elsewhere in the passage, but this question asks specifically about paragraph two. Choice (A) is discussed in paragraph one. Choice (B) is discussed in paragraph three. And choice (C) is discussed in paragraph one. Choice (E) overstates the content in paragraph four.

4 B—This question sends us to the third paragraph. There, the author says Cather's attitude toward slavery is somewhat ambiguous, and offers several bits of evidence. On the one hand, Cather never comes out and directly condemns slavery, and she displays ignorance of and indifference to its legal and political aspects. On the other hand, she sympathetically portrays characters opposed to slavery and clearly portrays the suffering of slaves and the cruelty of slave owners. Choice (A) captures only part of this evidence and is therefore wrong. Choice (B) sums the evidence up and is the right answer.

The author never says that Cather **sympathizes** with slave owners, so choice (C) is out. The passage says Cather's attitude toward slavery was ambiguous, not that she was **an enemy of slavery,** so choice (D) is wrong. And finally, choice (E) is out because the author is talking about Cather's attitude toward slavery as expressed in *Sapphira*, not in terms of what she did or did not do in her life.

5 B—Again, go back to the text. In the last paragraph the author refers to Cather as "a bit of a romantic" who cherished past creativity over the present emptiness. Choice (B) is a nice paraphrase of this, and is the right answer.

(A) can't be right, because the passage says Cather's views of slavery are "ambiguous." Nothing suggests Cather **disliked writing about the 1930s**, so choice (C) is wrong. Cather did dislike certain aspects of mid-19th-century life, but that's the opposite of romanticizing those times, so eliminate choice (D). Finally, Cather didn't **exaggerate the evils** of the past; if anything, she underestimated them. So choice (E) is wrong.

---

ambiguous: not clear; capable of being understood in two or more ways

---

KAPLAN

Suggested Time: 10 minutes

Directions—Answer the questions below based on the information in the accompanying passage.

Practice Passage 2: Sweet Track

The following passage is excerpted from a popular journal of archeology.

About fifty miles west of Stonehenge, buried in the peat bogs of the Somerset flatlands in southwestern England, lies the oldest road known to humanity. Dubbed the "Sweet Track" after its discoverer, Raymond Sweet, this painstakingly constructed 1,800-meter road dates back to the early Neolithic period, some 6,000 years ago. Thanks primarily to the overlying layer of acidic peat, which has kept the wood moist, inhibited the growth of decay bacteria, and discouraged the curiosity of animal life, the road is remarkably well preserved. Examination of its remains has provided extensive information about the people who constructed it.

The design of the Sweet Track indicates that its builders possessed extraordinary engineering skills. In constructing the road, they first hammered pegs into the soil in the form of upright X's. Single rails were slid beneath the pegs, so that the rails rested firmly on the soft surface of the bog. Then planks were placed in the V-shaped space formed by the upper arms of the pegs. This method of construction—allowing the underlying rail to distribute the weight of the plank above and thereby prevent the pegs from sinking into the marsh—is remarkably sophisticated, testifying to a surprisingly advanced level of technology.

Furthermore, in order to procure the materials for the road, several different species of tree had to be felled, debarked, and split. This suggests that the builders possessed high quality tools, and that they knew the differing properties of various roundwoods. It appears also that the builders were privy to the finer points of lumbering, maximizing the amount of wood extracted from a given tree by slicing logs of large diameter radially and logs of small diameter tangentially.

Studies of the Sweet Track further indicate a high level of social organization among its builders. This is supported by the observation that the road seems to have been completed in a very short time; tree-ring analysis confirms that the components of the Sweet Track were probably all felled within a single year. Moreover, the fact that such an involved engineering effort could be orchestrated in the first place hints at a complex social structure.

Finally, excavation of the Sweet Track has provided evidence that the people who built it comprised a community devoted to land cultivation. It appears that the road was built to serve as a footpath linking two islands—islands that provided a source of timber, cropland, and pastures for the community that settled the hills to the south. Furthermore, the quality of the pegs indicates that the workers knew enough to fell trees in such a way as to encourage the rapid growth of long, straight, rodlike shoots from the remaining stumps, to be used as pegs. This method is called coppicing and its practice by the settlers is the earliest known example of woodland management.

Undoubtedly, the discovery of the Sweet Track in 1970 added much to our knowledge of Neolithic technology. But while study of the remains has revealed unexpectedly high levels of engineering and social organization, it must be remembered that the Sweet Track represents the work of a single isolated community. One must be careful not to extrapolate sweeping generalizations from the achievements of such a small sample of Neolithic humanity.

1. In the first paragraph, the author claims that which of the following was primarily responsible for the preservation of the Sweet Track until modern times?

(A) It was located in an area containing very few animals.

(B) Its components were buried beneath the peat bog.

(C) It was only lightly traveled during its period of use.

(D) Local authorities prohibited development in the surrounding area.

(E) It was protected from excessive humidity.

Ⓐ Ⓑ Ⓒ Ⓓ Ⓔ

2 The author's reference to the peat bog as "acidic" (line 8) primarily serves to
(A) indicate the importance of protecting ancient ruins from the effects of modern pollution
(B) emphasize that the Sweet Track was constructed of noncorrosive materials
(C) distinguish between the effects of acidic and basic conditions on ancient ruins
(D) suggest that acidic conditions were important in inhibiting decay
(E) prove the relevance of knowledge of chemical properties to archaeological concerns
Ⓐ Ⓑ Ⓒ Ⓓ Ⓔ

3 In lines 16–26, the author describes the construction of the Sweet Track primarily in order to
(A) explain the unusual strength of the structure
(B) show how it could withstand 6,000 years buried underground
(C) prove that its builders cooperated efficiently
(D) indicate its builders' advanced level of technological expertise
(E) emphasize the importance of careful construction techniques
Ⓐ Ⓑ Ⓒ Ⓓ Ⓔ

4 The primary focus of the passage is on
(A) the high degree of social organization exhibited by earlier cultures
(B) the complex construction and composition of the Sweet Track
(C) an explanation for the survival of the Sweet Track over 6,000 years
(D) ways in which the Sweet Track reveals aspects of a particular Neolithic society
(E) the innovative methods of woodland management practiced by early builders
Ⓐ Ⓑ Ⓒ Ⓓ Ⓔ

5 In lines 32–33, the phrase *privy to* means
(A) close to
(B) expert at
(C) concealed from
(D) likely to
(E) familiar with
Ⓐ Ⓑ Ⓒ Ⓓ Ⓔ

6 In her discussion of social organization in paragraph four, the author mentions ring analysis primarily as evidence that
(A) the road is at least 6,000 years old
(B) the Sweet Track was constructed quickly
(C) the techniques used in building the road were quite sophisticated
(D) the builders knew enough to split thick trees radially and thin trees tangentially
(E) the builders felled a large variety of trees
Ⓐ Ⓑ Ⓒ Ⓓ Ⓔ

7 The cited example of "woodland management" (lines 58–59) is best described as a system in which trees are
(A) lumbered in controlled quantities
(B) planted only among trees of their own species
(C) cultivated in specialized ways for specific purposes
(D) felled only as they are needed
(E) harvested for use in construction only
Ⓐ Ⓑ Ⓒ Ⓓ Ⓔ

8 In the last paragraph, the author cautions that the Sweet Track
(A) is not as technologically advanced as is generally believed
(B) should not necessarily be regarded as representative of its time
(C) has not been studied extensively enough to support generalized conclusions
(D) is probably not the earliest road in existence
(E) will force historians to reevaluate their assumptions about the Neolithic technology
Ⓐ Ⓑ Ⓒ Ⓓ Ⓔ

SCORECARD	
Number of Questions Right:	
Number of Questions Wrong:	
Number of Questions Omitted:	
Number of Correct Guesses:	
Number of Wrong Guesses:	
Time Used:	

Answers and Explanations

Passage 2: Sweet Track

The next passage, which comes from "a popular journal of archeology," is about the "oldest road known to humanity," also known as the Sweet Track after its discoverer. The last sentence of the first paragraph makes the main point—that examination of the remains of the Sweet Track has revealed lots of information about the people who built it. The next four paragraphs provide examples and insights about the builders, revealed by studying the remains. Do you have to sweat the details of each example? No way. Don't waste time trying to understand the specific construction techniques, materials, tools, etcetera.

In the second paragraph, for instance, we hope you skimmed over all that description about wooden X-shaped pegs and the upper and lower rails. All you need to know is that the builders of the Sweet Track had a "surprisingly advanced level of technology."

The passage concludes with a little warning: Although the Sweet Track shows X, Y, and Z about the builders, this small group of people does not represent Neolithic peoples in general. You can't assume that all people in those long-ago days were as advanced as the builders of the Sweet Track.

1 **B**—This Little Picture question about the Sweet Track's preservation sends you back to the first paragraph. Right there in the third sentence you get the information you need. What accounts for the road's being so well preserved? The remains were **buried** under a layer of acidic peat, which kept the wood moist, prevented decay from bacteria, and kept nosy animals away. That should have led you to answer choice (B).

(A) may have given you pause, since a lack of interfering **animals** is mentioned in paragraph one. But it wasn't the location of the road that kept animals away; it was the fact that the road was **buried,** so the animals couldn't get to it. (C) and (D) might seem to offer reasonable explanations for the road's good condition, but the passage never mentions **light travel** patterns or **development** prohibitions. Finally, (E) gets it dead wrong; the road was kept "moist," according to the author, so it was hardly **protected from excessive humidity.**

2 **D**—Reread the sentence in which "acidic" is mentioned. It says that the "acidic peat" allowed for three conditions that caused the road to be preserved: It kept it moist, relatively free of bacteria, and free from animal interference. So the fact that the bog was "acidic" must have something to do with causing those conditions. When you check the answer choices, only (D) mentions one of those conditions, so it's the right answer. Incorrect choices (A) and (C) bring in unmentioned issues; (A) **modern pollution** and (C) **acidic** versus **basic conditions** are never discussed in the passage. You know (B) is wrong because the author never mentions **noncorrosive materials** as a factor that kept the road in such good shape. And (E) is too general; the author is not making a big point about chemicals and archeology.

3 **D**—The line reference directs you to the second paragraph. You're asked why the author describes the construction of the Sweet Track. Don't read all the details; just look to see what the author concludes. In the last sentence of the paragraph, the author claims the method of construction "is remarkably sophisticated, testifying to a surprisingly advanced level of technology." (D) is the answer you want.

Incorrect choices (B) and (C) point to conclusions the author makes elsewhere in the passage, not in the lines specified in question 3. (A) talks about the **unusual strength** of the road, which the author never discusses in any paragraph. (E)'s sweeping reference to the **importance of careful construction techniques** is too general, since the author is only drawing conclusions about this one specific culture.

4 **D**—The key to this Big Picture question is in the last sentence of the first paragraph. The author says she's going to discuss how Sweet Track's remains tell us a great deal about the Neolithic people who built it—a focus best summed up by correct choice (D).

Choice (B) is probably the closest wrong choice, but it's only half of the main focus. The author does focus on the **complex construction and composition** of the road, but for a purpose—to discuss what that **construction and composition** tells us about the builders of the road. Choice (A) is too broad. The passage only discusses the **social organization** of one isolated community. (C) and (E) are too narrow. The **survival** of the road over **6,000 years** (C) is the purpose of just the end of the first paragraph. And (E) is too narrow because **woodland management** is the topic of paragraph five only.

5 **E**—This is a Vocabulary-in-Context question, so go back and examine how *privy to* is used in the sentence *before* you try to answer.

The sentence says "the builders were privy to the finer points of lumbering" because they knew how to maximize the amount of wood extracted from a log by slicing it in different ways. That shows they were (E) **familiar with** the finer points of lumbering.

> Hint: You should look at the sentences around the word to figure out how the word is used.

If you plug choices (A), (C), and (D) into that sentence, they don't make sense. How can somebody be **close to, concealed from,** or **likely to** the finer points of lumbering? Choice (B) sounds possible, but **familiar with** is a more moderate choice, so it's a better bet. Remember, you're looking for the "best" answer. So (E) is correct.

6 **B**—To find out why the author brings up *ring analysis*, reread paragraph four. The author writes that the road "seems to have been completed in a very short time." How do we know? Because "tree-ring analysis," the topic of this question, confirms that the trees used to build the road were all felled within a single year. So tree-ring analysis offers evidence to support the claim that the Sweet Track was built **quickly;** choice (B).

Choice (A) may seem plausible, because we usually count tree-rings to find out how **old** trees are. But in paragraph four of this passage, tree-ring analysis was used for another purpose. The other choices raise issues discussed elsewhere. Those **sophisticated** building **techniques,** choice (C), were the subject of paragraph two, while the fancy lumbering technique mentioned in choice (D), as well as the **large variety** of felled trees mentioned in choice (E), were brought up in paragraph three and have nothing to do with the tree-ring analysis mentioned in paragraph four.

7 **C**—What's *the cited example of "woodland management"* the question refers to? When you go to the line reference given, you'll find it's called "coppicing." Coppicing is described as the process of felling trees "in such a way as to encourage the rapid growth of long, straight, rodlike shoots from the remaining stumps, to be used as pegs." In other words, trees are grown in a special way in order to yield special materials—that is, **the rodlike shoots.** Choice (C) best paraphrases that process.

Choices (A) and (D) have nothing to do with the paragraph; nowhere does the author talk about lumbering (A) **controlled quantities** of trees or cutting down trees (D) **only as they are needed.** (B) may sound plausible, but the process described here focuses not on the *kind* of trees being planted, but rather the *way* they are planted. And (E) may have been tempting, because the lumber in question *was* harvested for **use in construction,** but again, the point is how the trees were planted, not what they were used for.

8 **B**—This question directs you to that interesting last paragraph we discussed above—the one that cautions not to generalize too much from the Sweet Track. The author says the Sweet Track represents "the work of a single isolated community," and that therefore we shouldn't use it to make conclusions about all Neolithic communities. That's best paraphrased by choice (B).

Choices (A) and (D) are not the subject of the last paragraph; besides, they're just plain wrong. (C) is a distortion. The reason we shouldn't draw **generalized conclusions** from the Sweet Track is because it is the work of just one small community, not because the road has been studied too little. And (E) implies that the study of the Sweet Track will bring about a fundamental revolution in historical thought about the whole Neolithic period—just the kind of general conclusions that the author explicitly warns against.

Suggested Time: 9 minutes

Directions—Answer the questions below based on the information in the accompanying passage.

Practice Passage 3: Fallingwater

The following passage is excerpted from a study of modern architecture.

Fallingwater, a small country house constructed in 1936, stands as perhaps the greatest residential building achievement of the American architect
Line Frank Lloyd Wright. In designing the dwelling for
(5) the Pittsburgh millionaire Edgar J. Kaufmann, Wright was confronted with an unusually challenging site, beside a waterfall deep in a Pennsylvania ravine. However, Wright viewed this difficult location not as an obstacle, but as a unique opportunity
(10) to put his architectural ideals into concrete form. In the end, Wright was able to turn Fallingwater into an artistic link between untamed nature and domestic tranquility, and a masterpiece in his brilliant career.

(15) Edgar J. Kaufmann had originally planned for his house to sit at the bottom of the waterfall, where there was ample flat land on which to build. But Wright proposed a more daring response to the site. The architect convinced Kaufmann to build his
(20) house at the top of the waterfall on a small stone precipice. Further, Wright proposed extending the living room of the house out over the rushing water, and making use of modern building techniques so that no vertical supports would be needed to hold
(25) up the room. Rather than allowing the environment to determine the placement and shape of the house, Wright sought to construct a home that actually confronted and interacted with the landscape.

In one sense, Fallingwater can be viewed as a
(30) showcase for unconventional building tactics. In designing the living room, for example, Wright made brilliant use of a technique called the cantilever, in which steel rods are laid inside a shelf of concrete, eliminating the need for external supports.
(35) But Fallingwater also contains a great many traditional and natural building materials. The boulders which form the foundation for the house also extend up through the floor and form part of the fireplace. A staircase in the living room extends
(40) down to an enclosed bathing pool at the top of the waterfall. To Wright, the ideal dwelling in this spot was not simply a modern extravaganza or a direct extension of natural surroundings; rather, it was a little of both.

(45) Critics have taken a wide range of approaches to understanding this unique building. Some have postulated that the house exalts the artist's triumph over untamed nature. Others have compared Wright's building to a cave, providing a psycholog-
(50) ical and physical safe haven from a harsh, violent world. Edgar Kaufmann, Jr., the patron's son, may have summed up Fallingwater best when he said, "Wright understood that people were creatures of nature; hence an architecture which conformed to
(55) nature would conform to what was basic in people . . . . Sociability and privacy are both available, as are the comforts of home and the adventures of the seasons." This, then, is Frank Lloyd Wright's achievement in Fallingwater, a home which con-
(60) nects the human and the natural, for the invigoration and exaltation of both.

1. The primary purpose of the passage is to
   (A) showcase Wright's use of unconventional building tactics and techniques
   (B) describe the relationship between Wright and Edgar J. Kaufmann
   (C) judge the place of Fallingwater in the history of architecture
   (D) describe Fallingwater as Wright's response to a challenging building site
   (E) evaluate various critical responses to Fallingwater

   Ⓐ Ⓑ Ⓒ Ⓓ Ⓔ

2. The word *concrete* in line 10 could best be replaced by
   (A) dense
   (B) hard
   (C) substantial
   (D) durable
   (E) reinforced

   Ⓐ Ⓑ Ⓒ Ⓓ Ⓔ

3 The passage suggests that Edgar J. Kaufmann's original plans for the site were
(A) conservative
(B) inexpensive
(C) daring
(D) idealistic
(E) architecturally unsound

Ⓐ Ⓑ Ⓒ Ⓓ Ⓔ

4 The author includes a description of a cantilever (lines 30–34) in order to explain
(A) the technique used to create the fireplace in Fallingwater
(B) the use of traditional engineering techniques in Fallingwater
(C) an unusual design feature of Fallingwater
(D) modern technological advances in the use of concrete
(E) how Fallingwater conforms to nature

Ⓐ Ⓑ Ⓒ Ⓓ Ⓔ

5 The end of paragraph three indicates that, above all else, Wright wanted Kaufmann's home to be
(A) representative of its owner's wealth and position
(B) as durable as current construction techniques would allow
(C) a landmark in 20th century American architecture
(D) impressive yet in harmony with its surroundings
(E) a symbol of man's triumph over the natural landscape

Ⓐ Ⓑ Ⓒ Ⓓ Ⓔ

6 Critics' comparison of Fallingwater to a cave (lines 48–51) suggests that the house conveys a sense of
(A) warmth
(B) darkness
(C) simplicity
(D) claustrophobia
(E) security

Ⓐ Ⓑ Ⓒ Ⓓ Ⓔ

7 In context, the phrase "for the invigoration and exaltation of both" (lines 60–61) suggests that Fallingwater
(A) encourages visitors to appreciate the change of seasons
(B) benefits the environment as well as its occupants
(C) stands out as the most beautiful feature in the local landscape
(D) enables its owners to entertain in an impressive setting
(E) typifies Wright's efforts to infuse modern architecture with spirituality

Ⓐ Ⓑ Ⓒ Ⓓ Ⓔ

SCORECARD	
Number of Questions Right:	
Number of Questions Wrong:	
Number of Questions Omitted:	
Number of Correct Guesses:	
Number of Wrong Guesses:	
Time Used:	

Answers and Explanations

Passage 3: Fallingwater

This short passage is about Fallingwater, a house designed by the famous American architect Frank Lloyd Wright. Your initial quick skim should have told you that Fallingwater is regarded as a bold architectural statement, both because of its dramatic location atop a waterfall and because of various unconventional building techniques Wright used in the design. One running theme is the relationship of the house to the natural setting around it. Throughout the passage, the author comments on that relationship, indicating that Fallingwater "confronted and interacted with the landscape," so that the house was in part an extension of nature, but also an impressive "modern extravaganza."

1 **D**—This Big Picture question asks for the primary purpose of the passage. Your initial response might have been a general statement, such as "to describe the design of the Fallingwater house." But the correct answer should incorporate the running theme mentioned above—the relationship of the house to the natural setting. That's why choice (D) is correct.

Choice (A) is too broad. The author discusses Wright's **tactics and techniques** only in the design of one specific building, Fallingwater, which this choice does not specify. (B) is a distortion; although Kaufmann and Wright had different ideas about the ideal location for the house, describing the **relationship** between the two men is not *the purpose of* the passage. In (C), though the author says Fallingwater is unique, she never discusses its place in architectural **history**. And finally, (E) is the focus of the last paragraph only, where **critical responses** are discussed.

2 **C**—Next is a Vocabulary-in-Context question. To find a synonym for *concrete* that fits the context, go back to the actual sentence. You'll see *concrete* is used figuratively. Wright, the author says, regarded Fallingwater's site as an "opportunity to put his architectural ideals into concrete form"—out of the realm of ideals, in other words, and into the realm of real, tangible things. So (C) **substantial** is the best replacement word; Wright wanted to give substance to his ideals by incorporating them in an actual building.

Choices (A), (B), and (E) are all too literal. We talk about **reinforced** concrete, about something being **hard** or **dense** as *concrete*, but that's not the meaning of *concrete* here. Choice (D) **durable** doesn't work either; although concrete is a **durable** substance, durable isn't a synonym for this figurative sense of the word.

3 **A**—Kaufmann's original plans for the house are discussed only at the beginning of the second paragraph, so go back to that spot. The author writes that Kaufmann had originally planned to put the house on a flat place near the bottom of the waterfall, but Wright convinced him to accept the "more daring" response of building the house right over the waterfall. While she doesn't say so directly, the author implies that Kaufmann's original plans were less daring, less risky, or, as correct choice (A) has it, more **conservative.**

As for the wrong choices, (C) is the opposite of what you want, since it was Wright who had the **daring** plan for the house. Similarly, (D) better describes Wright's plan than Kaufmann's, since the author claims that Wright's plan "put his architectural ideals into concrete form." (B) may be true, but the cost of the two plans are never discussed in the passage. And nowhere is Kaufmann's plan criticized as (E) **architecturally unsound;** in fact, it was almost certainly regarded as *more* sound than Wright's daring idea.

4 **C**—Don't worry if you can't tell a cantilever from a cantaloupe. To answer this question, you don't have to know what a cantilever is. You just have to know *why* the author described the technique.

As always, go to the place in the passage specified in the line reference, where the cantilever process is explained. We're told it's an example of the "unconventional building tactics" mentioned in the sentence before. "Unconventional" translates nicely to **unusual,** so (C) is the best answer here.

The construction of the **fireplace,** choice (A), is mentioned as an example of the traditional elements used in the house; it has nothing to do with cantilevers. (B) is the opposite of what you want, since "unconventional" and **traditional** are virtual antonyms. (D) might seem logical, but it's not in the paragraph; the author isn't talking broadly about **modern technological advances** in **concrete;** she only describes the advances used in the Fallingwater house. Finally, (E) is offbase since there's nothing particularly natural about a cantilever; the discussion about **nature** comes later in the same paragraph and is not directly related.

5 **D**—At the end of the third paragraph, we learn that Wright's ideal dwelling for the waterfall site "was not simply a modern extravaganza or a direct extension of natural surroundings, [but] a little bit of both." So your answer has to incorporate both elements. And that makes (D) correct; Wright wanted the house to be **impressive** but still **harmonious.**

(A) is wrong because the passage offers no evidence that Kaufmann's **money and position** influenced Wright's thinking. (B)'s focus on **durability** makes it inappropriate; the end of paragraph three doesn't deal with Fallingwater's ability to survive over time. Nor does it deal with Wright's desire for the house to be considered an architectural **landmark,** so (C) is wrong. And (E) is a distortion; Wright wanted Fallingwater to be an "extension of [the] natural surroundings"—not a **triumph** over them.

6 **E**—The absolutely wrong way of approaching this question is to use your own impression of "cave[s]" as your guide. It's the critics' idea of a "cave" that's important here. According to the cited sentence, critics compared Fallingwater to a "cave" because the house provided "a psychological and physical safe haven from a harsh, violent world." So it's the quality of safety that's being equated here, leading you to correct choice (E) **security.**

(A) seems a possible choice, since **warmth** conveys a sense of refuge from the cold, but compare it with (E). Since security is more directly related to the mention of "safe haven," (A) is only second-best and will earn you no SAT points. (B) **darkness** and (D) **claustrophobia** are qualities that you personally may associate with "cave[s]," but they're not the qualities these "critics" had in mind. Finally, choice (C) **simplicity** is way offbase; first, there's nothing particularly simple about a cave, and second, the "safe haven" is not from a complex world, but a "harsh, violent" world.

7 **B**—The line reference refers you to the very end of the passage. To answer correctly, you need to see that "both" refers to both "the human

and the natural." This underlines the running theme we mentioned earlier—the interaction between the human, as represented by the house, and the natural, as represented by the natural setting. Wright wants to do justice to both, and so (B) best answers the question. It talks about **benefits to the environment** (the natural) as well as to the **occupants** (the human).

(A) and (D) miss half the message; they show how humans are "invigorated and exalted" by the natural setting, but not how nature benefits. (C) does the opposite, emphasizing how the house beautifies the setting but failing to mention how the setting beautifies the house. And (E) is an inference that goes too far. (B) is a better answer, and you need to go with the best choice.

Suggested Time: 13 minutes

Directions—Answer the questions below based on the information in the accompanying passages.

Practice Passage 4: Paired Parks

The following passages present two views of the city. Passage 1 focuses on the decline of the city park system. Passage 2 describes the decline of the city as a work of art.

Passage 1

City parks were originally created to provide the local populace with a convenient refuge from the crowding and chaos of its surroundings. Until quite
Line recently, these parks served their purpose
(5) admirably. Whether city dwellers wanted to sit under a shady tree to think or take a vigorous stroll to get some exercise, they looked forward to visiting these nearby oases. Filled with trees, shrubs, flowers, meadows, and ponds, city parks were a tranquil
(10) spot in which to unwind from the daily pressures of urban life. They were places where people met their friends for picnics or sporting events. And they were also places to get some sun and fresh air in the midst of an often dark and dreary environment,
(15) with its seemingly endless rows of steel, glass, and concrete buildings.

For more than a century, the importance of these parks to the quality of life in cities has been recognized by urban planners. Yet city parks around the
(20) world have been allowed to deteriorate to an alarming extent in recent decades. In many cases, they have become centers of crime; some city parks are now so dangerous that local residents are afraid even to enter them. And the great natural beauty
(25) which was once their hallmark has been severely damaged. Trees, shrubs, flowers, and meadows have withered under the impact of intense air pollution and littering, and ponds have been fouled by untreated sewage.
(30) This process of decline, however, is not inevitable. A few changes can turn the situation around. First, special police units, whose only responsibility would be to patrol city parks, should be created to ensure that they remain safe for those who wish to
(35) enjoy them. Second, more caretakers should be hired to care for the grounds and, in particular, to collect trash. Beyond the increased staffing require-

ments, it will also be necessary to insulate city parks from their surroundings. Total isolation is, of
(40) course, impossible; but many beneficial measures in that direction could be implemented without too much trouble. Vehicles, for instance, should be banned from city parks to cut down on air pollution. And sewage pipes should be rerouted away
(45) from park areas to prevent the contamination of land and water. If urban planners are willing to make these changes, city parks can be restored to their former glory for the benefit of all.

Passage 2

With the rise of the great metropolis in the indus-
(50) trial era, city planning in the West passed out of the hands of the architect and into the hands of the technocrat.* Unlike the architect who thought of the city as a work of art to be built up with an eye toward beauty, the technocrat has always taken a purely
(55) functional approach to city planning; the city exists for the sole purpose of serving the needs of its inhabitants. Its outward appearance has no intrinsic value.

Over the span of a few centuries, this new breed
(60) of urban planner has succeeded in forever changing the face of the Western city. A brief visit to any large metropolis is enough to confirm this grim fact. Even a casual observer could not fail to notice that the typical urban landscape is arranged along the lines
(65) of the tedious chessboard pattern, with its four-cornered intersections and long, straight and dull streets. Strict building codes have resulted in an overabundance of unsightly neighborhoods in which there is only slight variation among struc-
(70) tures. Rows of squat concrete apartment houses and files of gigantic steel and glass skyscrapers have almost completely replaced older, more personal buildings. Moreover, the lovely natural surroundings of many cities are no longer a part of the urban
(75) landscape. For the most part, the hills and rivers which were once so much a part of so many metropolitan settings have now been blotted out by thoughtless construction.

The lone bright spot amidst all of this urban blight
(80) has been the local park system, which is to be found in most Western cities. Large, centrally-located parks—for example, New York's Central Park or London's Hyde Park—and smaller, outlying parks bring a measure of beauty to Western cities by
(85) breaking up the man-made monotony. With their green pastures, dense woods, and pleasant ponds,

streams and waterfalls, local park systems also offer a vast array of opportunities for city dwellers to rest or recreate, free of the intense burdens of urban life. (90) If they have understood nothing else about the quality of life in urban areas, technocrats have at least had the good sense to recognize that people need a quiet refuge from the chaotic bustle of the city.

*technocrat: technical expert

1   The author of Passage 1 uses the phrase "convenient refuge" in line 2 to suggest that parks were
(A) built in order to preserve plant life in cities
(B) designed with the needs of city residents in mind
(C) meant to end the unpleasantness of city life
(D) supposed to help people make new friends
(E) intended to allow natural light to filter into cities
Ⓐ Ⓑ Ⓒ Ⓓ Ⓔ

2   By mentioning crime and pollution (lines 21–29), the author of Passage 1 primarily emphasizes
(A) how rapidly the city parks have deteriorated
(B) how city parks can once again be made safe and clean
(C) why people can no longer rest and relax in city parks
(D) why urban planners should not be in charge of city parks
(E) who is responsible for damaging the quality of life in cities
Ⓐ Ⓑ Ⓒ Ⓓ Ⓔ

3   In line 27, the word *intense* most nearly means
(A) severe
(B) fervent
(C) piercing
(D) strenuous
(E) meticulous
Ⓐ Ⓑ Ⓒ Ⓓ Ⓔ

4   In the last paragraph of Passage 1, the author acknowledges which problem in restoring city parks?
(A) The constant need to collect trash
(B) The difficulty in rerouting sewage pipes
(C) The congestion caused by banning vehicular traffic
(D) The lack of total separation from the surrounding city
(E) The expense of creating additional police patrol units
Ⓐ Ⓑ Ⓒ Ⓓ Ⓔ

5   In Passage 2, the reference to "a purely functional approach to city planning" (lines 54–55) serves to
(A) demonstrate that architects and technocrats should cooperate
(B) imply that architects are unconcerned about human comfort
(C) indicate that architects are obsolete in an industrial era
(D) stress that architects and technocrats have different priorities
(E) show that technocrats have destroyed the natural beauty of cities
Ⓐ Ⓑ Ⓒ Ⓓ Ⓔ

6   The word *face* in line 61 means
(A) reputation
(B) expression
(C) value
(D) dignity
(E) appearance
Ⓐ Ⓑ Ⓒ Ⓓ Ⓔ

7   In lines 63–78, the author's description of cities is
(A) tolerant
(B) surprised
(C) derogatory
(D) nostalgic
(E) bewildered
Ⓐ Ⓑ Ⓒ Ⓓ Ⓔ

KAPLAN

8   In context, "the good sense to recognize" (line 92) suggests that technocrats
   (A) want to get rid of urban blight
   (B) are aware of the stress of city life
   (C) support nature conservation programs
   (D) favor large city parks over smaller ones
   (E) think that greenery makes cities more attractive

   Ⓐ Ⓑ Ⓒ Ⓓ Ⓔ

9   Both passages focus primarily on
   (A) criticizing certain aspects of the city
   (B) romanticizing city life in a bygone era
   (C) exploring the origins of urban decay
   (D) blaming urban problems on city residents
   (E) pointing out how city life could be improved

   Ⓐ Ⓑ Ⓒ Ⓓ Ⓔ

10 The author of Passage 1 would most likely react to the characterization of city parks presented in lines 85–89 by pointing out that
   (A) this characterization is confirmed by the evidence
   (B) future reforms will render this characterization false
   (C) urban planners would reject this characterization
   (D) this characterization is in bad taste
   (E) recent developments have made this characterization obsolete

   Ⓐ Ⓑ Ⓒ Ⓓ Ⓔ

11 How would the author of Passage 1 respond to the way the author of Passage 2 uses the phrase "urban blight" (line 79) to describe the current state of cities?
   (A) This phrase is not supported by the facts.
   (B) It is being used to denounce what is best about cities.
   (C) It is an accurate description of the situation.
   (D) Choosing this phrase demonstrates very poor taste.
   (E) New studies show that this phrase will soon be outdated.

   Ⓐ Ⓑ Ⓒ Ⓓ Ⓔ

SCORECARD	
Number of Questions Right:	
Number of Questions Wrong:	
Number of Questions Omitted:	
Number of Correct Guesses:	
Number of Wrong Guesses:	
Time Used:	

Answers and Explanations

Passage 4: Paired Parks

Always read the introduction to paired passages first, because it will indicate how the two passages relate. Do the questions keyed to Passage 1 after you read it. Then read the second passage and answer the rest of the questions. That way, you'll be answering questions while the general impressions from each passage are fresh in your mind.

Passage 1, on the decline of the city park system, is not wholly pessimistic. After depicting the parks as a once-ideal place for people to escape from the city, the author describes city parks around the world as ruined by crime and pollution. But the final paragraph expresses hope that the parks can be restored and offers suggestions for accomplishing this.

In contrast, Passage 2 sees parks as the "lone bright spot" amid cities marred by technocrats' "purely functional approach" to city planning. Technocrats get blamed for the ugly, unnatural, and impersonal look of the urban landscape of Western cities. The only good thing the technocrats have done is recognize that people need a park system as a refuge from city life.

1 B—The question stem directs you back to the first sentence of Passage 1. The author says parks were created to give people a "refuge" from the city. Scanning quickly through the answer choices, (B) jumps out because it fits the opening statement: Parks were **designed with the needs of city residents in mind.**

Choices (A), (D), and (E) are misleading bits of information from the rest of the first paragraph. Although parks may house **plant life, allow natural light into cities,** and provide a place to make or meet **friends,** that's not what "convenient refuge" means. As for (C), the author never suggests that parks are supposed to **end the unpleasantness of city life.** They merely provide a refuge.

2 C—To answer this question, you have to understand the context in which crime and pollution are mentioned in the second paragraph. The author describes the deterioration of parks, including the effects of crime and pollution, to show that people can no longer use the parks as they were meant to be used. In other words, the author is talk-

ing about (C) **why people can no longer rest and relax** in the parks.

The author mentions that parks have deteriorated in recent decades, but the information on *crime and pollution* doesn't emphasize how **rapidly,** so (A) is out. Making parks cleaner and safer is the topic of the third paragraph, not the second, so (B) is wrong. The passage says nothing negative about **urban planners,** nor does it blame anyone in particular for **damaging the quality of life in [the] cities,** so eliminate (D) and (E).

3 A—This is a Vocabulary-in-Context question. Since all the answer choices except (E) **meticulous** are possible synonyms for *intense,* you have to figure out how the word is used in the sentence. The author says greenery in the parks has been destroyed by *intense* pollution and littering. Pollution and littering clearly can't be (B) **fervent,** (C) **piercing,** or (D) **strenuous,** so (A) **severe** is the right choice.

4 D—The last paragraph of Passage 1 offers suggestions for reversing the decline of the parks: adding more police units and caretakers, banning vehicles, and rerouting sewage pipes. It is also necessary, the author says, to "insulate city parks from their surroundings," but the problem here is that "total isolation" is "impossible." This is paraphrased in the right choice, (D).

Choices (A), (B), (C), and (E) all twist information from the author's suggestions. Trash does need to be collected, but the author never says that (A) **the constant need to collect trash** would be a problem. Nor does the paragraph say that (B) **rerouting sewage pipes** will be difficult, (C) **banning traffic** will cause congestion, or (E) **additional police units** will be expensive.

5 D—This is the first question about Passage 2. Look again at the sentence that describes "a purely functional approach to city planning." The author contrasts architects, who view building a city as an artistic endeavor, to technocrats, who focus only on "serving the needs of . . . inhabitants." In other words, the author is (D) **stressing that architects and technocrats have different priorities.**

The author does not imply here that (A) **architects and technocrats should cooperate** or that architects do not care (B) **about human comfort.** Certainly, the author does not think (C) **architects are obsolete;** if anything, he regrets they no longer do city planning. As for (E), the author does think **technocrats have destroyed the natural beauty of the cities,** but this point comes up in the second and third paragraphs, not the first. In keyed questions like this, concentrate on the few sentences around the quoted phrase.

6 E—Once again, before you answer a Vocabulary-in-Context question, reread the sentence that contains the line reference. If you didn't do that here, several answer choices may have looked tempting. The author is talking about how the *face,* or **appearance,** of the Western city has been changed forever, so (E) is the only choice that fits.

7 C—Skim quickly over the sentence referred to in the second paragraph of Passage 2. You'll see phrases like *tedious chessboard pattern, straight and dull streets,* and *an overabundance of unsightly neighborhoods.* Clearly, the author has a low opinion of modern cities; the tone is disparaging, or (C) **derogatory.** (A) **Tolerant,** (B) **surprised,** and (E) **bewildered** are clearly wrong. Nor are the comments (D) **nostalgic,** or wistful. Although the author states that older, more personal buildings and lovely natural surroundings can no longer be found in cities, the tone is critical, rather than yearning.

8 B—Passage 2 concludes by saying that technocrats "have at least had the good sense to recognize that people need a quiet refuge" from the chaos of the city. The inference is that technocrats (B) **are aware of the stress of city life.**

The author certainly doesn't believe technocrats (A) **want to get rid of urban blight;** according to him, the technocrats caused it all. Nor does the final sentence indicate that technocrats (C) **support nature conservation programs,** or (D) **favor large city parks over smaller ones,** or (E) **think that greenery makes cities more attractive.**

9 A—The last three questions ask you to compare and contrast the two passages. To answer this one, look for the choice that accurately covers the subject matter of *both* passages, not just one.

Both passages certainly **criticize aspects of the city,** so (A) seems the right answer, but check out the other choices. (B) is wrong because it doesn't fit *both* passages: Although Passage 1 may **romanticize** parks of a bygone era, Passage 2 focuses on the present. (C) can be eliminated because it's not the primary focus of either passage; besides, only Passage 2 discusses **the origin of urban decay;** Passage 1 talks about the decline of parks. Passage 2 blames **urban problems** on technocrats, not **city residents,** so (D) is out. Finally, (E) doesn't fit because only Passage 1 points out **how city life can be improved.**

10 E—The final paragraph of Passage 2 offers a vision of a beautiful park system, very similar to the description in Passage 1 of the way parks used to be. But Passage 1 says parks have deteriorated considerably in recent decades. So the author of Passage 1 would probably point out that (E) **recent developments have made this [idealized] characterization obsolete.**

(A) is contrary to the evidence of Passage 1. (B) is wrong because **reforms** would improve parks, so the **characterization** in Passage 2 might be true, not **false.** Finally, since the parks in Passage 2 are presented as delightful places, the author of Passage 1 would be foolish to think that (C) **urban planners would reject this characterization** or that (D) **this characterization is in bad taste.**

11 C—The phrase *this urban blight* refers back to the bleak landscape described in the paragraph just above: "rows of squat concrete apartments" and "files of gigantic steel and glass skyscrapers." The author of Passage 1 portrays cities, aside from the parks, as "dark and dreary" environments, with "seemingly endless rows of steel, glass, and concrete buildings." The two pictures are very similar, so the author of Passage 1 would probably find *urban blight* to be (C) **an accurate description of the situation.**

Since the two authors agree on this point, choices (A), (B), and (D) can be eliminated. Finally, neither passage mentions any **new studies,** so (E) is wrong.

Suggested Time: 10 minutes

Directions—Answer the questions below based on the information in the accompanying passage.

Practice Passage 5: Life on Mars

The following passage discusses the possibility that there is life on Mars. Interest in the subject reached a peak when the National Aeronautics and Space Administration sent two unmanned spacecraft to Mars in 1975. After ten months, Vikings 1 and 2 entered orbits around the red planet and released landers.

When the first of the two Viking landers touched down on Martian soil on July 20, 1976, and began to send camera images back to Earth, the scientists at
Line the Jet Propulsion Laboratory could not suppress a
(5) certain nervous anticipation, like people who hold a ticket to a lottery they have a one-in-a-million chance of winning. The first photographs that arrived, however, did not contain any evidence of life. What revealed itself to them was merely a bar-
(10) ren landscape littered with rocks and boulders. The view resembled nothing so much as a flat section of desert—in fact, the winning entry in a contest at J.P.L. for the photograph most accurately predicting what Mars would look like was a snapshot taken in
(15) a particularly arid section of the Mojave Desert.

The scientists were soon ready to turn their attention from visible life to microorganisms. The twin Viking landers carried three experiments designed to detect current biological activity and one to
(20) detect organic compounds, because researchers thought it possible that life had developed on early Mars just as it is thought to have developed on Earth, through the gradual chemical evolution of complex organic molecules. To detect biological
(25) activity, Martian soil samples were treated with various nutrients that would produce characteristic by-products if life forms were active in the soil. The results from all three experiments were inconclusive. The fourth experiment heated a soil sample to
(30) look for signs of organic material but found none, an unexpected result because at least organic compounds from the steady bombardment of the Martian surface by meteorites were thought to have been present.
(35) The absence of organic materials, some scientists speculated, was the result of intense ultraviolet

radiation penetrating the atmosphere of Mars and destroying organic compounds in the soil. Although Mars' atmosphere was at one time rich in carbon
(40) dioxide and thus thick enough to protect its surface from the harmful rays of the Sun, the carbon dioxide had gradually left the atmosphere and been converted into rocks. This means that even if life had gotten a start on early Mars, it could not have sur-
(45) vived the exposure to ultraviolet radiation when the atmosphere thinned. Mars never developed a protective layer of ozone as Earth did.

Despite the disappointing Viking results, there are those who still keep open the possibility of life on
(50) Mars. They point out that the Viking data cannot be considered the final word on Martian life because the two landers only sampled two limited—and uninteresting—sites. The Viking landing sites were not chosen for what they might tell of the planet's
(55) biology. They were chosen primarily because they appeared to be safe for landing a spacecraft. The landing sites were on parts of the Martian plains that appeared relatively featureless from orbital photographs.
(60) The type of Martian terrain that these researchers suggest may be a possible hiding place for active life has an Earthly parallel: the ice-free region of southern Victoria Land, Antarctica, where the temperatures in some dry valleys average below zero.
(65) Organisms known as endoliths, a form of blue-green algae that has adapted to this harsh environment, were found living inside certain translucent, porous rocks in these Antarctic valleys. The argument based on this discovery is that if life did exist
(70) on early Mars, it is possible that it escaped worsening conditions by similarly seeking refuge in rocks. Skeptics object, however, that Mars in its present state is simply too dry, even compared with Antarctic valleys, to sustain any life whatsoever.
(75) Should Mars eventually prove to be completely barren of life, as some suspect, then this would have a significant impact on the current view of the chemical origin of life. It could be much more difficult to get life started on a planet than scientists
(80) thought before the Viking landings.

1. The major purpose of the passage is to
   (A) relate an account of an extraordinary scientific achievement
   (B) undermine the prevailing belief that life may exist on Mars
   (C) discuss the efforts of scientists to determine whether Martian life exists
   (D) show the limitations of the scientific investigation of other planets
   (E) examine the relationship between theories about Martian life and evolutionary theory
   Ⓐ Ⓑ Ⓒ Ⓓ Ⓔ

2. In line 4, the word *suppress* most nearly means
   (A) oppose
   (B) vanquish
   (C) prohibit
   (D) stifle
   (E) disguise
   Ⓐ Ⓑ Ⓒ Ⓓ Ⓔ

3. The reference to "people who hold a ticket to a lottery" (lines 5–6) serves to
   (A) point out the human facet of a scientific enterprise
   (B) indicate the expected likelihood of visible Martian life
   (C) show that there was doubt as to whether the camera would function
   (D) imply that any mission to another planet is a risky venture
   (E) reveal how the success of the Viking mission depended largely on chance
   Ⓐ Ⓑ Ⓒ Ⓓ Ⓔ

4. The author uses the evidence from the four Viking experiments (lines 24–34) to establish that
   (A) meteorites do not strike the surface of Mars as often as scientists had thought
   (B) current theory as to how life developed on Earth is probably flawed
   (C) there was no experimental confirmation of the theory that life exists on Mars
   (D) biological activity has been shown to be absent from the surface of Mars
   (E) the experiments were more fruitful than was examination of camera images
   Ⓐ Ⓑ Ⓒ Ⓓ Ⓔ

5. The third paragraph of the passage provides
   (A) an analysis of a theory proposed earlier
   (B) evidence supporting a statement made earlier
   (C) a theory about findings presented earlier
   (D) criticism of experiments discussed earlier
   (E) a synthesis of facts reviewed earlier
   Ⓐ Ⓑ Ⓒ Ⓓ Ⓔ

6. The author suggests that an important difference between Mars and Earth is that, unlike Earth, Mars
   (A) accumulated organic compounds from the steady bombardment of meteorites
   (B) possessed at one time an atmosphere rich in carbon dioxide
   (C) is in the path of the harmful rays of ultraviolet radiation
   (D) has an atmospheric layer that protects organic compounds
   (E) could not have sustained any life that developed
   Ⓐ Ⓑ Ⓒ Ⓓ Ⓔ

7. In the fourth paragraph, the author mentions the Viking landing sites (lines 53–56) in order to emphasize which point?
   (A) Although evidence of life was not found by the landers, this does not mean that Mars is devoid of life.
   (B) Although the landing sites were uninteresting, they could have harbored Martian life.
   (C) The Viking mission was unsuccessful largely due to poor selection of the landing sites.
   (D) The detection of life on Mars was not a primary objective of the scientists who sent the Viking landers.
   (E) Scientists were not expecting to discover life on the Martian plains.
   Ⓐ Ⓑ Ⓒ Ⓓ Ⓔ

8 In lines 68–71, the researchers' argument that life may exist in Martian rocks rests on the idea that
(A) organisms may adopt identical survival strategies in comparable environments
(B) life developed in the form of blue-green algae on Mars
(C) life evolved in the same way on two different planets
(D) endoliths are capable of living in the harsh environment of Mars
(E) organisms that have survived in Antarctica could survive the Martian environment
Ⓐ Ⓑ Ⓒ Ⓓ Ⓔ

SCORECARD	
Number of Questions Right:	
Number of Questions Wrong:	
Number of Questions Omitted:	
Number of Correct Guesses:	
Number of Wrong Guesses:	
Time Used:	

Answers and Explanations

Passage 5: Life on Mars

The subject of this science passage is the possibility that life exists, or has existed, on Mars. The first paragraph begins with a description of the scene at the Jet Propulsion Lab when pictures first arrived from the Viking landers on Mars. The second paragraph discusses the Viking experiments designed to detect microscopic signs of life on Mars, and the inconclusive or negative results of these experiments. The theory that some scientists have advanced to explain the negative results is discussed in the third paragraph: Organic materials on Mars might have been destroyed by the lack of protection from ultraviolet radiation.

The topic of the fourth paragraph is the possibility that there is life on Mars, and the two landers simply missed it. The fifth paragraph discusses the suggestion that if life can survive in Antarctica by living inside rocks, maybe life does the same thing on Mars. The author concludes the passage in the sixth paragraph by remarking that the evidence we have from Mars influences scientific theory regarding the chemical origin of life on Earth.

Some of this may have seemed difficult to wade through if you tried to get all of it the first time around, but remember, it isn't necessary to do that. The questions tell you where to go back to get the information you need.

1 C—For this Big Picture question, the answer has to be broad enough to cover the entire passage. We just reviewed the topics of the individual paragraphs; scientists get pictures, scientists run experiments, scientists propose theories and make suggestions throughout the passage. Clearly, the author is discussing the (C) **efforts of scientists.**

Although the Viking mission may have been **an extraordinary scientific achievement,** the author does much more than relate an account of the mission, so (A) is wrong. (B) is out, because the passage presents a balanced view on the question of life on Mars. (D) is wrong, because the only time the author discusses **limitations of the scientific investigation** of Mars is in the fourth paragraph. (E) is wrong for a similar reason: The **relationship between** life on Mars and **evolutionary theory** is mentioned only in the second and sixth paragraphs.

2 D—This Vocabulary-in-Context question refers to the first sentence of the passage. Go back and read it to understand how *suppress* is being used. The scientists are trying in vain to *suppress,* or (D) **stifle,** their nervous anticipation. (A), (B), and (C) can all be synonyms of *suppress,* but none of them works in the context of the sentence. (E) **disguise** is not a synonym for *suppress.*

3 B—This question focuses on the same sentence as the last did, but you have to read a little further to figure it out. The word *however* in the next sentence indicates that what the scientists hardly dared to hope for (and didn't get) was some visible sign of Martian life. Therefore, the reference to "people who hold a ticket to the lottery" is there to show how **likely** it was that the photographs would show Martian life (B).

Although the first paragraph does give you a glimpse of scientists as **human**s, this is not why the author uses the lottery-ticket analogy, so (A) is wrong. (C) is a misreading of the first two sentences; there is nothing there to suggest that the scientists thought the **camera** might mal**function.** (D) and (E) miss the mark completely by being far too broad.

4 C—You know by the end of the second paragraph that the experiments designed to detect biological life were inconclusive, and that no organic materials were found, either. There was, therefore, (C) **no experimental confirmation of the theory that life exists on Mars,** and that is all that the author is establishing here.

Several of the other choices may have tempted you, but they all involve making unsupported inferences. Just because there weren't organic materials from meteorites on Mars doesn't mean that (A) **meteorites do not strike the surface of Mars as often as scientists thought.** The author never implies that the (B) **theory as to how life developed on Earth is probably flawed.** (D) is off because it is too sweeping. These four experiments were not the evidence to prove or disprove the existence of life on Mars. Finally, (E) can be eliminated because the experiments certainly didn't tell scientists much more than the photographs did.

5 C—Here you need an understanding of the role the third paragraph plays in the context of the passage as a whole. Reread the end of the second paragraph and the beginning of the third. In the second paragraph, the author states that a Viking experiment turned up no trace of organic material on the Martian surface. The third paragraph presents the theory that UV radiation may have destroyed any organic materials once present in the Martian soil. So the third paragraph provides (C) **a theory about findings presented earlier.**

The **theory** is not **proposed earlier** in the passage, so (A) is out. The third paragraph does not give (B) **evidence supporting a statement made earlier,** nor does it (D) **criticize** anything. Finally, there is nothing like **facts reviewed earlier** in the third paragraph, so (E) can be eliminated.

6 E—The author mentions Earth in the passage at the end of the third paragraph, where he says that Mars "never developed a protective layer of ozone as Earth did." Since it is life that the ozone layer protected on Earth, you can infer that Mars was not able to support life, (E), as Earth was.

(A) is wrong because it contradicts information from the passage that says that no organic compounds were found on Mars. (B) is out, because although Mars **possessed at one time an atmosphere rich in carbon dioxide,** the author never suggests that Earth *didn't.* Mars and Earth are both **in the path of the ultraviolet radiation** of the Sun, so (C) is out. Finally, (D) reverses Mars and Earth: Earth is the planet with **an atmospheric layer that protects organic compounds** from UV radiation, not Mars.

7 A—Reread the sentences surrounding the reference to Viking landing sites, and look for a paraphrase among the answer choices. Those who still think that there might be life on Mars point out that there were only two Viking landers, that the experimental sites were limited and uninteresting, and that scientists were not concerned about finding life when they chose the landing spots. In other words, they are saying that (A) **although evidence of life was not found by the landers, this does not mean that Mars is devoid of life.**

Forget about choice (B); although the statement is true, this isn't why the author mentions the landing sites. The author never says that the Viking mission was **unsuccessful** or that the selection of landing sites was **poor,** so (C) is wrong. Choices (D) and (E) focus on the intentions and expectations of the scientists. All you know is that they wanted to land the spacecrafts safely, not whether they thought detection of life was a (D) **primary objective** or whether they (E) **expected to discover life on the Martian plains.**

8 A—The argument of the researchers in the fifth paragraph is that, if endoliths could adapt to the harsh conditions of Antarctica by living in rocks, maybe some form of life did the same thing to survive on early Mars. The idea here is that Mars and Antarctica are (A) **comparable environments** and that life may adapt in the same way, or **adopt identical strategies**, to survive.

All of the wrong choices are based on distortions of the argument. Choices (B) and (D) are both wrong because the argument never states that **endoliths** or **blue-green algae** have anything to do with Mars; they were found in Antarctica and merely became the subject of speculation for the researchers. Choice (C) is too broad: Scientists think that organisms may have adapted to similar environments in similar ways, but this doesn't mean that all of **life evolved in the same way** on the two planets. That idea comes into play in the second paragraph, not in the fifth. As for (E), the author never suggests that the endoliths or any other type of organism **that has survived in Antarctica could survive** on Mars.

Suggested Time: 7 minutes

Directions—Answer the questions below based on the information in the accompanying passage.

Practice Passage 6: TV in Courts

The role of television in the courtroom has been debated by members of the judicial system for the last two decades. Those who favor its presence are of the opinion that broadcasting courtroom proceedings is fully consistent with the ideal of the "public's right to know." Others believe that television distorts the judicial process by creating a theatrical atmosphere in the courtroom.

The following are excerpts from a speech about this issue given by a retired Chief Judge of New York State at a Pre-law Association meeting.

Justice is the most profound aspiration of men and women on earth; it is the allotment to each person of that to which he or she is entitled; it exists
Line only when there has been adherence to principles of
(5) honesty and fairness and disregard of other considerations.

Down through the centuries, the character of a particular government or civilization could be measured best by the sort of justice meted out to its cit-
(10) izens. In the more advanced and more humane governances, trials have taken place in courtrooms to which the public has been admitted. On the other hand, secret trials have almost invariably been the telltale sign of oppressive and autocratic regimes.
(15) Indeed, the grant of a fair trial is the greatest contribution of any jurisprudence.

The difference in openness is not without significance. It is not a matter of mere entertainment. It is far more serious than that. First, and foremost,
(20) unobstructed courtrooms are a guarantee of fairness and justice. Furthermore, the public officials functioning therein can be observed so that those performing well may be retained and those not may be replaced.

(25) Courtrooms with "open doors" have always been a fetish for me. I stood here in this city sixteen years ago and in an interview announced that I favored cameras in the courts. Broadcasting from courtrooms was unpopular then and there were only
(30) four states in the Union permitting television of judicial proceedings. My response shocked many in this state. When the Chief Judgeship came my way,

a rule was adopted permitting television and still cameras in the appellate courts of our jurisdiction
(35) and it was a success. I worked long and hard in favor of an amendment of the Civil Rights Law to allow photography in the trial courts. I am pleased that that is now reality.

However, I am worried. I am worried about what
(40) seems to be an increasing antipathy toward the media and concurrent attempts to narrow the doors leading into courtrooms by distinguishing ancillary or supplemental proceedings from trials themselves. Freedom of the press and open courtrooms
(45) go together.

I believe in the First Amendment. I believe with might and main in the constitutional guarantee of freedom of the press, not merely to curry favor with those of the "Fourth Estate," not merely as an aid to
(50) the media in its varied shapes and forms, but more as a benefit for all the people. A broadly defined freedom of the press assures the maintenance of our political system of democracy, social equality, and public exposure. Indeed, the strength of America,
(55) different from any nation in the world, lies in its openness.

---

1 In line 17, the word *openness* most probably means
(A) candor
(B) tolerance
(C) receptivity
(D) friendliness
(E) accessibility

    Ⓐ Ⓑ Ⓒ Ⓓ Ⓔ

2 The information in lines 39–45 suggests that the judge is very concerned about
(A) restrictions being placed upon people opposed to media participation in the judicial process
(B) undermining the rights of the accused by giving the media too much access to the judicial process
(C) media abuse of the First Amendment to distort the judicial process
(D) harm being caused to the judicial process by a distaste for the media
(E) encouraging those who favor a narrow definition of civil rights by allowing the media to participate in the judicial process

    Ⓐ Ⓑ Ⓒ Ⓓ Ⓔ

3 The judge's point about the role of the media in the judicial process is made mainly through
(A) general statements
(B) specific examples
(C) statistical data
(D) long citations
(E) scientific evidence

Ⓐ Ⓑ Ⓒ Ⓓ Ⓔ

SCORECARD	
Number of Questions Right:	
Number of Questions Wrong:	
Number of Questions Omitted:	
Number of Correct Guesses:	
Number of Wrong Guesses:	
Time Used:	

4 In lines 46–56, the judge reflects on the
(A) strengths and weaknesses of the judicial system
(B) attitude of the judicial system toward the media
(C) role of a free press in maintaining a democratic society
(D) ability of the media to function effectively in the courtroom
(E) connection between the First Amendment and the Civil Rights Law

Ⓐ Ⓑ Ⓒ Ⓓ Ⓔ

5 Which best describes the judge's view of cameras in the courtroom?
(A) Cameras do not play a useful part in determining which members of the judicial system are competent and which members are incompetent.
(B) While the First Amendment gives the media the right to bring cameras into the courtroom, their use has impaired the proper functioning of the judicial system.
(C) Judicial systems that allow cameras into the courtroom are no more likely to be fair than judicial systems which do not admit them.
(D) Regardless of the fact that many members of the judicial system do not approve of their presence, cameras should be permitted in every courtroom.
(E) Oppressive and autocratic regimes are likely to place cameras in the courtroom to deter their subjects from committing criminal acts.

Ⓐ Ⓑ Ⓒ Ⓓ Ⓔ

Answers and Explanations

Practice Passage 6: TV in Courts

This is a strong statement of an individual point of view. You may naturally respond by taking a stand yourself, for or against the author. But the questions never ask for your personal point of view. They ask only about the author's opinion.

In reading, skim over the first few paragraphs. Look for a definite statement of the author's opinion, which you get in paragraph four—the author favors cameras in court. This puts the rest of the passage in perspective. Don't worry about the details of the argument. Questions about details will be easy to answer based on specific context.

1 E—This is another Vocabulary-in-Context question. As used in paragraph three, *openness* refers to the discussion in paragraph two about whether the public can be admitted to the courtroom. (E) **accessibility** best defines this sense of *openness.*

The other choices are all possible meanings of *openness*, but none fits the context. (A) **candor,** or frankness, refers to openness of one's own opinions; (B) **tolerance** is openness to other people or their views; (C) **receptivity** implies a willingness to be convinced. (D) **friendliness** suggests an outgoing nature, which doesn't match what the author is saying here.

2 D—In paragraph five the author worries over "antipathy," or dislike, towards the media. This is paraphrased as **distaste** in (D). The **harm . . . to the judicial process** in this answer choice arises from the author's strong belief that media access is good for the judicial process, as expressed earlier.

If you know the author favors cameras, or *media participation*, you're likely to pick the right answer. The other four choices, in different ways, say the author worries about too *much* media participation; they contradict the author's point of view.

3 A—Paragraphs one through three and paragraph six all contain broad arguments about the nature of justice, the need for public trials, and the importance of freedom of the press—(A) **general statements.** The author gives no (B) **specific examples** of how courtroom openness works, though there is one example of the author's own activity (paragraph four). The passage never uses (C) **statistics** or (E) **scientific** findings, and never refers to judicial decisions or other writings or speeches (D).

4 C—This question asks about paragraph six, which discusses freedom of the press and its importance in upholding democracy, equality, and other American values (C).

Since the passage as a whole discusses **the attitude of the judicial system** to **the media,** you might be tempted to choose (B). But this is not a Big Picture question; you're asked to focus here only on certain lines from paragraph six. Similarly, (A) **strengths and weaknesses of the judicial system**—or strong and weak judicial systems—get discussed only in paragraph two. And while paragraph six mentions (E) **the First Amendment,** it never mentions **Civil Rights Laws.** Finally, (D) how **the media function in the courtroom** is never discussed.

5 D—Here's a Big Picture question. You're looking for the answer choice that *best describes* the overall point of view. Since the author strongly supports cameras in the courts (paragraph four) and the whole passage defends this view, your answer must be (D), the only pro-camera choice. (D) acknowledges the opposition to cameras that the author notes in paragraph five, but says this opposition should be disregarded—as the author implies, too (paragraph six).

Choice (A) contradicts a minor point the author raises in the last part of paragraph three. (B) distorts what paragraph six says about the First Amendment, as well as the author's pro-media position. (C) contradicts the general sense of paragraph two, though cameras are not specifically discussed there. (E) refers to the discussion of oppressive regimes in this same paragraph, but the author never raises this point.

Practice Passage 7: Rosemary

In the following excerpt from a novella, Rosemary, an elderly woman, reminisces about her childhood as she waits for her grandson to wake up.

Rosemary sat at her kitchen table, working a crossword puzzle. Crosswords were nice; they filled the time, and kept the mind active. She needed just one word to complete this morning's puzzle; the
Line clue was "a Swiss river," and the first of its three let-
(5) ters was "A." Unfortunately, Rosemary had no idea what the name of the river was, and could not look it up. Her atlas was on her desk, and the desk was in the guest room, currently being occupied by her grandson Victor. Looking up over the tops of her
(10) bifocals, Rosemary glanced at the kitchen clock: it was almost 10 a.m. *Land sakes!* Did the boy intend to sleep all day? She noticed that the arthritis in her wrist was throbbing, and put down her pen. At eighty-seven years of age, she was glad she could
(15) still write at all. She had decided long ago that growing old was like slowly turning to stone; you couldn't take anything for granted. She stood up slowly, painfully, and started walking to the guest room.
(20) The trip, though only a distance of about twenty-five feet, seemed to take a long while. Late in her ninth decade now, Rosemary often experienced an expanded sense of time, with present and past tense intermingling in her mind. One minute she was
(25) padding in her slippers across the living room carpet, the next she was back on the farm where she'd grown up, a sturdy little girl treading the path behind the barn just before dawn. In her mind's eye, she could still pick her way among the stones in the
(30) darkness, more than seventy years later . . . . Rosemary arrived at the door to the guest room. It stood slightly ajar, and she peered through the opening. Victor lay sleeping on his side, his arms bent, his expression slightly pained. *Get up, lazy*
(35) *bones*, she wanted to say. Even in childhood, Rosemary had never slept past 4 a.m.; there were too many chores to do. How different things were for Victor's generation! Her youngest grandson behaved as if he had never done a chore in his life.

(40) Twenty-one years old, he had driven down to Florida to visit Rosemary in his shiny new car, a gift from his doting parents. Victor would finish college soon, and his future appeared bright—if he ever got out of bed, that is.
(45) Something Victor had said last night over dinner had disturbed her. Now what was it? Oh yes; he had been talking about one of his college courses—a "gut," he had called it. When she had asked him to explain the term, Victor had said it was a course that
(50) you took simply because it was easy to pass. Rosemary, who had not even had a high school education, found the term repellent. If she had been allowed to continue her studies, she would never have taken a "gut" . . . The memory flooded back
(55) then, still painful as an open wound all these years later. It was the first day of high school. She had graduated from grammar school the previous year, but her father had forbidden her to go on to high school that fall, saying she was needed on the farm.
(60) After much tearful pleading, she had gotten him to promise that next year, she could start high school. She had endured a whole year of chores instead of books, with animals and rough farmhands for company instead of people her own age. Now, at
(65) last, the glorious day was at hand. She had put on her best dress (she owned two), her heart racing in anticipation. But her father was waiting for her as she came downstairs.
"Where do you think you're going?" he asked.
(70) "To high school, Papa."
"No you're not. Take that thing off and get back to work."
"But Papa, you promised!"
"Do as I say!" he thundered.
(75) There was no arguing with Papa when he spoke that way. Tearfully, she had trudged upstairs to change clothes. Rosemary still wondered what her life would have been like if her father had not been waiting at the bottom of the stairs that day, or if
(80) somehow she had found the strength to defy him . . . .
Suddenly, Victor stirred, without waking, and mumbled something unintelligible. Jarred from her reverie, Rosemary stared at Victor. She wondered if
(85) he were having a nightmare.

1   Rosemary's attitude toward the physical afflictions of old age can best be described as one of
    (A) acceptance
    (B) sadness
    (C) resentment
    (D) anxiety
    (E) optimism
    Ⓐ Ⓑ Ⓒ Ⓓ Ⓔ

2   Rosemary's walk to the guest room (lines 21–32) reveals that she
    (A) feels nostalgia for her family
    (B) is anxious about Victor
    (C) is determined to conquer her ailments
    (D) has an elastic perception of time
    (E) suffers from severe disorientation
    Ⓐ Ⓑ Ⓒ Ⓓ Ⓔ

3   In context, "if he ever got out of bed" (lines 44–45) suggests that Rosemary thinks Victor
    (A) lacks a sense of humor
    (B) is ashamed of what he said last night
    (C) is promising but undisciplined
    (D) works himself to exhaustion
    (E) has failed to plan for the future
    Ⓐ Ⓑ Ⓒ Ⓓ Ⓔ

4   The reason Rosemary finds Victor's use of the term *gut* (line 49) repellent is because it
    (A) has unpleasant digestive associations
    (B) is typical of Victor's disregard for traditional values
    (C) signifies a disrespect for education
    (D) reminds Rosemary of her grammar school classes
    (E) implies that Rosemary is lacking in education
    Ⓐ Ⓑ Ⓒ Ⓓ Ⓔ

5   Lines 63–65 indicate that, for Rosemary, the year after she graduated from grammar school was
    (A) marred by illness and hardship
    (B) filled with travel and adventure
    (C) a year of reading and study
    (D) spent isolated from her peers
    (E) difficult because of her father's temper
    Ⓐ Ⓑ Ⓒ Ⓓ Ⓔ

6   Rosemary's memory of the day she finally prepared to start high school indicates that she had
    (A) anticipated her father's command to stay home
    (B) hesitated over her choice of clothes
    (C) done especially well in grammar school
    (D) already decided to pursue a career
    (E) strongly desired to continue her education
    Ⓐ Ⓑ Ⓒ Ⓓ Ⓔ

7   The passage as a whole is most concerned with
    (A) Rosemary's affectionate concern for Victor
    (B) Rosemary's struggle to suppress painful memories
    (C) the abusive treatment Rosemary suffered at the hands of her father
    (D) the interplay in Rosemary's mind between present and past
    (E) whether Rosemary will wake Victor up
    Ⓐ Ⓑ Ⓒ Ⓓ Ⓔ

SCORECARD	
Number of Questions Right:	
Number of Questions Wrong:	
Number of Questions Omitted:	
Number of Correct Guesses:	
Number of Wrong Guesses:	
Time Used:	

Answers and Explanations

Practice Passage 7: Rosemary

Next up is a fiction passage about Rosemary, an elderly woman, who recalls parts of her childhood as she waits for her grandson Victor to wake up. There's nothing too difficult here. The most interesting thing about this passage is the way it swings back and forth between the present and the past, by way of Rosemary's wandering mind. Notice the contrast between Victor's cavalier attitude toward his schooling and Rosemary's painful memories of being denied an education—that's sure to generate some questions. Let's take a look at them now.

1 A—The last four sentences of paragraph one discuss Rosemary's attitude toward old age. Thankful that she could write at all, she decided that growing old was like turning to stone: "You couldn't take anything for granted." The attitude that best sums this up is (A) **acceptance.**

She doesn't talk about things she can't do or misses, so (B) **sadness** is incorrect. Since she's not **complaining** or **worrying,** (C) and (D) are wrong, too. And though Rosemary is not unhappy, (E) **optimism** is too positive. There's no sense that she believes her life is going to improve.

2 D—A Little Picture question. When we read the lines around the lines cited, we see that the trip, though short, "seemed to take a long while," and that Rosemary "often experienced an expanded sense of time." (D) restates this perfectly, since **elastic** means to be able to expand and contract.

(A) is wrong because at this point in the passage, she's just thinking about her life on the farm, not her **family.** Though Rosemary may be anxious about **Victor,** he is not mentioned in the lines cited in the stem, so (B) is also wrong. (C) tries to catch you because it picks up on the gist of the last question, but in lines 21–32, she is not thinking about her physical problems. Finally, (E) is much too strong, even though it's related to (D). Rosemary's mind is flooded with memories of her childhood, but she's not **severely disoriented.**

3 C—Rosemary refers to Victor as a "lazy bones" who's been given every advantage by his "doting parents . . . his future appeared bright—if he ever got out of bed, that is." (C) sums up that idea well.

> Hint: When you see the phrase *in context* in a question stem, always find the "keyed" part of the passage and start reading a few lines earlier.

There's nothing in the passage about Victor's **sense of humor,** so (A) is unsupported. (B) is out of context and remember, this is a context question. Victor's remark isn't discussed until paragraph three. (D) is almost the exact opposite of what the cited lines say about Rosemary's feelings towards Victor. (E) sounds right, but it makes an assumption that's not supported in the passage. Rosemary says his "future appeared bright." Victor may be lazy, but the only things we know about his future are positive.

4 C—The line reference points you to the start of paragraph three. Notice the definition of the term *gut*—"a course you took simply because it was easy to pass." Rosemary thinks the word is "repellent," a very strong word, and believes that "if she had been allowed to continue her studies, she would never had taken a 'gut.'" Obviously, Rosemary has different feelings about education than did Victor. Given her respect for education, you can infer that she is reacting to what she feels is Victor's lack of respect. (C) is the right choice.

No one is talking about anyone's stomach here, so (A) is just silly. (B) feels close, but since the passage is concerned only with education and not things like family, religious beliefs, and society, it's too vague to be correct. (D) suggests that Rosemary didn't enjoy her own schooling, which we know is false. It's true that the word upsets her because it makes her think about her experiences, but the experiences were good ones. She's not repelled by thinking about them. Finally, while Rosemary may not have a broad education, Victor was only referring to his own classes. (E) is definitely wrong.

5 D—Again, go straight to the lines cited in the question stem, here one sentence at the end of the third paragraph. "She had endured a whole year of chores instead of books, with animals and rough farmhands for company instead of people her own age." Comparing the answer choices to this clear statement, we see that (D) is the right selection. Her

peers are "people her own age."

Working on the farm may have been hard, but **illness** is never mentioned, so (A) is out. In fact, Rosemary is referred to as "a sturdy little girl." Since she was on the farm the whole time, she could not have been **traveling** and having **adventures,** as (B) claims. The phrase says that she spent the year with "chores instead of books," so (C) directly contradicts the stem. (E) may be tempting, because it's true that her **father** had a **temper.** This isn't mentioned, however, as a reason the year is so difficult, so (E) is wrong.

> Hint: If you have a choice between an answer that paraphrases something in the cited context and an answer that may be true but has no direct reference in the text, go with the paraphrase.

6 **E**—Even though the stem doesn't direct you to a specific point of reference, this is a relatively easy question. The question refers to Rosemary on that "glorious" day when she was going to high school, which is found near the end of paragraph three. She gets up, puts on her "best dress, her heart racing in anticipation." All together, these facts point to (E) as the right choice.

Though you may have **anticipated** that Rosemary's father would stop her from going to school, there's no evidence that Rosemary did, so (A) is wrong. Remember that Rosemary had only two dresses, which makes it unlikely that she **hesitated** in **her choice,** as (B) says. Again, as with (A) you may be tempted to make an assumption with (C) that's not supported. The passage makes it clear that Rosemary enjoyed **grammar school,** but nowhere does it says she did **especially well.** Same with (D): One can guess that she wanted a **career,** but nothing is said about it in the passage.

7 **D**—A Big Picture question. What is the primary concern of the passage?

Though Victor is important in this passage, his real role is to awaken thoughts in Rosemary about her past. Most of the passage is about Rosemary and her life. When you look at the answer choices, (D) is really the only one that addresses this in a wide enough way.

(A) is too narrow. It deals only with Victor and doesn't take into account all the memories

Rosemary has. (B) feels close, but we never get the sense that she's trying to **suppress** the **unhappy memories.** (C) is a distortion; we're told that Rosemary was forbidden from attending school, but there's no suggestion she was **victimized** by her father. (E) is too trivial. This is a small and incorrect answer to a Big Picture question.

> Hint: Take a few seconds (no more) to predict an answer. Then find a choice that best matches your prediction.

Suggested Time: 13 minutes

Directions—Answer the questions below based on the information in the accompanying passages.

Practice Passage 8: Miles Davis Pair

This pair of passages presents contrasting views of the music of jazz trumpeter Miles Davis, who died in 1993. The author of Passage 1 argues that Davis's artistry reached its peak in the 1950s. The author of Passage 2 claims that Davis remained an important creative force in jazz to the end of his life.

Passage 1

The recent death of trumpeter Miles Davis brought an end to one of the most celebrated careers in the history of jazz. Few musicians have ever
Line enjoyed such popularity for so long. Much has been
(5) made of Davis's influence on the historical development of jazz, his ability to "show the way" to other musicians. Yet it must be said that Miles reached the artistic high point of his career in the 1950s.

Davis came to New York City from the Midwest
(10) in the mid-1940s while still a teenager. Studying at the Juilliard School of Music by day, he haunted the city's jazz clubs by night, receiving another education entirely. Bebop, the hot, frantic new sound in jazz, was being played by such musical revolution-
(15) aries as Charlie Parker, Dizzy Gillespie, and Thelonious Monk, and Davis was sometimes invited up on the bandstand to play with them. Though obviously talented, Davis had to struggle to keep up with these musicians, and he worked tirelessly to
(20) perfect his technique.

Even at this early stage, Davis's sound and style on trumpet set him apart. Rather than filling the air with a headlong rush of musical notes, as other bebop musicians did, Davis played sparingly. He
(25) seemed more interested in the silences between the notes than in the notes themselves. This less-is-more approach became the basis of "Cool" jazz, the counter-revolution Davis led which dominated West Coast jazz in the 1950s. The Miles Davis quin-
(30) tet set the standard for all other jazz combos of the era, and produced a series of recordings culminating in the classic *Kind of Blue*.

Although *Kind of Blue* represents the high-water mark of Davis's career, his artistic decline was not
(35) immediately apparent. In the early 1960s, playing with a different set of musicians, he produced some excellent albums. But the end was near. His last pure jazz album is named, fittingly enough, *In a Silent Way*. After issuing this recording in 1969,
(40) Davis turned his back on traditional jazz, disappointingly opting for an electronic "fusion" sound that blurred the lines between jazz and rock. Yes, he continued to enjoy a lucrative recording career and public adulation. But for all those who learned to
(45) love jazz by listening to the plaintive sounds of the Miles Davis of the 1950s, it was as if he had already fallen silent.

Passage 2

Miles Davis was a protean* figure in jazz; like some musical Picasso, he mastered and then shed a
(50) series of styles throughout the course of his career. This is rare in any artist, but almost unheard of in the world of jazz, where a musician's style is usually formed extremely early, and then refined and repeated for the remainder of his or her life.
(55) Although Davis could have earned millions by continuing to play the music that had first made him famous in the 1950s, he refused to repeat himself. He consistently sought to expand his musical horizons, working with young, emerging musicians,
(60) restlessly searching for new sounds.

After cutting his teeth on the bebop jazz of the 1940s, Davis developed a "cooler" style and made his name in the 1950s with a five-man combo. The so-called "purists" have often claimed that this peri-
(65) od represents the zenith of Davis's achievement. But this argument reveals more about the narrow tastes of certain critics than it does about the supposed limitations of Miles Davis. The groups Davis led in the 1960s featured a new generation of superb
(70) musicians such as Wayne Shorter and Herbie Hancock, and produced music that explored new and complex rhythmic textures.

Yet critics continued to complain. And when Davis released *Bitches Brew* in 1970, the jazz
(75) "purists" were horrified: His band was using electronic instruments, and its music borrowed heavily from rock rhythms and the psychedelic sound of "acid" rock. Typically, Davis ignored the storm of protest, secure in his artistic vision. Throughout the
(80) early 1970s, he continued to attract the best new players to his side. They benefited from his vast experience and mastery, and he from their youthful energy and fresh approach to the music.

After a six-year retirement brought on by illness,
(85) Davis re-emerged in 1981. Ever willing to court controversy, he wore outrageous clothes, grew his hair long, and even did a television commercial. But musically, Davis was as exciting as ever. Once again, he sought out some of the finest young musicians,
(90) and played to great acclaim. A restless innovator to the end of his life, Miles Davis deserves his place as the dominant figure in jazz in the second half of the 20th century.

*protean: able to assume different shapes or roles

1 In paragraph 1, the phrase *show the way* most nearly means
(A) lead a band
(B) bring publicity to
(C) teach novice musicians
(D) affect the creative development of
(E) compose music of high quality

Ⓐ Ⓑ Ⓒ Ⓓ Ⓔ

2 The author suggests that "Cool" jazz was a "counter-revolution" (lines 26–29) because it
(A) reflected Davis's unique sound on trumpet
(B) improved the quality of jazz on the West Coast
(C) marked Davis's emergence as the premier trumpeter of his generation
(D) represented a stylistic alternative to bebop jazz
(E) grew out of Davis's disagreements with Parker, Gillespie, and Monk

Ⓐ Ⓑ Ⓒ Ⓓ Ⓔ

3 In lines 35–37, when discussing the Davis group of the early 1960s, the author of Passage 1 suggests that
(A) critics persuaded Davis that he should reject the "Cool" sound of the 1950s
(B) Davis's individual style of play became even more spare and economical
(C) Davis continued to produce music of high quality even though past his prime
(D) musicians and audiences alike began treating Davis with increased respect
(E) Davis gave up electronic instruments and returned to playing traditional jazz

Ⓐ Ⓑ Ⓒ Ⓓ Ⓔ

4 The author of Passage 1 suggests that the music Miles Davis played after *In a Silent Way*
(A) ignored current musical trends
(B) alienated most of his listeners
(C) revived bebop jazz
(D) disappointed influential music critics
(E) remained highly profitable

Ⓐ Ⓑ Ⓒ Ⓓ Ⓔ

5 By saying that "it was as if he had already fallen silent" (lines 46–47), the author of Passage 1 suggests that
(A) it would have been preferable if Davis had not played at all, rather than play "fusion" jazz
(B) by 1970, Davis no longer had the ability to play in the plaintive style that had made him famous
(C) people who loved traditional jazz stopped buying recordings after the use of electronic instruments became popular
(D) Davis lost most of his popular following when he began to blur the lines between jazz and rock music
(E) younger listeners learned about jazz in a completely different way than those who had first heard it in the 1950s

Ⓐ Ⓑ Ⓒ Ⓓ Ⓔ

6 The author of Passage 2 suggests that, unlike Miles Davis, most jazz musicians
(A) find it difficult to earn a living playing music
(B) know very little about the tradition of jazz
(C) solidify their playing style early in life
(D) refuse to work with musicians younger than themselves
(E) prefer to play a "hot" style of jazz

Ⓐ Ⓑ Ⓒ Ⓓ Ⓔ

7 The phrase *cutting his teeth* (line 61) most nearly means
(A) getting excited about
(B) acquiring skill
(C) becoming injured by
(D) memorizing fully
(E) criticizing sharply

Ⓐ Ⓑ Ⓒ Ⓓ Ⓔ

8   The references in Passage 2 to "purists" (line 64) and "supposed limitations" (lines 67–68) serve to
(A) emphasize the shortcomings of Miles Davis as a bebop player
(B) show what Davis might have accomplished had he continued to play "cool" jazz
(C) give an assessment of Davis's reaction to his critics
(D) criticize those who would say negative things about Miles Davis
(E) prove that Davis entered a period of artistic decline in the 1960s
Ⓐ Ⓑ Ⓒ Ⓓ Ⓔ

9   According to the author of Passage 2, the relationship between Davis and the musicians he played with in the early 1970s can best be summarized as which of the following?
(A) It was similar to that of teacher and pupil.
(B) It was filled with dissension and conflict.
(C) It was the focus of critical acclaim.
(D) It lacked the "chemistry" of Davis's earlier groups.
(E) It was mutually beneficial.
Ⓐ Ⓑ Ⓒ Ⓓ Ⓔ

10   The author of Passage 1 would most likely react to the characterization of Miles Davis as a "restless innovator" (line 90) by arguing that
(A) Davis was no longer the dominant figure in jazz after 1950
(B) only a critic can properly judge the extent of a musician's artistic achievement
(C) Davis should have concentrated less on innovation and more on perfecting his technique
(D) the artistic quality of any musical innovation depends largely on the caliber of the musicians involved
(E) Davis should have realized that change for change's sake is not always a positive thing
Ⓐ Ⓑ Ⓒ Ⓓ Ⓔ

11   Both passages are primarily concerned with
(A) describing the evolution of jazz from the 1940s onward
(B) explaining why Miles Davis continually played with new groups of musicians
(C) showing how the music of Miles Davis was heavily influenced by bebop jazz
(D) evaluating the career and achievements of Miles Davis
(E) indicating the high point of Miles Davis's career
Ⓐ Ⓑ Ⓒ Ⓓ Ⓔ

SCORECARD	
Number of Questions Right:	
Number of Questions Wrong:	
Number of Questions Omitted:	
Number of Correct Guesses:	
Number of Wrong Guesses:	
Time Used:	

Answers and Explanations

Practice Passage 8: Miles Davis Pair

In this pair of passages about jazz trumpet player Miles Davis, each author has a different take on Davis's career. Passage 1 says Davis played his best music in the 1950s and then went off in the wrong direction—eventually switching to electronic instruments and borrowing from rock music. Passage 2 celebrates the very thing Passage 1 criticizes: Davis's ability to change styles over the course of his career. You don't need to be a musical expert to do well here. The paragraphs of each passage are organized chronologically, which makes it doubly easy to go back and relocate material pertinent to the questions.

1 **D**—Look at the entire third sentence in which the *keyed* phrase occurs: "Much has been made of Davis's influence on the historical development of jazz, his ability to 'show the way' to other musicians." "Show the way" is *equivalent in meaning to* "influenc[ing] the historical development of jazz." So (D) is best: Davis was able to **affect the creative development of** other musicians, even his peers, which is one reason he was so influential.

(A) **leading a band,** (B) **bringing publicity to** jazz, and even (E) **composing** excellent **music** can all be done without necessarily being *historically* influential. Likewise, (C) **teaching novice** jazz players influences *their* development, but not necessarily the historical development of jazz.

2 **D**—Paragraph three of Passage 1 says Davis played differently from other bebop players. Earlier, paragraph two describes bebop jazz as "the hot, frantic new sound" being played by "revolutionaries." So the "Cool" sound Davis developed was "counter-revolutionary" because stylistically it differed dramatically from bebop. Correct choice (D) restates this idea.

(A) and (B) touch on other details mentioned in paragraph three, but neither creates the direct opposition of "revolution" and "counter-revolution." (C) distorts the final sentence of paragraph three, which says that Davis's quintet "set the standard" for all other jazz combos of the era. The author of Passage 1 never calls Davis the premier trumpeter of his generation. Finally, (E) is plausible but unsupported by the text. We don't know whether Davis dis-

agreed with beboppers Parker, Gillespie, and Monk or simply followed his own instincts.

3 **C**—This inference question is *keyed* to the top of the last paragraph of Passage 1. The author says that, after the "high-water mark" of *Kind of Blue*, Davis's "artistic decline was not immediately apparent"; that in the early 1960s he played with another group and "produced some excellent albums." So (C) is correct: In the 1960s Davis still made **high-quality music, although he was past his prime.**

Critics are not mentioned in Passage 1, so choice (A) is a poor guess. Nor does the author say Davis's playing became (B) **more economical.** (D) distorts the assertion, near the end of Passage 1, that Davis "continued to enjoy . . . public adulation." This suggests that his popularity remained high, not that it increased. And (E) gets it backwards: Davis gave up traditional jazz and turned to electronic instruments.

4 **E**—This is a question about Davis's music after 1969. In Passage 1, the second half of the last paragraph says that after *In a Silent Way*, Davis "turned his back on traditional jazz," so you can eliminate choice (C). (A) is wrong because Davis *was* influenced during this time by **current trends**—i.e., by rock music. (B) is wrong because Davis "continued to enjoy . . . public adulation."

(D) is tempting, but we don't know that Passage 1 was written by a critic, and the author never suggests that **influential music critics** were **disappointed.** That leaves (E) as correct. It's based on the reference to Davis continuing to enjoy a "lucrative recording career."

5 **A**—This is a question about the last line of Passage 1. The phrase *fallen silent* intentionally echoes the title of *In a Silent Way*, the album that marked the end of Davis's traditional jazz playing. The suggestion is that Davis *should have* fallen silent, rather than make music the author disliked. Correct choice (A) restates this.

(B) is wrong because there's no suggestion that Davis was *unable* to play traditional jazz. Rather, he *chose* to play a different style. (C) is completely unwarranted; we know nothing about the record-buying habits of people who love traditional jazz.

(D) is contradicted by the reference to Davis continuing to enjoy public adulation. And (E) has nothing to do with the issue of Davis falling silent.

6 C—Now you're into Passage 2. The first paragraph says Davis "mastered and then shed a variety of styles" during his career. It goes on to say that this is rare in the jazz world, "where a musician's style is usually formed extremely early, and then refined and repeated for the remainder of his or her life." So choice (C) is correct: Davis is different from most jazz players, who **solidify their playing style early in life.**

(A) is wrong: We're told Davis earned "millions," but the passage never mentions whether most jazz musicians find it hard **to earn a living.** There's no evidence for (B) or (D). And (E) refers only to bebop players, not *most jazz musicians.*

7 B—We talk about babies teething or cutting their first teeth. The figurative use of the phrase conveys the image of a beginner learning and improving, which points to (B) **acquiring skill** as correct. If you aren't familiar with this expression, information in Passage 1 can help you answer correctly. Davis "cut his teeth" on the bebop in the 1940s, at the earliest phase of his career.

(A) has nothing to do with "cutting one's teeth." (C) and (E) try to distract you by playing off the use of the verb *cut,* (C) literally and (E) figuratively. Memorization (D) is related to learning, but doesn't fit the cliché; you don't always need to memorize in order to acquire skill.

8 D—The question stem quotes from two successive sentences in paragraph two of Passage 2, and a careful reading of context helps here. Responding to critics who think Davis's 1950s music was the "zenith," or highest point, of his career, the author argues that this "reveals more about the narrow tastes of . . . critics than it does about the supposed limitations of Miles Davis." In other words, the author is attacking Davis's critics; (D) is correct.

(A), (B), and (E) incorrectly focus on Davis's music instead of his detractors, and (C) wrongly puts the author's words in Davis's mouth.

9 E—Always check the context—in this case, the last two sentences of paragraph three. During the early 70s, Davis played with the best young jazz musicians, who "benefited from his vast experience and mastery," as he did from their "youthful energy and fresh approach." In other words, both sides got something good; the relationship **was mutually beneficial,** and (E) is correct.

(A) fails on two counts: First, Davis was playing with the younger musicians as peers, and second, **teacher-pupil** relationships are not necessarily mutually beneficial. The passage suggests neither (B) **conflict** between Davis and the young players, nor a drop-off in (D) **"chemistry."** Finally, in (C), the critics did not praise the work of Davis and the musicians he played with; on the contrary, in 1970 purists complained when his band was using electronic instruments, so (C) is wrong.

10 E—Here you're asked to compare the viewpoints in Passages 1 and 2. An "innovator" introduces something new, or changes the way things are done. While Author 2 praises Davis for restlessly changing musical styles, Author 1 wishes Davis had continued playing traditional jazz. So Author 1 would argue that Davis's "innovations" were a mistake, and this suggests (E): **Davis [failed to] realize that change for the sake of change is not always [good].**

(A) doesn't address whether Davis's innovations were a good thing; in addition, Author 1 thought Davis reached his peak *after* 1950. (B) is a poor guess, since the author of Passage 1 never takes this position. The first half of (C) is accurate, but the second half is untrue: Author 1 thinks Davis's decline stemmed from the kind of music he chose to play, *not* from imperfect technique. Nor does Author 1 suggest that Davis's mistake was playing with inferior musicians, as (D) suggests.

11 D—This Big Picture question asks about the main point of *both* passages. The wording suggests they share the same primary purpose. Though each author has a different opinion of Davis, both evaluate his music and trace the arc of his career, so (D) is correct.

(A) is too broad; it doesn't even mention Davis. (B) reflects Passage 2, but not Passage 1, which argues that Davis should have stayed with his '50s music. (C) relates only to a minor point in each passage—how Davis got started in jazz. And (E) accurately describes Passage 1, but not Passage 2, which argues that Davis's career was a succession of high points.

SAT

VOCABULARY

How to Use the SAT Word and Root Lists

The Kaplan SAT Word List is a minidictionary of SAT-level vocabulary words. These are the right words to study, with brief definitions based on the meanings likely to be tested. The SAT Root List breaks these words into their component parts. Use the Kaplan Word List and Root List in three ways to help build your vocabulary:

1. Anytime you come across a word or root in this workbook that you don't know, look it up on the appropriate list. Think about the word or root for a moment. Try to come up with a way to remember it. Put a check mark next to anything you look up so that you can come back to review. Here are some ways to help lodge new words or roots in your head:

- Create and use flashcards
- Make a vocabulary notebook
- Make a vocabulary tape
- Use rhymes, mental pictures, or other mnemonics (memory aids)

2. Use these Lists to study from, concentrating on the things you check off. It takes repetition and review to memorize new words. Cover up the definitions, and quiz yourself every now and then to make sure you still remember what you've studied.

3. Read through the Lists whenever you have some time. Relax. Browse around. The more familiar you get with the look and feel of SAT-level vocabulary, the more comfortable you'll be on Test Day.

You don't need to use any particular method to build your vocabulary. Use whatever works for you. All of the Verbal question types will become easier for you as your word mastery grows.

A

- ABANDON (n)—total lack of inhibition
- ABASE—to humble, disgrace
- ABATEMENT—decrease, reduction
- ABDICATE—to give up a position, right, or power
- ABERRATION—something different from the usual or normal
- ABET—to aid, act as accomplice
- ABEYANCE—temporary suppression or suspension
- ABHOR—to loathe, detest
- ABJECT—miserable, pitiful
- ABJURE—to reject, abandon formally
- ABLUTION—act of cleansing
- ABNEGATE—to deny, renounce
- ABOLITIONIST—one who opposes the practice of slavery
- ABORTIVE—interrupted while incomplete
- ABRIDGE—to condense, shorten
- ABROGATE—to abolish or invalidate by authority
- ABSCOND—to depart secretly
- ABSOLVE—to forgive, free from blame
- ABSTEMIOUS—moderate in appetite
- ABSTRACT (adj)—theoretical; complex, difficult
- ABSTRUSE—difficult to comprehend
- ACCEDE—to express approval; agree to
- ACCESSIBLE—attainable, available; approachable
- ACCESSORY—attachment, ornament; accomplice, partner
- ACCOLADE—praise, distinction
- ACCOST—to approach and speak to someone
- ACCRETION—growth in size or increase in amount
- ACCRUE—to accumulate, grow by additions
- ACERBIC—bitter, sharp in taste or temper
- ACME—highest point; summit
- ACQUIESCE—to agree, comply quietly
- ACQUITTAL—release from blame
- ACRID—harsh, bitter
- ACRIMONY—bitterness, animosity
- ACUITY—sharpness
- ACUMEN—sharpness of insight
- ACUTE—sharp, pointed
- ADAGE—old saying or proverb
- ADAMANT—uncompromising, unyielding
- ADAPT—to accommodate, adjust
- ADHERE—to cling to or follow without deviation
- ADJACENT—next to
- ADJUNCT—something added, attached, or joined
- ADMONISH—to caution or reprimand
- ADROIT—skillful, accomplished, highly competent
- ADULATION—high praise
- ADULTERATE—to corrupt or make impure
- ADUMBRATE—to sketch, outline in a shadowy way
- ADVANTAGEOUS—favorable, useful
- ADVERSARIAL—antagonistic, competitive
- ADVERSE—unfavorable, unlucky, harmful
- AERIAL—having to do with the air
- AERIE—nook or nest built high in the air
- AERODYNAMIC—relating to objects moving through the air
- AESTHETIC—pertaining to beauty or art
- AFFABLE—friendly, easy to approach
- AFFECTED (adj)—pretentious, phony
- AFFINITY—fondness, liking; similarity
- AFFLUENT—rich, abundant
- AFFRONT (n)—personal offense, insult
- AGENDA—plan, schedule
- AGGRANDIZE—to make larger or greater in power
- AGGREGATE (n)—collective mass or sum; total
- AGGRIEVE—to afflict, distress
- AGILE—well-coordinated, nimble
- AGITATION—commotion, excitement; uneasiness
- AGNOSTIC—one doubting that God exists
- AGRARIAN—relating to farming or rural matters
- ALACRITY—cheerful willingness, eagerness; speed
- ALCHEMY—medieval chemical philosophy based on changing metal into gold
- ALGORITHM—mechanical problem-solving procedure
- ALIAS—assumed name
- ALIENATED—distanced, estranged
- ALIGNED—precisely adjusted; committed to one side
- ALLAY—to lessen, ease, or soothe

- ALLEGORY—symbolic representation
- ALLEVIATE—to relieve, improve partially
- ALLITERATION—repetition of the beginning sounds of words
- ALLOCATION—allowance, portion, share
- ALLURE (v)—to entice by charm; attract
- ALLUSION—indirect reference
- ALLUSIVENESS—quality of making many indirect references
- ALOOF—detached, indifferent
- ALTERCATION—noisy dispute
- ALTRUISM—unselfish concern for others' welfare
- AMALGAM—mixture, combination, alloy
- AMBIDEXTROUS—able to use both hands equally well
- AMBIGUOUS—uncertain; subject to multiple interpretations
- AMBIVALENCE—attitude of uncertainty; conflicting emotions
- AMELIORATE—to make better, improve
- AMENABLE—agreeable, cooperative
- AMEND—to improve or correct flaws in
- AMENITY—pleasantness; something increasing comfort
- AMIABLE—friendly, pleasant, likable
- AMICABLE—friendly, agreeable
- AMITY—friendship
- AMORAL—unprincipled, unethical
- AMOROUS—strongly attracted to love; showing love
- AMORPHOUS—having no definite form
- AMORTIZE—to diminish by installment payments
- AMPHIBIAN—creature equally at home on land or in water
- AMPHITHEATER—arena theater with rising tiers around a central open space
- AMPLE—abundant, plentiful
- AMPLIFY—increase, intensify
- AMULET—ornament worn as a charm against evil spirits
- ANACHRONISM—something chronologically inappropriate
- ANACHRONISTIC—outdated
- ANALOGOUS—comparable, parallel
- ANARCHY—absence of government or law; chaos
- ANATHEMA—ban, curse; something shunned or disliked
- ANCILLARY—accessory, subordinate, helping

- ANECDOTE—short, usually funny account of an event
- ANGULAR—characterized by sharp angles; lean and gaunt
- ANIMATION—enthusiasm, excitement
- ANIMOSITY—hatred, hostility
- ANNUL—to cancel, nullify, declare void, or make legally invalid
- ANODYNE—something that calms or soothes pain
- ANOINT—to apply oil to, especially as a sacred rite
- ANOMALY—irregularity or deviation from the norm
- ANONYMITY—condition of having no name or an unknown name
- ANTAGONIST—foe, opponent, adversary
- ANTECEDENT (adj)—coming before in place or time
- ANTEDILUVIAN—prehistoric, ancient beyond measure
- ANTEPENULTIMATE—third from last
- ANTERIOR—preceding, previous, before, prior (to)
- ANTHOLOGY—collection of literary works
- ANTHROPOMORPHIC—attributing human qualities to nonhumans
- ANTIPATHY—dislike, hostility; extreme opposition or aversion
- ANTIQUATED—outdated, obsolete
- ANTIQUITY—ancient times; the quality of being old or ancient
- ANTITHESIS—exact opposite or direct contrast
- APATHETIC—indifferent, unconcerned
- APATHY—lack of feeling or emotion
- APHASIA—inability to speak or use words
- APHELION—point in a planet's orbit that is farthest from the sun
- APHORISM—old saying or short pithy statement
- APOCRYPHAL—not genuine; fictional
- APOSTATE—one who renounces a religious faith
- APOSTROPHE—an address to the reader or someone not present
- APOTHEOSIS—glorification; glorified ideal
- APPEASE—to satisfy, placate, calm, pacify
- APPROBATION—praise; official approval
- APPROPRIATE (v)—to take possession of
- AQUATIC—belonging or living in water

❑ ARABLE—suitable for cultivation
❑ ARBITRARY—depending solely on individual will; inconsistent
❑ ARBITRATOR—mediator, negotiator
❑ ARBOREAL—relating to trees; living in trees
❑ ARBORETUM—place where trees are displayed and studied
❑ ARCANE—secret, obscure, known only to a few
❑ ARCHAIC—antiquated, from an earlier time; outdated
❑ ARCHIPELAGO—large group of islands
❑ ARDENT—passionate, enthusiastic, fervent
❑ ARDOR—great emotion or passion
❑ ARDUOUS—extremely difficult, laborious
❑ ARID—extremely dry or deathly boring
❑ ARRAIGN—to call to court to answer an indictment
❑ ARROGATE—to demand, claim arrogantly
❑ ARSENAL—ammunition storehouse
❑ ARTICULATE (adj)—well-spoken, expressing oneself clearly
❑ ARTIFACT—historical relic, item made by human craft
❑ ARTISAN—craftsperson; expert
❑ ASCEND—to rise or climb
❑ ASCENDANCY—state of rising, ascending; power or control
❑ ASCERTAIN—to determine, discover, make certain of
❑ ASCETIC—self-denying, abstinent, austere
❑ ASCRIBE—to attribute to, assign
❑ ASHEN—resembling ashes; deathly pale
❑ ASKEW—crooked, tilted
❑ ASPERSION—false rumor, damaging report, slander
❑ ASPIRE—to have great hopes; to aim at a goal
❑ ASSAIL—to attack, assault
❑ ASSENT—to express agreement
❑ ASSERT—to affirm, attest
❑ ASSIDUOUS—diligent, persistent, hard-working
❑ ASSIGNATION—appointment for lovers' meeting; assignment
❑ ASSIMILATION—act of blending in, becoming similar
❑ ASSONANCE—resemblance in sound, especially in vowel sounds; partial rhyme
❑ ASSUAGE—to make less severe, ease, relieve
❑ ASTRINGENT—harsh, severe, stern
❑ ASTUTE—having good judgment

❑ ASUNDER (adv)—into different parts
❑ ASYMMETRICAL—not corresponding in size, shape, position, etc.
❑ ATONE—to make amends for a wrong
❑ ATROCIOUS—monstrous, shockingly bad, wicked
❑ ATROPHY—to waste away, wither from disuse
❑ ATTAIN—to accomplish, gain
❑ ATTENUATE—to make thin or slender; weaken
❑ ATTEST—to testify, stand as proof of, bear witness
❑ AUDACIOUS—bold, daring, fearless
❑ AUDIBLE—capable of being heard
❑ AUDIT—formal examination of financial records
❑ AUDITORY—having to do with hearing
❑ AUGMENT—to expand, extend
❑ AUGURY—prophecy, prediction of events
❑ AUGUST—dignified, awe-inspiring, venerable
❑ AUSPICIOUS—having favorable prospects, promising
❑ AUSTERE—stern, strict, unadorned
❑ AUTHORITARIAN—extremely strict, bossy
❑ AUTOCRAT—dictator
❑ AUTONOMOUS—separate, independent
❑ AUXILIARY—supplementary, reserve
❑ AVARICE—greed
❑ AVENGE—to retaliate, take revenge for an injury or crime
❑ AVER—to declare to be true, affirm
❑ AVERSION—intense dislike
❑ AVERT—to turn (something) away; prevent, hinder
❑ AVIARY—large enclosure housing birds
❑ AVOW—to state openly or declare
❑ AWRY—crooked, askew, amiss
❑ AXIOM—premise, postulate, self-evident truth

B

❑ BALEFUL—harmful, with evil intentions
❑ BALK—to refuse, shirk; prevent
❑ BALLAD—folk song, narrative poem
❑ BALM—soothing, healing influence
❑ BAN—to forbid, outlaw
❑ BANAL—trite and overly common
❑ BANE—something causing death, destruction, or ruin
❑ BANTER—playful conversation
❑ BASTION—fortification, stronghold

❏ BAY (v)—to bark, especially in a deep, prolonged way

❏ BECALM—to make calm or still; keep motionless by lack of wind

❏ BECLOUD—to confuse; darken with clouds

❏ BEGUILE—to deceive, mislead; charm

❏ BEHEMOTH—huge creature

❏ BELABOR—to insist repeatedly or harp on

❏ BELATED—late

❏ BELEAGUER—to harass, plague

❏ BELFRY—bell tower, room in which a bell is hung

❏ BELIE—to misrepresent; expose as false

❏ BELITTLE—to represent as unimportant, make light of

❏ BELLICOSE—warlike, aggressive

❏ BELLIGERENT—hostile, tending to fight

❏ BELLOW—to roar, shout

❏ BEMUSE—to confuse, stupefy; plunge deep into thought

❏ BENCHMARK—standard of measure

❏ BENEFACTOR—someone giving aid or money

❏ BENEFICENT—kindly, charitable; doing good deeds; producing good effects

❏ BENIGHTED—unenlightened

❏ BENIGN—kindly, gentle, or harmless

❏ BEQUEATH—to give or leave through a will; to hand down

❏ BERATE—to scold harshly

❏ BESEECH—to beg, plead, implore

❏ BESTIAL—beastly, animal-like

❏ BESTOW—to give as a gift

❏ BETOKEN—to indicate, signify, give evidence of

❏ BEVY—group

❏ BIAS—prejudice, slant

❏ BIBLIOGRAPHY—list of books

❏ BIBLIOPHILE—book lover

❏ BILATERAL—two-sided

❏ BILK—to cheat, defraud

❏ BILLET—board and lodging for troops

❏ BIPED—two-footed animal

❏ BISECT—to cut into two (usually equal) parts

❏ BLANCH—to pale; take the color out of

❏ BLANDISH—to coax with flattery

❏ BLASPHEMOUS—cursing, profane, irreverent

❏ BLATANT—glaring, obvious, showy

❏ BLIGHT (v)—to afflict, destroy

❏ BLITHE—joyful, cheerful, or without appropriate thought

❏ BLUDGEON—to hit as with a short, heavy club

❏ BOISTEROUS—rowdy, loud, unrestrained

❏ BOMBASTIC—using high-sounding but meaningless language

❏ BONANZA—extremely large amount; something profitable

❏ BONHOMIE—good-natured geniality; atmosphere of good cheer

❏ BOON—blessing, something to be thankful for

❏ BOOR—crude person, one lacking manners or taste

❏ BOTANIST—scientist who studies plants

❏ BOUNTIFUL—plentiful

❏ BOURGEOIS—middle-class

❏ BOVINE—cowlike; relating to cows

❏ BRAZEN—bold, shameless, impudent; of or like brass

❏ BREACH—act of breaking, violation

❏ BRIGAND—bandit, outlaw

❏ BROACH—to mention or suggest for the first time

❏ BRUSQUE—rough and abrupt in manner

❏ BUFFET (v)—to toss about

❏ BUFFOON—clown or fool

❏ BULWARK—defense wall; anything serving as defense

❏ BURGEON—to sprout or flourish

❏ BURLY—brawny, husky

❏ BURNISH—to polish, make smooth and bright

❏ BURSAR—treasurer

❏ BUSTLE—commotion, energetic activity

❏ BUTT—person or thing that is object of ridicule

❏ BUTTRESS (v)—to reinforce or support

❏ BYWAY—back road

C

❏ CACOPHONOUS—jarring, unpleasantly noisy

❏ CADENCE—rhythmic flow of poetry; marching beat

❏ CAJOLE—to flatter, coax, persuade

❏ CALAMITOUS—disastrous, catastrophic

❏ CALLOUS—thick-skinned, insensitive

❏ CALLOW—immature, lacking sophistication

❏ CALUMNY—false and malicious accusation, misrepresentation, slander

❏ CANDOR—honesty of expression

❏ CANNY—smart; founded on common sense

❏ CANONIZE—to declare a person a saint; raise to highest honors

❏ CANVASS—to examine thoroughly; conduct a poll

- CAPACIOUS—large, roomy; extensive
- CAPITULATE—to submit completely, surrender
- CAPRICIOUS—impulsive, whimsical, without much thought
- CARDIOLOGIST—physician specializing in diseases of the heart
- CARICATURE—exaggerated portrait, cartoon
- CARNAL—of the flesh
- CARNIVOROUS—meat-eating
- CARP (v)—to find fault, complain constantly
- CARTOGRAPHY—science or art of making maps
- CAST (n)—copy, replica
- CAST (v)—to fling, to throw
- CASTIGATE—to punish, chastise, criticize severely
- CATALYST—something causing change without being changed
- CATEGORICAL—absolute, without exception
- CATHARSIS—purification, cleansing
- CATHOLIC—universal; broad and comprehensive
- CAUCUS—smaller group within an organization; a meeting of such a group
- CAULK—to make watertight
- CAUSALITY—cause-and-effect relationship
- CAUSTIC—biting, sarcastic; able to burn
- CAVALIER—carefree, happy; with lordly disdain
- CAVORT—to frolic, frisk
- CEDE—to surrender possession of something
- CELEBRITY—fame, widespread acclaim
- CENSORIOUS—severely critical
- CENTRIPETAL—directed or moving toward the center
- CERTITUDE—assurance, certainty
- CESSATION—temporary or complete halt
- CESSION—act of surrendering something
- CHAGRIN—shame, embarrassment, humiliation
- CHALICE—goblet, cup
- CHAMPION (v)—to defend or support
- CHAOTIC—extremely disorderly
- CHARLATAN—quack, fake
- CHARY—watchful, cautious, extremely shy
- CHASTISE—to punish, discipline, scold
- CHERUBIC—sweet, innocent, resembling a cherub angel
- CHICANERY—trickery, fraud, deception
- CHIDE—to scold, express disapproval

- CHIMERICAL—fanciful, imaginary, visionary, impossible
- CHOLERIC—easily angered, short-tempered
- CHOICE (adj)—specially selected, preferred
- CHORTLE—to chuckle
- CHROMATIC—relating to color
- CHRONICLER—one who keeps records of historical events
- CIRCUITOUS—roundabout
- CIRCUMFERENCE—boundary or distance around a circle or sphere
- CIRCUMLOCUTION—roundabout, lengthy way of saying something
- CIRCUMNAVIGATE—to sail completely around
- CIRCUMSCRIBE—to encircle; set limits on, confine
- CIRCUMSPECT—cautious, wary
- CIRCUMVENT—to go around; avoid
- CISTERN—tank for rainwater
- CITADEL—fortress or stronghold
- CIVIL—polite; relating to citizens
- CIVILITY—courtesy, politeness
- CLAIRVOYANT (adj)—having ESP, psychic
- CLAMOR (v)—to make a noisy outcry
- CLAMOR (n)—noisy outcry
- CLANDESTINE—secretive, concealed for a darker purpose
- CLARITY—clearness; clear understanding
- CLAUSTROPHOBIA—fear of small, confined places
- CLEAVE—to split or separate; to stick, cling, adhere
- CLEMENCY—merciful leniency
- CLOISTER (v)—to confine, seclude
- COAGULATE—to clot or change from a liquid to a solid
- COALESCE—to grow together or cause to unite as one
- CODDLE—to baby, treat indulgently
- COERCE—to compel by force or intimidation
- COFFER—strongbox, large chest for money
- COGENT—logically forceful, compelling, convincing
- COGNATE—related, similar, akin
- COGNITION—mental process by which knowledge is acquired
- COGNOMEN—family name; any name, especially a nickname
- COHABIT—to live together
- COHERENT—intelligible, lucid, understandable

- COLLATERAL—accompanying
- COLLOQUIAL—characteristic of informal speech
- COLLOQUY—dialogue or conversation, conference
- COLLUSION—collaboration, complicity, conspiracy
- COMELINESS—physical grace and beauty
- COMMEND—to compliment, praise
- COMMENSURATE—proportional
- COMMISSION—fee payable to an agent; authorization
- COMMODIOUS—roomy, spacious
- COMMONPLACE—ordinary, found every day
- COMMUNICABLE—transmittable
- COMMUTE—to change a penalty to a less severe one
- COMPATRIOT—fellow countryman
- COMPELLING (adj)—having a powerful and irresistible effect
- COMPENSATE—to repay or reimburse
- COMPLACENT—self-satisfied, smug, affable
- COMPLEMENT—to complete, perfect
- COMPLIANT—submissive and yielding
- COMPLICITY—knowing partnership in wrongdoing
- COMPOUND (adj)—complex; composed of several parts
- COMPOUND (v)—to combine, augment
- COMPRESS—to reduce, squeeze
- COMPULSIVE—obsessive, fanatic
- COMPUNCTION—feeling of uneasiness caused by guilt or regret
- CONCAVE—curving inward
- CONCEDE—to yield, admit
- CONCEPTUALIZE—to envision, imagine
- CONCERTO—musical composition for orchestra and soloist(s)
- CONCILIATORY—overcoming distrust or hostility
- CONCORD—agreement
- CONCUR—to agree
- CONDONE—to pardon or forgive; overlook, justify, or excuse a fault
- CONDUIT—tube, pipe, or similar passage
- CONFECTION—something sweet to eat
- CONFISCATE—to appropriate, seize
- CONFLAGRATION—big, destructive fire
- CONFLUENCE—meeting place; meeting of two streams
- CONFOUND—to baffle, perplex

- CONGEAL—to become thick or solid, as a liquid freezing
- CONGENIAL—similar in tastes and habits
- CONGENITAL—existing since birth
- CONGLOMERATE—collected group of varied things
- CONGRESS—formal meeting or assembly
- CONGRUITY—correspondence, harmony, agreement
- CONJECTURE—speculation, prediction
- CONJUGAL—pertaining to marriage
- CONJURE—to evoke a spirit, cast a spell
- CONNIVE—to conspire, scheme
- CONSANGUINEOUS—of the same origin; related by blood
- CONSCIENTIOUS—governed by conscience; careful and thorough
- CONSECRATE—to declare sacred; dedicate to a goal
- CONSENSUS—unanimity, agreement of opinion or attitude
- CONSIGN—to commit, entrust
- CONSOLATION—something providing comfort or solace for a loss or hardship
- CONSOLIDATE—to combine, incorporate
- CONSONANT (adj)—consistent with, in agreement with
- CONSTITUENT—component, part; citizen, voter
- CONSTRAINED—forced, compelled; confined, restrained
- CONSTRAINT—something that forces or compels; something that restrains or confines
- CONSTRUE—to explain or interpret
- CONSUMMATE (adj)—accomplished, complete, perfect
- CONSUMMATE (v)—to complete, fulfill
- CONTEND—to battle, clash; compete
- CONTENTIOUS—quarrelsome, disagreeable, belligerent
- CONTINENCE—self-control, self-restraint
- CONTRAVENE—to contradict, deny, act contrary to
- CONTRITE—deeply sorrowful and repentant for a wrong
- CONTUSION—bruise
- CONUNDRUM—riddle, puzzle, or problem with no solution
- CONVALESCENCE—gradual recovery after an illness
- CONVENE—to meet, come together, assemble

- CONVENTIONAL—typical, customary, commonplace
- CONVEX—curved outward
- CONVIVIAL—sociable; fond of eating, drinking, and people
- CONVOKE—to call together, summon
- CONVOLUTED—twisted, complicated, involved
- COPIOUS—abundant, plentiful
- COQUETTE—woman who flirts
- CORPOREAL—having to do with the body; tangible, material
- CORPULENCE—obesity, fatness, bulkiness
- CORRELATION—association, mutual relation of two or more things
- CORROBORATE—to confirm, verify
- CORRUGATE—to mold in a shape with parallel grooves and ridges
- COSMETIC (adj)—relating to beauty; affecting the surface of something
- COSMOGRAPHY—science that deals with the nature of the universe
- COSMOPOLITAN—sophisticated, free from local prejudices
- COSSET—to pamper, treat with great care
- COTERIE—small group of persons with a similar purpose
- COUNTENANCE (n)—facial expression; look of approval or support
- COUNTENANCE (v)—to favor, support
- COUNTERMAND—to annul, cancel, make a contrary order
- COUNTERVAIL—to counteract, to exert force against
- COVEN—group of witches
- COVERT—hidden; secret
- COVET—to desire strongly something possessed by another
- CRASS—crude, unrefined
- CRAVEN—cowardly
- CREDENCE—acceptance of something as true or real
- CREDIBLE—plausible, believable
- CREDULOUS—gullible, trusting
- CREED—statement of belief or principle
- CRESCENDO—gradual increase in volume of sound
- CRITERION—standard for judging
- CRYPTIC—puzzling
- CUISINE—characteristic style of cooking
- CULMINATION—climax, final stage

- CULPABLE—guilty, responsible for wrong
- CULPRIT—guilty person
- CUMULATIVE—resulting from gradual increase
- CUPIDITY—greed
- CURATOR—caretaker and overseer of an exhibition, especially in a museum
- CURMUDGEON—cranky person
- CURSORY—hastily done, superficial
- CURT—abrupt, blunt
- CURTAIL—to shorten
- CUTLERY—cutting instruments; tableware
- CYGNET—young swan
- CYNIC—person who distrusts the motives of others

D

- DAINTY—delicate, sweet
- DAUNT—to discourage, intimidate
- DEARTH—lack, scarcity, insufficiency
- DEBASE—to degrade or lower in quality or stature
- DEBAUCH—to corrupt, seduce from virtue or duty; indulge
- DEBILITATE—to weaken, enfeeble
- DEBUNK—to discredit, disprove
- DEBUTANTE—young woman making her debut in high society
- DECAPITATE—to behead
- DECATHLON—athletic contest with ten events
- DECIDUOUS—losing leaves in the fall; short-lived, temporary
- DECLIVITY—downward slope
- DECOROUS—proper, tasteful, socially correct
- DECORUM—proper behavior, etiquette
- DECRY—to belittle, openly condemn
- DEFACE—to mar the appearance of, vandalize
- DEFAMATORY—slanderous, injurious to the reputation
- DEFENDANT—person required to answer a legal action or suit
- DEFERENTIAL—respectful and polite in a submissive way
- DEFILE—to dirty, spoil; to disgrace, dishonor
- DEFINITIVE—clear-cut, explicit or decisive
- DEFLATION—decrease, depreciation
- DEFORM—to disfigure, distort
- DEFT—skillful, dexterous
- DEFUNCT—no longer existing, dead, extinct
- DELECTABLE—appetizing, delicious

- DELEGATE (v)—to give powers to another
- DELETERIOUS—harmful, destructive, detrimental
- DELINEATION—depiction, representation
- DELTA—tidal deposit at the mouth of a river
- DELUGE (n)—flood
- DELUGE (v)—to submerge, overwhelm
- DEMAGOGUE—leader, rabble-rouser, usually using appeals to emotion or prejudice
- DEMARCATION—borderline; act of defining or marking a boundary or distinction
- DEMEAN—to degrade, humiliate, humble
- DEMOGRAPHICS—data relating to study of human population
- DEMOTE—to reduce to a lower grade or rank
- DEMOTION—lowering in rank or grade
- DEMUR—to express doubts or objections
- DEMYSTIFY—to remove mystery from, clarify
- DENIGRATE—to slur or blacken someone's reputation
- DENOUNCE—to accuse, blame
- DENUDE—to make bare, uncover, undress
- DENUNCIATION—public condemnation
- DEPICT—to describe, represent
- DEPLETE—to use up, exhaust
- DEPLORE—to express or feel disapproval of; regret strongly
- DEPLOY—to spread out strategically over an area
- DEPOSE—to remove from a high position, as from a throne
- DEPRAVITY—sinfulness, moral corruption
- DEPRECATE—to lessen in value, belittle, disparage
- DEPRECIATE—to lose value gradually
- DERIDE—to mock, ridicule, make fun of
- DERIVATIVE—copied or adapted; not original
- DERIVE—to originate; take from a certain source
- DEROGATE—to belittle, disparage
- DESECRATE—to abuse something sacred
- DESICCATE—to dry completely, dehydrate
- DESIST—to stop doing something
- DESPONDENT—feeling discouraged and dejected
- DESPOT—tyrannical ruler
- DESTITUTE—very poor, poverty-stricken
- DESULTORY—at random, rambling, unmethodical
- DETER—to discourage; prevent from happening

- DETERMINATE—having defined limits; conclusive
- DETRIMENTAL—causing harm or injury
- DEVIATE—to stray, wander
- DEVIATION—departure, exception, anomaly
- DEVOID—totally lacking
- DEVOUT—deeply religious
- DEXTEROUS—skilled physically or mentally
- DIABOLICAL—fiendish; wicked
- DIALECT—regional style of speaking
- DIAPHANOUS—allowing light to show through; delicate
- DIATRIBE—bitter verbal attack
- DICHOTOMY—division into two parts
- DICTUM—authoritative statement; popular saying
- DIDACTIC—excessively instructive
- DIFFERENTIATE—to distinguish between two items
- DIFFIDENCE—shyness, lack of confidence
- DIFFRACT—to cause to separate into parts, especially light
- DIFFUSE—widely spread out
- DIGRESS—to turn aside; to stray from the main point
- DILAPIDATED—in disrepair, run down, neglected
- DILATE—to enlarge, swell, extend
- DILATORY—slow, tending to delay
- DILUVIAL—relating to a flood
- DIMINUTIVE—small
- DIPLOMACY—discretion, tact
- DIRGE—funeral hymn
- DISAFFECTED—discontented and disloyal
- DISARRAY—clutter, disorder
- DISBAND—to break up
- DISBAR—to expel from legal profession
- DISBURSE—to pay out
- DISCERN—to perceive something obscure
- DISCLAIM—to deny, disavow
- DISCLOSE—to confess, divulge
- DISCONCERTING—bewildering, perplexing, slightly disturbing
- DISCORDANT—harsh-sounding, badly out of tune
- DISCREDIT—to dishonor or disgrace
- DISCREDITED—disbelieved, discounted; disgraced, dishonored
- DISCREPANCY—difference between
- DISCRETIONARY—subject to one's own judgment

- DISCURSIVE—wandering from topic to topic
- DISDAIN—to regard with scorn and contempt
- DISDAINFUL—contemptuous, scornful
- DISENGAGED—disconnected, disassociated
- DISGORGE—to vomit, discharge violently
- DISHEVELED—untidy, disarranged, unkempt
- DISINCLINED—averse, unwilling, lacking desire
- DISPARAGE—to belittle, speak disrespectfully about
- DISPARATE—dissimilar, different in kind
- DISPARITY—contrast, dissimilarity
- DISPASSIONATE—free from emotion; impartial, unbiased
- DISPEL—to drive out or scatter
- DISPENSE—to distribute, administer
- DISPENSE WITH—to suspend the operation of, do without
- DISPERSE—to break up, scatter
- DISPIRIT—to dishearten, make dejected
- DISREPUTE—disgrace, dishonor
- DISSEMBLE—to pretend, disguise one's motives
- DISSEMINATE—to spread far and wide
- DISSENSION—difference of opinion
- DISSIPATE—to scatter; to dissolve; to pursue pleasure to excess
- DISSOCIATE—to separate; remove from an association
- DISSONANT—harsh and unpleasant sounding
- DISSUADE—to persuade someone to alter original intentions
- DISTEND—to swell, inflate, bloat
- DISTRAUGHT—very worried and distressed
- DISTRUST (n)—disbelief and suspicion
- DITHER—to move or act confusedly or without clear purpose
- DIURNAL—daily
- DIVINE (v)—to foretell or know by inspiration
- DIVISIVE—creating disunity or conflict
- DOCILE—tame, willing to be taught
- DOCTRINAIRE—rigidly devoted to theories
- DOGMATIC—rigidly fixed in opinion, opinionated
- DOLEFUL—sad, mournful
- DOLT—idiot, dimwit, foolish person
- DOMINEER—to rule over something in a tyrannical way
- DONOR—benefactor, contributor
- DORMANT—at rest, inactive, in suspended animation

- DOTARD—senile old person
- DOTING—excessively fond, loving to excess
- DOUR—sullen and gloomy; stern and severe
- DOWRY—money or property given by a bride to her husband
- DRAFT (v)—to plan, outline; to recruit, conscript
- DRIVEL—stupid talk; slobber
- DROLL—amusing in a wry, subtle way
- DROSS—waste produced during metal smelting; garbage
- DULCET—pleasant sounding, soothing to the ear
- DUPE (v)—to deceive, trick
- DUPE (n)—fool, pawn
- DUPLICITY—deception, dishonesty, double-dealing
- DURABILITY—strength, sturdiness
- DURATION—period of time that something lasts
- DURESS—threat of force or intimidation; imprisonment
- DYSPEPTIC—suffering from indigestion; gloomy and irritable

E

- EBB—to fade away, recede
- EBULLIENT—exhilarated, full of enthusiasm and high spirits
- ECLECTIC—selecting from various sources
- ECSTATIC—joyful
- EDDY—air or wind current
- EDICT—law, command, official public order
- EDIFICE—building
- EDIFY—to instruct morally and spiritually
- EDITORIALIZE—to express an opinion on an issue
- EFFACE—to erase or make illegible
- EFFERVESCENT—bubbly, lively
- EFFICACIOUS—effective, efficient
- EFFIGY—stuffed doll; likeness of a person
- EFFLUVIA—outpouring of gases or vapors
- EFFRONTERY—impudent boldness; audacity
- EFFULGENT—brilliantly shining
- EFFUSIVE—expressing emotion without restraint
- EGOCENTRIC—acting as if things are centered around oneself
- EGREGIOUS—conspicuously bad
- EGRESS—exit
- ELATION—exhilaration, joy

- ELEGY—mournful poem, usually about the dead
- ELICIT—to draw out, provoke
- ELOQUENCE—fluent and effective speech
- ELUCIDATE—to explain, clarify
- EMACIATED—skinny, scrawny, gaunt, especially from hunger
- EMANCIPATION—the act of setting free or liberating
- EMBELLISH—to ornament; make attractive with decoration or details; add details to a statement
- EMBEZZLE—to steal money in violation of a trust
- EMBROIL—to involve in; cause to fall into disorder
- EMEND—to correct a text
- EMINENT—celebrated, distinguished; outstanding, towering
- EMOLLIENT—having soothing qualities, especially for skin
- EMOTIVE—appealing to or expressing emotion
- EMPATHY—sympathy, identification with another's feelings
- EMULATE—to copy, imitate
- ENCIPHER—to translate a message into code
- ENCORE—additional performance, often demanded by audience
- ENCUMBER—to hinder, burden, restrict motion
- ENDEMIC—belonging to a particular area, inherent
- ENDURANCE—ability to withstand hardships
- ENERVATE—to weaken, sap strength from
- ENGENDER—to produce, cause, bring about
- ENIGMATIC—puzzling, inexplicable
- ENJOIN—to urge, order, command; forbid or prohibit, as by judicial order
- ENMITY—hostility, antagonism, ill will
- ENNUI—boredom, lack of interest and energy
- ENORMITY—state of being gigantic or terrible
- ENSCONCE—to settle comfortably into a place
- ENSHROUD—to cover, enclose with a dark cover
- ENTAIL—to involve as a necessary result, necessitate
- ENTHRALL—to captivate, enchant, enslave
- ENTITY—something with its own existence or form
- ENTOMOLOGIST—scientist who studies insects
- ENTREAT—to plead, beg
- ENUMERATE—to count, list, itemize
- ENUNCIATE—to pronounce clearly
- EPHEMERAL—momentary, transient, fleeting
- EPICURE—person with refined taste in food and wine
- EPIGRAM—short, witty saying or poem
- EPIGRAPH—quotation at the beginning of a literary work
- EPILOGUE—concluding section of a literary work
- EPITOME—representative of an entire group; summary
- EPOCHAL—very significant or influential; defining an epoch or time-period
- EQUANIMITY—calmness, composure
- EQUESTRIAN—one who rides on horseback
- EQUINE—relating to horses
- EQUIVOCAL—ambiguous, open to two interpretations
- EQUIVOCATE—to use vague or ambiguous language intentionally
- ERADICATE—to erase or wipe out
- ERRANT—straying, mistaken, roving
- ERUDITE—learned, scholarly
- ESCHEW—to abstain from, avoid
- ESOTERIC—understood only by a learned few
- ESPOUSE—to support or advocate; to marry
- ESTRANGE—to alienate, keep at a distance
- ETHEREAL—not earthly, spiritual, delicate
- ETHOS—beliefs or character of a group
- ETYMOLOGY—origin and history of a word; study of words
- EULOGY—high praise, often in a public speech
- EUPHEMISM—use of an inoffensive word or phrase in place of a more distasteful one
- EUPHONY—pleasant, harmonious sound
- EUPHORIA—feeling of well-being or happiness
- EURYTHMICS—art of harmonious bodily movement
- EUTHANASIA—mercy killing; intentional, easy, and painless death
- EVADE—to avoid, dodge
- EVANESCENT—momentary, transitory, short-lived
- EVICT—to put out or force out
- EVINCE—to show clearly, display, signify

- EVOKE—to inspire memories; to produce a reaction
- EXACERBATE—to aggravate, intensify the bad qualities of
- EXASPERATION—irritation
- EXCERPT (n)—selection from a book or play
- EXCOMMUNICATE—to bar from membership in the church
- EXCRUCIATING—agonizing, intensely painful
- EXCULPATE—to clear of blame or fault, vindicate
- EXECRABLE—utterly detestable, abhorrent
- EXHILARATION—state of being energetic or filled with happiness
- EXHORT—to urge or incite by strong appeals
- EXHUME—to remove from a grave; uncover a secret
- EXIGENT—urgent; excessively demanding
- EXONERATE—to clear of blame, absolve
- EXORBITANT—extravagant, greater than reasonable
- EXORCISE—to expel evil spirits
- EXOTIC—foreign; romantic, excitingly strange
- EXPANSIVE—sweeping, comprehensive; tending to expand
- EXPATRIATE (n)—one who lives outside one's native land
- EXPATRIATE (v)—to drive someone from his/her native land
- EXPEDIENT (adj)—convenient, efficient, practical
- EXPIATE—to atone for, make amends for
- EXPIRE—to come to an end; die; breathe out
- EXPLICABLE—capable of being explained
- EXPLICIT—clearly defined, specific; forthright in expression
- EXPLODE—to debunk, disprove; blow up, burst
- EXPONENT—one who champions or advocates
- EXPOUND—to elaborate; to expand or increase
- EXPUNGE—to erase, eliminate completely
- EXPURGATE—to censor
- EXTEMPORANEOUS—unrehearsed, on the spur of the moment
- EXTENUATE—to lessen the seriousness, strength or effect of
- EXTINCTION—end of a living thing or species
- EXTOL—to praise

- EXTORT—to obtain something by threats
- EXTRANEOUS—irrelevant, unrelated, unnecessary
- EXTREMITY—outermost or farthest point
- EXTRICATE—to free from, disentangle, free
- EXTRINSIC—not inherent or essential, coming from without
- EXUBERANT—lively, happy, and full of good spirits
- EXUDE—to give off, ooze
- EXULT—to rejoice

F

- FABRICATE—to make or devise; construct
- FABRICATED—constructed, invented; faked, falsified
- FACADE—face, front; mask, superficial appearance
- FACILE—very easy
- FACILITATE—to aid, assist
- FACILITY—aptitude, ease in doing something
- FALLACIOUS—wrong, unsound, illogical
- FALLOW—uncultivated, unused
- FANATICISM—extreme devotion to a cause
- FARCICAL—absurd, ludicrous
- FASTIDIOUS—careful with details
- FATHOM (v)—to measure the depth of, gauge
- FATUOUS—stupid; foolishly self-satisfied
- FAULT—break in a rock formation; mistake or error
- FAWN (v)—to flatter excessively, seek the favor of
- FAZE—to bother, upset, or disconcert
- FEASIBLE—possible, capable of being done
- FECKLESS—ineffective, careless, irresponsible
- FECUND—fertile, fruitful, productive
- FEDERATION—union of organizations; union of several states, each of which retains local power
- FEIGN—to pretend, give a false impression; to invent falsely
- FEISTY—excitable, easily drawn into quarrels
- FELICITOUS—suitable, appropriate; well-spoken
- FELL (v)—to chop, cut down
- FERVID—passionate, intense, zealous
- FETID—foul-smelling, putrid
- FETTER—to bind, chain, confine
- FIASCO—disaster, utter failure
- FICTIVE—fictional, imaginary
- FIDELITY—loyalty

KAPLAN

- ❏ FILCH—to steal
- ❏ FILIBUSTER—use of obstructive tactics in a legislative assembly to prevent adoption of a measure
- ❏ FINICKY—fussy, difficult to please
- ❏ FISSION—process of splitting into two parts
- ❏ FITFUL—intermittent, irregular
- ❏ FLACCID—limp, flabby, weak
- ❏ FLAGRANT—outrageous, shameless
- ❏ FLAMBOYANT—flashy, garish; exciting, dazzling
- ❏ FLAMMABLE—combustible, being easily burned
- ❏ FLAUNT—to show off
- ❏ FLEDGLING—young bird just learning to fly; beginner, novice
- ❏ FLORA—plants
- ❏ FLORID—gaudy, extremely ornate; ruddy, flushed
- ❏ FLOUNDER—to falter, waver; to muddle, struggle
- ❏ FLOUT—to treat contemptuously, scorn
- ❏ FLUCTUATE—to alternate, waver
- ❏ FODDER—raw material; feed for animals
- ❏ FOIBLE—minor weakness or character flaw
- ❏ FOIL (v)—to defeat, frustrate
- ❏ FOLIATE—to grow, sprout leaves
- ❏ FOMENT—to arouse or incite
- ❏ FORBEARANCE—patience, restraint, leniency
- ❏ FORECLOSE—to rule out; to seize debtor's property for lack of payments
- ❏ FORD (v)—to cross a body of water at a shallow place
- ❏ FOREBODING—dark sense of evil to come
- ❏ FORENSIC—relating to legal proceedings; relating to debates
- ❏ FORSAKE—to abandon, withdraw from
- ❏ FORESTALL—to prevent, delay; anticipate
- ❏ FORETHOUGHT—anticipation, foresight
- ❏ FORGO—to go without, refrain from
- ❏ FORLORN—dreary, deserted; unhappy; hopeless, despairing
- ❏ FORMULATE—to conceive, devise; to draft, plan; to express, state
- ❏ FORSWEAR—to repudiate, renounce, disclaim, reject
- ❏ FORTE—strong point, something a person does well
- ❏ FORTUITOUS—happening by luck, fortunate
- ❏ FOSTER—to nourish, cultivate, promote
- ❏ FOUNDATION—groundwork, support; institution established by donation to aid a certain cause
- ❏ FOUNDER (v)—to fall helplessly; sink
- ❏ FRACAS—noisy dispute
- ❏ FRACTIOUS—unruly, rebellious
- ❏ FRAGMENTATION—division, separation into parts, disorganization
- ❏ FRANK—honest and straightforward
- ❏ FRAUD—deception, hoax
- ❏ FRAUDULENT—deceitful, dishonest, unethical
- ❏ FRAUGHT—full of, accompanied by
- ❏ FRENETIC—wildly frantic, frenzied, hectic
- ❏ FRENZIED—feverishly fast, hectic, and confused
- ❏ FRIVOLOUS—petty, trivial; flippant, silly
- ❏ FROND—leaf
- ❏ FULSOME—excessive, overdone, sickeningly abundant
- ❏ FUNEREAL—mournful, appropriate to a funeral
- ❏ FURTIVE—secret, stealthy
- ❏ FUSION—process of merging things into one

G

- ❏ GALL (n)—bitterness; careless nerve
- ❏ GALL (v)—to exasperate and irritate
- ❏ GAMBOL—to dance or skip around playfully
- ❏ GAMELY—courageously
- ❏ GARGANTUAN—giant, tremendous
- ❏ GARNER—to gather and store
- ❏ GARRULOUS—very talkative
- ❏ GAUNT—thin and bony
- ❏ GAVEL—mallet used for commanding attention
- ❏ GENRE—type, class, category
- ❏ GERMINATE—to begin to grow (used of a seed or idea)
- ❏ GESTATION—growth process from conception to birth
- ❏ GIBE—to make heckling, taunting remarks
- ❏ GIRTH—distance around something
- ❏ GLIB—fluent in an insincere manner; off-hand, casual
- ❏ GLOBAL—involving the entire world; relating to a whole
- ❏ GLOWER—to glare, stare angrily and intensely
- ❏ GLUTTONY—eating and drinking to excess

- ❑ GNARL—to make knotted, deform
- ❑ GNOSTIC—having to do with knowledge
- ❑ GOAD—to prod or urge
- ❑ GRADATION—process occurring by regular degrees or stages; variation in color
- ❑ GRANDILOQUENCE—pompous talk, fancy but meaningless language
- ❑ GRANDIOSE—magnificent and imposing; exaggerated and pretentious
- ❑ GRANULAR—having a grainy texture
- ❑ GRASP (v)—to perceive and understand; to hold securely
- ❑ GRATIS—free, costing nothing
- ❑ GRATUITOUS—free, voluntary; unnecessary and unjustified
- ❑ GRATUITY—something given voluntarily, tip
- ❑ GREGARIOUS—outgoing, sociable
- ❑ GRIEVOUS—causing grief or sorrow; serious and distressing
- ❑ GRIMACE—facial expression showing pain or disgust
- ❑ GRIMY—dirty, filthy
- ❑ GROSS (adj)—obscene; blatant, flagrant
- ❑ GROSS (n)—total before deductions
- ❑ GROVEL—to humble oneself in a demeaning way
- ❑ GUILE—trickery, deception
- ❑ GULLIBLE—easily deceived
- ❑ GUSTATORY—relating to sense of taste

H

- ❑ HABITAT—dwelling place
- ❑ HACKNEYED—worn out by over-use
- ❑ HALLOW—to make holy; treat as sacred
- ❑ HAMLET—small village
- ❑ HAPLESS—unfortunate, having bad luck
- ❑ HARBINGER—precursor, sign of something to come
- ❑ HARDY—robust, vigorous
- ❑ HARROWING—extremely distressing, terrifying
- ❑ HASTEN—to hurry, to speed up
- ❑ HAUGHTY—arrogant and condescending
- ❑ HEADSTRONG—reckless; insisting on one's own way
- ❑ HEATHEN—pagan; uncivilized and irreligious
- ❑ HECTIC—hasty, hurried, confused
- ❑ HEDONISM—pursuit of pleasure as a goal
- ❑ HEGEMONY—leadership, domination, usually by a country
- ❑ HEIGHTEN—to raise

- ❑ HEINOUS—shocking, wicked, terrible
- ❑ HEMICYCLE—semicircular form or structure
- ❑ HEMORRHAGE (n)—heavy bleeding
- ❑ HEMORRHAGE (v)—to bleed heavily
- ❑ HERETICAL—opposed to an established religious orthodoxy
- ❑ HERMETIC—tightly sealed
- ❑ HETERODOX—unorthodox, not widely accepted
- ❑ HETEROGENEOUS—composed of unlike parts, different, diverse
- ❑ HEW—to cut with an ax
- ❑ HIATUS—break, interruption, vacation
- ❑ HIDEBOUND—excessively rigid; dry and stiff
- ❑ HINDSIGHT—perception of events after they happen
- ❑ HINTERLAND—wilderness
- ❑ HOARY—very old; whitish or gray from age
- ❑ HOLISTIC—emphasizing importance of the whole and interdependence of its parts
- ❑ HOLOCAUST—widespread destruction, usually by fire
- ❑ HOMAGE—public honor and respect
- ❑ HOMOGENEOUS—composed of identical parts
- ❑ HOMONYM—word identical in pronunciation and spelling but different in meaning
- ❑ HONE—to sharpen
- ❑ HONOR—to praise, glorify, pay tribute to
- ❑ HUMANE—merciful, kindly
- ❑ HUSBAND (v)—to farm, manage carefully and thriftily
- ❑ HUTCH—pen or coop for animal; shack, shanty
- ❑ HYDRATE—to add water to
- ❑ HYGIENIC—clean, sanitary
- ❑ HYMN—religious song, usually of praise or thanks
- ❑ HYPERBOLE—purposeful exaggeration for effect
- ❑ HYPERVENTILATE—to breathe abnormally fast
- ❑ HYPOCHONDRIA—unfounded belief that one is often ill
- ❑ HYPOCRITE—person claiming beliefs or virtues he or she doesn't really possess
- ❑ HYPOTHERMIA—abnormally low body temperature
- ❑ HYPOTHESIS—assumption subject to proof
- ❑ HYPOTHETICAL—theoretical, speculative

I

- ICONOCLAST—one who attacks traditional beliefs
- IDEALISM—pursuit of noble goals
- IDIOSYNCRASY—peculiarity of temperament, eccentricity
- IGNOBLE—dishonorable, not noble in character
- IGNOMINIOUS—disgraceful and dishonorable
- ILK—type or kind
- ILLICIT—illegal, improper
- ILLIMITABLE—limitless
- ILLUSORY—unreal, deceptive
- ILLUSTRIOUS—famous, renowned
- IMBUE—to infuse; dye, wet, moisten
- IMMACULATE—spotless; free from error
- IMMATERIAL—extraneous, inconsequential, nonessential; not consisting of matter
- IMMENSE—enormous, huge
- IMMERSE—to bathe, dip; to engross, preoccupy
- IMMOBILE—not moveable; still
- IMMUNE—exempt; protected from harm or disease; unresponsive to
- IMMUNOLOGICAL—relating to immune system
- IMMUTABLE—unchangeable, invariable
- IMPAIR—to damage, injure
- IMPASSE—blocked path, dilemma with no solution
- IMPASSIONED—with passion
- IMPASSIVE—showing no emotion
- IMPEACH—to charge with misdeeds in public office; accuse
- IMPECCABLE—flawless, without fault
- IMPECUNIOUS—poor, having no money
- IMPEDIMENT—barrier, obstacle; speech disorder
- IMPERATIVE—essential; mandatory
- IMPERIOUS—arrogantly self-assured, domineering, overbearing
- IMPERTINENT—rude
- IMPERTURBABLE—not capable of being disturbed
- IMPERVIOUS—impossible to penetrate; incapable of being affected
- IMPETUOUS—quick to act without thinking
- IMPIOUS—not devout in religion
- IMPLACABLE—inflexible, incapable of being pleased

- IMPLANT—to set securely or deeply; to instill
- IMPLAUSIBLE—improbable, inconceivable
- IMPLICATE—to involve in a crime, incriminate
- IMPLICIT—implied, not directly expressed
- IMPORTUNE—to ask repeatedly, beg
- IMPOSE—to inflict, force upon
- IMPOSING—dignified, grand
- IMPOTENT—powerless, ineffective, lacking strength
- IMPOUND—to seize and confine
- IMPOVERISH—to make poor or bankrupt
- IMPRECATION—curse
- IMPREGNABLE—totally safe from attack, able to resist defeat
- IMPRESSIONABLE—easily influenced or affected
- IMPROMPTU—spontaneous, without rehearsal
- IMPROVIDENT—without planning or foresight, negligent
- IMPUDENT—arrogant, audacious
- IMPUGN—to call into question, attack verbally
- IMPULSE—sudden tendency, inclination
- IMPULSIVE—spontaneous, unpredictable
- INADVERTENTLY—unintentionally
- INANE—foolish, silly, lacking significance
- INAUGURATE—to begin or start officially; to induct into office
- INCANDESCENT—shining brightly
- INCARCERATE—to put in jail; to confine
- INCARCERATION—imprisonment
- INCARNADINE—blood-red in color
- INCARNATE—having bodily form
- INCENDIARY—combustible, flammable, burning easily
- INCENSE (v)—to infuriate, enrage
- INCEPTION—beginning
- INCESSANT—continuous, never ceasing
- INCHOATE—imperfectly formed or formulated
- INCIPIENT—beginning to exist or appear; in an initial stage
- INCISIVE—perceptive, penetrating
- INCLINATION—tendency towards
- INCLUSIVE—comprehensive, all-encompassing
- INCOGNITO—in disguise, concealing one's identity
- INCONCEIVABLE—impossible, unthinkable

- INCONSEQUENTIAL—unimportant, trivial
- INCONTROVERTIBLE—unquestionable, beyond dispute
- INCORRIGIBLE—incapable of being corrected
- INCREDULOUS—skeptical, doubtful
- INCULCATE—to teach, impress in the mind
- INCULPATE—to blame, charge with a crime
- INCUMBENT—holding a specified office, often political
- INCURSION—sudden invasion
- INDEFATIGABLE—never tired
- INDEFENSIBLE—inexcusable, unforgivable
- INDELIBLE—permanent, not erasable
- INDICATIVE—showing or pointing out, suggestive of
- INDICT—to accuse formally, charge with a crime
- INDIGENOUS—native, occurring naturally in an area
- INDIGENT—very poor
- INDIGNANT—angry, incensed, offended
- INDOLENT—habitually lazy, idle
- INDOMITABLE—fearless, unconquerable
- INDUBITABLE—unquestionable
- INDUCE—to persuade; bring about
- INDUCT—to place ceremoniously in office
- INDULGE—to give in to a craving or desire
- INDUSTRY—business or trade; diligence, energy
- INEBRIATED—drunk, intoxicated
- INEPT—clumsy, awkward
- INERT—unable to move, tending to inactivity
- INESTIMABLE—too great to be estimated
- INEVITABLE—certain, unavoidable
- INEXORABLE—inflexible, unyielding
- INEXTRICABLE—incapable of being disentangled
- INFALLIBLE—incapable of making a mistake
- INFAMY—reputation for bad deeds
- INFANTILE—childish, immature
- INFATUATED—strongly or foolishly attached to, inspired with foolish passion, overly in love
- INFER—to conclude, deduce
- INFILTRATE—to pass secretly into enemy territory
- INFINITESIMAL—extremely tiny
- INFIRMITY—disease, ailment
- INFRINGE—to encroach, trespass; to transgress, violate
- INFURIATE—to anger, provoke, outrage
- INFURIATING—provoking anger or outrage

- INGENIOUS—original, clever, inventive
- INGENUOUS—straightforward, open; naive and unsophisticated
- INGRATE—ungrateful person
- INGRATIATE—to bring oneself purposely into another's good graces
- INGRESS—entrance
- INHIBIT—to hold back, prevent, restrain
- INIMICAL—hostile, unfriendly
- INIQUITY—sin, evil act
- INITIATE—to begin, introduce; to enlist, induct
- INJECT—to force into; to introduce into conversation
- INJUNCTION—command, order
- INKLING—hint; vague idea
- INNATE—natural, inborn
- INNATENESS—state of being natural or inborn
- INNOCUOUS—harmless; inoffensive
- INNOVATE—to invent, modernize, revolutionize
- INNUENDO—indirect and subtle criticism, insinuation
- INNUMERABLE—too many to be counted
- INOFFENSIVE—harmless, innocent
- INOPERABLE—not operable; incurable by surgery
- INQUEST—investigation; court or legal proceeding
- INSATIABLE—never satisfied
- INSCRUTABLE—impossible to understand fully
- INSENTIENT—unfeeling, unconscious
- INSIDIOUS—sly, treacherous, devious
- INSINUATE—to suggest, say indirectly, imply
- INSIPID—bland, lacking flavor; lacking excitement
- INSOLENT—insulting and arrogant
- INSOLUBLE—not able to be solved or explained
- INSOLVENT—bankrupt, unable to pay one's debts
- INSTIGATE—to incite, urge, agitate
- INSUBSTANTIAL—modest, insignificant
- INSULAR—isolated, detached
- INSUPERABLE—insurmountable, unconquerable
- INSURGENT—rebellious, insubordinate
- INSURRECTION—rebellion
- INTEGRAL—central, indispensable

❑ INTEGRITY—decency, honest; wholeness
❑ INTEMPERATE—not moderate
❑ INTER—to bury
❑ INTERDICT—to forbid, prohibit
❑ INTERJECT—to interpose, insert
❑ INTERLOCUTOR—someone taking part in a dialogue
❑ INTERLOPER—trespasser; meddler in others' affairs
❑ INTERMINABLE—endless
❑ INTERMITTENT—starting and stopping
❑ INTERNECINE—deadly to both sides
❑ INTERPOLATE—to insert; change by adding new words or material
❑ INTERPOSE—to insert; to intervene
❑ INTERREGNUM—interval between reigns
❑ INTERROGATE—to question formally
❑ INTERSECT—to divide by passing through or across
❑ INTERSPERSE—to distribute among, mix with
❑ INTIMATION—clue, suggestion
❑ INTRACTABLE—not easily managed
❑ INTRAMURAL—within an institution like a school
❑ INTRANSIGENT—uncompromising, refusing to be reconciled
❑ INTREPID—fearless
❑ INTRINSIC—inherent, internal
❑ INTROSPECTIVE—contemplating one's own thoughts and feelings
❑ INTROVERT—someone given to self-analysis
❑ INTRUSION—trespass, invasion of another's privacy
❑ INTUITIVE—instinctive, untaught
❑ INUNDATE—to cover with water; overwhelm
❑ INURE—to harden; accustom; become used to
❑ INVALIDATE—to negate or nullify
❑ INVECTIVE—verbal abuse
❑ INVESTITURE—ceremony conferring authority
❑ INVETERATE—confirmed, long-standing, deeply rooted
❑ INVIDIOUS—likely to provoke ill will, offensive
❑ INVINCIBLE—invulnerable, unbeatable
❑ INVIOLABLE—safe from violation or assault
❑ INVOKE—to call upon, request help
❑ IOTA—very tiny amount
❑ IRASCIBLE—easily angered
❑ IRIDESCENT—showing many colors
❑ IRRESOLVABLE—unable to be resolved; not analyzable

❑ IRREVERENT—disrespectful
❑ IRREVOCABLE—conclusive, irreversible
❑ ITINERANT—wandering from place to place, unsettled
❑ ITINERARY—route of a traveler's journey

J

❑ JADED—tired by excess or overuse; slightly cynical
❑ JANGLING—clashing, jarring; harshly unpleasant (in sound)
❑ JARGON—nonsensical talk; specialized language
❑ JAUNDICE—yellowish discoloration of skin
❑ JAUNDICED—affected by jaundice; prejudiced or embittered
❑ JETTISON—to cast off, throw cargo overboard
❑ JINGOISM—belligerent support of one's country
❑ JOCULAR—jovial, playful, humorous
❑ JUBILEE—special anniversary
❑ JUDICIOUS—sensible, showing good judgment
❑ JUGGERNAUT—huge force destroying everything in its path
❑ JUNCTURE—point where two things are joined
❑ JURISPRUDENCE—philosophy of law
❑ JUXTAPOSITION—side-by-side placement

K

❑ KEEN—having a sharp edge; intellectually sharp, perceptive
❑ KERNEL—innermost, essential part; seed grain, often in a shell
❑ KEYNOTE—note or tone on which a musical key is founded; main idea of a speech, program, etc.
❑ KINDLE—to set fire to or ignite; excite or inspire
❑ KINETIC—relating to motion; characterized by movement
❑ KNELL—sound of a funeral bell; omen of death or failure
❑ KUDOS—fame, glory, honor

L

❑ LABYRINTH—maze
❑ LACERATION—cut or wound
❑ LACHRYMOSE—tearful

- LACKADAISICAL—idle, lazy; apathetic, indifferent
- LACONIC—using few words
- LAGGARD—dawdler, loafer, lazy person
- LAMENT (v)—to deplore, grieve
- LAMPOON—to attack with satire, mock harshly
- LANGUID—lacking energy, indifferent, slow
- LAP (v)—to drink using the tongue; to wash against
- LAPIDARY—relating to precious stones
- LARCENY—theft of property
- LARDER—place where food is stored
- LARGESS—generosity; gift
- LARYNX—organ containing vocal cords
- LASSITUDE—lethargy, sluggishness
- LATENT—present but hidden; potential
- LAUDABLE—deserving of praise
- LAXITY—carelessness
- LEERY—suspicious
- LEGERDEMAIN—trickery
- LEGIBLE—readable
- LEGISLATE—to decree, mandate, make laws
- LENIENT—easygoing, permissive
- LETHARGY—indifferent inactivity
- LEVITATE—to rise in the air or cause to rise
- LEVITY—humor, frivolity, gaiety
- LEXICON—dictionary, list of words
- LIBERAL—tolerant, broad-minded; generous, lavish
- LIBERATION—freedom, emancipation
- LIBERTARIAN—one who believes in unrestricted freedom
- LIBERTINE—one without moral restraint
- LICENTIOUS—immoral; unrestrained by society
- LIEN—right to possess and sell the property of a debtor
- LIMPID—clear, transparent
- LINEAGE—ancestry
- LINGUISTICS—study of language
- LINIMENT—medicinal liquid used externally to ease pain
- LIONIZE—to treat as a celebrity
- LISSOME—easily flexed, limber, agile
- LISTLESS—lacking energy and enthusiasm
- LITERATE—able to read and write; well-read and educated
- LITHE—moving and bending with ease; graceful
- LITIGATION—lawsuit

- LIVID—discolored from a bruise; reddened with anger
- LOATHE—to abhor, despise, hate
- LOCOMOTION—movement from place to place
- LOGO—corporate symbol
- LOITER—to stand around idly
- LOQUACIOUS—talkative
- LOW (v)—to make a sound like a cow, moo
- LUCID—clear and easily understood
- LUDICROUS—laughable, ridiculous
- LUGUBRIOUS—sorrowful, mournful
- LUMBER (v)—to move slowly and awkwardly
- LUMINARY—bright object; celebrity; source of inspiration
- LUMINOUS—bright, brilliant, glowing
- LUNAR—relating to the moon
- LURID—harshly shocking, sensational; glowing
- LURK—to prowl, sneak
- LUSCIOUS—very tasty
- LUXURIANCE—elegance, lavishness
- LYRICAL—suitable for poetry and song; expressing feeling

M

- MACHINATION—plot or scheme
- MACROBIOTICS—art of prolonging life by special diet of organic, nonmeat substances
- MACROCOSM—system regarded as an entity with subsystems
- MAELSTROM—whirlpool; turmoil; agitated state of mind
- MAGNANIMOUS—generous, noble in spirit
- MAGNATE—powerful or influential person
- MAGNITUDE—extent, greatness of size
- MALADROIT—clumsy, tactless
- MALADY—illness
- MALAPROPISM—humorous misuse of a word
- MALCONTENT—discontented person, one who holds a grudge
- MALEDICTION—curse
- MALEFACTOR—evildoer; culprit
- MALEVOLENT—ill-willed; causing evil or harm to others
- MALFUNCTION (v)—to fail to work
- MALFUNCTION (n)—breakdown, failure
- MALICE—animosity, spite, hatred
- MALINGER—to evade responsibility by pretending to be ill

- MALNUTRITION—undernourishment
- MALODOROUS—foul-smelling
- MANDATORY—necessary, required
- MANIFEST (adj)—obvious
- MANIFOLD—diverse, varied, comprised of many parts
- MANNERED—artificial or stilted in character
- MANUAL (adj)—hand-operated; physical
- MAR—to damage, deface; spoil
- MARGINAL—barely sufficient
- MARITIME—relating to the sea or sailing
- MARTIAL—warlike, pertaining to the military
- MARTINET—strict disciplinarian, one who rigidly follows rules
- MARTYR—person dying for his/her beliefs
- MASOCHIST—one who enjoys pain or humiliation
- MASQUERADE—disguise; action that conceals the truth
- MATERIALISM—preoccupation with material things
- MATRICULATE—to enroll as a member of a college or university
- MATRILINEAL—tracing ancestry through mother's line rather than father's
- MAUDLIN—overly sentimental
- MAWKISH—sickeningly sentimental
- MEDDLER—person interfering in others' affairs
- MEDIEVAL—relating to the Middle Ages
- MEGALITH—huge stone used in prehistoric structures
- MEGALOMANIA—mental state with delusions of wealth and power
- MELANCHOLY—sadness, depression
- MELODY—pleasing musical harmony; related musical tunes
- MENAGERIE—various animals kept together for exhibition
- MENDACIOUS—dishonest
- MENDICANT—beggar
- MENTOR—experienced teacher and wise adviser
- MERCENARY (n)—soldier for hire in foreign countries
- MERCENARY (adj)—motivated only by greed
- MERCURIAL—quick, shrewd, and unpredictable
- MERETRICIOUS—gaudy, falsely attractive
- MERIDIAN—circle passing through the two poles of the earth

- MERITORIOUS—deserving reward or praise
- METAMORPHOSIS—change, transformation
- METAPHOR—figure of speech comparing two different things
- METICULOUS—extremely careful, fastidious, painstaking
- METRONOME—time-keeping device used in music
- METTLE—courageousness; endurance
- MICROBE—microorganism
- MICROCOSM—tiny system used as analogy for larger system
- MIGRATORY—wandering from place to place with the seasons
- MILITATE—to operate against, work against
- MINIMAL—smallest in amount, least possible
- MINUSCULE—very small
- MIRTH—frivolity, gaiety, laughter
- MISANTHROPE—person who hates human beings
- MISAPPREHEND—to misunderstand, fail to know
- MISCONSTRUE—to misunderstand, fail to discover
- MISERLINESS—extreme stinginess
- MISGIVING—apprehension, doubt, sense of foreboding
- MISHAP—accident; misfortune
- MISNOMER—an incorrect name or designation
- MISSIVE—note or letter
- MITIGATE—to soften, or make milder
- MNEMONIC—relating to memory; designed to assist memory
- MOBILITY—ease of movement
- MOCK—to deride, ridicule
- MODERATE (adj)—reasonable, not extreme
- MODERATE (v)—to make less excessive, restrain; regulate
- MOLLIFY—to calm or make less severe
- MOLLUSK—sea animal with soft body
- MOLT (v)—to shed hair, skin, or an outer layer periodically
- MONASTIC—extremely plain or secluded, as in a monastery
- MONOCHROMATIC—having one color
- MONOGAMY—custom of marriage to one person at a time
- MONOLITH—large block of stone
- MONOLOGUE—dramatic speech performed by one actor

- MONTAGE—composite picture
- MOOT—debatable; previously decided
- MORBID—gruesome; relating to disease; abnormally gloomy
- MORES—customs or manners
- MORIBUND—dying, decaying
- MOROSE—gloomy, sullen, or surly
- MORSEL—small bit of food
- MOTE—small particle, speck
- MOTLEY—many-colored; composed of diverse parts
- MOTTLE—to mark with spots
- MULTIFACETED—having many parts, many-sided
- MULTIFARIOUS—diverse
- MUNDANE—worldly; commonplace
- MUNIFICENT—generous
- MUNITIONS—ammunition
- MUTABILITY—changeability
- MYOPIC—nearsighted
- MYRIAD—immense number, multitude

N

- NADIR—lowest point
- NARRATIVE—account, story
- NASCENT—starting to develop, coming into existence
- NATAL—relating to birth
- NEBULOUS—vague, cloudy
- NECROMANCY—black magic
- NEFARIOUS—vicious, evil
- NEGLIGENT—careless, inattentive
- NEGLIGIBLE—not worth considering
- NEOLOGISM—new word or expression
- NEONATE—newborn child
- NEOPHYTE—novice, beginner
- NETHER—located under or below
- NETTLE (v)—to irritate
- NEUTRALITY—disinterest, impartiality
- NEUTRALIZE—to balance, offset
- NICETY—elegant or delicate feature; minute distinction
- NICHE—recess in a wall; best position for something
- NIGGARDLY—stingy
- NIHILISM—belief that existence and all traditional values are meaningless
- NOCTURNAL—pertaining to night; active at night
- NOISOME—stinking, putrid
- NOMADIC—moving from place to place

- NOMENCLATURE—terms used in a particular science or discipline
- NOMINAL—existing in name only; negligible
- NON SEQUITUR—conclusion not following from apparent evidence
- NONDESCRIPT—lacking interesting or distinctive qualities; dull
- NOTORIETY—unfavorable fame
- NOVICE—apprentice, beginner
- NOVITIATE—state of being a beginner or novice
- NOXIOUS—harmful, unwholesome
- NUANCE—shade of meaning
- NULLIFY—to make legally invalid; to counteract the effect of
- NUMISMATICS—coin collecting
- NUPTIAL—relating to marriage
- NUTRITIVE—relating to nutrition or health

O

- OBDURATE—stubborn
- OBFUSCATE—to confuse, obscure
- OBLIQUE—indirect, evasive; misleading, devious
- OBLITERATE—demolish, wipe out
- OBLIVIOUS—unaware, inattentive
- OBSCURE (adj)—dim, unclear; not well-known
- OBSCURITY—place or thing that's hard to perceive
- OBSEQUIOUS—overly submissive, brownnosing
- OBSEQUY—funeral ceremony
- OBSESSIVE—preoccupying, all-consuming
- OBSOLETE—no longer in use
- OBSTINATE—stubborn
- OBSTREPEROUS—troublesome, boisterous, unruly
- OBTRUSIVE—pushy, too conspicuous
- OBTUSE—insensitive, stupid, dull
- OBVIATE—to make unnecessary; to anticipate and prevent
- OCCLUDE—to shut, block
- ODIOUS—hateful, contemptible
- OFFICIOUS—too helpful, meddlesome
- OFFSHOOT—branch
- OMINOUS—menacing, threatening, indicating misfortune
- OMNIPOTENT—having unlimited power
- OMNISCIENT—having infinite knowledge
- OMNIVOROUS—eating everything; absorbing everything

- ONEROUS—burdensome
- ONTOLOGY—theory about the nature of existence
- OPALESCENT—iridescent, displaying colors
- OPAQUE—impervious to light; difficult to understand
- OPERATIVE—functioning, working
- OPINE—to express an opinion
- OPPORTUNE—appropriate, fitting
- OPPORTUNIST—one who takes advantage of circumstances
- OPPROBRIOUS—disgraceful, contemptuous
- OPULENCE—wealth
- ORACLE—person who foresees the future and gives advice
- ORATION—lecture, formal speech
- ORATOR—lecturer, speaker
- ORB—spherical body; eye
- ORCHESTRATE—to arrange music for performance; to coordinate, organize
- ORDAIN—to make someone a priest or minister; to order
- ORNITHOLOGIST—scientist who studies birds
- OSCILLATE—to move back and forth
- OSSIFY—to turn to bone; to become rigid
- OSTENSIBLE—apparent
- OSTENTATIOUS—showy
- OSTRACISM—exclusion, temporary banishment
- OUSTER—expulsion, ejection
- OVERSTATE—to embellish, exaggerate
- OVERTURE—musical introduction; proposal, offer
- OVERWROUGHT—agitated, overdone

P

- PACIFIC—calm, peaceful
- PACIFIST—one opposed to war
- PACIFY—to restore calm, bring peace
- PALATIAL—like a palace, magnificent
- PALAVER—idle talk
- PALEONTOLOGY—study of past geological eras through fossil remains
- PALETTE—board for mixing paints; range of colors
- PALISADE—fence made up of stakes
- PALL (n)—covering that darkens or obscures; coffin
- PALL (v)—to lose strength or interest
- PALLIATE—to make less serious, ease

- PALLID—lacking color or liveliness
- PALPABLE—obvious, real, tangible
- PALPITATION—trembling, shaking
- PALTRY—pitifully small or worthless
- PANACEA—cure-all
- PANACHE—flamboyance, verve
- PANDEMIC—spread over a whole area or country
- PANEGYRIC—elaborate praise; formal hymn of praise
- PANOPLY—impressive array
- PANORAMA—broad view; comprehensive picture
- PARADIGM—ideal example, model
- PARADOX—contradiction, incongruity; dilemma, puzzle
- PARADOXICAL—self-contradictory but true
- PARAGON—model of excellence or perfection
- PARAMOUNT—supreme, dominant, primary
- PARAPHRASE—to reword, usually in simpler terms
- PARASITE—person or animal that lives at another's expense
- PARCH—to dry or shrivel
- PARE—to trim
- PARIAH—outcast
- PARITY—equality
- PARLEY—discussion, usually between enemies
- PAROCHIAL—of limited scope or outlook, provincial
- PARODY—humorous imitation
- PAROLE—conditional release of a prisoner
- PARRY—to ward off or deflect
- PARSIMONY—stinginess
- PARTISAN (n)—strong supporter
- PARTISAN (adj)—biased in favor of
- PASTICHE—piece of literature or music imitating other works
- PATENT (adj)—obvious, unconcealed
- PATENT (n)—official document giving exclusive right to sell an invention
- PATERNITY—fatherhood; descent from father's ancestors
- PATHOGENIC—causing disease
- PATHOS—pity, compassion
- PATRICIAN—aristocrat
- PATRICIDE—murder of one's father
- PATRIMONY—inheritance or heritage derived from one's father

- PATRONIZE—to condescend to, disparage; to buy from
- PAUCITY—scarcity, lack
- PAUPER—very poor person
- PAVILION—tent or light building used for shelter or exhibitions
- PECCADILLO—minor sin or offense
- PECULATION—theft of money or goods
- PEDAGOGUE—teacher
- PEDANT—uninspired, boring academic
- PEDESTRIAN (adj)—commonplace
- PEDIATRICIAN—doctor specializing in children and their ailments
- PEDIMENT—triangular gable on a roof or facade
- PEER (n)—contemporary, equal, match
- PEERLESS—unequaled
- PEJORATIVE—having bad connotations; disparaging
- PELLUCID—transparent; translucent; easily understood
- PENANCE—voluntary suffering to repent for a wrong
- PENCHANT—inclination
- PENDING (adj)—not yet decided, awaiting decision
- PENITENT—expressing sorrow for sins or offenses, repentant
- PENSIVE—thoughtful
- PENULTIMATE—next to last
- PENUMBRA—partial shadow
- PENURY—extreme poverty
- PERAMBULATOR—baby carriage
- PERCIPIENT—discerning, able to perceive
- PERDITION—complete and utter loss; damnation
- PEREGRINATE—to wander from place to place
- PERENNIAL—present throughout the years; persistent
- PERFIDIOUS—faithless, disloyal, untrustworthy
- PERFUNCTORY—done in a routine way; indifferent
- PERIHELION—point in orbit nearest to the sun
- PERIPATETIC—moving from place to place
- PERJURE—to tell a lie under oath
- PERMEABLE—penetrable
- PERNICIOUS—very harmful
- PERPETUAL—endless, lasting

- PERSONIFICATION—act of attributing human qualities to objects or abstract qualities
- PERSPICACIOUS—shrewd, astute, keen-witted
- PERT—lively and bold
- PERTINACIOUS—persistent, stubborn
- PERTINENT—relevant, applicable
- PERTURBATION—disturbance
- PERUSAL—close examination
- PERVERT (v)—to cause to change in immoral way; to misuse
- PESTILENCE—epidemic, plague
- PETULANCE—rudeness, peevishness
- PHALANX—massed group of soldiers, people, or things
- PHILANDERER—pursuer of casual love affairs
- PHILANTHROPY—love of humanity; generosity to worthy causes
- PHILISTINE—narrow-minded person, someone lacking appreciation for art or culture
- PHILOLOGY—study of words
- PHLEGMATIC—calm in temperament; sluggish
- PHOBIA—anxiety, horror
- PHOENIX—mythical, immortal bird that lives for 500 years, burns itself to death, and rises from its ashes
- PHONETICS—study of speech sounds
- PHONIC—relating to sound
- PIETY—devoutness
- PILFER—to steal
- PILLAGE—to loot, especially during a war
- PINNACLE—peak, highest point of development
- PIOUS—dedicated, devout, extremely religious
- PIQUE—fleeting feeling of hurt pride
- PITHY—profound, substantial; concise, succinct, to the point
- PITTANCE—meager amount or wage
- PLACATE—to soothe or pacify
- PLACID—calm
- PLAGIARIST—one who steals words or ideas
- PLAINTIFF—injured person in a lawsuit
- PLAIT—to braid
- PLATITUDE—stale, overused expression
- PLEBEIAN—crude, vulgar, low-class
- PLENITUDE—abundance, plenty
- PLETHORA—excess, overabundance
- PLIANT—pliable, yielding

❑ PLUCK—to pull strings on musical instrument
❑ PLUCKY—courageous, spunky
❑ PLUMMET—to fall, plunge
❑ PLURALISTIC—including a variety of groups
❑ PLY (v)—to use diligently; to engage; to join together
❑ PNEUMATIC—relating to air; worked by compressed air
❑ POACH—to steal game or fish; cook in boiling liquid
❑ PODIUM—platform or lectern for orchestra conductors or speakers
❑ POIGNANT—emotionally moving
❑ POLAR—relating to a geographic pole; exhibiting contrast
❑ POLARIZE—to tend towards opposite extremes
❑ POLEMIC—controversy, argument; verbal attack
❑ POLITIC—discreet, tactful
❑ POLYGLOT—speaker of many languages
❑ PONDEROUS—weighty, heavy, large
❑ PONTIFICATE—to speak in a pretentious manner
❑ PORE (v)—to study closely or meditatively
❑ POROUS—full of holes, permeable to liquids
❑ PORTENT—omen
❑ PORTLY—stout, dignified
❑ POSIT—to put in position; to suggest an idea
❑ POSTERIOR—bottom, rear
❑ POSTERITY—future generations; all of a person's descendants
❑ POTABLE—drinkable
❑ POTENTATE—monarch or ruler with great power
❑ PRAGMATIC—practical; moved by facts rather than abstract ideals
❑ PRATTLE—meaningless, foolish talk
❑ PRECARIOUS—uncertain
❑ PRECEPT—principle; law
❑ PRECIPICE—edge, steep overhang
❑ PRECIPITATE (adj)—sudden and unexpected
❑ PRECIPITATE (v)—to throw down from a height; to cause to happen
❑ PRECIPITOUS—hasty, quickly, with too little caution
❑ PRÉCIS—short summary of facts
❑ PRECISION—state of being precise
❑ PRECLUDE—to rule out
❑ PRECOCIOUS—unusually advanced at an early age

❑ PRECURSOR—forerunner, predecessor
❑ PREDATOR—one that preys on others, destroyer, plunderer
❑ PREDICAMENT—difficult situation
❑ PREDICATE (v)—to found or base on
❑ PREDICTIVE—relating to prediction, indicative of the future
❑ PREDILECTION—preference, liking
❑ PREDISPOSITION—tendency, inclination
❑ PREEMINENT—celebrated, distinguished
❑ PREFACE—introduction to a book; introductory remarks to a speech
❑ PREMEDITATE—to consider, plan beforehand
❑ PREMONITION—forewarning; presentiment
❑ PREPONDERANCE—majority in number; dominance
❑ PREPOSSESSING—attractive, engaging, appealing
❑ PREPOSTEROUS—absurd, illogical
❑ PRESAGE—to foretell, indicate in advance
❑ PRESCIENT—having foresight
❑ PRESCRIBE—to set down a rule; to recommend a treatment
❑ PRESENTIMENT—premonition, sense of foreboding
❑ PRESTIDIGITATION—sleight of hand
❑ PRESUMPTUOUS—rude, improperly bold
❑ PRETEXT—excuse, pretended reason
❑ PREVALENT—widespread
❑ PREVARICATE—to lie, evade the truth
❑ PRIMEVAL—ancient, primitive
❑ PRIMORDIAL—original, existing from the beginning
❑ PRISTINE—untouched, uncorrupted
❑ PRIVATION—lack of usual necessities or comforts
❑ PROBITY—honesty, high-mindedness
❑ PROCLIVITY—tendency, inclination
❑ PROCRASTINATOR—one who continually and unjustifiably postpones
❑ PROCURE—to obtain
❑ PRODIGAL—wasteful, extravagant, lavish
❑ PRODIGIOUS—vast, enormous, extraordinary
❑ PROFANE—impure; contrary to religion; sacrilegious
❑ PROFICIENT—expert, skilled in a certain subject
❑ PROFLIGATE—corrupt, degenerate
❑ PROFUSE—lavish, extravagant
❑ PROGENITOR—originator, forefather, ancestor in a direct line

- PROGENY—offspring, children
- PROGNOSIS—prediction of disease outcome; any prediction
- PROGRESSIVE—favoring progress or change; moving forward, going step-by-step
- PROLIFERATION—propagation, reproduction; enlargement, expansion
- PROLIFIC—productive, fertile
- PROLOGUE—introductory section of a literary work or play
- PROMONTORY—piece of land or rock higher than its surroundings
- PROMULGATE—to make known publicly
- PROPENSITY—inclination, tendency
- PROPINQUITY—nearness
- PROPITIATE—to win over, appease
- PROPITIOUS—favorable, advantageous
- PROPONENT—advocate, defender, supporter
- PROSAIC—relating to prose; dull, commonplace
- PROSCRIBE—to condemn; to forbid, outlaw
- PROSE—ordinary language used in everyday speech
- PROSECUTOR—person who initiates a legal action or suit
- PROSELYTIZE—to convert to a particular belief or religion
- PROSTRATE—lying face downward, lying flat on ground
- PROTAGONIST—main character in a play or story, hero
- PROTEAN—readily assuming different forms or characters
- PROTESTATION—declaration
- PROTOCOL—ceremony and manners observed by diplomats
- PROTRACT—to prolong, draw out, extend
- PROTRUSION—something that sticks out
- PROVINCIAL—rustic, unsophisticated, limited in scope
- PROVOCATION—cause, incitement to act or respond
- PROWESS—bravery, skill
- PROXIMITY—nearness
- PROXY—power to act as a substitute for another
- PRUDE—one who is excessively proper or modest
- PRUDENT—careful, cautious
- PRURIENT—lustful, exhibiting lewd desires

- PRY—to intrude into; force open
- PSEUDONYM—pen name; fictitious or borrowed name
- PSYCHIC (adj)—perceptive of nonmaterial, spiritual forces
- PUERILE—childish, immature, silly
- PUDGY—chubby, overweight
- PUGILISM—boxing
- PUGNACIOUS—quarrelsome, eager, and ready to fight
- PULCHRITUDE—beauty
- PULVERIZE—to pound, crush, or grind into powder; destroy
- PUMMEL—to pound, beat
- PUNCTILIOUS—careful in observing rules of behavior or ceremony
- PUNGENT—strong or sharp in smell or taste
- PUNITIVE—having to do with punishment
- PURGATION—catharsis, purification
- PURGE—to cleanse or free from impurities
- PURITANICAL—adhering to a rigid moral code
- PURPORT—to profess, suppose, claim

Q

- QUACK—faker; one who falsely claims to have medical skill
- QUADRILATERAL—four-sided polygon
- QUADRUPED—animal having four feet
- QUAGMIRE—marsh; difficult situation
- QUALIFY—to provide with needed skills; modify, limit
- QUANDARY—dilemma, difficulty
- QUARANTINE—isolation period, originally 40 days, to prevent spread of disease
- QUATERNARY—consisting of or relating to four units or members
- QUELL—to crush or subdue
- QUERULOUS—inclined to complain, irritable
- QUERY (n)—question
- QUIBBLE—to argue about insignificant and irrelevant details
- QUICKEN (v)—to hasten, arouse, excite
- QUIESCENCE—inactivity, stillness
- QUINTESSENCE—most typical example; concentrated essence
- QUIVER—to shake slightly, tremble, vibrate
- QUIXOTIC—overly idealistic, impractical
- QUOTIDIAN—occurring daily; commonplace

R

- RACONTEUR—witty, skillful storyteller
- RADICAL—fundamental; drastic
- RAIL (v)—to scold with bitter or abusive language
- RALLY (v)—to assemble; recover, recuperate
- RAMBLE—to roam, wander; to babble, digress
- RAMIFICATION—an implication, outgrowth, or consequence
- RAMSHACKLE—likely to collapse
- RANCID—spoiled, rotten
- RANCOR—bitter hatred
- RANT—to harangue, rave, forcefully scold
- RAPPORT—relationship of trust and respect
- RAPT—deeply absorbed
- RAREFY—to make thinner, purer, or more refined
- RASH (adj)—careless, hasty, reckless
- RATIFY—to approve formally, confirm
- RATIOCINATION—methodical, logical reasoning
- RATION (n)—portion, share
- RATION (v)—to supply; to restrict consumption of
- RATIONAL—logical, reasonable
- RAUCOUS—harsh-sounding; boisterous
- RAVAGE—to destroy, devastate
- RAVENOUS—extremely hungry
- RAVINE—deep, narrow gorge
- RAZE—to tear down, demolish
- REACTIONARY—marked by extreme conservatism, especially in politics
- REBUFF (n)—blunt rejection
- REBUKE—to reprimand, scold
- REBUT—to refute by evidence or argument
- RECALCITRANT—resisting authority or control
- RECANT—to retract a statement, opinion, etc.
- RECAPITULATE—to review by a brief summary
- RECEPTIVE—open to others' ideas; congenial
- RECLUSIVE—shut off from the world
- RECONDITE—relating to obscure learning; known to only a few
- RECOUNT—to describe facts or events
- RECRUIT (v)—to draft, enlist; to seek to enroll
- RECTIFY—to correct
- RECTITUDE—moral uprightness
- RECURRENCE—repetition
- REDRESS—relief from wrong or injury
- REDUNDANCY—unnecessary repetition
- REFECTORY—room where meals are served
- REFLECTION—image, likeness; opinion, thought, impression
- REFORM—to change, correct
- REFRACT—to deflect sound or light
- REFUGE—escape, shelter
- REFURBISH—to renovate
- REFUTE—to contradict, discredit
- REGIMEN—government rule; systematic plan
- REGRESS—to move backward; revert to an earlier form or state
- REHABILITATE—to restore to good health or condition; reestablish a person's good reputation
- REITERATE—to say or do again, repeat
- REJOINDER—response
- REJUVENATE—to make young again; renew
- RELEGATE—to assign to a class, especially an inferior one
- RELINQUISH—to renounce or surrender something
- RELISH (v)—to enjoy greatly
- REMEDIABLE—capable of being corrected
- REMEDY (v)—to cure, correct
- REMINISCENCE—remembrance of past events
- REMISSION—lessening, relaxation
- REMIT—to send (usually money) as payment
- REMOTE—distant, isolated
- REMUNERATION—pay or reward for work, trouble, etc.
- RENASCENT—reborn, coming into being again
- RENEGE—to go back on one's word
- RENEGADE—traitor, person abandoning a cause
- RENOUNCE—to give up or reject a right, title, person, etc.
- RENOWN—fame, widespread acclaim
- REPAST—meal or mealtime
- REPEAL—to revoke or formally withdraw (often a law)
- REPEL—to rebuff, repulse; disgust, offend
- REPENT—to regret a past action
- REPENTANT—apologetic, guilty, remorseful
- REPLETE—abundantly supplied
- REPLICATE—to duplicate, repeat
- REPOSE—relaxation, leisure
- REPRESS—to restrain or hold in
- REPRESSION—act of restraining or holding in
- REPREHENSIBLE—blameworthy, disreputable

❑ REPRISE—repetition, especially of a piece of music

❑ REPROACH—to find fault with; blame

❑ REPROBATE—morally unprincipled person

❑ REPROVE—to criticize or correct

❑ REPUDIATE—to reject as having no authority

❑ REPULSE—repel, fend off; sicken, disgust

❑ REQUIEM—hymns or religious service for the dead

❑ REQUITE—to return or repay

❑ RESCIND—to repeal, cancel

❑ RESIDUE—remainder, leftover, remnant

❑ RESILIENT—able to recover quickly after illness or bad luck; able to bounce back to shape

❑ RESOLUTE—determined; with a clear purpose

❑ RESOLVE (n)—determination, firmness of purpose

❑ RESOLVE (v)—to conclude, determine

❑ RESONATE—to echo

❑ RESPIRE—to breathe

❑ RESPITE—interval of relief

❑ RESPLENDENT—splendid, brilliant

❑ RESTITUTION—act of compensating for loss or damage

❑ RESTIVE—impatient, uneasy, restless

❑ RESTORATIVE—having the power to renew or revitalize

❑ RESTRAINED—controlled, repressed, restricted

❑ RESUSCITATE—to revive, bring back to life

❑ RETAIN—to hold, keep possession of

❑ RETARD (v)—to slow, hold back

❑ RETICENT—not speaking freely; reserved

❑ RETINUE—group of attendants with an important person

❑ RETIRING—shy, modest, reserved

❑ RETORT—cutting response

❑ RETRACT—to draw in or take back

❑ RETRENCH—to regroup, reorganize

❑ RETRIEVE—to bring, fetch; reclaim

❑ RETROACTIVE—applying to an earlier time

❑ RETROGRADE—having a backward motion or direction

❑ RETROSPECTIVE—review of the past

❑ REVELRY—boisterous festivity

❑ REVERE—to worship, regard with awe

❑ REVERT—to backslide, regress

❑ REVILE—to criticize with harsh language, verbally abuse

❑ REVITALIZE—to renew; reenergize

❑ REVOKE—to annul, cancel, call back

❑ REVULSION—strong feeling of repugnance or dislike

❑ RHAPSODY—emotional literary or musical work

❑ RHETORIC—persuasive use of language

❑ RHYTHM—regular pattern or variation of sounds and stresses

❑ RIBALD—humorous in a vulgar way

❑ RIDDLE (v)—to make many holes in; permeate

❑ RIFE—widespread, prevalent; abundant

❑ RISQUÉ—bordering on being inappropriate or indecent

❑ ROBUST—strong and healthy; hardy

❑ ROCOCO—very highly ornamented

❑ ROOT (v)—to dig with a snout (like a pig)

❑ ROSTRUM—stage for public speaking

❑ ROTUND—round in shape; fat

❑ RUE—to regret

❑ RUMINATE—to contemplate, reflect upon

❑ RUSTIC—rural

S

❑ SACCHARINE—excessively sweet or sentimental

❑ SACROSANCT—extremely sacred; beyond criticism

❑ SAGACIOUS—shrewd

❑ SALIENT—prominent or conspicuous

❑ SALLOW—sickly yellow in color

❑ SALUBRIOUS—healthful

❑ SALUTATION—greeting

❑ SANCTION—permission, support; law; penalty

❑ SANCTUARY—haven, retreat

❑ SANGUINE—ruddy; cheerfully optimistic

❑ SARDONIC—cynical, scornfully mocking

❑ SATIATE—to satisfy

❑ SAUNTER—to amble; walk in a leisurely manner

❑ SAVANT—learned person

❑ SAVORY—agreeable in taste or smell

❑ SCABBARD—sheath for sword or dagger

❑ SCALE (v)—to climb to the top of

❑ SCATHING—harshly critical; painfully hot

❑ SCENARIO—plot outline; possible situation

❑ SCINTILLA—trace amount

❑ SCINTILLATE—to sparkle, flash

❑ SCOFF—to deride, ridicule

❑ SCORE (n)—notation for a musical composition

❑ SCORE (v)—to make a notch or scratch

- SCRIVENER—professional copyist
- SCRUPULOUS—restrained; careful and precise
- SCRUTINY—careful observation
- SCURRILOUS—vulgar, low, indecent
- SECANT—straight line intersecting a curve at two points
- SECEDE—to withdraw formally from an organization
- SECLUDED—isolated and remote
- SECTARIAN—narrow-minded; relating to a group or sect
- SECULAR—not specifically pertaining to religion
- SEDENTARY—inactive, stationary; sluggish
- SEDITION—behavior promoting rebellion
- SEISMOLOGY—science of earthquakes
- SEMINAL—relating to the beginning or seeds of something
- SENESCENT—aging, growing old
- SENSUAL—satisfying or gratifying the senses; suggesting sexuality
- SENTENTIOUS—having a moralizing tone
- SENTIENT—aware, conscious, able to perceive
- SEQUEL—anything that follows
- SEQUESTER—to remove or set apart; put into seclusion
- SERAPHIC—angelic, pure, sublime
- SERENDIPITY—habit of making fortunate discoveries by chance
- SERENITY—calm, peacefulness
- SERPENTINE—serpentlike; twisting, winding
- SERRATED—saw-toothed, notched
- SERVILE—submissive, obedient
- SHARD—piece of broken glass or pottery
- SHEEPISH—timid, meek, or bashful
- SHIRK—to avoid a task due to laziness or fear
- SIGNIFY—denote, indicate; symbolize
- SIMIAN—apelike; relating to apes
- SIMPER—to smirk, smile foolishly
- SINECURE—well-paying job or office that requires little or no work
- SINGE—to burn slightly, scorch
- SINUOUS—winding; intricate, complex
- SKEPTICAL—doubtful, questioning
- SKULK—to move in a stealthy or cautious manner; sneak
- SLIGHT—to treat as unimportant; insult
- SLIPSHOD—careless, hasty
- SLOTH—sluggishness, laziness
- SLOUGH—to discard or shed
- SLOVENLY—untidy, messy
- SLUGGARD—lazy, inactive person
- SMELT (v)—to melt metal so as to refine it
- SNIPPET—tiny part, tidbit
- SOBRIETY—seriousness
- SOBRIQUET—nickname
- SODDEN—thoroughly soaked; saturated
- SOJOURN—visit, stay
- SOLACE—comfort in distress; consolation
- SOLARIUM—room or glassed-in area exposed to the sun
- SOLECISM—grammatical mistake
- SOLICITOUS—concerned, attentive; eager
- SOLIDARITY—unity based on common aims or interests
- SOLILOQUY—literary or dramatic speech by one character, not addressed to others
- SOLIPSISM—belief that the self is the only reality
- SOLSTICE—shortest and longest day of the year
- SOLUBLE—capable of being solved or dissolved
- SOMBER—dark and gloomy; melancholy, dismal
- SOMNAMBULIST—sleepwalker
- SOMNOLENT—drowsy, sleepy; inducing sleep
- SONIC—relating to sound
- SONOROUS—producing a full, rich sound
- SOPHIST—person good at arguing deviously
- SOPHISTRY—deceptive reasoning or argumentation
- SOPHOMORIC—immature and overconfident
- SOPORIFIC—sleepy or tending to cause sleep
- SORDID—filthy; contemptible and corrupt
- SOVEREIGN—having supreme power
- SPARTAN—austere, severe, grave; simple, bare
- SPAWN—to generate, produce
- SPECULATION—contemplation; act of taking business risks for financial gain
- SPECULATIVE—involving assumption; uncertain; theoretical
- SPONTANEOUS—on the spur of the moment, impulsive
- SPORADIC—infrequent, irregular
- SPORTIVE—frolicsome, playful
- SPRIGHTLY—lively, animated, energetic
- SPUR (v)—to prod
- SPURIOUS—lacking authenticity; counterfeit, false

- ❑ SPURN—to reject or refuse contemptuously; scorn
- ❑ SQUALID—filthy; morally repulsive
- ❑ SQUANDER—to waste
- ❑ STACCATO—marked by abrupt, clear-cut sounds
- ❑ STAGNANT—immobile, stale
- ❑ STAID—self-restrained to the point of dullness
- ❑ STAND (n)—group of trees
- ❑ STALK (v)—to hunt, pursue
- ❑ STARK—bare, empty, vacant
- ❑ STASIS—motionless state; standstill
- ❑ STIFLE—to smother or suffocate; suppress
- ❑ STIGMA—mark of disgrace or inferiority
- ❑ STILTED—stiff, unnatural
- ❑ STINT (n)—period of time spent doing something
- ❑ STINT (v)—to be sparing or frugal
- ❑ STIPEND—allowance; fixed amount of money paid regularly
- ❑ STOCKADE—enclosed area forming defensive wall
- ❑ STOIC—indifferent to or unaffected by emotions
- ❑ STOLID—having or showing little emotion
- ❑ STRATAGEM—trick designed to deceive an enemy
- ❑ STRATIFY—to arrange into layers
- ❑ STRICTURE—something that restrains; negative criticism
- ❑ STRIDENT—loud, harsh, unpleasantly noisy
- ❑ STRINGENT—imposing severe, rigorous standards
- ❑ STULTIFY—to impair or reduce to uselessness
- ❑ STUNTED—having arrested growth or development
- ❑ STUPEFY—to dull the senses of; stun, astonish
- ❑ STYLIZE—to fashion, formalize
- ❑ STYMIE—to block or thwart
- ❑ SUAVE—smoothly gracious or polite; blandly ingratiating
- ❑ SUBDUED—suppressed, stifled
- ❑ SUBJECTION—dependence, obedience, submission
- ❑ SUBJUGATE—to conquer, subdue; enslave
- ❑ SUBLIME—awe-inspiring; of high spiritual or moral value
- ❑ SUBLIMINAL—subconscious; imperceptible
- ❑ SUBMISSIVE—tending to be meek and submit
- ❑ SUBPOENA—notice ordering someone to appear in court
- ❑ SUBSEQUENT—following in time or order
- ❑ SUBTERFUGE—trick or tactic used to avoid something
- ❑ SUBTERRANEAN—hidden, secret; underground
- ❑ SUBTLE—hard to detect or describe; perceptive
- ❑ SUBVERT—to undermine or corrupt
- ❑ SUCCINCT—terse, brief, concise
- ❑ SUCCULENT—juicy; full of vitality or freshness
- ❑ SUFFERABLE—bearable
- ❑ SUFFRAGIST—one who advocates extended voting rights
- ❑ SULLEN—brooding, gloomy
- ❑ SULLY—to soil, stain, tarnish; taint
- ❑ SUMPTUOUS—lavish, splendid
- ❑ SUPERANNUATED—too old, obsolete, outdated
- ❑ SUPERCILIOUS—arrogant, haughty, overbearing, condescending
- ❑ SUPERFLUOUS—extra, more than necessary
- ❑ SUPERSEDE—to take the place of; replace
- ❑ SUPERVISE—to direct or oversee the work of others
- ❑ SUPPLANT—replace, substitute
- ❑ SUPPLE—flexible, pliant
- ❑ SUPPLICANT—one who asks humbly and earnestly
- ❑ SURFEIT—excessive amount
- ❑ SURLY—rude and bad-tempered
- ❑ SURMISE—to make an educated guess
- ❑ SURMOUNT—to conquer, overcome
- ❑ SURPASS—to do better than, be superior to
- ❑ SUPERFICIAL—hasty; shallow and phony
- ❑ SURPLUS—excess
- ❑ SURREPTITIOUS—characterized by secrecy
- ❑ SURVEY (v)—to examine in a comprehensive way
- ❑ SUSCEPTIBLE—vulnerable, unprotected
- ❑ SUSPEND—to defer, interrupt; dangle, hang
- ❑ SUSTAIN—support, uphold; endure, undergo
- ❑ SWARTHY—having a dark complexion
- ❑ SYBARITE—person devoted to pleasure and luxury
- ❑ SYCOPHANT—self-serving flatterer, yes-man
- ❑ SYLLABUS—outline of a course
- ❑ SYMBIOSIS—cooperation, mutual helpfulness
- ❑ SYMPOSIUM—meeting with short presentations on related topics

- SYNCOPATION—temporary irregularity in musical rhythm
- SYNOPSIS—plot summary
- SYNTHESIS—blend, combination
- SYNTHETIC—artificial, imitation

T

- TABLEAU—vivid description, striking incident or scene
- TACIT—silently understood or implied
- TACITURN—uncommunicative, not inclined to speak much
- TACTILE—relating to the sense of touch
- TAINT—to spoil or infect; to stain honor
- TAINTED—stained, tarnished; corrupted, poisoned
- TALON—claw of an animal, especially a bird of prey
- TANG—sharp flavor or odor
- TANGENTIAL—digressing, diverting
- TANGIBLE—able to be sensed; perceptible, measurable
- TANTAMOUNT—equivalent in value or significance; amounting to
- TARNISHED—corroded, discolored; discredited, disgraced
- TAWDRY—gaudy, cheap, showy
- TAXONOMY—science of classification
- TECHNOCRAT—strong believer in technology; technical expert
- TEMPERANCE—restraint, self-control, moderation
- TEMPERED—moderated, restrained
- TEMPESTUOUS—stormy, raging, furious
- TENABLE—defensible, reasonable
- TENACIOUS—stubborn, holding firm
- TENET—belief, doctrine
- TENSILE—capable of withstanding physical stress
- TENUOUS—weak, insubstantial
- TEPID—lukewarm; showing little enthusiasm
- TERMINAL (adj)—concluding, final; fatal
- TERMINAL (n)—depot, station
- TERRESTRIAL—earthly; down-to-earth, commonplace
- TERSE—concise, brief, free of extra words
- TESTAMENT—statement of belief; will
- TESTIMONIAL—statement testifying to a truth; something given in tribute to a person's achievement
- TETHER—to bind, tie
- THEOCRACY—government by priests representing a god
- THEOLOGY—study of God and religion
- THEORETICAL—abstract
- THERAPEUTIC—medicinal
- THESAURUS—book of synonyms and antonyms
- THESIS—theory or hypothesis; dissertation or long, written composition
- THWART—to block or prevent from happening; frustrate
- TIDINGS—news
- TIMOROUS—timid, shy, full of apprehension
- TINGE—to color slightly; slight amount
- TIRADE—long violent speech; verbal assault
- TITAN—person of colossal stature or achievement
- TOADY—flatterer, hanger-on, yes-man
- TOLERANCE—capacity to respect different values; capacity to endure or resist something
- TOME—book, usually large and academic
- TONAL—relating to pitch or sound
- TOPOGRAPHY—art of making maps or charts
- TORPID—lethargic; unable to move; dormant
- TORRID—burning hot; passionate
- TORSION—act of twisting and turning
- TORTUOUS—having many twists and turns; highly complex
- TOTTERING—barely standing
- TOXIN—poison
- TRACTABLE—obedient, yielding
- TRANSCEND—to rise above, go beyond
- TRANSCENDENT—rising above, going beyond
- TRANSCRIPTION—copy, reproduction; record
- TRANSGRESS—to trespass, violate a law
- TRANSIENT—temporary, short-lived, fleeting
- TRANSITORY—short-lived, existing only briefly
- TRANSLUCENT—partially transparent
- TRANSMUTE—to change in appearance or shape
- TRANSPIRE—to happen, occur; become known
- TRAVESTY—parody, exaggerated imitation, caricature
- TREMULOUS—trembling, quivering; fearful, timid
- TRENCHANT—acute, sharp, incisive; forceful, effective
- TREPIDATION—fear and anxiety

- TRIFLING—of slight worth, trivial, insignificant
- TRITE—shallow, superficial
- TROUNCE—to beat severely, defeat
- TROUPE—group of actors
- TRUNCATE—to cut off, shorten by cutting
- TRYING—difficult to deal with
- TRYST—agreement between lovers to meet; rendezvous
- TUMULT—state of confusion; agitation
- TUNDRA—treeless plain found in arctic or subarctic regions
- TURBULENCE—commotion, disorder
- TURGID—swollen, bloated
- TURPITUDE—inherent vileness, foulness, depravity
- TYRO—beginner, novice

U

- UBIQUITOUS—being everywhere simultaneously
- UMBRAGE—offense, resentment
- UNADULTERATED—absolutely pure
- UNANIMITY—state of total agreement or unity
- UNAPPEALING—unattractive, unpleasant
- UNAVAILING—hopeless, useless
- UNCONSCIONABLE—unscrupulous; shockingly unfair or unjust
- UNCTUOUS—greasy, oily; smug and falsely earnest
- UNDERMINE—to sabotage, thwart
- UNDOCUMENTED—not certified, unsubstantiated
- UNDULATING—moving in waves
- UNEQUIVOCAL—absolute, certain
- UNFROCK—to strip of priestly duties
- UNHERALDED—unannounced, unexpected, not publicized
- UNIDIMENSIONAL—having one size or dimension, flat
- UNIFORM (adj)—consistent and unchanging; identical
- UNIMPEACHABLE—beyond question
- UNINITIATED—not familiar with an area of study
- UNKEMPT—uncombed, messy in appearance
- UNOBTRUSIVE—modest, unassuming
- UNSCRUPULOUS—dishonest
- UNSOLICITED—unrequested
- UNWARRANTED—groundless, unjustified
- UNWITTING—unconscious; unintentional

- UNYIELDING—firm, resolute
- UPBRAID—to scold sharply
- UPROARIOUS—loud and forceful
- URBANE—courteous, refined, suave
- USURP—to seize by force
- USURY—practice of lending money at exorbitant rates
- UTILITARIAN—efficient, functional, useful
- UTOPIA—perfect place

V

- VACILLATE—to waver, show indecision
- VACUOUS—empty, void; lacking intelligence, purposeless
- VAGRANT—poor person with no home
- VALIDATE—to authorize, certify, confirm
- VANQUISH—to conquer, defeat
- VAPID—tasteless, dull
- VARIABLE—changeable, inconstant
- VARIEGATED—varied; marked with different colors
- VAUNTED—boasted about, bragged about
- VEHEMENTLY—strongly, urgently
- VENDETTA—prolonged feud marked by bitter hostility
- VENERABLE—respected because of age
- VENERATION—adoration, honor, respect
- VENT—to express, say out loud
- VERACIOUS—truthful, accurate
- VERACITY—accuracy, truth
- VERBATIM—word for word
- VERBOSE—wordy
- VERDANT—green with vegetation; inexperienced
- VERDURE—fresh, rich vegetation
- VERIFIED—proven true
- VERISIMILITUDE—quality of appearing true or real
- VERITY—truthfulness; belief viewed as true and enduring
- VERMIN—small creatures offensive to humans
- VERNACULAR—everyday language used by ordinary people; specialized language of a profession
- VERNAL—related to spring
- VERSATILE—adaptable, all-purpose
- VESTIGE—trace, remnant
- VETO—to reject formally
- VEX—to irritate, annoy; confuse, puzzle
- VIABLE—workable, able to succeed or grow

- ❑ VIADUCT—series of elevated arches used to cross a valley
- ❑ VICARIOUS—substitute, surrogate; enjoyed through imagined participation in another's experience
- ❑ VICISSITUDE—change or variation; ups and downs
- ❑ VIE—to compete, contend
- ❑ VIGILANT—attentive, watchful
- ❑ VIGNETTE—decorative design; short literary composition
- ❑ VILIFY—to slander, defame
- ❑ VIM—energy, enthusiasm
- ❑ VINDICATE—to clear of blame; support a claim
- ❑ VINDICATION—clearance from blame or suspicion
- ❑ VINDICTIVE—spiteful, vengeful, unforgiving
- ❑ VIRILE—manly, having qualities of an adult male
- ❑ VIRTUOSO—someone with masterly skill; expert musician
- ❑ VIRULENT—extremely poisonous; malignant; hateful
- ❑ VISCOUS—thick, syrupy, and sticky
- ❑ VITRIOLIC—burning, caustic; sharp, bitter
- ❑ VITUPERATE—to abuse verbally
- ❑ VIVACIOUS—lively, spirited
- ❑ VIVID—bright and intense in color; strongly perceived
- ❑ VOCIFEROUS—loud, vocal, and noisy
- ❑ VOID (adj)—not legally enforceable; empty
- ❑ VOID (n)—emptiness, vacuum
- ❑ VOID (v)—to cancel, invalidate
- ❑ VOLITION—free choice, free will; act of choosing
- ❑ VOLLEY (n)—flight of missiles, round of gunshots
- ❑ VOLUBLE—speaking much and easily, talkative; glib
- ❑ VOLUMINOUS—large, having great volume
- ❑ VORACIOUS—having a great appetite
- ❑ VULNERABLE—defenseless, unprotected; innocent, naive

W

- ❑ WAIVE—to refrain from enforcing a rule; to give up a legal right
- ❑ WALLOW—to indulge oneself excessively, luxuriate
- ❑ WAN—sickly pale
- ❑ WANTON—undisciplined, unrestrained, reckless
- ❑ WARRANTY—guarantee of a product's soundness
- ❑ WARY—careful, cautious
- ❑ WAYWARD—erratic, unrestrained, reckless
- ❑ WEATHER (v)—to endure, undergo
- ❑ WHET—to sharpen, stimulate
- ❑ WHIMSY—playful or fanciful idea
- ❑ WILY—clever, deceptive
- ❑ WINDFALL—sudden, unexpected good fortune
- ❑ WINSOME—charming, happily engaging
- ❑ WITHDRAWN—unsociable, aloof; shy, timid
- ❑ WIZENED—withered, shriveled, wrinkled
- ❑ WRIT—written document, usually in law
- ❑ WRY—amusing, ironic

X

- ❑ XENOPHOBIA—fear or hatred of foreigners or strangers

Y

- ❑ YOKE (v)—to join together

Z

- ❑ ZEALOT—someone passionately devoted to a cause
- ❑ ZENITH—highest point, summit
- ❑ ZEPHYR—gentle breeze
- ❑ ZOOLOGIST—scientist who studies animals

SAT Root List

A

- **A, AN**—not, without
  amoral, atrophy, asymmetrical, anarchy, anesthetic, anonymity, anomaly
- **AB, A**—from, away, apart
  abnormal, abdicate, aberration, abhor, abject, abjure, ablution, abnegate, abortive, abrogate, abscond, absolve, abstemious, abstruse, annul, avert, aversion
- **AC, ACR**—sharp, sour
  acid, acerbic, exacerbate, acute, acuity, acumen, acrid, acrimony
- **AD, A**—to, toward
  adhere, adjacent, adjunct, admonish, adroit, adumbrate, advent, abeyance, abet, accede, accretion, acquiesce, affluent, aggrandize, aggregate, alleviate, alliteration, allude, allure, ascribe, aspersion, aspire, assail, assonance, attest
- **ALI, ALTR**—another
  alias, alienate, inalienable, altruism
- **AM, AMI**—love
  amorous, amicable, amiable, amity
- **AMBI, AMPHI**—both
  ambiguous, ambivalent, ambidextrous, amphibious
- **AMBL, AMBUL**—walk
  amble, ambulatory, perambulator, somnambulist
- **ANIM**—mind, spirit, breath
  animal, animosity, unanimous, magnanimous
- **ANN, ENN**—year
  annual, annuity, superannuated, biennial, perennial
- **ANTE, ANT**—before
  antecedent, antediluvian, antebellum, antepenultimate, anterior, antiquity, antiquated, anticipate
- **ANTHROP**—human
  anthropology, anthropomorphic, misanthrope, philanthropy
- **ANTI, ANT**—against, opposite
  antidote, antipathy, antithesis, antacid, antagonist, antonym
- **AUD**—hear
  audio, audience, audition, auditory, audible
- **AUTO**—self
  autobiography, autocrat, autonomous

B

- **BELLI, BELL**—war
  belligerent, bellicose, antebellum, rebellion
- **BENE, BEN**—good
  benevolent, benefactor, beneficent, benign
- **BI**—two
  bicycle, bisect, bilateral, bilingual, biped
- **BIBLIO**—book
  Bible, bibliography, bibliophile
- **BIO**—life
  biography, biology, amphibious, symbiotic, macrobiotics
- **BURS**—money, purse
  reimburse, disburse, bursar

C

- **CAD, CAS, CID**—happen, fall
  accident, cadence, cascade, deciduous
- **CAP, CIP**—head
  captain, decapitate, capitulate, precipitous, precipitate
- **CARN**—flesh
  carnal, carnage, carnival, carnivorous, incarnate
- **CAP, CAPT, CEPT, CIP**—take, hold, seize
  capable, capacious, recapitulate, captivate, deception, intercept, precept, inception, anticipate, emancipation, incipient, percipient
- **CED, CESS**—yield, go
  cease, cessation, incessant, cede, precede, accede, recede, antecedent, intercede, secede, cession
- **CHROM**—color
  chrome, chromatic, monochrome
- **CHRON**—time
  chronology, chronic, anachronism
- **CIDE**—murder
  suicide, homicide, regicide, patricide
- **CIRCUM**—around
  circumference, circumlocution, circumnavigate, circumscribe, circumspect, circumvent
- **CLIN, CLIV**—slope
  incline, declivity, proclivity
- **CLUD, CLUS, CLAUS, CLOIS**—shut, close
  conclude, reclusive, claustrophobia, cloister, preclude, occlude
- **CO, COM, CON**—with, together
  coeducation, coagulate, coalesce, coerce, cogent, cognate, collateral, colloquial, colloquy,

commensurate, commodious, compassion, compatriot, complacent, compliant, complicity, compunction, concerto, conciliatory, concord, concur, condone, conflagration, congeal, congenial, congenital, conglomerate, conjure, conjugal, conscientious, consecrate, consensus, consonant, constrained, contentious, contrite, contusion, convalescence, convene, convivial, convoke, convoluted, congress

❑ COGN, GNO—know
recognize, cognition, cognizance, incognito, diagnosis, agnostic, prognosis, gnostic, ignorant

❑ CONTRA—against
controversy, incontrovertible, contravene

❑ CORP—body
corpse, corporeal, corpulence

❑ COSMO, COSM—world
cosmopolitan, cosmos, microcosm, macrocosm

❑ CRAC, CRAT—rule, power
democracy, bureaucracy, theocracy, autocrat, aristocrat, technocrat

❑ CRED—trust, believe
incredible, credulous, credence

❑ CRESC, CRET—grow
crescent, crescendo, accretion

❑ CULP—blame, fault
culprit, culpable, inculpate, exculpate

❑ CURR, CURS—run
current, concur, cursory, precursor, incursion

D

❑ DE—down, out, apart
depart, debase, debilitate, declivity, decry, deface, defamatory, defunct, delegate, demarcation, demean, demur, deplete, deplore, depravity, deprecate, deride, derivative, desist, detest, devoid

❑ DEC—ten, tenth
decade, decimal, decathlon, decimate

❑ DEMO, DEM—people
democrat, demographics, demagogue, epidemic, pandemic, endemic

❑ DI, DIURN—day
diary, diurnal, quotidian

❑ DIA—across
diagonal, diatribe, diaphanous

❑ DIC, DICT—speak
diction, interdict, predict, abdicate, indict, verdict

❑ DIS, DIF, DI—not, apart, away

disaffected, disband, disbar, disburse, discern, discordant, discredit, discursive, disheveled, disparage, disparate, dispassionate, dispirit, dissemble, disseminate, dissension, dissipate, dissonant, dissuade, distend, differentiate, diffidence, diffuse, digress, divert

❑ DOC, DOCT—teach
doctrine, docile, doctrinaire

❑ DOL—pain
condolence, doleful, dolorous, indolent

❑ DUC, DUCT—lead
seduce, induce, conduct, viaduct, induct

E

❑ EGO—self
ego, egoist, egocentric

❑ EN, EM—in, into
enter, entice, encumber, endemic, ensconce, enthrall, entreat, embellish, embezzle, embroil, empathy

❑ ERR—wander
erratic, aberration, errant

❑ EU—well, good
eulogy, euphemism, euphony, euphoria, eurythmics, euthanasia

❑ EX, E—out, out of
exit, exacerbate, excerpt, excommunicate, exculpate, execrable, exhume, exonerate, exorbitant, exorcise, expatriate, expedient, expiate, expunge, expurgate, extenuate, extort, extremity, extricate, extrinsic, exult, evoke, evict, evince, elicit, egress, egregious

F

❑ FAC, FIC, FECT, FY, FEA—make, do
factory, facility, benefactor, malefactor, fiction, fictive, beneficent, affect, confection, refectory, magnify, unify, rectify, vilify, feasible

❑ FAL, FALS—deceive
false, infallible, fallacious

❑ FERV—boil
fervent, fervid, effervescent

❑ FID—faith, trust
confident, diffidence, perfidious, fidelity

❑ FLU, FLUX—flow
fluent, flux, affluent, confluence, effluvia, superfluous

❑ FORE—before
forecast, foreboding, forestall

❑ FRAG, FRAC—break
fragment, fracture, diffract, fractious, refract

❏ FUS—pour
profuse, infusion, effusive, diffuse

G

❏ GEN—birth, class, kin
generation, congenital, homogeneous,
heterogeneous, ingenious, engender,
progenitor, progeny
❏ GRAD, GRESS—step
graduate, gradual, retrograde, centigrade,
degrade, gradation, gradient, progress,
congress, digress, transgress, ingress, egress
❏ GRAPH, GRAM—writing
biography, bibliography, epigraph, grammar,
epigram
❏ GRAT—pleasing
grateful, gratitude, gratis, ingrate,
congratulate, gratuitous, gratuity
❏ GRAV, GRIEV—heavy
grave, gravity, aggravate, grieve, aggrieve,
grievous
❏ GREG—crowd, flock
segregate, gregarious, egregious, congregate,
aggregate

H

❏ HABIT, HIBIT—have, hold
habit, inhibit, cohabit, habitat
❏ HAP—by chance
happen, haphazard, hapless, mishap
❏ HELIO, HELI—sun
heliocentric, helium, heliotrope, aphelion,
perihelion
❏ HETERO—other
heterosexual, heterogeneous, heterodox
❏ HOL—whole
holocaust, catholic, holistic
❏ HOMO—same
homosexual, homogenize, homogeneous,
homonym
❏ HOMO—man
homo sapiens, homicide, bonhomie
❏ HYDR—water
hydrant, hydrate, dehydration
❏ HYPER—too much, excess
hyperactive, hyperbole, hyperventilate
❏ HYPO—too little, under
hypodermic, hypothermia, hypochondria,
hypothesis, hypothetical

I

❏ IN, IG, IL, IM, IR—not
incorrigible, indefatigable, indelible,
indubitable, inept, inert, inexorable, insatiable,
insentient, insolvent, insomnia, interminable,
intractable, incessant, inextricable, infallible,
infamy, innumerable, inoperable, insipid,
intemperate, intrepid, inviolable, ignorant,
ignominious, ignoble, illicit, illimitable,
immaculate, immutable, impasse, impeccable,
impecunious, impertinent, implacable,
impotent, impregnable, improvident,
impassioned, impervious, irregular
❏ IN, IL, IM, IR—in, on, into
infusion, ingress, innate, inquest, inscribe,
insinuate, inter, illustrate, imbue, immerse,
implicate, irrigate, irritate, invade, inaugurate,
incandescent, incarcerate, incense, indenture,
induct, ingratiate, introvert, incarnate,
inception, incisive, infer
❏ INTER—between, among
intercede, intercept, interdiction, interject,
interlocutor, interloper, intermediary,
intermittent, interpolate, interpose,
interregnum, interrogate, intersect, intervene
❏ INTRA, INTR—within
intrastate, intravenous, intramural, intrinsic
❏ IT, ITER—between, among
transit, itinerant, reiterate, transitory

J

❏ JECT, JET—throw
eject, interject, abject, trajectory, jettison
❏ JOUR—day
journal, adjourn, sojourn
❏ JUD—judge
judge, judicious, prejudice, adjudicate
❏ JUNCT, JUG—join
junction, adjunct, injunction, conjugal,
subjugate
❏ JUR—swear, law
jury, abjure, adjure, conjure, perjure,
jurisprudence

L

❏ LAT—side
lateral, collateral, unilateral, bilateral,
quadrilateral
❏ LAV, LAU, LU—wash
lavatory, laundry, ablution, antediluvian

- ❑ LEG, LEC, LEX—read, speak
  legible, lecture, lexicon
- ❑ LEV—light
  elevate, levitate, levity, alleviate
- ❑ LIBER—free
  liberty, liberal, libertarian, libertine
- ❑ LIG, LECT—choose, gather
  eligible, elect, select
- ❑ LIG, LI, LY—bind
  ligament, oblige, religion, liable, liaison, lien, ally
- ❑ LING, LANG—tongue
  lingo, language, linguistics, bilingual
- ❑ LITER—letter
  literate, alliteration, literal
- ❑ LITH—stone
  monolith, lithograph, megalith
- ❑ LOQU, LOC, LOG—speech, thought
  eloquent, loquacious, colloquial, colloquy, soliloquy, circumlocution, interlocutor, monologue, dialogue, eulogy, philology, neologism
- ❑ LUC, LUM—light
  lucid, illuminate, elucidate, pellucid, translucent
- ❑ LUD, LUS—play
  ludicrous, allude, delusion, allusion, illusory

M

- ❑ MACRO—great
  macrocosm, macrobiotics
- ❑ MAG, MAJ, MAS, MAX—great
  magnify, majesty, master, maximum, magnanimous, magnate, magnitude
- ❑ MAL—bad
  malady, maladroit, malevolent, malodorous
- ❑ MAN—hand
  manual, manuscript, emancipate, manifest
- ❑ MAR—sea
  submarine, marine, maritime
- ❑ MATER, MATR—mother
  maternal, matron, matrilineal
- ❑ MEDI—middle
  intermediary, medieval, mediate
- ❑ MEGA—great
  megaphone, megalomania, megaton, megalith
- ❑ MEM, MEN—remember
  memory, memento, memorabilia, reminisce
- ❑ METER, METR, MENS—measure
  meter, thermometer, perimeter, metronome, commensurate

- ❑ MICRO—small
  microscope, microorganism, microcosm, microbe
- ❑ MIS—wrong, bad, hate
  misunderstand, misanthrope, misapprehension, misconstrue, misnomer, mishap
- ❑ MIT, MISS—send
  transmit, emit, missive
- ❑ MOLL—soft
  mollify, emollient, mollusk
- ❑ MON, MONIT—warn
  admonish, monitor, premonition
- ❑ MONO—one
  monologue, monotonous, monogamy, monolith, monochrome
- ❑ MOR—custom, manner
  moral, mores, morose
- ❑ MOR, MORT—dead
  morbid, moribund, mortal, amortize
- ❑ MORPH—shape
  amorphous, anthropomorphic, metamorphosis, morphology
- ❑ MOV, MOT, MOB, MOM—move
  remove, motion, mobile, momentum, momentous
- ❑ MUT—change
  mutate, mutability, immutable, commute

N

- ❑ NAT, NASC—born
  native, nativity, natal, neonate, innate, cognate, nascent, renascent, renaissance
- ❑ NAU, NAV—ship, sailor
  nautical, nauseous, navy, circumnavigate
- ❑ NEG—not, deny
  negative, abnegate, renege
- ❑ NEO—new
  neoclassical, neophyte, neologism, neonate
- ❑ NIHIL—none, nothing
  annihilation, nihilism
- ❑ NOM, NYM—name
  nominate, nomenclature, nominal, cognomen, misnomer, ignominious, antonym, homonym, pseudonym, synonym, anonymity
- ❑ NOX, NIC, NEC, NOC—harm
  obnoxious, noxious, pernicious, internecine, innocuous
- ❑ NOV—new
  novelty, innovation, novitiate
- ❑ NUMER—number
  numeral, numerous, innumerable, enumerate

O

- ❑ OB—against
  obstruct, obdurate, obfuscate, obnoxious, obsequious, obstinate, obstreperous, obtrusive
- ❑ OMNI—all
  omnipresent, omnipotent, omniscient, omnivorous
- ❑ ONER—burden
  onerous, onus, exonerate
- ❑ OPER—work
  operate, cooperate, inoperable

P

- ❑ PAC—peace
  pacify, pacifist, pacific
- ❑ PALP—feel
  palpable, palpitation
- ❑ PAN—all
  panorama, panacea, panegyric, pandemic, panoply
- ❑ PATER, PATR—father
  paternal, paternity, patriot, compatriot, expatriate, patrimony, patricide, patrician
- ❑ PATH, PASS—feel, suffer
  sympathy, antipathy, empathy, apathy, pathos, impassioned
- ❑ PEC—money
  pecuniary, impecunious, peculation
- ❑ PED, POD—foot
  pedestrian, pediment, expedient, biped, quadruped, tripod
- ❑ PEL, PULS—drive
  compel, compelling, expel, propel, compulsion
- ❑ PEN—almost
  peninsula, penultimate, penumbra
- ❑ PEND, PENS—hang
  pendant, pendulous, compendium, suspense, propensity
- ❑ PER—through, by, for, throughout
  perambulator, percipient, perfunctory, permeable, perspicacious, pertinacious, perturbation, perusal, perennial, peregrinate
- ❑ PER—against, destruction
  perfidious, pernicious, perjure
- ❑ PERI—around
  perimeter, periphery, perihelion, peripatetic
- ❑ PET—seek, go toward
  petition, impetus, impetuous, petulant, centripetal
- ❑ PHIL—love
  philosopher, philanderer, philanthropy, bibliophile, philology

- ❑ PHOB—fear
  phobia, claustrophobia, xenophobia
- ❑ PHON—sound
  phonograph, megaphone, euphony, phonetics, phonics
- ❑ PLAC—calm, please
  placate, implacable, placid, complacent
- ❑ PON, POS—put, place
  postpone, proponent, exponent, preposition, posit, interpose, juxtaposition, depose
- ❑ PORT—carry
  portable, deportment, rapport
- ❑ POT—drink
  potion, potable
- ❑ POT—power
  potential, potent, impotent, potentate, omnipotence
- ❑ PRE—before
  precede, precipitate, preclude, precocious, precursor, predilection, predisposition, preponderance, prepossessing, presage, prescient, prejudice, predict, premonition, preposition
- ❑ PRIM, PRI—first
  prime, primary, primal, primeval, primordial, pristine
- ❑ PRO—ahead, forth
  proceed, proclivity, procrastinator, profane, profuse, progenitor, progeny, prognosis, prologue, promontory, propel, proponent, propose, proscribe, protestation, provoke
- ❑ PROTO—first
  prototype, protagonist, protocol
- ❑ PROX, PROP—near
  approximate, propinquity, proximity
- ❑ PSEUDO—false
  pseudoscientific, pseudonym
- ❑ PYR—fire
  pyre, pyrotechnics, pyromania

Q

- ❑ QUAD, QUAR, QUAT—four
  quadrilateral, quadrant, quadruped, quarter, quarantine, quaternary
- ❑ QUES, QUER, QUIS, QUIR—question
  quest, inquest, query, querulous, inquisitive, inquiry
- ❑ QUIE—quiet
  disquiet, acquiesce, quiescent, requiem
- ❑ QUINT, QUIN—five
  quintuplets, quintessence

R

- ❏ RADI, RAMI—branch
  radius, radiate, radiant, eradicate, ramification
- ❏ RECT, REG—straight, rule
  rectangle, rectitude, rectify, regular
- ❏ REG—king, rule
  regal, regent, interregnum
- ❏ RETRO—backward
  retrospective, retroactive, retrograde
- ❏ RID, RIS—laugh
  ridiculous, deride, derision
- ❏ ROG—ask
  interrogate, derogatory, abrogate, arrogate, arrogant
- ❏ RUD—rough, crude
  rude, erudite, rudimentary
- ❏ RUPT—break
  disrupt, interrupt, rupture

S

- ❏ SACR, SANCT—holy
  sacred, sacrilege, consecrate, sanctify, sanction, sacrosanct
- ❏ SCRIB, SCRIPT, SCRIV—write
  scribe, ascribe, circumscribe, inscribe, proscribe, script, manuscript, scrivener
- ❏ SE—apart, away
  separate, segregate, secede, sedition
- ❏ SEC, SECT, SEG—cut
  sector, dissect, bisect, intersect, segment, secant
- ❏ SED, SID—sit
  sedate, sedentary, supersede, reside, residence, assiduous, insidious
- ❏ SEM—seed, sow
  seminar, seminal, disseminate
- ❏ SEN—old
  senior, senile, senescent
- ❏ SENT, SENS—feel, think
  sentiment, nonsense, assent, sentient, consensus, sensual
- ❏ SEQU, SECU—follow
  sequence, sequel, subsequent, obsequious, obsequy, non sequitur, consecutive
- ❏ SIM, SEM—similar, same
  similar, semblance, dissemble, verisimilitude
- ❏ SIGN—mark, sign
  signal, designation, assignation
- ❏ SIN—curve
  sine curve, sinuous, insinuate
- ❏ SOL—sun
  solar, parasol, solarium, solstice

- ❏ SOL—alone
  solo, solitude, soliloquy, solipsism
- ❏ SOMN—sleep
  insomnia, somnolent, somnambulist
- ❏ SON—sound
  sonic, consonance, dissonance, assonance, sonorous, resonate
- ❏ SOPH—wisdom
  philosopher, sophistry, sophisticated, sophomoric
- ❏ SPEC, SPIC—see, look
  spectator, circumspect, retrospective, perspective, perspicacious
- ❏ SPER—hope
  prosper, prosperous, despair, desperate
- ❏ SPERS, SPAR—scatter
  disperse, sparse, aspersion, disparate
- ❏ SPIR—breathe
  respire, inspire, spiritual, aspire, transpire
- ❏ STRICT, STRING—bind
  strict, stricture, constrict, stringent, astringent
- ❏ STRUCT, STRU—build
  structure, construe, obstruct
- ❏ SUB—under
  subconscious, subjugate, subliminal, subpoena, subsequent, subterranean, subvert
- ❏ SUMM—highest
  summit, summary, consummate
- ❏ SUPER, SUR—above
  supervise, supercilious, supersede, superannuated, superfluous, insurmountable, surfeit
- ❏ SURGE, SURRECT—rise
  surge, resurgent, insurgent, insurrection
- ❏ SYN, SYM—together
  synthesis, sympathy, synonym, syncopation, synopsis, symposium, symbiosis

T

- ❏ TACIT, TIC—silent
  tacit, taciturn, reticent
- ❏ TACT, TAG, TANG—touch
  tact, tactile, contagious, tangent, tangential, tangible
- ❏ TEN, TIN, TAIN—hold, twist
  detention, tenable, tenacious, pertinacious, retinue, retain
- ❏ TEND, TENS, TENT—stretch
  intend, distend, tension, tensile, ostensible, contentious

- ❑ TERM—end
  terminal, terminus, terminate, interminable
- ❑ TERR—earth, land
  terrain, terrestrial, extraterrestrial, subterranean
- ❑ TEST—witness
  testify, attest, testimonial, testament, detest, protestation
- ❑ THE—god
  atheist, theology, apotheosis, theocracy
- ❑ THERM—heat
  thermometer, thermal, thermonuclear, hypothermia
- ❑ TIM—fear, frightened
  timid, intimidate, timorous
- ❑ TOP—place
  topic, topography, utopia
- ❑ TORT—twist
  distort, extort, tortuous
- ❑ TORP—stiff, numb
  torpedo, torpid, torpor
- ❑ TOX—poison
  toxic, toxin, intoxication
- ❑ TRACT—draw
  tractor, intractable, protract
- ❑ TRANS—across, over, through, beyond
  transport, transgress, transient, transitory, translucent, transmutation
- ❑ TREM, TREP—shake
  tremble, tremor, tremulous, trepidation, intrepid
- ❑ TURB—shake
  disturb, turbulent, perturbation

U

- ❑ UMBR—shadow
  umbrella, umbrage, adumbrate, penumbra
- ❑ UNI, UN—one
  unify, unilateral, unanimous
- ❑ URB—city
  urban, suburban, urbane

V

- ❑ VAC—empty
  vacant, evacuate, vacuous
- ❑ VAL, VAIL—value, strength
  valid, valor, ambivalent, convalescence, avail, prevail, countervail
- ❑ VEN, VENT—come
  convene, contravene, intervene, venue, convention, circumvent, advent, adventitious
- ❑ VER—true
  verify, verity, verisimilitude, veracious, aver, verdict
- ❑ VERB—word
  verbal, verbose, verbiage, verbatim
- ❑ VERT, VERS—turn
  avert, convert, pervert, revert, incontrovertible, divert, subvert, versatile, aversion
- ❑ VICT, VINC—conquer
  victory, conviction, evict, evince, invincible
- ❑ VID, VIS—see
  evident, vision, visage, supervise
- ❑ VIL—base, mean
  vile, vilify, revile
- ❑ VIV, VIT—life
  vivid, vital, convivial, vivacious
- ❑ VOC, VOK, VOW—call, voice
  vocal, equivocate, vociferous, convoke, evoke, invoke, avow
- ❑ VOL—wish
  voluntary, malevolent, benevolent, volition
- ❑ VOLV, VOLUT—turn, roll
  revolve, evolve, convoluted
- ❑ VOR—eat
  devour, carnivore, omnivorous, voracious

KAPLAN

PRACTICE TESTS

PRACTICE TEST A

Before taking this practice test, find a quiet room where you can work uninterrupted for 90 minutes. Make sure you have a comfortable desk and several #2 pencils.

Use the answer sheet on the following page to record your answers. (You can tear it out or photocopy it.)

Once you start this practice test, don't stop until you've finished. Remember—you can review any questions within a section, but you may not go back or forward a section.

Good luck.

ANSWER SHEET

Start with number 1 for each new section. If a section has fewer questions than answer spaces, leave the extra spaces blank.

SECTION 1

1 Ⓐ Ⓑ Ⓒ Ⓓ Ⓔ	11 Ⓐ Ⓑ Ⓒ Ⓓ Ⓔ	21 Ⓐ Ⓑ Ⓒ Ⓓ Ⓔ	31 Ⓐ Ⓑ Ⓒ Ⓓ Ⓔ
2 Ⓐ Ⓑ Ⓒ Ⓓ Ⓔ	12 Ⓐ Ⓑ Ⓒ Ⓓ Ⓔ	22 Ⓐ Ⓑ Ⓒ Ⓓ Ⓔ	32 Ⓐ Ⓑ Ⓒ Ⓓ Ⓔ
3 Ⓐ Ⓑ Ⓒ Ⓓ Ⓔ	13 Ⓐ Ⓑ Ⓒ Ⓓ Ⓔ	23 Ⓐ Ⓑ Ⓒ Ⓓ Ⓔ	33 Ⓐ Ⓑ Ⓒ Ⓓ Ⓔ
4 Ⓐ Ⓑ Ⓒ Ⓓ Ⓔ	14 Ⓐ Ⓑ Ⓒ Ⓓ Ⓔ	24 Ⓐ Ⓑ Ⓒ Ⓓ Ⓔ	34 Ⓐ Ⓑ Ⓒ Ⓓ Ⓔ
5 Ⓐ Ⓑ Ⓒ Ⓓ Ⓔ	15 Ⓐ Ⓑ Ⓒ Ⓓ Ⓔ	25 Ⓐ Ⓑ Ⓒ Ⓓ Ⓔ	35 Ⓐ Ⓑ Ⓒ Ⓓ Ⓔ
6 Ⓐ Ⓑ Ⓒ Ⓓ Ⓔ	16 Ⓐ Ⓑ Ⓒ Ⓓ Ⓔ	26 Ⓐ Ⓑ Ⓒ Ⓓ Ⓔ	36 Ⓐ Ⓑ Ⓒ Ⓓ Ⓔ
7 Ⓐ Ⓑ Ⓒ Ⓓ Ⓔ	17 Ⓐ Ⓑ Ⓒ Ⓓ Ⓔ	27 Ⓐ Ⓑ Ⓒ Ⓓ Ⓔ	37 Ⓐ Ⓑ Ⓒ Ⓓ Ⓔ
8 Ⓐ Ⓑ Ⓒ Ⓓ Ⓔ	18 Ⓐ Ⓑ Ⓒ Ⓓ Ⓔ	28 Ⓐ Ⓑ Ⓒ Ⓓ Ⓔ	38 Ⓐ Ⓑ Ⓒ Ⓓ Ⓔ
9 Ⓐ Ⓑ Ⓒ Ⓓ Ⓔ	19 Ⓐ Ⓑ Ⓒ Ⓓ Ⓔ	29 Ⓐ Ⓑ Ⓒ Ⓓ Ⓔ	39 Ⓐ Ⓑ Ⓒ Ⓓ Ⓔ
10 Ⓐ Ⓑ Ⓒ Ⓓ Ⓔ	20 Ⓐ Ⓑ Ⓒ Ⓓ Ⓔ	30 Ⓐ Ⓑ Ⓒ Ⓓ Ⓔ	40 Ⓐ Ⓑ Ⓒ Ⓓ Ⓔ

right in section 1

wrong in section 1

SECTION 2

1 Ⓐ Ⓑ Ⓒ Ⓓ Ⓔ	11 Ⓐ Ⓑ Ⓒ Ⓓ Ⓔ	21 Ⓐ Ⓑ Ⓒ Ⓓ Ⓔ	31 Ⓐ Ⓑ Ⓒ Ⓓ Ⓔ
2 Ⓐ Ⓑ Ⓒ Ⓓ Ⓔ	12 Ⓐ Ⓑ Ⓒ Ⓓ Ⓔ	22 Ⓐ Ⓑ Ⓒ Ⓓ Ⓔ	32 Ⓐ Ⓑ Ⓒ Ⓓ Ⓔ
3 Ⓐ Ⓑ Ⓒ Ⓓ Ⓔ	13 Ⓐ Ⓑ Ⓒ Ⓓ Ⓔ	23 Ⓐ Ⓑ Ⓒ Ⓓ Ⓔ	33 Ⓐ Ⓑ Ⓒ Ⓓ Ⓔ
4 Ⓐ Ⓑ Ⓒ Ⓓ Ⓔ	14 Ⓐ Ⓑ Ⓒ Ⓓ Ⓔ	24 Ⓐ Ⓑ Ⓒ Ⓓ Ⓔ	34 Ⓐ Ⓑ Ⓒ Ⓓ Ⓔ
5 Ⓐ Ⓑ Ⓒ Ⓓ Ⓔ	15 Ⓐ Ⓑ Ⓒ Ⓓ Ⓔ	25 Ⓐ Ⓑ Ⓒ Ⓓ Ⓔ	35 Ⓐ Ⓑ Ⓒ Ⓓ Ⓔ
6 Ⓐ Ⓑ Ⓒ Ⓓ Ⓔ	16 Ⓐ Ⓑ Ⓒ Ⓓ Ⓔ	26 Ⓐ Ⓑ Ⓒ Ⓓ Ⓔ	36 Ⓐ Ⓑ Ⓒ Ⓓ Ⓔ
7 Ⓐ Ⓑ Ⓒ Ⓓ Ⓔ	17 Ⓐ Ⓑ Ⓒ Ⓓ Ⓔ	27 Ⓐ Ⓑ Ⓒ Ⓓ Ⓔ	37 Ⓐ Ⓑ Ⓒ Ⓓ Ⓔ
8 Ⓐ Ⓑ Ⓒ Ⓓ Ⓔ	18 Ⓐ Ⓑ Ⓒ Ⓓ Ⓔ	28 Ⓐ Ⓑ Ⓒ Ⓓ Ⓔ	38 Ⓐ Ⓑ Ⓒ Ⓓ Ⓔ
9 Ⓐ Ⓑ Ⓒ Ⓓ Ⓔ	19 Ⓐ Ⓑ Ⓒ Ⓓ Ⓔ	29 Ⓐ Ⓑ Ⓒ Ⓓ Ⓔ	39 Ⓐ Ⓑ Ⓒ Ⓓ Ⓔ
10 Ⓐ Ⓑ Ⓒ Ⓓ Ⓔ	20 Ⓐ Ⓑ Ⓒ Ⓓ Ⓔ	30 Ⓐ Ⓑ Ⓒ Ⓓ Ⓔ	40 Ⓐ Ⓑ Ⓒ Ⓓ Ⓔ

right in section 2

wrong in section 2

SECTION 3

1 Ⓐ Ⓑ Ⓒ Ⓓ Ⓔ	11 Ⓐ Ⓑ Ⓒ Ⓓ Ⓔ	21 Ⓐ Ⓑ Ⓒ Ⓓ Ⓔ	31 Ⓐ Ⓑ Ⓒ Ⓓ Ⓔ
2 Ⓐ Ⓑ Ⓒ Ⓓ Ⓔ	12 Ⓐ Ⓑ Ⓒ Ⓓ Ⓔ	22 Ⓐ Ⓑ Ⓒ Ⓓ Ⓔ	32 Ⓐ Ⓑ Ⓒ Ⓓ Ⓔ
3 Ⓐ Ⓑ Ⓒ Ⓓ Ⓔ	13 Ⓐ Ⓑ Ⓒ Ⓓ Ⓔ	23 Ⓐ Ⓑ Ⓒ Ⓓ Ⓔ	33 Ⓐ Ⓑ Ⓒ Ⓓ Ⓔ
4 Ⓐ Ⓑ Ⓒ Ⓓ Ⓔ	14 Ⓐ Ⓑ Ⓒ Ⓓ Ⓔ	24 Ⓐ Ⓑ Ⓒ Ⓓ Ⓔ	34 Ⓐ Ⓑ Ⓒ Ⓓ Ⓔ
5 Ⓐ Ⓑ Ⓒ Ⓓ Ⓔ	15 Ⓐ Ⓑ Ⓒ Ⓓ Ⓔ	25 Ⓐ Ⓑ Ⓒ Ⓓ Ⓔ	35 Ⓐ Ⓑ Ⓒ Ⓓ Ⓔ
6 Ⓐ Ⓑ Ⓒ Ⓓ Ⓔ	16 Ⓐ Ⓑ Ⓒ Ⓓ Ⓔ	26 Ⓐ Ⓑ Ⓒ Ⓓ Ⓔ	36 Ⓐ Ⓑ Ⓒ Ⓓ Ⓔ
7 Ⓐ Ⓑ Ⓒ Ⓓ Ⓔ	17 Ⓐ Ⓑ Ⓒ Ⓓ Ⓔ	27 Ⓐ Ⓑ Ⓒ Ⓓ Ⓔ	37 Ⓐ Ⓑ Ⓒ Ⓓ Ⓔ
8 Ⓐ Ⓑ Ⓒ Ⓓ Ⓔ	18 Ⓐ Ⓑ Ⓒ Ⓓ Ⓔ	28 Ⓐ Ⓑ Ⓒ Ⓓ Ⓔ	38 Ⓐ Ⓑ Ⓒ Ⓓ Ⓔ
9 Ⓐ Ⓑ Ⓒ Ⓓ Ⓔ	19 Ⓐ Ⓑ Ⓒ Ⓓ Ⓔ	29 Ⓐ Ⓑ Ⓒ Ⓓ Ⓔ	39 Ⓐ Ⓑ Ⓒ Ⓓ Ⓔ
10 Ⓐ Ⓑ Ⓒ Ⓓ Ⓔ	20 Ⓐ Ⓑ Ⓒ Ⓓ Ⓔ	30 Ⓐ Ⓑ Ⓒ Ⓓ Ⓔ	40 Ⓐ Ⓑ Ⓒ Ⓓ Ⓔ

right in section 3

wrong in section 3

Use the answer key following the test to count up the number of questions you got right and the number you got wrong. (Remember not to count omitted questions as wrong.) The "Compute Your Score" section at the back of the book will show you how to find your score.

For each of the following questions, choose the best answer and darken the corresponding oval on the answer sheet.

Select the lettered word or set of words that best completes the sentence.

Example:
Today's small, portable computers contrast markedly with the earliest electronic computers, which were ----.
(A) effective
(B) invented
(C) useful
(D) destructive
(E) enormous   Ⓐ Ⓑ Ⓒ Ⓓ ⬤

---

1 Most of those polled stated that they would vote to reelect their legislators; this response showed the public was ---- a change in leadership.
(A) partial to
(B) wary of
(C) inured to
(D) confident of
(E) receptive to

2 Mountain lions are very ---- creatures, able to run at high speed and capable of climbing any tree.
(A) agile
(B) passive
(C) capricious
(D) attentive
(E) dominant

3 Although organic farming is more labor intensive and thus initially quite ----, it may be less expensive in the long term than conventional farming.
(A) nutritious
(B) tasteful
(C) restrained
(D) costly
(E) arduous

4 Diego Rivera was one of the most ---- painters of the modern Mexican mural movement, ---- a generation of young artists with his bold, dramatic forms.
(A) famous . . displacing
(B) convoluted . . attracting
(C) antagonistic . . prompting
(D) influential . . inspiring
(E) observant . . thwarting

5 Although the Druids, an ancient Celtic priestly class, were ----, they preferred to use ---- teaching methods to educate the young.
(A) uneducated . . illegible
(B) enduring . . intelligent
(C) earnest . . unexceptional
(D) religious . . haphazard
(E) literate . . oral

6 Emphysema, a chronic lung disease, can occur in either a localized or ---- form.
(A) a contained
(B) an acute
(C) a restricted
(D) a diffuse
(E) a fatal

7 Famed for her ---- opposition to the consumption of alcohol, Carrie Nation used a hatchet to demolish barrooms in turn-of-the-century Kansas.
(A) characteristic
(B) feeble
(C) adamant
(D) perfunctory
(E) docile

8 Even though her friends described Becky as amiable and frank, she was really a very --- and ---- woman.
(A) dependable . . unfriendly
(B) rude . . calculating
(C) gregarious . . insignificant
(D) entertaining . . antagonistic
(E) frugal . . mysterious

9 Despite much educated ----, there remains no ---- relationship between sunspot cycles and the Earth's weather.
(A) argument . . decisive
(B) confusion . . clear
(C) conjecture . . proven
(D) evidence . . tenuous
(E) disagreement . . systematic

GO ON TO THE NEXT PAGE   183

Choose the lettered pair of words that is related in the same way as the pair in capital letters.

Example:
FLAKE : SNOW ::
(A)   storm : hail
(B)   drop : rain
(C)   field : wheat
(D)   stack : hay
(E)   cloud : fog

10 HOOF : HORSE ::
(A) lion : mane
(B) paw : cat
(C) pace : foot
(D) bicycle : rider
(E) dog : prairie

11 EMERALD : GEMSTONE ::
(A) hydrogen : gas
(B) granite : marble
(C) hue : tint
(D) diamond : ring
(E) iron : tool

12 LETTER : POSTSCRIPT ::
(A) manuscript : book
(B) address : envelope
(C) garden : plant
(D) building : addition
(E) landscape : house

13 SHIP : DOCK ::
(A) car : park
(B) wheel : steer
(C) horse : ride
(D) raft : float
(E) truck : drive

14 GROUCH : ILL-HUMOR ::
(A) creditor : bankruptcy
(B) chauffeur : speed
(C) official : arrogance
(D) writer : wit
(E) scholar : studiousness

15 LIMP : FIRMNESS ::
(A) sinful : weakness
(B) deep : thickness
(C) silky : softness
(D) old : dryness
(E) polished : roughness

GO ON TO THE NEXT PAGE

Answer the questions below based on the information in the accompanying passages.

Questions 16–24 are based on the following passage.

The following passage was written in 1992 by France Bequette, a writer who specializes in environmental issues.

The ozone layer, the fragile layer of gas surrounding our planet between 7 and 30 miles above the Earth's surface, is being rapidly depleted.
Line Seasonally occurring holes have appeared in it over
(5) the Poles and, recently, over densely populated temperate regions of the northern hemisphere. The threat is serious because the ozone layer protects the Earth from the sun's ultraviolet radiation, which is harmful to all living organisms.
(10) Even though the layer is many miles thick, the atmosphere in it is tenuous and the total amount of ozone, compared with other atmospheric gases, is small. Ozone is highly reactive to chlorine, hydrogen, and nitrogen. Of these chlorine is the
(15) most dangerous since it is very stable and long-lived. When chlorine compounds reach the stratosphere, they bond with and destroy ozone molecules, with consequent repercussions for life on Earth.
(20) In 1958, researchers began noticing seasonal variations in the ozone layer above the South Pole. Between June and October the ozone content steadily fell, followed by a sudden increase in November. These fluctuations appeared to result from the nat-
(25) ural effects of wind and temperature. But while the low October levels remained constant until 1979, the total ozone content over the Pole was steadily diminishing. In 1985, public opinion was finally roused by reports of a "hole" in the layer.
(30) The culprits responsible for the hole were identified as compounds known as chlorofluorocarbons, or CFCs. CFCs are compounds of chlorine and fluorine. Nonflammable, nontoxic and noncorrosive, they have been widely used in industry since the
(35) 1950s, mostly as refrigerants and propellants and in making plastic foam and insulation.
In 1989 CFCs represented a sizeable market valued at over $1.5 billion and a labor force of 1.6 million. But with CFCs implicated in ozone depletion,
(40) the question arose as to whether we were willing to risk an increase in cases of skin cancer, eye ailments, even a lowering of the human immune defense system—all effects of further loss of the ozone layer. And not only humans would suffer. So would plant
(45) life. Phytoplankton, the first link in the ocean food chain and vital to the survival of most marine species, would not be able to survive near the ocean surface, which is where these organisms grow.

In 1990, 70 countries agreed to stop producing
(50) CFCs by the year 2000. In late 1991, however, scientists noticed a depletion of the ozone layer over the Arctic. In 1992 it was announced that the layer was depleting faster than expected and that it was also declining over the northern hemisphere. Scientists
(55) believe that natural events are making the problem worse. The Pinatubo volcano in the Philippines, which erupted in June 1991, released 12 million tons of damaging volcanic gases into the atmosphere.
Even if the whole world agreed today to stop all
(60) production and use of CFCs, this would not solve the problem. A single chlorine molecule can destroy 10,000–100,000 molecules of ozone. Furthermore, CFCs have a lifespan of 75–400 years and they take ten years to reach the ozone layer. In other words,
(65) what we are experiencing today results from CFCs emitted ten years ago.
Researchers are working hard to find substitute products. Some are too dangerous because they are highly flammable; others may prove to be toxic and
(70) to contribute to the greenhouse effect—to the process of global warming. Nevertheless, even if there is no denying that the atmosphere is in a state of disturbance, nobody can say that the situation will not improve, either in the short or the long
(75) term, especially if we ourselves lend a hand.

---

16 As it is described in the passage, the major function of the ozone layer is closest to that of
   (A) an emergency evacuation plan for a skyscraper
   (B) a central information desk at a convention center
   (C) a traffic light at a busy intersection
   (D) the structural support for a suspension bridge
   (E) the filtering system for a city water supply

17 The word *tenuous* in line 11 most nearly means
   (A) doubtful
   (B) tense
   (C) clear
   (D) thin
   (E) hazy

18 The passage implies which of the following about the "seasonal variations in the ozone layer" (lines 20–21) observed by scientists in 1958?
(A) They were caused by industrial substances other than CFCs.
(B) They created alarm among scientists but not the public.
(C) They were least stable in the months between June and November.
(D) They opened the public's eye to the threat of ozone depletion.
(E) They focused attention on the dangers posed by CFCs.

19 In context, the word *constant* in line 26 means
(A) gentle
(B) steady
(C) pestering
(D) unerring
(E) considerable

20 The author mentions market and workforce figures related to CFC production in lines 37–39 in order to point out that
(A) responsibility for the problem of ozone depletion lies primarily with industry
(B) the disadvantages of CFCs are obvious while the benefits are not
(C) the magnitude of profits from CFCs has turned public opinion against the industry's practices
(D) while the economic stakes are large, they are overshadowed by the effects of CFCs
(E) curbing the use of CFCs will lead to a crippling loss of jobs worldwide

21 In paragraph six, the author cites the evidence of changes in the ozone layer over the northern hemisphere to indicate that
(A) the dangers of ozone depletion appear to be intensifying
(B) ozone depletion is posing an immediate threat to many marine species
(C) scientists are unsure about the ultimate effects of ozone loss on plants
(D) CFCs are not the primary cause of ozone depletion in such areas
(E) ozone levels are beginning to stabilize at the poles

22 Scientists apparently believe which of the following about the "volcanic gases" mentioned in lines 56–58?
(A) They contribute more to global warming than to ozone loss.
(B) They pose a greater long-term threat than CFCs.
(C) They are hastening ozone loss at present.
(D) They are of little long-term consequence.
(E) They contain molecules that are less destructive of ozone than CFCs.

23 The author's reference to the long life of chlorine molecules (lines 62–64) is meant to show that
(A) CFCs are adaptable to a variety of industrial uses
(B) there is more than adequate time to develop a long-term strategy against ozone loss
(C) the long-term effects of ozone loss on human health may never be known
(D) it is doubtful that normal levels of ozone can ever be reestablished
(E) the positive effects of actions taken against ozone loss will be gradual

24 In the final paragraph, the author tries to emphasize that
(A) researchers are unlikely to find effective substitutes for CFCs
(B) human action can alleviate the decline of the ozone layer
(C) people must to learn to live with the damaging effects of industrial pollutants
(D) people have more control over ozone depletion than over the greenhouse effect
(E) atmospheric conditions are largely beyond human control

KAPLAN

GO ON TO THE NEXT PAGE

Questions 25–30 are based on the following passage.

In this excerpt from a short story, the narrator describes an afternoon visit to the farm of Mrs. Hight and her daughter, Esther. The narrator is accompanied on her visit by William, a fisherman.

Mrs. Hight, like myself, was tired and thirsty. I brought a drink of water, and remembered some fruit that was left from my lunch. She revived vigorously, and told me the
Line history of her later years since she had been been struck in
(5) the prime of her life by a paralyzing stroke, and her husband had died and left her with Esther and a mortgage on their farm. There was only one field of good land, but they owned a large area of pasture and some woodland. Esther had always been laughed at for her belief in sheep-raising
(10) when one by one their neighbors were giving up their flocks. When everything had come to the point of despair she had raised some money and bought all the sheep she could, insisting that Maine lambs were as good as any, and that there was a straight path by sea to the Boston market.
(15) By tending her flock herself she had managed to succeed; she had paid off the mortgage five years ago, and now what they did not spend was in the bank. "It has been stubborn work, day and night, summer and winter, and now she's beginning to get along in years," said the old
(20) mother. "She's tended me along with the sheep, and she's been good right along, but she should have been a teacher."
We heard voices, and William and Esther entered; they did not know that it was so late in the afternoon. William
(25) looked almost bold, like a young man rather than an ancient boy. As for Esther, she might have been Joan of Arc returned to her sheep*, touched with age and gray. My heart was moved by the sight of her face, weather-worn and gentle, her thin figure in its close dress, and the strong
(30) hand that clasped a shepherd's staff, and I could only hold William in new awe; this silent fisherman who alone knew the heart that beat within her. I am not sure that they acknowledged even to themselves that they had always been lovers. Esther was untouched by the fret and fury of
(35) life; she had lived in sunshine and rain among her sheep and been refined instead of coarsened, while her patience with an angry old mother, stung by defeat and mourning her lost activities, had given back a self-possession and habit of sweet temper. I had seen enough of Mrs. Hight to
(40) know that nothing a sheep might do could vex a person who was used to the severities of her companionship.

*Joan of Arc (1412–31): a young shepherdess who led the French army against the English during the Hundred Years' War.

25 The main purpose of the passage is to
(A) suggest some of the essential attributes of a character
(B) speculate about a romantic link between two people
(C) show that people's lives are determined by events beyond their control
(D) identify the major causes of Mrs. Hight's unhappiness
(E) recount an incident that changed the narrator's life

26 Mrs. Hight's description of Esther's sheep-raising efforts (lines 8–14) reveals her daughter's
(A) desire to succeed no matter what the cost
(B) humility and grace in accepting defeat
(C) considerable regard for her neighbors' opinions
(D) calm determination in meeting difficulties
(E) dogged refusal to admit a mistake

27 In lines 32–34, the narrator speculates that Esther and William may be
(A) resigned to being permanently separated from one another
(B) apprehensive about each other's true feelings
(C) impatient to make a formal commitment to one another
(D) ambivalent in their regard for one another
(E) unaware of the extent of their attachment

28 The narrator is most impressed with Esther's
(A) aloofness and reserve
(B) serenity and devotion
(C) lively sense of humor
(D) stubborn pride
(E) material success

29 Lines 34–41 are meant to convey Mrs. Hight's
(A) strength in the face of adversity
(B) inability to carry on a conversation
(C) dissatisfaction with her life
(D) distrust of her neighbors
(E) ingratitude toward her daughter

30 The "person" referred to in line 40 is
(A) the narrator
(B) William
(C) Esther
(D) Mrs. Hight
(E) Mrs. Hight's husband

STOP IF YOU FINISH BEFORE TIME IS CALLED, YOU MAY CHECK YOUR WORK ON THIS SECTION ONLY. **DO NOT** TURN TO ANY OTHER SECTION IN THE TEST.

For each of the following questions, choose the best answer and darken the corresponding oval on the answer sheet.

Select the lettered word or set of words that best completes the sentence.

Example:

Today's small, portable computers contrast markedly with the earliest electronic computers, which were ----.
(A) effective
(B) invented
(C) useful
(D) destructive
(E) enormous

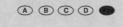

1. Liz is ---- person who loves to attend parties and is always full of ----.
(A) a saturnine . . melancholy
(B) a querulous . . zest
(C) a convivial . . bonhomie
(D) an eloquent . . vitriol
(E) an affable . . choler

2. Negritude, a literary movement emphasizing the importance and value of African culture and history, was founded in Paris in the 1930s by a group of ---- students from Martinique, Senegal, and other French-speaking colonies.
(A) animated
(B) didactic
(C) expatriate
(D) radical
(E) sophisticated

3. Maria's performance was so ---- that even Mr. Rhodes, her teacher and harshest critic, was forced to ---- her talent.
(A) magnificent . . denigrate
(B) tentative . . concede
(C) superb . . deny
(D) indifferent . . praise
(E) compelling . . laud

4. Though the Greek author Thucydides used psychological insight rather than documented information to ---- speeches to historical figures, he is still considered an impartial and ---- historian.
(A) dictate . . endless
(B) transmit . . illustrious
(C) disseminate . . relevant
(D) attribute . . accurate
(E) promote . . inventive

5. Clint Eastwood made his reputation playing tough, ---- characters, notable for their expressive yet ---- speech.
(A) laconic . . pithy
(B) narcissistic . . obtuse
(C) pragmatic . . enthusiastic
(D) esoteric . . trite
(E) monotonous . . interesting

6. Though George Balanchine's choreography stayed within a classical context, he challenged convention by recombining ballet idioms in ---- ways.
(A) naive
(B) effective
(C) redundant
(D) unexpected
(E) awkward

7. While many Americans enjoy ---- lifestyle, the official number of Americans living in poverty has been ---- for several years.
(A) an opulent . . increasing
(B) a leisurely . . developing
(C) an acerbic . . varying
(D) a provincial . . ignored
(E) a peripheral . . stabilized

8. The participants allowed the debate to degenerate into ---- dispute; the urgency of the topic precluded the cordiality expected at such events.
(A) an inconsequential
(B) a depraved
(C) an acrimonious
(D) a prudent
(E) a reticent

9. He claimed to usher in a new era of literature, but his novels were mostly ----, resembling those of many other contemporary authors.
(A) realistic
(B) emotional
(C) pastoral
(D) theoretical
(E) derivative

188 **KAPLAN**

GO ON TO THE NEXT PAGE

10 Nearly all epiphytic ferns are ---- tropical rain-forests; while they do not require soil, they cannot survive without constant moisture.
(A) uprooted to
(B) steeped in
(C) appointed to
(D) decorative in
(E) endemic to

> **Choose the lettered pair of words that is related in the same way as the pair in capital letters.**
>
> Example:
> FLAKE : SNOW ::
> (A) storm : hail
> (B) drop : rain
> (C) field : wheat
> (D) stack : hay
> (E) cloud : fog

11 MARE : STALLION ::
(A) fawn : buck
(B) ewe : ram
(C) mule : donkey
(D) alligator : crocodile
(E) goat : nanny

12 MESS : SOLDIERS ::
(A) infirmary : patients
(B) museum : artists
(C) library : intellectuals
(D) cafeteria : students
(E) courtroom : lawyers

13 DAUNTLESS : HERO ::
(A) ill : hypochondriac
(B) servile : waiter
(C) credulous : agnostic
(D) abstemious : teetotaler
(E) mendacious : politician

14 QUARANTINE : EPIDEMIC ::
(A) barricade : building
(B) cloister : isolation
(C) boil : bacteria
(D) eat : famine
(E) sterilize : infection

15 LION : PRIDE ::
(A) violinist : quartet
(B) worker : syndicate
(C) goose : gaggle
(D) beaver : dam
(E) elephant : circus

16 AFFLUENCE : MENDICANT ::
(A) conformity : maverick
(B) generosity : altruist
(C) banality : demagogue
(D) vanity : sycophant
(E) innocence : defendant

17 HERBIVORE : PLANT ::
(A) omnivore : poultry
(B) historian : history
(C) choreographer : dance
(D) carnivore : meat
(E) vegetarian : calorie

18 TEPID : HEAT ::
(A) basic : simplicity
(B) lukewarm : wateriness
(C) plain : blandness
(D) regular : familiarity
(E) mild : spiciness

19 ADMIRE : ADULATION ::
(A) bore : sadness
(B) deplete : lending
(C) hope : adoration
(D) save : hoarding
(E) grow : satisfaction

20 MESMERIZING : INTERESTING ::
(A) incredible : dull
(B) vile : unpleasant
(C) wholesome : sour
(D) nutritious : unwholesome
(E) unexpected : evil

21 PEERLESS : EQUAL ::
(A) painless : gain
(B) unique : consequence
(C) shapeless : form
(D) inanimate : object
(E) inconceivable : idea

22 DESICCATE : MOISTURE ::
(A) debilitate : strength
(B) augur : future
(C) exonerate : verdict
(D) stem : tide
(E) exaggerate : confidence

23 ABSTINENT : RESTRAINT ::
(A) compassionate : sympathy
(B) eloquent : terseness
(C) enraged : mistrust
(D) subservient : deviance
(E) indifferent : attitude

GO ON TO THE NEXT PAGE

Answer the questions below based on the information in the accompanying passages.

Questions 24–35 are based on the following passage.

The author of the following passage is Juan Carlos Langlois, an Argentine artist whose work has been exhibited in Latin America, North America, and Europe.

With the spread of industry, the exodus of people from the countryside, and the resultant transformation of the urban landscape, city-dwellers of the
Line twentieth century have found themselves living in
(5) an increasingly colorless environment. Veiled in soot, towns and suburbs have lapsed into grimy taciturnity as an all-pervading drabness has overcome our great, sprawling urban complexes.

From the time of the first industrial revolution,
(10) western societies have favored the use of somber, neutral colors in their towns and cities, judging them to be more functional. This anti-color attitude has been accentuated by the desire to imitate the supposed canons of Greek and Roman classicism.
(15) As we now know, however, the city-dwellers of antiquity loved color. Our vision of the temples and market-places of old, built solely in white marble, is wrong. On the contrary, judging by the rich and subtle palette found in the art of ancient civiliza-
(20) tions, the use of color as a symbolic language seems to have been an important development in human culture. In later times, Romanesque and Gothic architecture also featured great use of color—witness the cathedrals of Siena, Florence, and Venice,
(25) with their stained-glass windows, frescoes, mosaics, and precious colored marble.

The facades embellished with traditional paintings still to be seen today in many countries of the world are an indication of the extent to which other
(30) peoples continue to nourish their spiritual and imaginative vision through contact with color. This extraordinary ornamental richness can be seen in the cities of Islam, the villages of Greece, the cities, villages and temples of India and Southeast Asia,
(35) and the fishing villages of the Caribbean, to name but a few examples. Sensitivity of this kind has found little place in the monotonous environments of our great western cities.

Fortunately, in recent decades the notion of
(40) bringing decorative color back into building projects has been gaining some ground. Bold and judicious use of color has an important role to play in the public art of our urban streets, providing a favorable background for a revived form of "urban-
(45) ity" in its original, positive sense. The whole city becomes more understandable and more convivial as color, the poetry of the street, triumphs over drabness.

Public murals and trompe-l'oeil* facades, which
(50) are able to strike a chord in the collective memory by alluding to the important political, religious or artistic events of our cultures, are gradually making a comeback. The first influential muralists of the twentieth century were three great Mexican
(55) artists—Diego Rivera, José Clemente Orozco, and David Alfaro Siqueiros. In the 1920s, in search of an art form that would be monumental yet human and popular, they began to paint gigantic frescoes that retraced the major episodes in the history of Mexico.
(60) Their initiative brought them many commissions in their own country and, later, in the United States, where they inspired a vast program of publicly financed commissions in the 1930s, designed to provide work for unemployed American artists during
(65) the Great Depression. More than 2,500 murals were completed throughout the United States over the next few years under New Deal programs begun by the administration of Franklin D. Roosevelt.

During the 1960s, the creation of murals in pub-
(70) lic places became the spearhead of an authentic popular art movement. This movement was a community response to the need for expression felt by ethnic and other minority groups to whom access to visual creativity and expression had previously
(75) been barred. In 1967, a mural conceived as a "collage" of portraits, photographs and poetic verse was created on a derelict building in the southern suburbs of Chicago by a group of Black American artists led by William Walker. Entitled "Wall of
(80) Respect," the work paid tribute to public figures who had fought for civil rights for Black Americans. This group effort by minority artists inspired other similar projects in American cities such as Los Angeles, San Francisco, Baltimore, and New York,
(85) and marked a new point of departure for public mural painting in this country.

Improving the quality of life in the city is one of the primary objectives of street art. Color can help to save, rehabilitate or otherwise give new life to
(90) neighborhoods and other urban sites doomed to demolition, dereliction or anonymity. The aim is to provide the city-dweller with the opportunity to participate in the rebirth of a more human environment. By its very nature as communal space, the
(95) street lends itself to collective creativity which, in

GO ON TO THE NEXT PAGE

turn, leads to an enhanced sense of community pride and well-being.

*Trompe l'oeil (literally, "deception of the eye"): a highly decorative style of mural painting that often depicts architectural or other three-dimensional forms.

24 The "transformation of the urban landscape" (lines 2–3) most likely refers to the
(A) diversity of urban ethnic populations
(B) spread and greater density of urban areas
(C) loss of manufacturing jobs in cities
(D) improved visual appearance of cities
(E) loss of parks in modern cities

25 In lines 6–7, the phrase "lapsed into grimy taciturnity" refers to the
(A) growing violence of city life
(B) decay of urban areas
(C) unresponsiveness of politicians to city problems
(D) increasing development of rural areas
(E) passive acceptance by city-dwellers of their surroundings

26 Which of the following best explains why "somber, neutral colors" (lines 10–11) came into wider use in western cities?
(A) They were intended to accentuate other bolder colors.
(B) They were viewed as more modern than the colors of Greece and Rome.
(C) They were considered more beautiful than brighter colors.
(D) They were judged more suitable for an industrial environment.
(E) They recalled the muted colors of Romanesque and Gothic architecture.

27 The author suggests that the admiration of western societies for "the supposed canons of Greek and Roman classicism" (line 14) was
(A) a reaction to the widespread use of functional colors
(B) based on a mistaken belief about the use of color in antiquity
(C) consistent with our love of the colors of Siena, Florence, and Venice
(D) founded on respect for the art of ancient civilizations
(E) inspired by their use of color as a symbolic language

28 In line 16, *vision* most nearly means
(A) image
(B) display
(C) fixation
(D) personal wish
(E) clear-sightedness

29 The cities and villages mentioned in lines 33–36 are noted for their
(A) breathtaking natural scenery
(B) complex histories
(C) uniform architecture
(D) decorative lushness
(E) religious convictions

30 In line 36, the word *sensitivity* most nearly means
(A) sense of community spirit
(B) imaginative use of color
(C) understanding of different cultures
(D) consideration for other people
(E) knowledge of art history

31 *Judicious* in lines 41–42 is best understood as meaning
(A) controversial
(B) objective
(C) determined
(D) informed
(E) judgmental

32 The phrase "strike a chord in the collective memory" (line 50) is used to signify the
(A) adaptability of people living in unfamiliar surroundings
(B) willingness of people to make sacrifices for the good of a community
(C) loyalty shown by people living in small communities
(D) tendency of city-dwellers to lose touch with their cultural roots
(E) ability of art to portray the variety and history of a culture

33 The reference in paragraph 5 to the painters Diego Rivera, José Clemente Orozco, and David Alfaro Siquieros serves to
(A) highlight the poor quality of mural painting in the United States
(B) indicate the wide range of colors and styles to be found in mural painting
(C) shed light on the revival of mural painting in two countries
(D) show the important role that artists have played in Mexican history
(E) emphasize the lack of government funding for public mural painting

34 William Walker's "Wall of Respect" project is described as a "new point of departure" (line 85) because
(A) artists who began painting murals went on to success in other art forms
(B) public mural painting had never before been attempted in the United States
(C) other minority groups were inspired to undertake similar community projects
(D) the project popularized a new use for derelict buildings
(E) the artists involved led a revival of the civil rights movement

35 The author most likely considers the street an appropriate location for art because the street
(A) encourages a natural reserve in city-dwellers
(B) carries few traces of past events
(C) is naturally a place of shared activities
(D) forces people to be more alert about their surroundings
(E) features subjects that are interesting to paint

STOP IF YOU FINISH BEFORE TIME IS CALLED, YOU MAY CHECK YOUR WORK ON THIS SECTION ONLY. **DO NOT** TURN TO ANY OTHER SECTION IN THE TEST.

Answer the questions below based on the information in the accompanying passages.

Questions 1–12 are based on the following passages.

The following two passages discuss closely linked periods in European history. In passage 1, the author describes the organization of the guild, an important feature of town life in medieval Europe. The author of passage 2 identifies a fundamental social change that began taking place in Italian towns in the late 1200s.

Passage 1

The membership of guilds in medieval European towns was made up of masters, journeymen, and apprentices. Each guild differed from
Line town to town in its social and political influence,
(5) but its primary economic function was the same everywhere—to protect the merchant and artisan, not just from the competition of foreign merchants, but also from the competition of fellow guild members. Town markets were closed to foreign products,
(10) and individual members were prevented from growing rich at the expense of others.

Each guild adopted strict rules, including fixed hours of work, fixed prices and wages, limits on the numbers of workers in workshops, and regular
(15) workshop inspections. These tightly enforced rules had the effect of dampening personal ambition and initiative. No one was allowed to employ methods of production that were cheaper or more efficient than those used by fellow guild members. In fact,
(20) technical progress and those who favored it were looked on with suspicion.

Each local guild was organized hierarchically. The dominant members were the masters—small merchant proprietors of workshops who owned
(25) their tools, raw materials, products, and all the profits from the sale of those products. Journeymen were wage-earning workers who had completed an apprenticeship. Apprentices were brought into a trade under a master's direction. The number of
(30) masters in each local guild was limited, determined by the needs of the local market and by certain requirements, including citizenship, that were hard to fulfill.

The master functioned as a small, independent
(35) entrepreneur whose primary capital included a house, a workshop, tools, and equipment. The number of workshop employees was restricted, usually to one or two apprentices and journeymen. If a master happened to inherit or marry into a fortune, it
(40) could not be used against other masters, because the guild system left no room for competition. But material inequality among guild merchants was rare. For most of them, the economic structure of the guild meant the same kind of existence and the
(45) same measured resources. While it gave them a secure position, it also prevented them from rising

above it. In this sense, the guild system might be described as non-capitalist.

Passage 2

Throughout most of Europe in the late Middle
(50) Ages, human consciousness as we know it today was really only half awake. People thought of themselves as members of a family, organization, or community, but not as individuals. In most countries, the different classes of society lived apart, each with
(55) its own sense of values. Throughout their lives, people tended to remain in the class in which they were born. But in Italy social fluidity appeared early. By the late 1200s, Italy was brimming with the notion of individuality. The Italians of the next two cen-
(60) turies—the period that we now call the Renaissance—were unafraid of being and appearing different from their neighbors.

Italian towns, primarily because of their control of the Mediterranean trade, were the busiest in
(65) Europe. Town crafts included such sophisticated trades as goldsmithing and stonecarving. Competition between artisans grew so acute that masterpieces began to proliferate, and love of art spread throughout society. A few merchants made
(70) great fortunes, lent their money to foreign princes, and thus became international bankers.

Italy was a place in which the potential for individual achievement—for a privileged few, anyway—seemed unlimited. Since there was no central
(75) Italian government, wealthy merchants were unchecked in their political and social ambitions. They competed for civic power and fame, sponsored public works and cultural institutions, hired armies, and forged alliances. The typical Italian
(80) merchant was fluent in Latin and Greek and read the classic works of Rome and Greece. It was in these circles that private, secular education got its start.

The story of the Medici family of Florence illus-
(85) trates these changes. Giovanni, an obscure merchant born in 1360, created the family banking fortune. His son Cosimo became ruler of Florence by scheming against rivals in other Florentine families. Cosimo's grandson and heir, Lorenzo the
(90) Magnificent, was an able politician, a famous patron of the arts and learning, and a reputable

scholar and poet. The Medici family's rise to prominence coincided with the decline of the guild and the growth of capitalist individualism in Italy.

1. The most important function of the "rules" discussed in lines 12–15 was probably to
   (A) guarantee that masters retained strict control over their employees
   (B) broaden the political influence of guilds within a town
   (C) minimize competition among local artisans and merchants
   (D) stimulate the development of more efficient production methods
   (E) improve the quality of merchandise in local markets

2. The "requirements" mentioned in line 32 had the effect of
   (A) opening local markets to foreign products
   (B) controlling the number of those who advanced beyond journeyman status
   (C) enlarging the number of those qualified to become town citizens
   (D) prohibiting trade with foreign merchants
   (E) encouraging economic rivalry among small entrepreneurs

3. In line 45, the word *measured* most nearly means
   (A) deliberate
   (B) inadequate
   (C) rhythmical
   (D) cautious
   (E) limited

4. The author of Passage 1 describes the guild system as an economic system that was
   (A) open and permissive
   (B) innovative and energetic
   (C) fluid and unpredictable
   (D) restrictive and stable
   (E) unfair and exploitative

5. In describing human consciousness in most of Europe as being "only half awake" (line 51), the author of Passage 2 seeks to
   (A) contrast prevailing social conditions in Europe to those in Italy
   (B) criticize a lack of interest in education in medieval European society
   (C) imply that some people have always opposed social progress
   (D) stress the role of individuality in contemporary society
   (E) suggest that a common belief about medieval Europe is wrong

6. The author of Passage 2 uses the term *social fluidity* in line 57 mainly to describe the
   (A) dangerous conditions of urban life in Italy
   (B) intense competition between families in Italian towns
   (C) great disparities of wealth among social classes in Italy
   (D) rapid spread of democratic institutions in Italy
   (E) unfixed character of social life in Italy

7. The meaning of the word *acute* in line 67 is
   (A) chaotic
   (B) dangerous
   (C) wise
   (D) keen
   (E) sudden

8. The author discusses the Medici primarily to illustrate which of the following?
   (A) The guild system in Italy rewarded individual effort and competitiveness.
   (B) There were few restraints on the aspirations of people in Italy.
   (C) Political power in Italy was held by a small number of wealthy families.
   (D) Family rivalry in Florence was a major social phenomenon.
   (E) It was easy for individuals to capture wealth and power in Italy.

KAPLAN

GO ON TO THE NEXT PAGE

9 The author's discussion of the Medici (lines 84–94) is
(A) nostalgic
(B) disapproving
(C) dispassionate
(D) ironic
(E) defensive

10 Both passages seek to explain the
(A) expanding role of commerce in Italian towns during the Middle Ages
(B) economic structure of the guild system during the Middle Ages
(C) growing importance of individuality in the Middle Ages
(D) circumstances of merchants during the Middle Ages
(E) fast growth of capitalism during the Middle Ages

11 What position would the author of Passage 1 most likely take regarding the description of European society in lines 49–53 of Passage 2?
(A) The structure of the medieval guild and its effects support the description.
(B) The description underestimates the extent to which the medieval guild system favored individual initiative.
(C) Trying to describe the complexities of human consciousness is not an appropriate task for historians.
(D) The accuracy of the description cannot be determined without further investigation.
(E) It is unwise to describe European society in such sweeping terms.

12 The merchants discussed in Passage 1 are most different from those discussed in Passage 2 in their
(A) concern for the economic welfare of their towns
(B) interest in exercising their rights as citizens
(C) views regarding the right to own private property
(D) patriotic loyalty to their towns
(E) attitudes regarding personal ambition

STOP IF YOU FINISH BEFORE TIME IS CALLED, YOU MAY CHECK YOUR WORK ON THIS SECTION ONLY. **DO NOT** TURN TO ANY OTHER SECTION IN THE TEST.

SECTION 1

1 **B**—The clue words here are *reelect* and *change*. If those polled are planning to reelect their legislators, then they are not eager for a change in leadership. The public could not have been **partial to** *a change in leadership*, since they're intending to bring back the same people. And if they were **confident of** or **receptive to** replacing their legislators, they would vote for someone other than the current office holders. (B) and (C) are the only remaining options. If anything, the public is getting used to keeping the same people around, so (C) doesn't fit the blank either. But if *the public was* **wary of** *a change* (that is, cautious or nervous about it), voters might well decide to reelect their legislators.

inured to: accustomed to something
receptive: open, welcoming
partial to: having a preference or liking for

2 **A**—The missing word has to describe an animal that can run at high speed and climb any tree. We could predict that a word like *nimble* would work. (A) **agile** matches our prediction. None of the other choices makes sense—the mountain lion certainly isn't a **passive** creature if it can run at high speed and climb any tree. It makes no sense to call the lion a **capricious** animal. And while the lion may very well be an **attentive** or **dominant** creature, these choices don't make sense in the context of the sentence.

capricious: inconsistent

3 **D**—The sentence says that organic *farming* is *labor intensive*, that is, it requires a lot of work by human beings (as opposed to machines). It is *thus initially quite* ----. If the sentence ended right after the blank, choice (E) might be the best answer. But the conjunction *although* signals a contrast between the two halves of this sentence. Since the second clause is concerned with how expensive organic farming is compared to conventional farming, the word that fills the blank must have something to do with expense, not labor. **Costly** means "expensive," so (D) is correct.

arduous: laborious, involving very hard work

> Hint: Remember to read the whole sentence. An answer choice that may make sense with one clause of the sentence may not work for the whole sentence.

4 **D**—We know that Rivera used *bold, dramatic forms*, so one possible prediction for the first blank would be something like *vivid* or *creative*. But none of the answer choices has a first word that matches this prediction. And it's hard to tell what Rivera did to the *generation of young artists*. We won't be able to pick a choice based on one blank.

We'll just have to see which answer choice contains two words that go together *and* make sense when we plug them into the sentence. The other important hint is that the overall tone of the sentence is positive, so whichever pair we choose will probably be positive as well. Choice (D) is the only answer that contains two positive words. When we plug them into the sentence, the two words do reinforce each other: An **influential** artist would be **inspiring** to other painters.

In (A), a famous artist could make it hard for younger artists. But nothing in the sentence indicates that Rivera's fame or his *bold, dramatic forms* **displac**ed other artists. In (B), **convoluted** doesn't really fit with *bold* and *dramatic*. And (C) and (E) both contain highly negative words: **antagonistic** and **thwarting**.

convoluted: complex, intricate
antagonistic: hostile, opposing
thwarting: blocking, hindering

5 **E**—The backbone of this sentence is a contrast: *Although the Druids . . . were* ----, *they preferred to use* ---- *teaching methods to educate the young*. The two words in the correct answer should contrast with each other somehow. The only answer choice that contains two contrasting words is (E). *The Druids . . . were* **literate**—they knew how to read—but they imparted *information* **orally**, that is, by speaking, rather than by writing. The word pairs in (A) and (B) may have a relation in some contexts, but they never contrast each other.

literate: able to read and write
oral: using speech
enduring: lasting
haphazard: random

6 **D**—The clue words here are *either* and *or*. This offers a choice of two options which do not mean the same thing. If one of the options is *a localized . . . form*, the other has to be *a [nonlocalized] form*. So the correct answer will mean "nonlocalized."

> Hint: If you don't know a vocabulary word, try to remember any similar or related words that you might know.

Let's say you didn't know the word *localized*. You probably do know the word *local*. It means near you, in your area, and not all over the place. So *localized* will have something to do with a limited space. The answer has to be "nonlocalized," so (A) and (C) won't work. (D) **diffuse** means "spread out," the opposite of *localized*, so it's correct.

> *localized: restricted to a given area*
> *diffuse: spread out*

7 **C**—The second part of this sentence states that Carrie Nation demolished barrooms with a hatchet. It's fair to say that this is a "militant," "violent," or "strong" response to alcohol consumption. We can predict that whatever fills the blank will be close to one of those three words.

Right away we can eliminate (B), (D), and (E). None of them describes a strong or violent action. We can eliminate (A) too. **Characteristic** is much too neutral. It's not really saying anything. **Adamant** means "inflexible or unyielding." That's what we were looking for. **Adamant** is close to *strong*.

> *temperance: abstinence from alcohol*
> *characteristic: typical*
> *adamant: inflexible, unyielding*
> *perfunctory: apathetic, mechanical*
> *docile: obedient, well-behaved*

8 **B**—The clue words here are *even though*. There must be a strong contrast between the way Becky's friends describe her and the way the author of the sentence sees her. So the words that go in the blanks should be the opposite of *amiable and frank*. We might predict that the correct answer would be something like *disagreeable and secretive*. No matter what, both words should certainly be negative. That lets us eliminate (A), (C), and (D) right away, since each of them contains a positive word. And in (E), **frugal** and **mysterious** aren't really negative or positive. Therefore, (B) must be the right answer. A

rude person is certainly not *amiable*; a **calculating** person isn't *frank*, either.

> *gregarious: sociable, friendly*
> *frugal: thrifty*
> *calculating: scheming*
> *amiable: pleasing, agreeable*
> *frank: open, honest*

9 **C**—It seems pretty clear that the second blank is going to be filled by something like *definite*. On the basis of that prediction alone, choice (D) is wrong.

That still leaves us with four choices in the second words that more or less match the prediction. We need to look at the first blank. The word *despite* is a major clue word. There will be an opposition or contrast between the two parts of the sentence. To contrast with the fact that there is still no definite *relationship between sunspot cycles and the earth's weather*, the first blank should probably set up a phrase like *educated guessing*. Though **clear** makes sense in (B), it's out, because *educated* **confusion** doesn't make sense. And (E) won't work, because it wouldn't set up a contrast either. The only remaining choices are (A) and (C). (C) makes the internal logic of the sentence work better. **Conjecture** is pretty close to *guessing* and contrasts very well with **proven**. Also, **proven** is closer to the meaning of *definite* that we had in mind.

> *tenuous: flimsy, slender*
> *conjecture: speculation, guessing*

10 **B**—A **HORSE's** foot is called a **HOOF**; a **cat's** foot is called a **paw**.

11 **A**—An **EMERALD** is a particular type of **GEMSTONE**; **hydrogen** is a particular kind of **gas**. **Granite** and **marble** are two different types of rock. Both **hue** and **tint** mean "a gradation of color," although **tint** can also mean more specifically "a lighter shade of color."

12 **D**—A **POSTSCRIPT** (abbreviated as *P.S.*) is an afterthought that's added to a **LETTER** after the closing and signature. Similarly, an **addition** is a room or wing that's added to a **building** after the initial construction is finished.

13 **A**—**Steer** here has got to be a verb, so you know that all the second position words, including **dock,** are verbs. When you **DOCK** a **SHIP,** you stop and leave it someplace temporarily; when you **park** a **car,** you stop and leave it someplace temporarily.

14 **E**—The defining characteristic of a **GROUCH** is **ILL-HUMOR;** the defining characteristic of a **scholar** is **studiousness. Bankruptcy** is not characteristic of a **creditor;** the **creditor** is the person to whom the debtor owes money.

15 **E**—Something that's **LIMP** has no **FIRM-NESS;** something that's **polished** has no **roughness.**

The Ozone Passage

Here's a straightforward but somewhat sobering science passage on the topical subject of damage to the ozone layer. Paragraph one summarizes the problem; the layer of ozone, which protects the earth from the sun's ultraviolet rays, is being depleted. Paragraph two explains the chemical reaction that causes the problem. Paragraph three traces the problem from the first time scientists noticed that something was wrong to the point that the public became aware of it. Paragraph four identifies industry-produced CFCs as the chief culprits in ozone depletion, and paragraph five lists some of the threats the problem poses to life on earth. Paragraphs six and seven give us the latest news—even though CFCs are being phased out, the long lifespan of CFC molecules means that the effects on the ozone layer can be expected to worsen for the time being. There's a note of optimism at the end of the passage, though—the author advocates continued effort to improve the situation.

16 **E**—The author describes the *function* of the ozone layer (in lines 7–8). We're told that the ozone layer "protects the earth from UV radiation," which is "harmful to all living organisms." Choice (E) is the closest analogy here. It captures the idea of something which constantly provides protection against a life-threatening force. The **evacuation plan** mentioned in (A) only helps in *emergencies.* None of the other choices—(B) **information desks,** (C) **traffic lights**—or (D) **suspension bridge supports**—are facilities designed to provide protection

against specific threats.

17 **D**—The author uses *tenuous* to describe the quality of the atmosphere at the ozone layer. Even though the ozone layer is several miles thick, leading us to expect that the atmophere would be thick too, we're told that the atmosphere is *tenuous.* And so *tenuous* here means *thin,* the opposite of *thick.*

(A) **doubtful** is the closest wrong answer because of its negative connotation, but it is not specific enough. (B) **tense** doesn't fit in a discussion of atmosphere. (C) **clear** would contradict the passage by implying that there was no atmosphere at all at this level. Finally, (E) **hazy** is a term that would apply more to the weather than to atmospheric density.

18 **C**—The "seasonal variations" noticed in 1958 were initially regarded as the "natural effects of wind and temperature" (lines 24–25). According to the passage, it was only much later that the connection between CFCs and ozone depletion became known (lines 30–32). Therefore, we can infer that in 1958, these seasonal variations *were not regarded as a threat,* making (C) correct and (B), (D), and (E) wrong. No other ozone depletants are mentioned (A).

19 **B**—The key word in line 25 is *while,* because it indicates a *contrast.* We're told that *while* low October levels stayed *constant,* ozone levels as a whole *diminished,* or fell. *Unlike* the overall figures, in other words, the October levels did not fluctuate—they remained (B) **steady.** (A) **gentle** and (C) **pestering** are unlikely words to use to describe atmospheric measurements. (D) **unerring** suggests that the accuracy of scientists' measurements is the issue. (E) presents a contradiction—the October levels couldn't be both low *and* **considerable** in size.

20 **D**—The author's point is *implied* in the first two lines of the paragraph. We're told that CFCs represent a sizeable market. Then we're told that *in spite of this,* people began to question the risks to human health when CFCs were implicated in ozone depletion. So the author's point in mentioning the CFC market is that the *dangers* of using CFCs overshadowed the *economic considerations* (D).

(A) can't be inferred from the context. The author doesn't explicitly *blame* industry for the problem.

(B) is out because the author makes *no* mention of benefits. (C) gets the issue wrong; it was the health risks, not industry profits, that turned public opinion. And (E) distorts the author's point of view, since ozone depletion, not job losses, is the author's main concern.

21 **A**—Here the author's giving us a progress report on ozone depletion in the 1990s. We're told that the layer was "depleting faster than expected" in addition to natural events "making the problem worse" (lines 55–56). (A) summarizes this idea that the situation is worsening.

Paragraph six describes the problem as a whole, without relating it to any particular species, even though threats to marine species (B) and plant life (C) are mentioned elsewhere. (D) goes against the gist of the passage, which basically identifies CFCs as the main culprits. Finally, we're told that the ozone layer is depleting over the Arctic, too (E).

22 **C**—Lines 55–56 say that scientists believe that natural events are "making the problem worse," and the volcanic gases emitted by the Pinatubo volcano are mentioned as one example. (C) is the correct answer.

(A) **Global warming** isn't mentioned until paragraph eight. (B) distorts the author's point; CFCs are still the biggest threat. Since the gases are adding to a long-term problem, (D) must be wrong. Finally, (E) can't be inferred here, since the author tells us nothing about how destructive the molecules in volcanic gases are.

23 **E**—Even stopping all CFC production today wouldn't solve the problem, we're told, because CFCs can live for up to 400 years. (E) captures the underlying point here; measures against ozone depletion may take years to have an effect.

Choice (A) doesn't fit with the passage at all. (B) is too positive; the author's saying that the problem's going to take years to fix, not that there's *plenty* of time to deal with it. There's no mention of the implications for human health (C) in paragraph seven. (D), finally, is too extreme. The author never states that the problem is *insoluble*.

24 **B**—The last paragraph focuses on what scientists are doing about the problem. Even if things are bad, the author says, "nobody can say the situation will *not* improve" if people lend a hand.

(B) captures this positive note.

(A) exaggerates the obstacles to research discussed at the beginning of the paragraph. Choices (C) and (E) just accept ozone depletion as a fact of life, which is not the author's position at all. And finally, ozone depletion and greenhouse warming are never compared in terms of our control over them (D).

The Mrs. Hight Passage

This fiction passage is about Mrs. Hight and her daughter Esther, who live together on a farm. Through a conversation with Mrs. Hight, paragraph one gives us some background detail on how Esther saved the family farm by raising sheep singlehandedly. Paragraph two centers on the narrator's admiration for Esther, for her achievement on the farm, and her steadfast loyalty to her mother.

25 **A**—From line 6 onwards, the story of the passage is really about Esther—her success with sheep farming, and her patience in looking after her mother. The purpose of the passage is to (A) **suggest some of the essential attributes** of her character—determination, good nature, and so on.

Both (B)—the romance between William and Esther, and (D)—**the causes of Mrs. Hight's unhappiness**—are topics only *briefly* touched on. (C) is not supported by the story at all—Esther's success in sheep raising seems to show that people's lives are very much under their own control. And (E) is too extreme—there's no indication that the visit to the farm has changed the narrator's life in any major way.

26 **D**—In *Mrs. Hight's* words, we're told that even though raising the sheep had been "stubborn work," Esther had been "good right along" (lines 18–21). Choice (D) captures Esther's approach here—not only did she overcome **difficulties** with **determination**—she kept **calm** throughout.

(A) is too extreme; Esther didn't put success before all other considerations. She wasn't defeated (B), and she didn't bow to her neighbors' opinions (C). And her success suggests that her efforts were not a mistake (E).

27 **E**—The author speculates that William and Esther had "always been lovers" but had not acknowledged it "even to themselves." In other

KAPLAN

words, she thinks that William and Esther have a strong attachment that they're not fully aware of. (E) captures this situation.

(B) is wrong because it's their *own* feelings that William and Esther haven't acknowledged, which also makes (C) a formal commitment unlikely as yet. (D) **ambivalence** is wrong because there's no suggestion of uncertainty or *contradictory* feelings. Finally, there's no evidence of a **permanent separation** (A).

28 **B**—This question touches again on the qualities Esther showed in managing to raise sheep *and* look after her mother at the same time. We're told that she had been "refined instead of coarsened" by her work, and had shown "patience," "self-possession," and "sweet temper" in caring for her mother. (B) **Serenity and devotion** fits the bill here.

(B) **Aloofness and reserve** sounds like the opposite of "sweet temper." Esther's (C) **sense of humor** is never mentioned, and the author doesn't seem particulary impressed by her (E) **material success.** Finally, (D) **stubborn pride** exaggerates Esther's determination in overcoming adversity, without acknowledging her good points.

29 **C**—Mrs. Hight, we're told, was an "angry old mother, stung by defeat and mourning her lost activities." (C) captures the point here—Mrs. Hight is difficult to live with because she's dissatisfied with the way her life has run.

(A) **Strength in adversity** applies to Esther, but not to her mother. (B) **Carrying on a conversation** doesn't seem to be a problem for Mrs. Hight. Mrs. Hight is angry because of her *own* defeats—not because she (D) **distrusts her neighbors** or (E) **lacks gratitude towards her daughter.**

30 **C**—The author's focus at the end of the passage is on Esther's relationship with her mother. It's (C) **Esther** who will probably find sheep easier to deal with than the "severity" of Mrs. Hight's company. None of the other characters deals with sheep, or interacts closely with Mrs. Hight.

SECTION 2

1 **C**—How would you describe someone who likes to attend parties? Probably as (C) **convivial,** (E) **affable,** or (a little less likely), as (D) **eloquent.** You certainly would not describe her as (A) **saturnine** or (B) **querulous.** Now you've eliminated (A) and (B). Looking at (C), (D), and (E), this person would have to be full of (C) **bonhomie.** She definitely wouldn't be full of (D) **vitriol** or (E) **choler.**

> *convivial: sociable*
> *affable: friendly, approachable*
> *eloquent: well-spoken*
> *saturnine: gloomy*
> *querulous: complaining, irritable*
> *bonhomie: good nature, geniality*
> *vitriol: bitterness*
> *choler: anger*

2 **C**—The clue here is that Negritude was founded in Paris and the students who created it were from French-speaking colonies. Thus they must have been **expatriates.** Nothing in the sentence suggests they were (A) **animated,** (D) **radical,** or (E) **sophisticated.**

> *expatriates: people who've left their*
> *   native land*
> *didactic: factual to the point of dullness;*
> *   instructive*

3 **E**—There are two things to look for in this sentence. The first is the construction *so ---- that.* It tells us that whatever word fills the first blank *forced [Mr. Rhodes] to ----* her talent. The second is the clue word *even.* If Maria's teacher was her *harshest critic,* and *even* he was forced to say something about *her talent,* chances are that the performance was too good to criticize. Therefore, we can predict that both words will be positive.

Although **praise** appears in choice (D), **indifferent** is not the kind of strongly positive word that would be suitable for the first blank. Similarly, the first word in (B), **tentative** wouldn't fit the first blank. The first words in (A), (C), and (E) are all strongly positive words, but the second words in (A) and (C) are negative. (E) is the only choice with positive words for both blanks.

---

tentative: hesitant
denigrate: to put down or insult
indifferent: mediocre
compelling: riveting
laud: to honor or praise highly
concede: to admit

---

4 **D**—The clue words *though* and *still* point to a contrast between what *Thucydides* did and how he is viewed today. We know that *he is still considered an impartial and ---- historian.* Since *impartial* is a good thing for historians to be, the second blank will probably be filled by another positive word. That doesn't help us much, though, since none of the second words in the answer choices is negative. But in (A), it doesn't make much sense to attach **endless** to *historian*. (E) can go, too. How can you **promote** a speech to a historical figure?

With (A) and (E) out of the running, let's go to the first blank. *Thucydides* used speculation or invention rather than *documented* fact, to ---- speeches to historical figures. So *Thucydides* must have ascribed *to historical figures* words that they never actually spoke. The only choice that gives us that meaning when plugged into the first blank is (D): *Thucydides* **attribute**d *speeches to historical figures* that they may never have made. Historians are supposed to be *impartial and* **accurate,** so (D) fills the sentence well all the way around. (B) doesn't work; *Thucydides* may be *considered* **illustrious,** but there is no evidence in the sentence that he **transmit**ted *speeches to historical figures.* Nor does (C) work; the sentence never hints that *Thucydides* **disseminate**d *speeches.*

---

impartial: fair, not taking sides
illustrious: notable
transmit: send
disseminate: distribute

---

5 **A**—The key to completing a sentence is to tie up loose ends without adding any new or unrelated information. The clue word *yet* should help you limit the choices up front. The second word will be something not usually associated with *expressive.* The first word will be one that goes well with *tough.* That lets you eliminate (C) and (E) based on their second blanks.

That leaves (A), (B), and (D) for the first blank. Someone *tough* isn't necessarily be (B) **narcissistic** or (E) **monotonous.** But he could very well be (A)

---

laconic. The two words in (A), **laconic** and **pithy,** best fit our predictions.

---

laconic: using as few words as possible, curt
pithy: concise and to the point
narcissistic: self-centered and vain
obtuse: blunt, dull, or stupid
pragmatic: practical
esoteric: relating to knowledge that
    few people have acquired

---

6 **D**—The problem with the wrong choices here is that they add new information and don't fit the logic of the existing sentence. We're told that *Balanchine stayed within* the format of a particular style of dance, but that he *challenged convention* by doing something new or creative within the established form. **Unexpected** ties the whole sentence together—*Balanchine's choreography* was **unexpected** and un*conventiona*l, but still *stayed within* the *context* of *classical* ballet.

> HINT—Remember that your job is to find the one answer that best fits the logic of the sentence.

---

naive: innocent, inexperienced
redundant: repetitive

---

7 **A**—The first clause says that *Americans enjoy ---- lifestyle.* Since *enjoy* is a very positive verb, the first blank should be filled by a positive adjective. This lets us eliminate (C), (D), and (E).

Now, if the sentence simply read *the official number of Americans has been ---- for several years,* you might generally predict that the blank would be filled by any verb or adjective having to do with quantity, e.g., **increasing,** *decreasing,* or *stable.* But the clue word *while* expresses a contrast or opposition between how *Americans* are depicted in the two main clauses. So if the first clause describes the *lifestyle* in positive terms, the second clause must describe it in negative terms. Therefore, we can predict that *the official number of Americans living in poverty has been* rising or increasing. In (B), **leisurely,** which means "without haste," doesn't work as well in the first blank; nor does it seem quite right to say that *the official number . . . has been* **developing.** That leaves us with (A) as the right choice.

acerbic: sharp or bitter
provincial: unsophisticated or closed-minded
peripheral: on the periphery or outer
  boundary, not essential
opulent: wealthy or luxurious
leisurely: without haste

8 **C**—A *debate* is normally orderly and rational, but this one apparently *degenerate[d] into ----dispute*. What we have of the sentence before filling in the blank implies that this *debate* became a bitter argument. Therefore, something like *bitter* should go in the blank. (A) won't work; since the sentence talks about *the urgency,* or pressing importance, *of the topic,* the *dispute* would hardly be **inconsequential. Depraved** seems a bit far-fetched. (D) **prudent** means "careful," which would go better with rational *debate* than with an uncordial *dispute.* And in (E), a **reticent** dispute means just the opposite of the tumultuous argument we predicted. But (C) **acrimonious** fulfills the prediction exactly.

degenerate: to deteriorate or sink to
  a lower level
preclude: to prevent
cordiality: affection and kindness
inconsequential: insignificant
depraved: sinful or corrupt
prudent: careful
reticent: silent, reserved
acrimonious: bitter

9 **E**—This unnamed novelist had delusions of grandeur. *He claimed to usher in a new era of literature,* that is, to be the first to write in a new style or format. But *his novels . . . [resembled] those of many other contemporary authors.* To complete this sentence correctly, you need a choice that reinforces the existing content of the sentence. Whatever fills the blank must support the idea that the author wasn't as innovative as he thought. (E) **derivative** fits the sentence well.

derivative: taken or received from
  another source
pastoral: relating to the countryside, especially to shepherds or to an idyllic scene

10 **E**—You don't have to know anything about *epiphytic ferns* to complete this sentence. The heart of a sentence completion is its internal logic, not its scientific topic or specialized technical vocabulary. Look at the parts of the sentence you do understand, and try to figure out how they might fit together with the rest of the sentence. Whatever *epiphytic ferns* are, we know that *they do not require soil* and that *they cannot survive without constant moisture.* What could either of those statements have to do with *tropical rainforests? Tropical rainforests* are extremely humid, so they're probably good places to find plants that need *constant moisture.* Look for an answer that means "found in" or "native to." You should be able to rule out most of the choices, because they don't fit that predicted meaning. But **endemic to** fits; it means "native to" or "found only in."

endemic: native, found only in
steep: to soak or saturate

11 **B**—A **MARE** is a female horse, while a **STALLION** is a male horse. So a **MARE** is the female counterpart of a **STALLION,** just as a **ewe** is the female counterpart of a **ram.** (A) **fawn** means a baby deer, not a female deer. (E) is wrong in part because **goat** can be a male or female. A male goat is a billy goat.

12 **D**—The **MESS** is the place where **SOLDIERS** eat; the **cafeteria** is the place where **students** eat. None of the other choices is functionally similar to the stem pair. For example, (A), you might find **patients** in an **infirmary,** or (E), **lawyers** in a **courtroom,** but those aren't the places where they eat.

13 **D**—Bridge: **DAUNTLESS** means "brave," and the quality is thus a characteristic of a **HERO.** Likewise, the quality of being **abstemious** is a characteristic of a **teetotaler.** The other choices present pairs that are not necessarily connected: In (A), a **hypochondriac** is not necessarily **ill;** in (B), a waiter can **serve** you without being **servile.** In (E), a **politician** may or may not be **mendacious.** As for (C), an **agnostic,** one who doubts the existence of God, would certainly not be **credulous.**

teetotaler: one who totally avoids alcohol
abstemious: moderate in eating or drinking
agnostic: one who doubts that God exists
dauntless: brave
hypochondriac: one who always imagines
    that he or she is ill
servile: submissive
mendacious: dishonest
credulous: trusting

14 E—You **QUARANTINE** someone or something in order to prevent an **EPIDEMIC;** just as you **sterilize** in order to prevent an **infection.** (C) is close but doesn't fit the bridge. In (D), **eating** doesn't prevent a **famine** from occurring, although it might prevent you from starving.

15 C—A group of **LIONS** is called a **PRIDE;** a group of **geese** is called a **gaggle.** (B), a group of **workers** may or may not be a **syndicate,** or union. You might find (A) **violinists** in a **quartet** or (E) **elephants** in a **circus,** but groups of **violinists** are not **quartets** and groups of **elephants** are not **circus**es.

syndicate: union

16 A—A good bridge is: A **MENDICANT** is notcharacterized by **AFFLUENCE;** a **maverick** is not characterized by **conformity.** (B) is the opposite of the relationship in the stem pair: An **altruist** is interested in others' welfare and would certainly not lack **generosity.** (D), a **sycophant** appeals to others' **vanity,** but does not necessarily lack vanity. (C), a **demagogue** may or may not possess **banality,** just as (E), a **defendant** may or may not be **innocent.**

affluence: wealth
mendicant: beggar
maverick: nonconformist
sycophant: flatterer
demagogue: rabble rouser
banality: quality of lacking originality
    or freshness

17 D—Bridge: an **HERBIVORE** is an animal that eats **PLANT**s.
Since the prefix **OMNI-** means "all" or "everything," an **omnivore** eats both **PLANT**s and animals. But there's no specific or necessary connection

between **omnivore** and **poultry.** An **historian** is not someone who eats **history;** nor is a **choreographer** someone who eats **dance**s. But a **carnivore** is a **meat**eater. The root **CARN** means **meat,** and **VOR** or **VOUR** (as in *devour*) means "eat." (D) fits the stem bridge: A **carnivore** is an animal that eats **meat.**

herbivore: an animal that eats plants
carnivore: an animal that eats meat

18 E—If you didn't know what **TEPID** meant, your best bet here was to work backwards by defining a bridge for each answer choice. Rule out any answer for which you can't create a strong bridge or whose bridge couldn't possibly fit the stem pair.
Something that's **basic** has **simplicity;** could something **TEPID** have **HEAT?** Possibly . . . .
Lukewarm has nothing to do with **wateriness,** so eliminate (B).
Blandness is the quality of being **plain** in taste. **HEAT** is not the quality of being **TEPID** in flavor, so (C)'s out.
(D) has a rather wishy-washy bridge; **familiarity** *might* stem from a **regular** occurrence of an event or a **regular** association, but the two words don't have to go together.
Finally, something **mild** lacks **spiciness;** could something **TEPID** lack **HEAT?**
As you can see, only the bridges for (A) and (E) sound as though they might fit the stem pair. If you guessed between the two strongest possibilities, you'd have a fifty-fifty chance of picking the right answer. Since **TEPID** means "barely warm," it also means "lacking in **HEAT.**" Thus, the words in the stem pair have the same relationship to each other as the words in choice (E).

lukewarm: almost cool, only slightly warm
tepid: barely warm

19 D—Let's try the same technique here.
The verb **bore** has nothing to do with **sadness,** so (A) is out. **Lending** may or may not **deplete** your resources. (B)'s out. Scratch (C)—**adoration** has nothing to do with **hoping.**
But (D) has a strong bridge: Someone who engages in **hoarding saves** excessively. Could it be that someone who engages in **ADULATION**

ADMIREs excessively? That sounds like a reasonable possibility. Since there's no direct connection between **grow** and **satisfaction**, and we've already eliminated the other choices, (D) must be the answer.

> *deplete: to drain, empty, or lessen*
> *adulation: excessive flattery or admiration*
> *hoarding: accumulating things of value*
> *in a greedy, often secretive, way*

20 **B**—Although **MESMERIZING** can be used to mean "hypnotizing," it can also mean "extraordinarily **INTERESTING**." The best option is (B), because something that's **vile** is extraordinarily **unpleasant**.

> *mesmerizing: hypnotizing, or*
> *extraordinarily interesting*

21 **C**—Bridge: **PEERLESS** means "without **EQUAL**." Despite the time-honored slogan used at gyms everywhere, **painless** doesn't mean "without **gain**," so (A) is wrong. But **shapeless** means "without **form**," so (C) is correct.

> *peerless: without equal inanimate: not alive*
> *inconceivable: unbelievable or impossible*
> *to imagine*

22 **A**—In general, the analogies at the end of a set contain more difficult words than the earlier ones. The bridge here is: To **DESICCATE** is to suck all the **MOISTURE** out of something. (A) is right, since to **debilitate** is to take the strength from something or someone. You really had to know the definitions of **DESICCATE** and **debilitate** to get this one right. The only small clue was the negative **DE-** prefix that they share in common.

> *dessicate: to take all the moisture*
> *out of something*
> *debilitate: to weaken, sap all the strength*
> *augur: to predict the future, especially by*
> *interpreting omens or signs*
> *exonerate: to prove innocent of charges*

> Hint: Study the Kaplan Word and Root
> Lists in this book.

23 **A**—The adjective **ABSTINENT** means "showing **RESTRAINT**." Similarly, **compassionate** means "showing **sympathy**."

Although **eloquent** and **terseness** both have to do with speech, there's not much of a connection between them, and **subservient** has nothing to do with **deviance**. If you tried to use roots and prefixes to set the meaning of **indifferent,** you would have been misled. Its negative **IN-** prefix would seem to give it a meaning of "the same," or "not different," but its actual meaning is "apathetic or neutral."

> *abstinent: refraining from indulging an*
> *appetite or drinking alcohol*
> *compassionate: showing sympathy*
> *eloquent: expressive and moving*
> *terseness: the quality of using few words*
> *subservient: menial, subordinate,*
> *overly submissive*
> *indifferent: apathetic or neutral*

The Murals Passage

This passage is about the lack of decorative color in our cities. Paragraph one tells us that modern cities have become "increasingly colorless environments." Paragraph two explains why—not only were somber colors believed to be more *functional,* but architects adopted them in order to imitate the traditions of ancient Greece and Rome. Midway through paragraph two, however, we're told that the architects were wrong—that the ancients *had* used a lot of color in their cities. In fact, according to paragraph three, vibrant colors are used almost everywhere outside the monotonous cities of the west. Paragraphs four through six state, however, that color in various forms is coming back; we're told that the work of Mexican mural painters sparked a revival of mural painting in the United States, and the work of William Walker is listed as the first of several mural projects by minority groups undertaken during the 1960s. Paragraph seven concludes the passage by affirming the benefits of street art.

24 **B**—*Resultant* is the key word here. We're told that the transformation of the landscape *was a result of* "the spread of industry" and "the exodus of the people from the countryside." (B)'s the correct answer here. If industry was growing, and people were moving from the country into the towns, we can infer that urban areas were spreading and growing in density.

Ethnic diversity (A) is discussed later in the passage. Loss of manufacturing jobs (C) goes against the idea of industry spreading. Improved visual appearance (D) goes against the author's critique of "an increasingly colorless environment." Loss of parks (E) isn't mentioned at all.

25 **B**—The author explains the phrase in question in lines 6–8. "Veiled in soot," we're told, towns have "lapsed into grimy taciturnity," as "all-pervading drabness" overcomes our "urban complexes." (B) captures the idea here.

City violence (A) isn't an issue in the passage at all. Politicians (C) aren't explicitly blamed for the situation and neither are city-dwellers (E). It's the *state* of our cities, not who's responsible, that the author is interested in. Finally, (D)'s out because the author's talking about urban areas, not rural ones.

26 **D**—Two things we're told about "somber, neutral colors" are relevant here. One, they've been widely used since the Industrial Revolution. Two, they were judged to be "more functional." Choice (D) captures these points.

(B)'s wrong because we're *also* told that somber, neutral colors were favored because people wanted to imitate Greek and Roman traditions. There's no basis for (C) in the passage. (A) takes the word *accentuate* (line 13) out of context; the author's point is that somber colors have been used almost exclusively. Finally, we're told that Romanesque and Gothic architecture featured "great use of color" (line 23), so (E) is out.

27 **B**—Western societies' admiration for Greek and Roman classicism was based on *mistaken beliefs*. We're told that somber, neutral colors were used for a long time out of a desire to imitate the Greeks and Romans, but historians *now know* that they loved color. Therefore (B) is correct.

(A) is wrong because we're told that these beliefs *accentuated* the widespread preference for functional colors. The cathedrals of Siena, Florence, and Venice (C) are described as featuring "great use of color"—so admiring the ancients for *neutral* colors wouldn't be a consistent attitude. Nor was a respect for ancient art (D) the basis of somber color schemes, since we're told that ancient art used a "rich and subtle palette." (E) is wrong for the same

reason—using color as a "symbolic language" is using a *lot of* color, and the admiration for the Greek and Roman canons was based on the idea that they used somber, neutral colors.

28 **A**—The word *vision* relates to the reverence for Greek and Roman classicism. We're told that our "vision" of marble market places in ancient Rome was all wrong. So *vision* in this context means (A) **image**—our mental picture of what ancient Rome was like.

(B) **Display** doesn't make sense. Neither does (D) **personal wish.** (C)'s too extreme; we're not *obsessed* with the classical colors—we just have a certain *idea* about them that happens to be wrong. (E) **clear-sightedness,** finally, doesn't fit with the author's acknowledgement that the vision is *wrong*.

29 **D**—In line 32, we're told that "extraordinary ornamental richness" can be seen in the cities and villages mentioned. The phrase "to name but a few examples" is the giveaway. The cities and villages are listed as *examples of* the (D) **decorative lushness** the author's discussing in the paragraph as a whole.

The author is interested in *colorful* architecture, not architecture that is all the same (C). (A) **natural scenery** is never discussed in the passage. (B) **complex history** only figures later in paragraph 5 in the discussion of mural painting. Finally, (E) **religious convictions** is a bit of a distortion—we're told that people from these societies derive spiritual nourishment from all the different *colors* they use.

30 **B**—The way he introduces the word—"sensitivity of this kind"—tells us that the author's referring to a sensitivity that he has *just discussed*. The topic of the paragraph is the decorative use of color in different cultures—something that has little place in "our great western cities." So the author is talking about sensitivity in the (B) **use of color** in our cities. (A) **sense of community spirit,** (C) **understanding of different cultures,** and (D) **consideration for other people** all suggest possible meanings for sensitivity in *other* contexts. But the author is talking specifically about the extent to which different societies use decorative color here. Finally, choice (E) is incorrect. We're told that all these people from different cultures are nourished by "contact with color," not that they're all versed in **art history.**

31 D—In lines 41–42, we're told that "bold and judicious" use of color makes cities better places to live. Judicious, then, is a *positive* quality. (D) **Informed,** meaning knowledgeable, is the best choice here, since judicious means *resulting in good decisions*. (A) **controversial** and (E) **judgmental** are both poor choices because both have negative connotations. (B) **objective** conflicts with the word *bold*—could a city planner be *both* bold and objective about a project? Finally, (C) **determined** simply restates the idea of being bold.

32 E—The author uses the metaphor "striking a chord" here to illustrate how murals work. By "alluding to the important political, religious or artistic events of our cultures," murals make us remember historical events that are significant in our cultures. (E) captures this idea.

It's the function of the mural, not the benefits they present for the community—choices (A), (B), (C)—nor the monotony of cities without murals (D), that the author's referring to here.

33 C—In the lines *surrounding* the quote in question, the author's talking about public murals "making a comeback" (lines 52–53). We're told that the three great Mexican artists were the "first influential muralists of the century" and that "their initiative" subsequently inspired American artists. (C)'s the answer here—the author mentions the Mexican artists to explain why there was a revival in mural painting in Mexico and the United States.

(A) is wrong because the author never implies any criticism of American mural painting. (B) is wrong because the history of this revival is the issue in paragraph five. (D)'s a distortion. We're never told that the Mexican artists themselves influenced historical events. Finally, paragraph five *does* mention the Mexican artists inspiring government funding for murals in the United States (E).

34 C—Turning lines 79–86 around, we're told that Walker's project inspired similar projects in various cities. In other words, it was a "point of departure" since it led to other group projects involving minorities (C).

There's no evidence for (A) at all—we're told nothing about specific artists. (B) contradicts paragraph 5; murals *had* been commissioned thirty years earlier during the New Deal. (D)'s a bit off the point—the author's more concerned with the

revival in murals than with public housing issues. (E) finally, is a distortion; Walker *portrayed* the civil rights pioneers, he didn't lead the movement himself.

35 C—The question ties quite clearly to the last paragraph's discussion of street art. The author tells us that "by its very nature as communal space" the street "lends itself to collective creativity." So it's the fact that streets are places shared by everyone that makes them ideal for this kind of mural painting (C).

(A) **Encouraging reserve** goes against the gist of the passage. (B) **Carrying few traces of past events** goes against the gist too, since part of the function of murals, according to paragraph five, is to make people aware of their own cultural history. (D) is wrong because the author describes many urban areas as "doomed to demolition, dereliction, or anonymity." If streets *already* made people aware of their surroundings, then presumably murals wouldn't be necessary. (E) is tempting, but the author doesn't mention using the street scenes themselves as subjects for painting.

SECTION 3

The Medieval-Guilds Passage

Unlike many others, these paired passages on medieval European society don't present two different perspectives on a single topic. Rather, the second passage here seems to grow out of the first, by depicting the beginning of the transition away from the historical situation described in Passage 1. Author 1 talks about the closed, stable world of the medieval guild, while author 2 talks about what was going on in Italy in the 13th century, when that world was giving way to the more open, more fluid world of the Renaissance. So Passage 2 is almost like an outgrowth of Passage 1.

1 C—You're asked about the main function of the rules discussed in lines 12–15. In the passage, we read that these rules had the effect of "dampening personal ambition and initiative," which would protect the merchant and artisan from competition with other merchants and artisans. So (C) answers the question best.

Choice (A) is perhaps the closest wrong choice, but the impression given in the passage is that the rules imposed as much control on masters as on the people under those masters. (B) is out, since the "political influence" of the guilds is never discussed at length. (D) and (E), meanwhile, work against the thrust of Passage 1, which is that the guild system *discouraged* the development and innovation.

2 **B**—We move to the third paragraph of Passage 1. In that last sentence of the paragraph, we read that "the number of masters in each local guild was limited . . . by certain requirements . . . that were hard to fulfill." So the requirements had the effect of limiting the number of masters, or, as correct choice (B) has it, of "controlling the number of those who advanced beyond journeyman status."

Choices (A) and (E) both contradict the passage, which claims that the guilds kept foreign products *out* of local markets (A) and actually *discouraged* economic rivalry (E). (C) is a distortion, since the guild requirements insisted only that one *be* a citizen to become a master. And in (D), the requirements mentioned in line 32 have to do with becoming a master, not with trade restrictions.

3 **E**—This Vocabulary-in-Context question asks about the adjective *measured* in line 45. It is used to describe the resources of guild merchants. The author has just written about restrictions on the number of workshop employees a merchant could employ, and limits on the amount of their personal wealth they could use against other masters. So their resources were (E) **limited.** (A) **Deliberate** and (C) **rhythmical** are other dictionary definitions of *measured*, but neither can be used to describe the word *resources* as it is used in this context. (B) **Inadequate** is a close wrong choice, but the passage implies that these resources, while subject to strict limits, were still adequate to get the job done. (D)'s suggestion of **cautious,** meanwhile, is off the mark, since it's not the resources that were cautious.

4 **D**—This question is asking us to characterize the author's general description of the guild system in economic terms. The author writes at great length of the restrictions the system placed on the guilds. And although these restrictions prevented guild members from "rising above" their position, they did ensure that those positions would be "secure." So choice (D), which incorporates both the restrictiveness and the security, looks good as our answer.

(A), (B), and (C) are the opposite of what we want;

they seem to describe the post-guild situation that appeared in Italy described in Passage 2—a situation variously described as **open** (A) and **fluid** (C), and one whose emphasis on competition led to the kind of **innovation** (B) that the guild system tended to stifle. Choice (E), on the other hand, goes too far in the other direction.

5 **A**—We switch to an examination of Passage 2. The author wants to contrast what was going on in most of Europe with the new developments in Italy. Individuality was replacing group mentality, openness was replacing restrictiveness, and fluidity was replacing social rigidity. So (A) is the best answer.

(B) brings up the red herring of "education," which isn't discussed until the end of paragraph three. (C) is a distortion, since the author's purpose is to describe the new attitudes in Italy rather than condemn the attitudes in the rest of medieval Europe. (D) is on the right track with its mention of individuality, but the author is not interested in "contemporary society." Finally, (E) fails because the author isn't debunking a common belief about medieval Europe.

6 **E**—The author sets up Italy's new "social fluidity" (line 57) as a contrast to what was going on in the rest of Europe, where social life was rigidly fixed. So it's the *un*fixed quality of social life in Italy that the author is describing with the term *social fluidity*, making (E) the best choice.

(A) misses the mark, since the author nowhere indicates that she regards life in Italy at this time as "dangerous." As for (B), the discussion of rivalries between Italian families doesn't come until much later. (C) is a distortion, since the phenomenon described by the author isn't the disparity in wealth between classes, but how individuals could jump from one class to another. (D) is closer in spirit, but it tries to fool you by playing to your outside knowledge, since nothing about "democratic institutions" is discussed by author 2.

7 **D**—What is described as *acute* in line 67? The competition between artisans, competition that was so sharp, or **keen,** as correct choice (D) says, that it spurred the artisans on to the creation of masterpieces.

As for (A) and (B): Although the competition described definitely could be characterized as energetic, it's not depicted as either out of control or perilous. (C) **wise** could perhaps be seen as a definition of the word *acute* in some contexts, but how can competition itself be described as wise? (E) **sudden** has sort of the opposite problem; it could be said to fit the context but there's no way that **sudden** is a synonym for *acute,* which means sharp, penetrating, or extreme.

8 B—Author 2 tells us explicitly in line 94 that the story of the Medici family is meant to illustrate "these changes." She means the changes mentioned in the previous paragraph, that showed how in Italy "the potential for individual achievement . . . seemed unlimited." Therefore (B) is the right choice.

Choice (A) is a distortion, since the Medici family's success is linked to the decline of the guild system, which actually hampered the kind of individual effort they represent. Although (C) and (D) are true statements, neither is something that the example of the Medicis is meant primarily to illustrate in the passage. (E), meanwhile, is another distortion; no one said that it was *easy* to become successful in Italy at this time, just that it was possible.

9 C—This question asks us to characterize the author's discussion of the Medici family. If you go back and examine that discussion, you'll see that the facts are reported without any kind of emotional slant, so (C) **dispassionate** is the best characterization.

Nostalgic implies a fondness for old times, but clearly there's nothing affectionate in this description. (B) **disapproving** suggests that the author is passing judgment on the Medicis, but there's no evidence of any such negative evaluation. Finally, choices (D) **ironic** and (E) **defensive** indicate emotions toward the Medici family that are just not supported by the sober delivery of facts in that last paragraph.

10 D—You're asked for a common denominator of the two passages. Passage 1 talks about the guild system and the limits it placed on medieval European merchants. Passage 2 deals with the throwing off of limits for artisans and merchants in Italy in the late Middle Ages. So both passages explain the circumstances of merchants in the Middle Ages, choice (D).

All of the wrong choices fail because they don't accurately describe something that's discussed in both passages. Choice (A) can't be the answer, since Italy isn't even mentioned in Passage 1. On the other hand, (B) talks about the structure of the guild system, which the author of Passage 2 never discusses. (C)'s mention of the growing importance of individuality misses the mark, since Passage 1 is about how the guild system discouraged individuality. Similarly, (E)'s mention of capitalism's "fast growth" runs afoul of the thrust of Passage 1.

11 A—We're looking for a likely position taken by author 1, so we must keep in mind what we know of author 1. He regards the guild system as closed, restrictive, and stifling of individuality and innovation. So what would he think of the description of most of European society in the first two lines of Passage 2? That's where we hear that human consciousness (in most of Europe) was "half awake," and that people regarded themselves in terms of groups rather than as individuals. Well, this description jibes pretty well with the situation described by author 1. So choices (A) looks good as the answer.

(B) is way off, since author 1 tells us how the guild system discouraged individual initiative. Meanwhile, there's no evidence that author 1 has such a restrictive view of the historian's job as choice (C) would imply. The wishy-washiness of (D) is also unfounded; we do have evidence that author 1 would agree with author 2's description. And the general statement in (E) seems unlike our author 1, who was perfectly willing to make sweeping statements about the entire system of medieval guilds.

12 E—The merchants discussed in Passage 1 are very different from the Italian merchants discussed in Passage 2, and this question wants to know in what way they are most different. Well, the merchants in Passage 1 were working within the closed system of the guild, which had numerous restrictions that actually discouraged individual initiative. On the other hand, the merchants in Passage 2 "were unchecked in their political and social ambitions." So individual ambitions were radically different, making choice (E) the best answer.

Since we don't hear anything about either kind of merchant's attitude toward the towns they lived in, we really can't choose either (A) or (D), both of which deal with such attitudes. As for (B), we know nothing about attitudes toward citizenship rights. And as for (C), both types of merchant seem to have had private property, so it's unclear how their views on the subject would have been vastly different.

PRACTICE TEST B

Before taking this practice test, find a quiet room where you can work uninterrupted for 75 minutes. Make sure you have a comfortable desk and several #2 pencils.

Use the answer sheet on the next page to record your answers. (You can tear it out, or photocopy it.)

Once you start this practice test, don't stop until you've finished Remember—you can review any questions within a section, but you may not go back or forward a section.

Good luck.

ANSWER SHEET

Start with number 1 for each new section. If a section has fewer questions than answer spaces, leave the extra spaces blank.

SECTION 1

1 Ⓐ Ⓑ Ⓒ Ⓓ Ⓔ	11 Ⓐ Ⓑ Ⓒ Ⓓ Ⓔ	21 Ⓐ Ⓑ Ⓒ Ⓓ Ⓔ	31 Ⓐ Ⓑ Ⓒ Ⓓ Ⓔ
2 Ⓐ Ⓑ Ⓒ Ⓓ Ⓔ	12 Ⓐ Ⓑ Ⓒ Ⓓ Ⓔ	22 Ⓐ Ⓑ Ⓒ Ⓓ Ⓔ	32 Ⓐ Ⓑ Ⓒ Ⓓ Ⓔ
3 Ⓐ Ⓑ Ⓒ Ⓓ Ⓔ	13 Ⓐ Ⓑ Ⓒ Ⓓ Ⓔ	23 Ⓐ Ⓑ Ⓒ Ⓓ Ⓔ	33 Ⓐ Ⓑ Ⓒ Ⓓ Ⓔ
4 Ⓐ Ⓑ Ⓒ Ⓓ Ⓔ	14 Ⓐ Ⓑ Ⓒ Ⓓ Ⓔ	24 Ⓐ Ⓑ Ⓒ Ⓓ Ⓔ	34 Ⓐ Ⓑ Ⓒ Ⓓ Ⓔ
5 Ⓐ Ⓑ Ⓒ Ⓓ Ⓔ	15 Ⓐ Ⓑ Ⓒ Ⓓ Ⓔ	25 Ⓐ Ⓑ Ⓒ Ⓓ Ⓔ	35 Ⓐ Ⓑ Ⓒ Ⓓ Ⓔ
6 Ⓐ Ⓑ Ⓒ Ⓓ Ⓔ	16 Ⓐ Ⓑ Ⓒ Ⓓ Ⓔ	26 Ⓐ Ⓑ Ⓒ Ⓓ Ⓔ	36 Ⓐ Ⓑ Ⓒ Ⓓ Ⓔ
7 Ⓐ Ⓑ Ⓒ Ⓓ Ⓔ	17 Ⓐ Ⓑ Ⓒ Ⓓ Ⓔ	27 Ⓐ Ⓑ Ⓒ Ⓓ Ⓔ	37 Ⓐ Ⓑ Ⓒ Ⓓ Ⓔ
8 Ⓐ Ⓑ Ⓒ Ⓓ Ⓔ	18 Ⓐ Ⓑ Ⓒ Ⓓ Ⓔ	28 Ⓐ Ⓑ Ⓒ Ⓓ Ⓔ	38 Ⓐ Ⓑ Ⓒ Ⓓ Ⓔ
9 Ⓐ Ⓑ Ⓒ Ⓓ Ⓔ	19 Ⓐ Ⓑ Ⓒ Ⓓ Ⓔ	29 Ⓐ Ⓑ Ⓒ Ⓓ Ⓔ	39 Ⓐ Ⓑ Ⓒ Ⓓ Ⓔ
10 Ⓐ Ⓑ Ⓒ Ⓓ Ⓔ	20 Ⓐ Ⓑ Ⓒ Ⓓ Ⓔ	30 Ⓐ Ⓑ Ⓒ Ⓓ Ⓔ	40 Ⓐ Ⓑ Ⓒ Ⓓ Ⓔ

☐ # right in section 1

☐ # wrong in section 1

SECTION 2

1 Ⓐ Ⓑ Ⓒ Ⓓ Ⓔ	11 Ⓐ Ⓑ Ⓒ Ⓓ Ⓔ	21 Ⓐ Ⓑ Ⓒ Ⓓ Ⓔ	31 Ⓐ Ⓑ Ⓒ Ⓓ Ⓔ
2 Ⓐ Ⓑ Ⓒ Ⓓ Ⓔ	12 Ⓐ Ⓑ Ⓒ Ⓓ Ⓔ	22 Ⓐ Ⓑ Ⓒ Ⓓ Ⓔ	32 Ⓐ Ⓑ Ⓒ Ⓓ Ⓔ
3 Ⓐ Ⓑ Ⓒ Ⓓ Ⓔ	13 Ⓐ Ⓑ Ⓒ Ⓓ Ⓔ	23 Ⓐ Ⓑ Ⓒ Ⓓ Ⓔ	33 Ⓐ Ⓑ Ⓒ Ⓓ Ⓔ
4 Ⓐ Ⓑ Ⓒ Ⓓ Ⓔ	14 Ⓐ Ⓑ Ⓒ Ⓓ Ⓔ	24 Ⓐ Ⓑ Ⓒ Ⓓ Ⓔ	34 Ⓐ Ⓑ Ⓒ Ⓓ Ⓔ
5 Ⓐ Ⓑ Ⓒ Ⓓ Ⓔ	15 Ⓐ Ⓑ Ⓒ Ⓓ Ⓔ	25 Ⓐ Ⓑ Ⓒ Ⓓ Ⓔ	35 Ⓐ Ⓑ Ⓒ Ⓓ Ⓔ
6 Ⓐ Ⓑ Ⓒ Ⓓ Ⓔ	16 Ⓐ Ⓑ Ⓒ Ⓓ Ⓔ	26 Ⓐ Ⓑ Ⓒ Ⓓ Ⓔ	36 Ⓐ Ⓑ Ⓒ Ⓓ Ⓔ
7 Ⓐ Ⓑ Ⓒ Ⓓ Ⓔ	17 Ⓐ Ⓑ Ⓒ Ⓓ Ⓔ	27 Ⓐ Ⓑ Ⓒ Ⓓ Ⓔ	37 Ⓐ Ⓑ Ⓒ Ⓓ Ⓔ
8 Ⓐ Ⓑ Ⓒ Ⓓ Ⓔ	18 Ⓐ Ⓑ Ⓒ Ⓓ Ⓔ	28 Ⓐ Ⓑ Ⓒ Ⓓ Ⓔ	38 Ⓐ Ⓑ Ⓒ Ⓓ Ⓔ
9 Ⓐ Ⓑ Ⓒ Ⓓ Ⓔ	19 Ⓐ Ⓑ Ⓒ Ⓓ Ⓔ	29 Ⓐ Ⓑ Ⓒ Ⓓ Ⓔ	39 Ⓐ Ⓑ Ⓒ Ⓓ Ⓔ
10 Ⓐ Ⓑ Ⓒ Ⓓ Ⓔ	20 Ⓐ Ⓑ Ⓒ Ⓓ Ⓔ	30 Ⓐ Ⓑ Ⓒ Ⓓ Ⓔ	40 Ⓐ Ⓑ Ⓒ Ⓓ Ⓔ

☐ # right in section 2

☐ # wrong in section 2

SECTION 3

1 Ⓐ Ⓑ Ⓒ Ⓓ Ⓔ	11 Ⓐ Ⓑ Ⓒ Ⓓ Ⓔ	21 Ⓐ Ⓑ Ⓒ Ⓓ Ⓔ	31 Ⓐ Ⓑ Ⓒ Ⓓ Ⓔ
2 Ⓐ Ⓑ Ⓒ Ⓓ Ⓔ	12 Ⓐ Ⓑ Ⓒ Ⓓ Ⓔ	22 Ⓐ Ⓑ Ⓒ Ⓓ Ⓔ	32 Ⓐ Ⓑ Ⓒ Ⓓ Ⓔ
3 Ⓐ Ⓑ Ⓒ Ⓓ Ⓔ	13 Ⓐ Ⓑ Ⓒ Ⓓ Ⓔ	23 Ⓐ Ⓑ Ⓒ Ⓓ Ⓔ	33 Ⓐ Ⓑ Ⓒ Ⓓ Ⓔ
4 Ⓐ Ⓑ Ⓒ Ⓓ Ⓔ	14 Ⓐ Ⓑ Ⓒ Ⓓ Ⓔ	24 Ⓐ Ⓑ Ⓒ Ⓓ Ⓔ	34 Ⓐ Ⓑ Ⓒ Ⓓ Ⓔ
5 Ⓐ Ⓑ Ⓒ Ⓓ Ⓔ	15 Ⓐ Ⓑ Ⓒ Ⓓ Ⓔ	25 Ⓐ Ⓑ Ⓒ Ⓓ Ⓔ	35 Ⓐ Ⓑ Ⓒ Ⓓ Ⓔ
6 Ⓐ Ⓑ Ⓒ Ⓓ Ⓔ	16 Ⓐ Ⓑ Ⓒ Ⓓ Ⓔ	26 Ⓐ Ⓑ Ⓒ Ⓓ Ⓔ	36 Ⓐ Ⓑ Ⓒ Ⓓ Ⓔ
7 Ⓐ Ⓑ Ⓒ Ⓓ Ⓔ	17 Ⓐ Ⓑ Ⓒ Ⓓ Ⓔ	27 Ⓐ Ⓑ Ⓒ Ⓓ Ⓔ	37 Ⓐ Ⓑ Ⓒ Ⓓ Ⓔ
8 Ⓐ Ⓑ Ⓒ Ⓓ Ⓔ	18 Ⓐ Ⓑ Ⓒ Ⓓ Ⓔ	28 Ⓐ Ⓑ Ⓒ Ⓓ Ⓔ	38 Ⓐ Ⓑ Ⓒ Ⓓ Ⓔ
9 Ⓐ Ⓑ Ⓒ Ⓓ Ⓔ	19 Ⓐ Ⓑ Ⓒ Ⓓ Ⓔ	29 Ⓐ Ⓑ Ⓒ Ⓓ Ⓔ	39 Ⓐ Ⓑ Ⓒ Ⓓ Ⓔ
10 Ⓐ Ⓑ Ⓒ Ⓓ Ⓔ	20 Ⓐ Ⓑ Ⓒ Ⓓ Ⓔ	30 Ⓐ Ⓑ Ⓒ Ⓓ Ⓔ	40 Ⓐ Ⓑ Ⓒ Ⓓ Ⓔ

☐ # right in section 3

☐ # wrong in section 3

Use the answer key following the test to count up the number of questions you got right and the number you got wrong. (Remember not to count omitted questions as wrong.) The "Compute Your Score" section at the back of the book will show you how to find your score.

For each of the following questions, choose the best answer and darken the corresponding oval on the answer sheet.

Select the lettered word or set of words that best completes the sentence.

Example:
Today's small, portable computers contrast markedly with the earliest electronic computers, which were ----.
(A) effective
(B) invented
(C) useful
(D) destructive
(E) enormous

1. More insurers are limiting the sale of property insurance in coastal areas and other regions ---- natural disasters.
(A) safe from
(B) according to
(C) despite
(D) which include
(E) prone to

2. Roman legions ---- the mountain ---- of Masada for three years before they were able to seize it.
(A) dissembled . . bastion
(B) assailed . . symbol
(C) besieged . . citadel
(D) surmounted . . dwelling
(E) honed . . stronghold

3. Unlike his calmer, more easygoing colleagues, the senator was ----, ready to quarrel at the slightest provocation.
(A) whimsical
(B) irascible
(C) gregarious
(D) ineffectual
(E) benign

4. Although historians have long thought of Genghis Khan as a ---- potentate, new research has shown he was ---- by many of his subjects.
(A) tyrannical . . abhorred
(B) despotic . . revered
(C) redundant . . venerated
(D) jocular . . esteemed
(E) peremptory . . invoked

5. Jill was ---- by her employees because she often ---- them for not working hard enough.
(A) deified . . goaded
(B) loathed . . berated
(C) disregarded . . eulogized
(D) cherished . . derided
(E) execrated . . lauded

6. Reconstructing the skeletons of extinct species like dinosaurs is ---- process that requires much patience and effort by paleontologists.
(A) a nascent
(B) an aberrant
(C) a disheveled
(D) a worthless
(E) an exacting

7. Nearly ---- by disease and the destruction of their habitat, koalas are now found only in isolated parts of eucalyptus forests.
(A) dispersed
(B) compiled
(C) decimated
(D) infuriated
(E) averted

8. Deep ideological ---- and internal power struggles ---- the government.
(A) disputes . . facilitated
(B) similarities . . protracted
(C) distortions . . accelerated
(D) agreements . . stymied
(E) divisions . . paralyzed

9. Medical experts have viewed high doses of vitamins as a popular remedy whose value is, as yet, ----.
(A) medicinal
(B) prescribed
(C) recommended
(D) unproven
(E) beneficial

GO ON TO THE NEXT PAGE

215

Choose the lettered pair of words that is related in the same way as the pair in capital letters.

Example:
FLAKE : SNOW ::
(A)   storm : hail
(B)   drop : rain
(C)   field : wheat
(D)   stack : hay
(E)   cloud : fog

10 TROUT : FISH ::
(A) grain : sand
(B) human : mammal
(C) river : stream
(D) chicken : egg
(E) frog : toad

11 INHALE : LUNGS ::
(A) swallow : stomach
(B) attack : heart
(C) ache : head
(D) pump : blood
(E) travel : foot

12 BRAGGART : BOAST ::
(A) laggard : tarry
(B) hypocrite : speak
(C) extrovert : brood
(D) mendicant : compromise
(E) boor : gratify

13 ALLEVIATE : PAIN ::
(A) soothe : antidote
(B) depreciate : value
(C) contract : job
(D) deviate : standard
(E) officiate : safety

14 INFURIATE : ANNOY ::
(A) admire : respect
(B) indulge : lure
(C) terrify : frighten
(D) satiate : deprive
(E) vex : startle

15 MISERLY : MAGNANIMITY ::
(A) greedy : mirth
(B) transient : stupefaction
(C) admirable : fastidiousness
(D) innocent : culpability
(E) offensive : avarice

KAPLAN

GO ON TO THE NEXT PAGE

Answer the questions below based on the information in the accompanying passages.

Questions 16–23 are based on the following passage.
In this excerpt, a Nobel Prize-winning scientist discusses ways of thinking about extremely long periods of time.

There is one fact about the origin of life which is reasonably certain. Whenever and wherever it happened, it started a very long time ago, so long ago that
Line it is extremely difficult to form any realistic idea of
(5) such vast stretches of time. The shortness of human life necessarily limits the span of direct personal recollection.

Human culture has given us the illusion that our memories go further back than that. Before writing
(10) was invented, the experience of earlier generations, embodied in stories, myths and moral precepts to guide behavior, was passed down verbally or, to a lesser extent, in pictures, carvings, and statues. Writing has made more precise and more extensive
(15) the transmission of such information and, in recent times, photography has sharpened our images of the immediate past. Even so, we have difficulty in contemplating steadily the march of history, from the beginnings of civilization to the present day, in such a
(20) way that we can truly experience the slow passage of time. Our minds are not built to deal comfortably with periods as long as hundreds or thousands of years.

Yet when we come to consider the origin of life, the time scales we must deal with make the whole span of
(25) human history seem but the blink of an eyelid. There is no simple way to adjust one's thinking to such vast stretches of time. The immensity of time passed is beyond our ready comprehension. One can only construct an impression of it from indirect and incomplete
(30) descriptions, just as a blind man laboriously builds up, by touch and sound, a picture of his immediate surroundings.

The customary way to provide a convenient framework for one's thoughts is to compare the age of
(35) the universe with the length of a single earthly day. Perhaps a better comparison, along the same lines, would be to equate the age of our earth with a single week. On such a scale the age of the universe, since the Big Bang, would be about two or three weeks. The old-
(40) est macroscopic fossils (those from the start of the Cambrian Period*) would have been alive just one day ago. Modern man would have appeared in the last ten seconds and agriculture in the last one or two. Odysseus** would have lived only half a second
(45) before the present time.

Even this comparison hardly makes the longer time scale comprehensible to us. Another alternative is to draw a linear map of time, with the different events marked on it. The problem here is to make the line
(50) long enough to show our own experience on a reasonable scale, and yet short enough for convenient reproduction and examination. But perhaps the most vivid method is to compare time to the lines of print themselves. Let us make a 200-page book equal in
(55) length to the time from the start of the Cambrian to the present; that is, about 600 million years. Then each full page will represent roughly 3 million years, each line about ninety thousand years and each letter or small space about fifteen hundred years. The origin of the
(60) earth would be about seven books ago and the origin of the universe (which has been dated only approximately) ten or so books before that. Almost the whole of recorded human history would be covered by the last two or three letters of the book.
(65) If you now turn back the pages of the book, slowly reading *one letter at a time*–remember, each letter is fifteen hundred years–then this may convey to you something of the immense stretches of time we shall have to consider. On this scale the span of your own
(70) life would be less than the width of a comma.

*Cambrian: the earliest period in the Paleozoic era, beginning about 600 million years ago.
**Odysseus: the most famous Greek hero of antiquity; he is the hero of Homer's *The Odyssey*, which describes the aftermath of the Trojan War (ca. 1200 B.C.).

16 The word *span* in line 6 most nearly means
(A) rate of increase
(B) value
(C) bridge
(D) extent
(E) accuracy

17 The phrase *to a lesser extent* in lines 12–13 indicates that, before the invention of writing, the wisdom of earlier generations was
(A) rejected by recent generations when portrayed in pictures, carvings, or statues
(B) passed down orally, or not at all
(C) transmitted more effectively by spoken word than by other means
(D) based on illusory memories that turned fact into fiction
(E) more strongly grounded in science than in the arts

18 The author most likely describes the impact of writing (lines 14–17) in order to
(A) illustrate the limitations of the human memory
(B) provide an example of how cultures transmit information
(C) indicate how primitive preliterate cultures were
(D) refute an opinion about the origin of human civilization
(E) explain the difference between historical facts and myth

19 The word *ready* in line 28 most nearly means
(A) set
(B) agreeable
(C) immediate
(D) apt
(E) willing

20 The analogy of the "blind man" (line 30) is presented primarily to show that
(A) humans are unable to comprehend long periods of time
(B) myths and legends fail to give an accurate picture of the past
(C) human history is only a fraction of the time since life began
(D) humans refuse to learn the lessons of the past
(E) long periods of time can only be understood indirectly

21 In lines 38–42, the author mentions the Big Bang and the Cambrian Period in order to demonstrate which point?
(A) The age of the earth is best understood using the time scale of a week.
(B) Agriculture was a relatively late development in human history.
(C) No fossil record exists before the Cambrian Period.
(D) Convenient time scales do not adequately represent the age of the earth.
(E) The customary framework for thinking about the age of the universe should be discarded permanently.

22 According to lines 49–52, one difficulty of using a linear representation of time is that
(A) linear representations of time do not meet accepted scientific standards of accuracy
(B) prehistoric eras overlap each other, making linear representation deceptive
(C) the more accurate the scale, the more difficult the map is to copy and study
(D) there are too many events to represent on a single line
(E) our knowledge of pre-Cambrian time is insufficient to construct an accurate linear map

23 The author of this passage discusses several kinds of time scales primarily in order to illustrate the
(A) difficulty of assigning precise dates to past events
(B) variety of choices faced by scientists investigating the origin of life
(C) evolution of efforts to comprehend the passage of history
(D) immensity of time since life began on earth
(E) development of the technology of communication

GO ON TO THE NEXT PAGE

Questions 24–30 are based on the following passage.
The following excerpt is from a speech delivered in 1873 by Susan B. Anthony, a leader in the women's rights movement of the 19th century.

Friends and fellow-citizens: I stand before you tonight under indictment for the alleged crime of having voted at the last Presidential election, without
Line having a lawful right to vote. It shall be my work this
(5) evening to prove to you that in thus voting, I not only committed no crime, but, instead, simply exercised my citizen's rights, guaranteed to me and all United States citizens by the National Constitution, beyond the power of any State to deny.
(10) The preamble of the Federal Constitution says:
"We, the people of the United States, in order to form a more perfect union, establish justice, insure domestic tranquillity, provide for the common defense, promote the general welfare, and secure the
(15) blessings of liberty to ourselves and our posterity, do ordain and establish this Constitution for the United States of America."
It was we, the people; not we, the white male citizens; nor yet we, the male citizens; but we, the
(20) whole people, who formed the Union. And we formed it, not to give the blessings of liberty, but to secure them; not to the half of ourselves and the half of our posterity, but to the whole people—women as well as men. And it is a downright mockery to talk to
(25) women of their enjoyment of the blessings of liberty while they are denied the use of the only means of securing them provided by this democratic-republican government—the ballot.
For any State to make sex a qualification that must
(30) ever result in the disfranchisement* of one entire half of the people is a violation of the supreme law of the land. By it the blessings of liberty are forever withheld from women and their female posterity. To them this government had no just powers derived from the
(35) consent of the governed. To them this government is not a democracy. It is not a republic. It is an odious aristocracy; a hateful oligarchy of sex; this oligarchy of sex, which makes father, brothers, husband, sons, the oligarchs over the mother and sisters, the wife
(40) and daughters of every household—which ordains all men sovereigns, all women subjects, carries dissension, discord and rebellion into every home of the nation.
Webster, Worcester and Bouvier all define a citizen
(45) to be a person in the United States, entitled to vote and hold office.

The one question left to be settled now is: Are women persons? And I hardly believe any of our opponents will have the hardihood to say they are
(50) not. Being persons, then, women are citizens; and no State has a right to make any law, or to enforce any old law, that shall abridge their privileges or immunities. Hence, every discrimination against women in the constitutions and laws of the several
(55) States is today null and void, precisely as is every one against Negroes.

*disfranchisement: to deprive of the right to vote.

24 In the first paragraph, Anthony states that her action in voting was
(A) illegal, but morally justified
(B) the result of her keen interest in national politics
(C) legal, if the Constitution is interpreted correctly
(D) an illustration of the need for a women's rights movement
(E) illegal, but worthy of leniency

25 Which best captures the meaning of the word *promote* in line 14?
(A) further
(B) organize
(C) publicize
(D) commend
(E) motivate

26 By saying "we, the people . . . the whole people, who formed the Union" (lines 18–20), Anthony means that
(A) the founders of the nation conspired to deprive women of their rights
(B) some male citizens are still being denied basic rights
(C) the role of women in the founding of the nation is generally ignored
(D) society is endangered when women are deprived of basic rights
(E) all people deserve to enjoy the rights guaranteed by the Constitution

GO ON TO THE NEXT PAGE

27 By "the half of our posterity" (line 22–23), Anthony means
(A) the political legacy passed down from her era
(B) future generations of male United States citizens
(C) those who wish to enjoy the blessings of liberty
(D) current and future opponents of the women's rights movement
(E) future members of the democratic-republican government

28 In the fifth paragraph, lines 29–43, Anthony's argument rests mainly on the strategy of convincing her audience that
(A) any state that denies women the vote undermines its status as a democracy
(B) women deprived of the vote will eventually raise a rebellion
(C) the nation will remain an aristocracy if the status of women does not change
(D) women's rights issues should be debated in every home
(E) even an aristocracy cannot survive without the consent of the governed

29 The word *hardihood* in line 49 could best be replaced by
(A) endurance
(B) vitality
(C) nerve
(D) opportunity
(E) stupidity

30 When Anthony warns that "no State . . . shall abridge their privileges" (line 50–52), she means that
(A) women should be allowed to live a life of privilege
(B) women on trial cannot be forced to give up their immunity
(C) every state should repeal its outdated laws
(D) governments may not deprive citizens of their rights
(E) the rights granted to women must be decided by the people, not the state

STOP IF YOU FINISH BEFORE TIME IS CALLED, YOU MAY CHECK YOUR WORK ON THIS SECTION ONLY. **DO NOT** TURN TO ANY OTHER SECTION IN THE TEST.

For each of the following questions, choose the best answer and darken the corresponding oval on the answer sheet.

Select the lettered word or set of words that best completes the sentence.

Example:
Today's small, portable computers contrast markedly with the earliest electronic computers, which were ----.
(A)   effective
(B)   invented
(C)   useful
(D)   destructive
(E)   enormous

---

1 The rain is so rare and the land is so ---- that few of the men who work there see much ---- in farming.
(A) plentiful . . hope
(B) barren . . difficulty
(C) productive . . profit
(D) infertile . . future
(E) dry . . danger

2 The principal declared that the students were not simply ignoring the rules, but openly ---- them.
(A) accepting
(B) redressing
(C) reviewing
(D) flouting
(E) discussing

3 Some critics believe that the ---- of modern art came with dadaism, while others insist that the movement was a ----.
(A) zenith . . sham
(B) pinnacle . . triumph
(C) decline . . disaster
(D) acceptance . . success
(E) originality . . fiasco

4 She would never have believed that her article was so ---- were it not for the ---- of correspondence which followed its publication.
(A) interesting . . dearth
(B) inflammatory . . lack
(C) controversial . . spate
(D) commonplace . . influx
(E) insignificant . . volume

5 The writings of the philosopher Descartes are ----; many readers have difficulty following his complex, intricately woven arguments.
(A) generic
(B) trenchant
(C) reflective
(D) elongated
(E) abstruse

6 The prisoner was ---- even though he presented evidence clearly proving that he was nowhere near the scene of the crime.
(A) abandoned
(B) indicted
(C) exculpated
(D) exhumed
(E) rescinded

7 Many biologists are critical of the film's ---- premise that dinosaurs might one day return.
(A) scientific
(B) tacit
(C) speculative
(D) unwitting
(E) ambiguous

8 Mozart composed music with exceptional ----; he left no rough drafts because he was able to write out his compositions in ---- form.
(A) audacity . . original
(B) facility . . finished
(C) incompetence . . ideal
(D) prestige . . orchestral
(E) independence . . concise

9 Known for their devotion, dogs were often used as symbols of ---- in Medieval and Renaissance painting.
(A) resistance
(B) benevolence
(C) generosity
(D) fidelity
(E) antagonism

10 It is ---- that a people so capable of treachery and brutality should also exhibit such a tremendous capacity for heroism.
(A) unfortunate
(B) explicable
(C) paradoxical
(D) distressing
(E) appalling

GO ON TO THE NEXT PAGE

Choose the lettered pair of words that is related in the same way as the pair in capital letters.

Example:
FLAKE : SNOW ::
(A)   storm : hail
(B)   drop : rain
(C)   field : wheat
(D)   stack : hay
(E)   cloud : fog

11 CHARLATAN : SCRUPULOUS ::
(A) confidant : virtuous
(B) laborer : stalwart
(C) officer : mutinous
(D) dullard : irritable
(E) tyrant : just

12 GREED : ACQUIRE ::
(A) fear : disguise
(B) inertia : persuade
(C) gluttony : eat
(D) conformity : agree
(E) ignorance : speak

13 PARRY : BLOW ::
(A) counter : argument
(B) sidestep : offense
(C) defer : ruling
(D) stumble : pitfall
(E) shine : light

14 MALIGN : SLURS ::
(A) satisfy : treaties
(B) persecute : complaints
(C) torment : whispers
(D) court : debates
(E) flatter : compliments

15 LENTIL : LEGUME ::
(A) rice : cereal
(B) nutrition : food
(C) horseshoe : pony
(D) husk : corn
(E) baker : cake

16 INDULGE : APPETITE ::
(A) filter : impurity
(B) infuriate : anger
(C) coddle : emotion
(D) humor : whim
(E) liberate : freedom

17 MELLIFLUOUS : SOUND ::
(A) musical : entertainment
(B) fragrant : smell
(C) pale : color
(D) raucous : discussion
(E) auspicious : occasion

18 GUFFAW : LAUGH ::
(A) sniffle : sneeze
(B) whoop : cough
(C) yell : talk
(D) snore : sleep
(E) chuckle : sigh

19 CELESTIAL : HEAVENS ::
(A) planetary : orbit
(B) scientific : experiment
(C) nautical : ships
(D) solar : heat
(E) viscous : matter

20 ENERVATE : VITALITY ::
(A) consolidate : power
(B) energize : action
(C) daunt : courage
(D) estimate : worth
(E) admit : guilt

21 OLIGARCHY : FEW ::
(A) government : majority
(B) authority : consent
(C) constitution : country
(D) monarchy : one
(E) discrimination : minority

22 UNTRUTHFUL : MENDACIOUSNESS ::
(A) circumspect : caution
(B) timid : behavior
(C) agile : physique
(D) sensitive : patient
(E) trusting : honesty

23 INEXCUSABLE : JUSTIFY ::
(A) isolated : abandon
(B) unassailable : attack
(C) affable : like
(D) famous : admire
(E) splendid : revere

GO ON TO THE NEXT PAGE

Answer the questions below based on the information in the accompanying passages.

Questions 24–35 are based on the following passage.
In the following passage, a nineteenth-century American writer recalls his boyhood in a small town along the Mississippi River.

My father was a justice of the peace, and I supposed he possessed the power of life and death over all men and could hang anybody that offended him. This was
Line distinction enough for me as a general thing; but the
(5) desire to be a steamboatman kept intruding, nevertheless. I first wanted to be a cabin boy, so that I could come out with a white apron on and shake a tablecloth over the side, where all my old comrades could see me. Later I thought I would rather be the deck hand who
(10) stood on the end of the stage plank with a coil of rope in his hand, because he was particularly conspicuous.

But these were only daydreams—too heavenly to be contemplated as real possibilities. By and by one of the boys went away. He was not heard of for a long
(15) time. At last he turned up as an apprentice engineer or "striker" on a steamboat. This thing shook the bottom out of all my Sunday-school teachings. That boy had been notoriously worldly and I had been just the reverse—yet he was exalted to this eminence, and I
(20) was left in obscurity and misery. There was nothing generous about this fellow in his greatness. He would always manage to have a rusty bolt to scrub while his boat was docked at our town, and he would sit on the inside guard and scrub it, where we could all see him
(25) and envy him and loathe him.

He used all sorts of steamboat technicalities in his talk, as if he were so used to them that he forgot common people could not understand them. He would speak of the "labboard" side of a horse in an easy, nat-
(30) ural way that would make you wish he was dead. And he was always talking about "St. Looy" like an old citizen. Two or three of the boys had long been persons of consideration among us because they had been to St. Louis once and had a vague general knowledge of its
(35) wonders, but the day of their glory was over now. They lapsed into a humble silence, and learned to disappear when the ruthless "cub" engineer approached. This fellow had money, too, and hair oil, and he wore a showy brass watch chain, a leather belt, and used no sus-
(40) penders. No girl could withstand his charms. He "cut out" every boy in the village. When his boat blew up at last, it diffused a tranquil contentment among us such as we had not known for months. But when he came home the next week, alive, renowned, and appeared in
(45) church all battered up and bandaged, a shining hero, stared at and wondered over by everybody, it seemed to us that the partiality of Providence for an undeserving reptile had reached a point where it was open to criticism.

(50) This creature's career could produce but one result, and it speedily followed. Boy after boy managed to get on the river. Four sons of the chief merchant, and two sons of the county judge became pilots, the grandest position of all. But some of us could not get on the
(55) river—at least our parents would not let us.

So by and by I ran away. I said I would never come home again till I was a pilot and could return in glory. But somehow I could not manage it. I went meekly aboard a few of the boats that lay packed together like
(60) sardines at the long St. Louis wharf, and very humbly inquired for the pilots, but got only a cold shoulder and short words from mates and clerks. I had to make the best of this sort of treatment for the time being, but I had comforting daydreams of a future when I should
(65) be a great and honored pilot, with plenty of money, and could kill some of these mates and clerks and pay for them.

24 The author makes the statement that "I supposed he . . . offended him" (lines 1–3) primarily to suggest the
(A) power held by a justice of the peace in a frontier town
(B) naive view that he held of his father's importance
(C) respect in which the townspeople held his father
(D) possibility of miscarriages of justice on the American frontier
(E) harsh environment in which he was brought up

25 As used in line 4, the word *distinction* most nearly means
(A) difference
(B) variation
(C) prestige
(D) desperation
(E) clarity

26 The author decides that he would rather become a deck hand than a cabin boy (lines 6–11) because
(A) the job offers higher wages
(B) he believes that the work is easier
(C) he wants to avoid seeing his older friends
(D) deck hands often go on to become pilots
(E) the job is more visible to passersby

27 The author most likely mentions his "Sunday-school teachings" in line 17 to emphasize
(A) the influence of his early education in later life
(B) his sense of injustice at the engineer's success
(C) his disillusionment with longstanding religious beliefs
(D) his determination to become an engineer at all costs
(E) the unscrupulous nature of the engineer's character

28 The author most likely concludes that the engineer is not "generous" (line 21) because he
(A) has no respect for religious beliefs
(B) refuses to share his wages with friends
(C) flaunts his new position in public
(D) takes a pride in material possessions
(E) ignores the disappointment of other people's ambitions

29 The author most probably mentions the use of "steamboat technicalities" (line 26) in order to emphasize the engineer's
(A) expertise after a few months on the job
(B) fascination for trivial information
(C) ignorance on most other subjects
(D) desire to appear sophisticated
(E) inability to communicate effectively

30 The word *consideration* in line 33 most nearly means
(A) generosity
(B) deliberation
(C) contemplation
(D) unselfishness
(E) reputation

31 According to the passage, the "glory" of having visited St. Louis (lines 33–35) was over because
(A) the boys' knowledge of St. Louis was much less detailed than the engineer's
(B) St. Louis had changed so much that the boys' stories were no longer accurate
(C) the boys realized that traveling to St. Louis was not a mark of sophistication
(D) the engineer's account revealed that the boys' stories were lies
(E) travel to St. Louis had become too commonplace to be envied

32 The author describes the engineer's appearance (lines 38–40) primarily in order to
(A) suggest one reason why many people found the engineer impressive
(B) convey the way steamboatmen typically dressed
(C) emphasize the inadequacy of his own wardrobe
(D) contrast the engineer's behavior with his appearance
(E) indicate his admiration for fashionable clothes

33 In lines 47–49, the author's response to the engineer's survival is one of
(A) thankfulness for what he believes is God's providence
(B) astonishment at the engineer's miraculous escape
(C) reflection on the occupational hazards of a steamboating career
(D) outrage at his rival's undeserved good fortune
(E) sympathy for the extent of the engineer's wounds

34 The major purpose of the passage is to
(A) sketch the peaceful life of a frontier town
(B) relate the events that led to a boy's first success in life
(C) portray the unsophisticated ambitions of a boy
(D) describe the characteristics of a small-town boaster
(E) give a humorous portrayal of a boy's conflicts with his parents

35 At the end of the passage, the author reflects on
(A) his new ambition to become either a mate or a clerk
(B) the wisdom of seeking a job in which advancement is easier
(C) the prospect of abandoning a hopeless search for fame
(D) the impossibility of returning home and asking his parents' pardon
(E) his determination to keep striving for success in a glorious career

STOP IF YOU FINISH BEFORE TIME IS CALLED, YOU MAY CHECK YOUR WORK ON THIS SECTION ONLY. **DO NOT** TURN TO ANY OTHER SECTION IN THE TEST.

Answer the questions below based on the information in the accompanying passages.

Questions 1–12 are based on the following passages.

The controversy over the authorship of Shakespeare's plays began in the 18th century and continues to this day. Here, the author of Passage 1 embraces the proposal that Francis Bacon actually wrote the plays, while the author of Passage 2 defends the traditional attribution to Shakespeare himself.

Passage 1

Anyone with more than a superficial knowledge of Shakespeare's plays must necessarily entertain some doubt concerning their true authorship. Can
Line scholars honestly accept the idea that such master-
(5) works were written by a shadowy actor with limited formal education and a social position that can most charitably be called "humble"? Obviously, the author of the plays must have traveled widely, yet there is no record that Shakespeare ever left his
(10) native England. Even more obviously, the real author had to have intimate knowledge of life within royal courts and palaces, yet Shakespeare was a commoner, with little firsthand experience of the aristocracy. No, common sense tells us that the
(15) plays must have been written by someone with substantial expertise in the law, the sciences, classics, foreign languages, and the fine arts—someone, in other words, like Shakespeare's eminent contemporary, Sir Francis Bacon.
(20) The first person to suggest that Bacon was the actual author of the plays was Reverend James Wilmot. Writing in 1785, Wilmot argued that someone of Shakespeare's educational background could hardly have produced works of such erudition and
(25) insight. But a figure like Bacon, a scientist and polymath* of legendary stature, would certainly have known about, for instance, the circulation of the blood as alluded to in *Coriolanus*. And as an aristocrat, Bacon would have possessed the familiarity
(30) with court life required to produce a *Love's Labour's Lost*.

Delia Bacon (no relation to Sir Francis) was next to make the case for Francis Bacon's authorship. In 1856, in collaboration with Nathaniel Hawthorne,
(35) she insisted that it was ridiculous to look for the creator of Hamlet among "that dirty, doggish group of players, who come into the scene [of the play Hamlet] summoned like a pack of hounds to his service." Ultimately, she concluded that the plays were
(40) actually composed by a committee consisting of Bacon, Edmund Spenser, Walter Raleigh, and several others.

Still, some might wonder why Bacon, if indeed the plays were wholly or partly his work, would not
(45) put his own name on them. But consider the political climate of England in Elizabethan times. Given that it would have been politically and personally damaging for a man of Bacon's position to associate himself with such controversial plays, it is quite
(50) understandable that Bacon would hire a lowly actor to take the credit—and the consequences.

But perhaps the most convincing evidence of all comes from the postscript of a 1624 letter sent to Bacon by Sir Tobie Matthew. "The most prodigious
(55) wit that I ever knew . . . is your lordship's name," Matthew wrote, "though he be known by another." That name, of course, was William Shakespeare.

*polymath: a person of wide and varied learning.

Passage 2

Over the years, there have been an astonishing number of persons put forth as the "true author" of
(60) Shakespeare's plays. Some critics have even gone so far as to claim that only a "committee" could have possessed the abundance of talent and energy necessary to produce Shakespeare's thirty-seven plays. Among the individual figures most seriously pro-
(65) moted as "the real Shakespeare" is Sir Francis Bacon. Apparently, the fact that Bacon wrote most of his own work in academic Latin does nothing to deter those who would crown him the premier stylist in the English language.
(70) Although the entire controversy reeks of scholarly gamesplaying, the issue underlying it is worth considering: How could an uneducated actor create such exquisite works? But the answer to that is easy. Shakespeare's dramatic gifts had little to do with
(75) encyclopedic knowledge, complex ideas, or a fluency with great systems of thought. Rather, Shakespeare's genius was one of common sense and perceptive intuition—a genius that grows not out of book-learning, but out of a deep understanding of
(80) human nature and a keen grasp of basic emotions, passions, and jealousies.

One of the most common arguments advanced by skeptics is that the degree of familiarity with the law exhibited in a *Hamlet* or a *Merchant of Venice* can
(85) only have been achieved by a lawyer or other man of affairs. The grasp of law evidenced in these plays, however, is not a detailed knowledge of formal law, but a more general understanding of so-called "country law." Shakespeare was a landowner—an

(90) extraordinary achievement in itself for an ill-paid Elizabethan actor—and so would have been knowledgeable about legal matters related to the buying, selling, and renting of real estate. Evidence of such a common understanding of land regulations can be (95) found, for instance, in the gravedigging scene of *Hamlet*.

So no elaborate theories of intrigue and secret identity are necessary to explain the accomplishment of William Shakespeare. Scholars who have (100) made a career of ferreting out "alternative bards" may be reluctant to admit it, but literary genius can flower in any socioeconomic bracket. Shakespeare, in short, was Shakespeare—an observation that one would have thought was obvious to everyone.

1. In line 2, *entertain* most nearly means
   (A) amuse
   (B) harbor
   (C) occupy
   (D) cherish
   (E) engage

2. In Passage 1, the author draws attention to Shakespeare's social standing as a "commoner" (line 13) in order to cast doubt on the Elizabethan actor's
   (A) aptitude for writing poetically
   (B) knowledge of foreign places and habits
   (C) ability to support himself by playwriting
   (D) familiarity with life among persons of high rank
   (E) understanding of the problems of government

3. *Coriolanus* and *Love's Labour's Lost* are mentioned in lines 28–31 as examples of works that
   (A) only Francis Bacon could have written
   (B) exhibit a deep understanding of human nature
   (C) resemble works written by Francis Bacon under his own name
   (D) portray a broad spectrum of Elizabethan society
   (E) reveal expertise more likely held by Bacon than Shakespeare

4. In Passage 1, the quotation from Delia Bacon (lines 36–39) conveys a sense of
   (A) disdain for the disreputable vulgarity of Elizabethan actors
   (B) resentment at the way Shakespeare's characters were portrayed
   (C) regret that conditions for Elizabethan actors were not better
   (D) doubt that Shakespeare could actually have created such unsavory characters
   (E) disappointment at the incompetence of Elizabethan actors

5. The author of Passage 1 maintains that Bacon did not put his own name on the plays attributed to Shakespeare because he
   (A) regarded writing as an unsuitable occupation for an aristocrat
   (B) wished to protect himself from the effects of controversy
   (C) preferred being known as a scientist and politician rather than as a writer
   (D) did not want to associate himself with lowly actors
   (E) sought to avoid the attention that fame brings

6. In the first paragraph of Passage 2, the author calls into question Bacon's likely ability to
   (A) write in a language with which he was unfamiliar
   (B) make the transition between scientific writing and playwriting
   (C) produce the poetic language evident in the plays
   (D) cooperate with other members of a committee
   (E) singlehandedly create thirty-seven plays

7. The word *premier* in line 68 most nearly means
   (A) earliest
   (B) influential
   (C) inaugural
   (D) greatest
   (E) original

GO ON TO THE NEXT PAGE

8 In line 75, the word *encyclopedic* most nearly means
(A) technical
(B) comprehensive
(C) abridged
(D) disciplined
(E) specialized

9 The author of Passage 2 cites Shakespeare's status as a landowner in order to
(A) prove that Shakespeare was a success as a playwright
(B) refute the claim that Shakespeare had little knowledge of aristocratic life
(C) prove that Shakespeare didn't depend solely on acting for his living
(D) dispute the notion that Shakespeare was a commoner
(E) account for Shakespeare's apparent knowledge of the law

10 In lines 99–102, the author maintains that literary genius
(A) is not dependent on a writer's external circumstances
(B) must be based on an inborn comprehension of human nature
(C) is enhanced by the suffering that poverty brings
(D) frequently goes unrecognized among those of modest means and position
(E) can be stifled by too much book-learning and academic training

11 The author of Passage 2 would probably respond to the speculation in the fourth paragraph of Passage 1 by pointing out that
(A) Shakespeare's plays would not have seemed particularly controversial to Elizabethan audiences
(B) The extent and range of Bacon's learning has been generally exaggerated
(C) such scenarios are farfetched and unnecessary if one correctly understands Shakespeare's genius
(D) Bacon would not have had the knowledge of the lower classes required to produce the plays
(E) the claim implies that Shakespeare was disreputable when in fact he was a respectable landowner

12 The author of Passage 1 would probably respond to the skepticism expressed in lines 66–69 by making which of the following statements?
(A) The similarities between English and Latin make it plausible that one person could write well in both languages.
(B) Plays written in Latin would not have been likely to attract a wide audience in Elizabethan England.
(C) The premier stylist in the English language is more likely to have been an eminent scholar than an uneducated actor.
(D) Writing the plays in Latin would have shielded Bacon from much of the political damage he wanted to avoid.
(E) The style of the plays is notable mostly for the clarity of thought behind the lines rather than their musicality or beauty.

STOP   IF YOU FINISH BEFORE TIME IS CALLED, YOU MAY CHECK YOUR WORK ON THIS SECTION ONLY. **DO NOT** TURN TO ANY OTHER SECTION IN THE TEST.

SECTION 1

1 **E**—It's easy enough to understand that insurers don't like to insure property in places where natural disasters are likely to happen. The term **prone to** in (E) means "having a tendency to," so it is correct.

2 **C**—If it took Roman legions three years to seize Masada, we can predict that they spent a long time "surrounding or isolating" the mountain "fortress or stronghold" of Masada before they were finally able to take it. (C) is the best choice. (B) **assailed,** meaning "attacked," would make sense in the first blank, and (E) **stronghold** and (A) **bastion** would fit, too. But (A), (B), and (E)'s first-position words don't make sense when plugged in.

> beseiged: surrounded with armed forces
> citadel: fortress
> assailed: attacked
> bastion: fortified area
> dissembled: concealed
> honed: sharpened

3 **B**—If the senator was **unlike** "his calmer, more easygoing colleagues" and "ready to quarrel at the slightest provocation," it's fair to infer that the senator was short-tempered or extremely irritable. The best choice is (B)—**irascible.**

> irascible: easily angered
> whimsical: fanciful, erratic, or unpredictable
> gregarious: sociable, friendly
> ineffectual: futile, unproductive
> benign: harmless or gentle

4 **B**—You don't have to know that Genghis Khan was a violent dictator to get this question right. What's important to know is that the first word of the sentence, *although,* implies that the two blanks have to contain words that contrast with each other. (B) is the best choice—although historians had thought that Genghis Khan was a **despotic** potentate, new research shows that many of his subjects nevertheless **revered** him. Although (A) **tyrannical** is synonymous with *despotic,* (A)'s second-blank choice, **abhorred,** doesn't provide the predicted contrast. Choice (C) **venerated** doesn't really contrast with **redundant.** And in (E), it doesn't make sense to say that Khan's subjects **invoked** him

despite his **peremptory** reputation.

> despotic: oppressive, dictatorial
> potentate: dictator
> revered: worshipped, adored
> abhorred: hated
> venerated: highly respected
> redundant: repetitive
> jocular: jolly
> peremptory: putting an end to debate
> invoke: call upon for help

5 **B**—The word *because* in the middle of the sentence lets us know that the words in the blanks will be consistent in meaning, which means that they will share the same type of charge. We can predict two positive words, like "Jill was appreciated by her employees because she often forgave" the fact that they were lazy, or two negative words like "Jill was disliked by her employees because she often scolded them" for being lazy. (B) matches the latter prediction—Jill was **loathed** by her employees because she often **berated** them for not working hard enough. No other choice besides (B) contains two like charges.

> loathed: hated
> berated: scolded
> deified: made godlike
> lauded: praised or celebrated
> derided: made fun of
> execrated: condemned, cursed

6 **E**—If "reconstructing the skeletons of extinct species like dinosaurs . . . requires much patience and effort by paleontologists," we can predict that such an acitivty is a "painstaking or tough, demanding process." (E) **exacting** is our best choice.

> exacting: requiring lots of attention and
>   extreme accuracy
> nascent: introductory or starting
> aberrant: abnormal

7 **C**—Because of disease and the destruction of their habitat, koalas are now found only in isolated parts of eucalyptus forests. The word in the blank must mean something like "killed off" or "destroyed," since things like "disease and habitat destruction" are destructive processes. (C) is our best choice—"nearly **decimated** or wiped out by disease and habitat destruction," koalas are now found only in isolated parts of eucalyptus forests. (A) **dispersed**, meaning "scattered," may have been a little tempting, but there's no reason to assume that the koalas were scattered around the forests due to "disease and habitat destruction."

---

dispersed: scattered
compiled: categorized, collected, arranged
averted: avoided

---

8 **E**—Looking at the first blank first, if there were "internal power struggles" in the government, then it's likely that the government had something like "deep ideological differences or conflicts." For the second blank, we can predict that these conflicts and power struggles harmed or crippled the government. Although choice (C)'s first-blank choice, **distortions,** sounds negative, like "differences or conflicts," choices (A) and (E) make *more* sense. We can easily imagine "deep ideological **disputes**" or "deep ideological **divisions**" going hand in hand with "internal power struggles," but it's hard to imagine ideological **distortions**.

Now we can turn to (A) and (E)'s second-blank choices. (A) doesn't make sense given the context of the sentence—why would "deep ideological **disputes** and internal power struggles **facilitate** the government"? (E) is the best choice—"deep ideological **divisions** and internal power struggles **paralyzed** the government."

---

distortions: perversions, twisted versions
facilitate: assist
stymied: frustrated, impeded

---

9 **D**—The terms *popular remedy* and *as yet* are key in this sentence. Large doses of vitamins are popularly thought to be good but their effectiveness has not been proven at this time. (D) **unproven** is the correct answer. Answer choices (A), (B), (C), and (E) are wrong because they imply that medical experts understand and approve of large doses, which clearly contradicts the sentence.

10 **B**—A **TROUT** is a type of **FISH,** just as a **human** is a type of **mammal**.

11 **A**—Bridge: If you **INHALE** something, it goes into your **LUNGS**. If you **swallow** something, it goes into your **stomach**.

12 **A**—A **BRAGGART** is, by definition, someone who **BOAST**s. A **laggard** is, by definition, someone who **tarries**. A speaker, not a **hypocrite**, is someone who, by definition, **speaks,** so (B) is wrong.

---

laggard: lingerer, one who lags behind
extrovert: someone very outgoing
tarry: to dawdle, be late, delay
hypocrite: someone who pretends to be
  what he or she is not

---

13 **B**—To **ALLEVIATE** is to reduce **PAIN,** just as to **depreciate** is to reduce **value**. In choice (D), to **deviate** is to move away from some set **standard**. That's not the same as lowering a **standard**.

14 **C**—Bridge: To **INFURIATE** someone is to **ANNOY** him or her a great deal. In correct choice (C), to **terrify** someone is to **frighten** him or her a great deal.

---

satiate: to satisfy

---

15 **D**—Someone **MISERLY** is not characterized by **MAGNANIMITY,** or generousness. Similarly, someone **innocent** is not characterized by **culpability**.

---

transient: wandering from place to place
stupefaction: overwhelming amazement
fastidiousness: the quality of being
  painstaking or particular
avarice: greed
magnanimity: generosity
culpability: guilt

The Time Passage

Next up is a fairly abstract science passage. This particular passage is perhaps a little bit harder than the ones you're going to encounter on Test Day—but don't be intimidated by the subject matter. Even if your passage is written by a Nobel Prize winner, it's going to contain ideas that you can relate to, and probably some ideas that you've seen before.

The topic of the passage is how difficult it is to comprehend long stretches of time. Paragraph two tells us that our minds aren't built to handle the idea of thousands of years passing. We have *some* conception of the past through the art, writing, and photography of previous generations, but the scale of longer time periods eludes us. Paragraphs four and five attempt to bridge this gap by providing a few everyday yardsticks; the time the human race has been around is compared to a few seconds in a week, or a few letters in a book. Essentially, that's all you need to take from your first reading of the passage; the details you can come back to later.

16 **D**—Here, in paragraph one, the author's talking about why we find it difficult to understand vast stretches of time. We're told that the "span" of what we can remember is limited because our lives are relatively short. So "span" in this context means the *amount* of time we're able to recollect—the (D) **extent.**

(A) **rate of increase,** (B) **value,** and (E) **accuracy** are all correct definitions of "span," but they're not aspects of memory as discussed in the passage. And (C) **bridge,** the most common definition, doesn't fit at all.

> Hint: The golden rule about vocabulary questions on the Critical Reading section is that they test vocabulary IN CONTEXT. You're being asked how a particular word is used in the passage, not how it's usually defined.

17 **C**—Before writing, we're told, the wisdom of generations was passed down in two ways—verbally, and "to a lesser extent," in pictures, carvings, and statues. This means that the wisdom of the past was transmitted less effectively by nonverbal means, and thus (C) **more effectively by the spoken word than by other means.**

Choices (A) and (B) *distort* this idea. Nowhere are we told that wisdom was rejected. And since spoken words *and* pictures were both used, it was obviously not an all or nothing proposition. (E) doesn't make much sense. How could there be an emphasis on science before writing existed? (D), finally, makes no sense at all—the author never says that all ancient wisdom was fiction.

18 **B**—This is a Little Picture question asking about the purpose of a detail. The question asks why the author discusses the impact of writing. Looking at the lines around the line reference given, we're told that writing has made the transmission of information about the past a lot more precise and extensive. Pictures and photography are also mentioned as ways in which the experience of the past has been passed down. So choice (B)'s correct here—writing is mentioned as an **example** of how cultures record knowledge about the past.

(A) is a distortion—the author is showing us something about the past, not why we remember hardly anything. He never implies any criticism of preliterate cultures, so choice (C) is out too. Choices (D) and (E) are wrong because the author never mentions them in the context referred to or in the whole passage.

19 **C**—Another Vocabulary-in-Context question. The word *ready* can mean several things—choices (A), (C), (D), and (E) are all possible meanings. In this context, however, it most nearly means **immediate,** choice (C). In the sentence before the cited line, the author says "there is no simple way" to understand vast stretches of time. And in the sentence following the cited line, the author compares the way we understand time to the way a blind man "laboriously" constructs a picture of his surroundings. This implies that our understanding of time is a difficult and time-consuming task, not something we can do *readily* or **immediately.**

20 **E**—Another question asking about the *purpose behind* part of the author is argument. Give the context a quick scan. Once again, the author's talking about how difficult it is to understand vast stretches of time. We're told that it's like a blind man building up a sensory picture of his surroundings. This is an **indirect** process, so choice (E) is right.

Choice (C) is dealt with later in paragraph four, so you can eliminate it right away.

Choice (A) is too sweeping. The author never says that human beings are *completely* **unable to comprehend time.** (B) and (D) have nothing to do with the passage.

21 **A**—Inference skills are required here. What is the author's underlying point in mentioning the Big Bang and the Cambrian Period? The author *introduces* this discussion in the cited passage by saying that **a week** provides a better yardstick for the age of the earth than a day. The Big Bang and the Cambrian Period are used as examples to support this point. So (A) is right—it's the point about the time scale that the author's trying to demonstrate.

Choices (D) and (E) both distort the point in different ways. The author is not suggesting that the time scale of a day should be totally abandoned—just that the week is a better scale. The development of (B) **agriculture** is another supporting example like the Big Bang and the Cambrian Period, but it's not the author's central point here. Finally, **fossils** have nothing to do with the question at hand, so (C) is easily eliminated.

22 C—A more straightforward comprehension question this time. When we go back to the lines referred to, we're told about the problem with linear maps: When you produce one that's big enough to show us on it, the map becomes too big to study and reproduce conveniently. (C) gets the right paraphrase here. Notice especially the match up in synonyms for "convenient reproduction" and "examination."

(A), (B), and (E) aren't supported here—there's nothing about **overlapping** periods, **scientific standards,** or ignorance about **pre-Cambrian times** in the passage. (D) doesn't address the problem. The question is about getting our human experience on the map.

23 D—What's the overall point the author is trying to prove?

The Big Picture is that life started on earth so long ago that it is difficult for us to comprehend. Everything that follows is meant to illustrate this point, including the time scales. Don't let the material confuse you. The point is (D)—**the immensity of time** since the origin of **life.**

(C) is tricky to reject because it's an aspect of the larger argument, but it's not the whole point. The other wrong choices mention issues that the author hardly touches on. In paragraphs four to six, the author's *not* concerned with getting dates right (A), the question of how life actually began (B), or the (E) **development of communication.**

The Susan B. Anthony Passage

This humanities passage is from a speech by Susan B. Anthony, a 19th-century women's rights leader. Anthony admits at the outset that she was recently charged with the "crime" of voting. Her intention is to prove that her vote was no crime, but rather the exercise of her Constitutional rights, which no state should be allowed to impinge upon. This generates the passage's big idea: that Anthony—and by exten-

sion all women—should be allowed to vote. You may have found Anthony's style a little dated or confusing. Don't worry; the questions will help you focus on specific details.

24 C—The important thing here is to see what exactly Anthony is saying. The question stem is keyed to the first paragraph. In the second sentence she states that she "not only committed no crime, but . . . simply exercised my citizen's rights, guaranteed me . . . by the National Constitution." The words *no crime* are the first important clue. You can immediately rule out (A) and (E) because they say she believes the act was illegal. The second part of the line discusses the Constitution, so (C) is clearly a restatement of her argument.

(B) and (D) both make sense, but she does not state these points in the first paragraph. Therefore, they are wrong.

25 A—The most common meaning of "promote" is to move up—to a higher position, rank, or job. This doesn't make sense, though, in the phrase "promote the general welfare." "General welfare" means the good of all people, so to (A) **further** it, makes the most sense.

(B) **organize** and (C) **publicize** both could apply to the general welfare, but not as well as (A). They refer more to promotion as you would do with a concert or sports event. (D) **commend** means "praise," which seems silly in the context given, as does (E) **motivate.**

> Hint: In Vocabulary-in-Context questions, the right answer is usually not the most common meaning of the given word. Be sure to reread the context.

26 E—Anthony points out that no subgroup was excluded by the wording of the preamble of the Constitution. ". . . we formed it . . . to secure [the blessings of liberty,] not to the half of ourselves . . . but to . . . women as well as men." Therefore (E) is correct. **All people deserve to enjoy the rights of the Constitution.**

Anthony never claims that the Founding Fathers plotted to deny women their rights (A). (B) is incorrect because the author's concern is women's rights and not rights of any other group. Though **some male citizens may still be denied basic rights,** (B) goes against the gist of what is being said. (C) is like (A) in that it's a claim Anthony never makes.

Finally, though (D) is a point that Anthony does make, she doesn't make it until the next paragraph.

27 **B**—We're still looking at the same part of the passage.
Look at the structure of the quoted sentence: "We didn't do it only for X, but for X *and* Y." "Posterity" means "future generations," which would include men and women. So the X, the "half of our posterity," refers to the posterity of those who already enjoy the blessings of liberty. In other words, men. (B) is the right choice.

(A) has nothing to do with what Anthony is discussing. Since the construction of the sentence makes it clear that the "half of our posterity" is not the whole of those who want to vote, (C) is out. There's no way of saying that one-half of the people are and will be opponents of women's rights, so (D) is wrong. And (E) wrongly suggests that in the future, one half of the country's population will be members of government.

28 **A**—Reread the keyed paragraph. Anthony is saying that a state that prohibits women from voting violates federal law—the Constitution. Therefore it becomes "an odious aristocracy, a hateful oligarchy." Neither of these things is a democracy. (A) is the correct answer.

Anthony mentions rebellion, but she doesn't mean the kind of violent rebellion (B) talks about. (C) is wrong because of the word *remain*. The nation is not and never has been an aristocracy. (D) plays off the same sentence as (B) does, but instead of going too far, it doesn't go far enough. Anthony wants the laws against women voting repealed; she doesn't want them merely discussed. (E) is totally wrong because at no point is Anthony arguing that an aristocracy should be preserved.

29 **C**—You might readily associate *hardihood* with (A) **endurance** and (B) **vitality**, but a quick check back in context shows you these aren't correct. Anthony says she doesn't believe her opponents would have the ---- to say women aren't "persons." Saying such an offensive thing would take a lot of **nerve**, choice (C). It might also take a lot of **stupidity** (E), but that's too strong a word, considering Anthony's diplomatic tone.

30 **D**—The stem keys you to the second to last sentence of the passage. *Abridge* means

"deprive," so Anthony is saying that no state can deprive citizens of their rights. (D) states exactly this.

In (A), *privilege* means "luxury," but voting is a basic right, not a luxury. (B) comes out of nowhere; there's no discussion of courts in this passage. (C) plays off Anthony's reference to "any old law." She's not talking about *any* outdated laws in this passage; she means any law *that prohibits women from voting*. Anthony never addresses how the laws will be changed, only that they must be changed, so (E) is out.

antagonism: hostility

SECTION 2

1 **D**—This is not a difficult question. The use of the word *and* tells us that we're looking for a word to fill the first blank which is consistent with "scarcity of rain"—a word like *dry*. We can, therefore, eliminate (A) and (C) at once. Since farming conditions are "bad," our second blank should express the idea that there's no point in trying to work there. By that criterion, choices (B) and (E) can be eliminated. This leaves us with (D) **future**. (D)'s first word, **infertile**, also fits perfectly, so (D) is the correct answer.

barren: not productive

2 **D**—The structural clue in this sentence is *not only . . . but*, which suggests that the students were doing something even worse than ignoring the rules. The only word that fits here is **flouting**, choice (D).

flouting: mocking, treating with contempt

3 **A**—The word *while* following the comma in the second part of the sentence tells us that there will be a contrast between what some critics believe about dadaism and what *others* "insist the movement was." The best choice is (A)—"some critics believe that the **zenith** of modern art came with dadaism, while others insist the movement was a **sham**." Other choices have single words that would make sense in one of the blanks, but none of the pairs except (A) expresses the contrast that is implied by the sentence.

zenith: highest point
sham: hoax

4 **C**—In this question you are asked to make a logical connection between two parts of a sentence. It is clear that the content of the journalist's article either had no impact, in which case there was little or no response from the public, or it attracted a great deal of attention and was followed by a lot of correspondence. (C) is the correct answer. The author would never have thought her article was **controversial** were it not for the **spate** of correspondence. The other answer choices are wrong because they sound contradictory when plugged into the sentence. For example, in choice (A), if the article were **interesting,** one would expect it to be followed by a lot of correspondence—not by a **dearth**, or lack of it. In choice (D), if the article were **commonplace** (ordinary), why would an **influx** of letters follow its publication?

spate: a sudden flood or rush
dearth: lack
inflammatory: likely to arouse strong
    feeling or anger
influx: flow coming in

5 **E**—If many readers have difficulty following Descartes' complex, intricately woven arguments, then it's likely that his writings are something like *complicated, esoteric,* or *obscure*. The best choice is (E) **abstruse**.

abstruse: difficult to understand
generic: common, general
trenchant: extremely perceptive, insightful

6 **B**—The phrase *even though* indicates contrast. So, even though the prisoner "presented evidence clearly proving that he was nowhere near the scene of the crime," he was **indicted** or formally charged with committing the crime.

exculpated: absolved, proved to be innocent
exhumed: removed from a grave
rescinded: cancelled, taken back

7 **C**—A premise is a proposition which is used as the basis for an argument—or a story. If scientists are critical of the premise for a movie, we can infer that they are so because they consider it to be unscientific, without basis in fact, or **speculative**. (C) is therefore the correct answer. (A) is wrong, because if the premise, or underlying argument, were scientific then it would hardly be open to criticism by scientists. (B) is wrong because there's no reason to think that the theme of the return of the dinosaurs is unexpressed in the movie.

tacit: silent; understood but unexpressed

8 **B**—Looking at the second blank first, if Mozart "left no rough drafts," it's probably "because he was able to write out his compositions in a complete, unrevised form." So, for the second blank, (B) **finished** looks best. (E) **concise** is also possible, so let's try (B) and (E) in the first blank. We've already seen that Mozart didn't need to revise his compositions—therefore, it makes sense to say that he "composed music with exceptional *ease* or **facility**." (E) **independence** is just too ambiguous to fit in to the context of the sentence.

concise: using as few words as possible,
    to the point

9 **D**—If dogs are "known for their devotion," than it's likely that they "were often used as symbols of *faithfulness, loyalty,* or *fidelity*" in Medieval and Renaissance paintings. (A) **resistance** and (E) **antagonism** are not what we're looking for, and choices (B) and (C), while positive, don't relate to the idea of *devotion*.

antagonism: hostility

10 **C**—In this sentence we find a description of two contradictory characteristics which exist in the same group of people. On the one hand, they are brutal; on the other, they are heroic. Such an occurrence is termed a *paradox* and therefore (C) **paradoxical** is the correct answer. Choices (A), (D), and (E) are wrong; it is **unfortunate, distressing,** and **appalling** that they are brutal—but not that they are heroic.

paradoxical: like a riddle; opposed to
    common sense but true
explicable: able to be explained

11 E—A **CHARLATAN** is, by definition not **SCRUPULOUS**. A **tyrant** is a ruler who uses power oppressively and unjustly. So a **tyrant** is, by definition, not **just**.

> *charlatan: a fraud or a quack, someone who pretends to have more knowledge or skill than he or she possesses*

12 C—**GREED** is the desire to **ACQUIRE** large amounts of things. **Gluttony** is the desire to **eat** large amounts, so (C) is the best answer.

(A) won't work; someone who experiences **fear** may or may not want to **disguise** him- or herself. In (B), it may be hard to **persuade** someone characterized by **inertia**, but **inertia** isn't the desire to **persuade** large amounts.

> *inertia: apathy, inactivity*

13 A—The word **BLOW** is being used to mean "a swipe or punch." To **PARRY** means "to deflect, ward off," so our bridge is "to **PARRY** a **BLOW** is to deflect it." (A) shares the same bridge— to **counter** an **argument** is to deflect it.

In choice (B), you might **sidestep** or avoid an argument or issue, but there isn't really any clear connection between **sidestep** and **offense**. In (C), to **defer** isn't to deflect or ward off a **ruling**.

> *pitfall: a trap or hidden danger*
> *defer: put off or delay*

14 E—**SLURS** are words that **MALIGN**, just as **compliments** are words that **flatter**. The other choices don't fit this bridge. For instance, in (C), **whispers** aren't necessarily words that **torment**.

15 A—A **LENTIL** is classified as a **LEGUME**, a bean or pea, in the same way that **rice** is classified as a **cereal**.

Even if you didn't know that a **LENTIL** is a **LEGUME**, you might have been able to arrive at the answer by eliminating all choices with no good bridges. For example, in (B) **food** may or may not provide **nutrition**, or nourishment.

> *husk: the outer covering of a kernel or seed*

16 D—To **INDULGE** an **APPETITE** is to satisfy it. Similarly, to **humor** a **whim** is to satisfy it.

In (A), you can **filter** out an **impurity**, but it doesn't make sense to say that to **filter** out an **impurity** is to satisfy it. (C) might have been a tempting choice, since the word **coddle** is similar to **indulge**. But **coddle** doesn't have a necessary connection to **emotion**.

> *coddle: to overindulge, pamper*

17 B—Bridge: **MELLIFLUOUS** means "sweet SOUND**ing**." **Fragrant** means "sweet smelling."

In (D), a **raucous** discussion would be a harsh-sounding, noisy debate.

> *mellifluous: sweet sounding, melodious*
> *fragrant: sweet smelling*
> *raucous: harsh or grating*

18 C—A **GUFFAW** is loud, unrestrained **LAUGH**ing. In the same way, a **yell** is loud, unrestrained **talk**ing.

19 C—The word **CELESTIAL** means "having to do with the **HEAVENS**." The word **nautical** means "having to do with **ships**."

> *celestial: having to do with the heavens*
> *nautical: having to do with ships*
> *viscous: thick and gluey*

20 C—To **ENERVATE** is to lessen or decrease **VITALITY**. In (C), to **daunt** is to lessen **courage**.

You could have worked backwards by eliminating answer choices with inappropriate or weak bridges. For example, in (A), one can **consolidate power** by securing and strengthening one's position, but that bridge doesn't work with the stem words. Choice (B) has a weak bridge, too: To **energize** is to fill with energy, but that doesn't always result in **action**. If you plug the stem words into (D)'s bridge, you get, "To enervate is to assess the vitality of something." It doesn't sound sensible, so (D) is out, too. In (E) to **admit guilt** is to confess. That couldn't be true of the stem as well. By process of elimination, (C) is correct.

enervate: to lessen or decrease vitality
daunt: to subdue or dismay
energize: to fill with energy
estimate: to assess the worth of something

21 **D**—An **OLIGARCHY** is, by definition, a form of government in which power is held by a **FEW** people. Answer choice (D) is analogous to this: A **monarchy** is a form of government in which power is held by **one** person.

If the definition of **OLIGARCHY** posed a problem, you could again eliminate wrong answers. For instance, in choice (A), the terms **government** and **majority** are not always linked. Similarly, in (B), **authority** and **consent** don't necessarily go together. In (C), a **country** may or may not have a **constitution**.

oligarchy: a form of government in which power is held by a few people
monarchy: a form of government in which power is held by one person
constitution: a set of principles according to which a nation is governed

22 **A**—Bridge: Someone who is **UNTRUTHFUL** is characterized by **MENDACIOUSNESS**. Choice (A) is correct: Someone who is **circumspect** is characterized by **caution**.

What if you don't know what mendaciousness or circumspect mean? You must try to eliminate wrong answers. Remember that the stem words and the correct answer choice will have the same strong bridge. Work backwards. Does (B) have a strong bridge? A person who is **timid** exhibits certain a type of **behavior**—that's not a strong connection. Similarly, (C)'s bridge is weak: Everyone has a **physique** of some kind, not just **agile** people. Answer choices (D) and (E) can also be eliminated because they have weak bridges. That leaves us with (A).

mendaciousness: lying
circumspect: cautious or watchful

23 **B**—The bridge can be stated as: Something that is **INEXCUSABLE** is impossible to **JUSTIFY**. Likewise, in (B), something that is **unassailable** is impossible to **attack**.

unassailable: not open to attack or question
affable: friendly and polite
revere: to feel deep respect or awe for

The Twain Passage

This excerpt from Mark Twain's *Life on the Mississippi* should be amusing and easy to read. All the humor comes from the same technique—using deadpan, matter-of-fact language to describe the exaggerated daydreams and jealousies of a boy's life.

The central point here is the author's envy of the engineer, and many of the questions focus on this. The author starts with his own glamorous ideas about steamboating, then spends most of the passage on the show-off engineer. The passage finishes with the author's own failure to find work as a pilot. The slightly old-fashioned style isn't hard to follow, but several questions focus on the author's figurative use of words.

24 **B**—The key word in the sentence is *supposed*. Of course, a justice of the peace *doesn't* possess unlimited power, but because of inexperience the author "supposed" he did. (B) accurately uses *naive* (inexperienced, gullible) to characterize the author's misconception. Three of the wrong choices assume that the father really *did* have unlimited powers and explain this in different ways—frontier justice (A, D), public support (C). (E) mistakenly views the boy's description of his father as an indication that the boy's childhood environment was harsh.

25 **C**—*Distinction* has several meanings, including those in (A), (B), (C), and (E). The key to its use here is context: In the previous sentence the author is talking about his naive ideas of his father's great power. **Prestige,** (C), suggesting high status and honor, fits this context; the other three don't. (D) is not a meaning of *distinction* at all.

26 **E**—This question asks about the literal meaning of the sentence, but inference and context help, too. The sentence explains that the author wanted the job because a deck hand was "conspicuous," or easily seen. The previous sentence stresses standing "where all my old comrades could see me," so you can deduce that the author wants to be seen and admired in what he imagines is a glamorous profession (E).

(A) and (B) invent advantages that are not mentioned, and miss the humor by suggesting common-sense economic motivations. (C) assumes that if the author could be seen by his "old comrades" in the first job, he must want *not* to be seen by them in a different job; but this is false, since he'd be "conspicuous" in the second job, too. (D) brings in an ambition—becoming a pilot—that the author doesn't develop until the end of the passage.

27 **B**—Again, context helps. The **Sunday-school** reference is explained in the next sentence. The engineer had been "worldly"— which is what Sunday-school probably taught students not to be— and the author had been "just the reverse." In other words, the author followed his Sunday-school teachings, the engineer didn't, yet the engineer gets the glory. The underlying idea is that this was unjust (B).

(A) is never mentioned. (C) takes the Sunday-school reference literally and misses the humorous tone. (D) invents an ambition that the author never mentions; his reaction is pure envy, not frustrated ambition. (E) misconstrues the reference to the engineer as "worldly"; it means he didn't take Sunday-school seriously, not that he was **unscrupulous** (dishonest or crooked).

28 **C**—To get this question, you need to read the sentence that follows. The engineer was not generous because he sat about where "we all could see him and envy him." The implication is that great people should be generous by not showing off or (C) **flaunting** their success.

(A) refers to the Sunday-school comment, but that was about undeserved greatness, not lack of generosity. (B) and (D) interpret *generous* in the literal sense of not caring for money, but the author is using the word figuratively. (E) relates to the author's unfulfilled desire to work on a steamboat, but the engineer is not thinking about the author, he is just showing off.

29 **D**—The engineer does everything for the purpose of showing off. He talks the jargon of the trade to make himself look knowledgeable, or (D) **sophisticated.**

Reading between the lines, we realize he's not an expert (A), and doesn't care about knowledge for its own sake (B). His (C) **ignorance** on other subjects is not mentioned; in fact, he has a working knowledge of St. Louis. (E) takes literally the phrase about how the engineer "forgot common people could not understand"—he couldn't **communicate effectively.** But the author says the engineer talked "as if" he forgot common people. In other words he didn't *fail* to communicate, he *chose not* to, to impress others.

30 **E**—The first four choices are all common meanings of *consideration*, but the context makes it clear that the figurative use in (E) is meant. The boys had "consideration" because they knew something about St. Louis, but their glory is over because the engineer knows much more. Prestige, respect, or (E) **reputation** supplies the meaning that fits. Boys are not likely to have the qualities of **generosity, deliberation, contemplation,** or **unselfishness** as a result of knowing a little about St. Louis.

31 **A**—The context makes it clear that the engineer had, or at least seemed to have, much more familiarity with St. Louis than the other boys with their "vague knowledge"; their "glory" is ended because he can talk rings around them about St. Louis (A).

There's no indication that (B) **St. Louis has changed,** or that the boys had been lying—their knowledge was "vague," not false (D). Reading between the lines, it's clear that travel to St. Louis was still rare enough to seem enviable (E). As for choice (C), the passage implies just the opposite.

32 **A**—With his "hair oil . . . showy brass watch chain, [and] leather belt," the engineer was obviously out to impress (A). The next sentence confirms that, telling us "no girl could withstand his charms."

The author never says the young man's dress is typical (B). (C) and (E) are both wrong; the emphasis here is on the engineer's charms, not the author's wardrobe or fashion ideas. (D) won't work because the engineer's behavior is as showy and superficial as his clothes.

33 **D**—As often in these questions, wrong choices give flatfooted, literal interpretations where the author is being humorous. (A) misunderstands the reference to Providence—the author is criticizing providence, not thanking it, because it has spared an "undeserving reptile," the engineer. So the author feels resentment, or (D) **outrage,** because the engineer's good luck seems **undeserved.**

Choice (B) sounds believable at first, but the passage doesn't emphasize the lucky escape—it focuses on people's sense that the engineer got better than he deserved. (C) and (E) are never mentioned.

34 **C**—The passage focuses on the author's ambition to work on a steamboat and his envy of the engineer. This makes (C) and (D) the strongest choices, so you need to decide between them. Looking at (D), the passage certainly emphasizes the engineer's **boastfulness,** but only within the framework of the author's dreams and ambitions (paragraphs one and five) and the author's reactions to the engineer. So (C) describes the *whole* passage whereas (D) describes only the long central paragraphs. In a *major purpose/major focus* question, the answer that sums up the *whole* passage will be correct.

The (A) **life** of the **town** is barely suggested. (B) is wrong because the passage's events don't end in **success**—although in reality, Mark Twain did go on to become a pilot. The author's (E) **conflict with his parents** is mentioned only briefly, toward the end of paragraph four.

35 **E**—The last paragraph discusses the author's failed attempts to become a pilot, and his daydreams that he will still become one, so (E) works best. Mates and clerks are mentioned as ignoring the author, but he never considers becoming either a (A) **mate or a clerk,** looking for some other job (B), giving up his aim of being a pilot (C), or asking his parents' forgiveness (D).

SECTION 3

The Shakespeare Pair

This paired passages present two opposing arguments on a single subject, the subject here being "Who Really Wrote Shakespeare's Plays?" The author of the first passage maintains that Francis Bacon actually wrote the plays, basing that conclusion on the assertion that Shakespeare didn't have the education and social experience necessary to create such sophisticated plays. The author of the second passage takes issue with that, claiming that Shakespeare's genius grew out of a deep understanding of human nature rather than any

wide learning or arcane knowledge.

1 **B**—A Vocabulary-in-Context question. Here we're asked the definition of the word *entertain* in line 2, where it is used in the phrase "entertain some doubt." Well, when you entertain doubt, or entertain an idea, you are holding it in your head. You are **harboring** it, in the sense of **to harbor** as "to be host to." So choice (B) is correct.

The other choices are all acceptable dictionary definitions of the verb *entertain*, but none fits the context as well as choice (B) does. (A) **amuse** is a common synonym for *entertain*, but how does one amuse doubt? (C) **occupy** and (E) **engage** are closer, but they don't fit the sentence either. One's *mind* is occupied or engaged, but the doubt itself is not occupied or engaged. Meanwhile, (D) **cherish** adds a sense of valuing the entertained thing, as if it were something desirable.

2 **D**—The author claims that the person who actually wrote the plays must have had "intimate knowledge of life within royal courts and palaces," but that Shakespeare was just a commoner, without that kind of "firsthand experience" of the aristocracy. He wants to cast doubt on Shakespeare's **familiarity with the life of [aristocrats],** or choice (D).

Shakespeare's ability to (A) **write poetically** and his (C) **ability to support himself as a playwright** never come up in Passage 1. The **knowledge of foreign places** mentioned in (B) does come up, but being a commoner is not necessarily related to Shakespeare's apparent lack of travel. Choice (E) is the closest wrong choice, since the aristocracy was the **government** in Elizabethan England, but the issue is his knowledge of all aspects of aristocratic life.

3 **E**—Two Shakespearian plays—*Coriolanus* and *Love's Labour's Lost*—are mentioned in lines 28–31 in connection with the allegedly specialized knowledge they contain. They support the point that the educated aristocrat Bacon was a more likely author than was the undereducated commoner Shakespeare. So (E) answers the question best.

Choice (A) is a clever wrong choice, but it's too extreme. The author's not trying to prove that *only* Bacon could have written these plays, just that Bacon was far more likely than Shakespeare to have written them. The **deep understanding of human** nature mentioned in (B) is something brought up in Passage 2, not Passage 1. The author is not comparing the two plays to **works written by Bacon,** as (C) claims. And (D) is wrong since nothing about society is mentioned with regard to *Coriolanus*. Also, it's not the **broad spectrum of society** the author alludes to with regard to *Love's Labour's Lost,* but rather the knowledge of just the upper range of society.

4 **A**—It's clear that Ms. Bacon is looking down on actors, of which Shakespeare was one, regarding them with the **disdain** expressed in correct choice (A).

She's not **resentful** at how the **characters are portrayed,** choice (B), since she's talking about the characters themselves and what they tell us about real-life actors. Given her opinion of actors, she certainly doesn't **regret that their conditions weren't better,** choice (C). (D) is closer, but it's a distortion. She never doubts that anyone could **create such characters;** she doubts that the author of the plays could *be like* such a character. And finally, in (E), there's no evidence in the quote that Ms. Bacon thinks the actors are inept at their art, just that they are vulgar and lowly persons.

5 **B**—This question sends you back to paragraph 4 of Passage 1, where Bacon's preference for anonymity is explained. The author claims that, because the plays were "controversial," Bacon felt that associating himself with them would have been "politically and personally damaging." So **he wished to protect himself from the effects of controversy,** choice (B).

(A) is wrong, since Bacon did publish a lot of writing under his own name. (C) is plausible, but it's not the reason given in paragraph 4 or anywhere else in the first passage. (D) tries to confuse us by introducing the subject of **lowly actors** from the preceding paragraph. And (E) is a fabrication since we know that Bacon was already famous from his other writings.

6 **C**—This question takes us to the first paragraph of Passage 2, where the emphasis is on language ability. The author doubts that Bacon, a writer primarily of academic Latin, would have had the ability to produce the exalted English in which the plays were written. That makes (C) the best answer.

(A) is a distortion. Just because Bacon wrote most of his own work in another language doesn't mean that he was **unfamiliar** with English. (B)'s emphasis on the difficult switch from **scientific writing** to **writing plays** is close, but language rather than the type of writing is the focus. There's no reason to surmise that the author doubts Bacon's ability to **cooperate** on a **committee,** choice (D). Finally, (E) is wrong because there is no evidence in the first paragraph that the author has doubts about Bacon's ability to produce that amount of work.

7 **D**—Back to Vocabulary-in-Context. This question asks about *premier* as it is used in the phrase "premier stylist in the English language." The author definitely wants to indicate the sublime language of the plays here, so *premier* is being used in the sense of "of the first rank," or, as choice (D) has it, **greatest.** (A), (C), and (E) all play on the sense of premier as "first in sequence,"(*inaugural,* by the way, means "marking the commencement or beginning") but the author is not referring here to *when* Shakespeare wrote. He's writing about how *well* Shakespeare wrote. On the other hand, (B) **influential** misses on two counts—first, it's not a definition of *premier* in any context, and second, the issue of influence on other writers is not brought up here.

8 **B**—The next Vocabulary-in-Context question concerns the adjective *encyclopedic* in line 75, where it's used to modify the noun "knowledge." The author says that Shakespeare's genius was one of common sense and perceptive intuition, not encyclopedic knowledge, which is related to great book-learning. So the knowledge described as "encyclopedic" is wide-ranging and in-depth—**comprehensive,** in other words, choice (B).

(A) **technical** is close to the sense of the context, but it's not a synonym of *encyclopedic,* so it really won't work here. (C) won't work either, since **abridged** (meaning "condensed") cannot describe the kind of exhaustive knowledge the author is describing here. And while it may take discipline to gain encyclopedic knowledge, *encyclopedic* itself cannot be defined as **disciplined,** so cut (D). Finally, (E) **specialized** isn't quite right, since it implies a narrowness of focus.

9 **E**—The reference to Shakespeare's status as a landowner comes in the third paragraph of Passage 2, where it is brought up to show that

Shakespeare would have been "knowledgeable about legal matters related to . . . real estate." That makes (E) the best answer, "legal matters" being equivalent to **the law.**

(A) is interesting, since the author does say that owning land was quite an accomplishment for a playwright, but it has nothing to do with his knowledge of the law. (B) is off, since owning land doesn't make one automatically friendly with the highborn set. (C) is wrong, because Shakespeare's financial state is just a side issue; it's not the point of bringing up Shakespeare's landowning status. And (D) doesn't fit, since no one doubts that **Shakespeare was a commoner.**

10 A—This question directs us to lines 99–102, where the author claims that literary genius "can flower in any socioeconomic bracket." That implies that genius has little to do with a person's social and financial position—or, as correct choice (A) has it—genius doesn't depend **on a writer's external circumstances.**

(B) fails by bringing in the notion of **comprehension of human nature** from elsewhere in the passage. (C) is a common cliché, but there's no evidence here that the author felt that Shakespeare's genius was **enhanced by poverty.** In fact, this author implies that Shakespeare wasn't even all that poor. (D) may be a true statement, but recognition of genius isn't really under discussion here; it's the simple existence of genius. And (E) is a distortion; the author claims that at least one kind of genius does not *stem* from **book-learning and academic training,** but that doesn't mean that those things would **stifle** *literary genius.*

11 C—Go back to the fourth paragraph of Passage 1, where our first author claims that Bacon may have "hired a lowly actor" like Shakespeare to put his name to the plays and take the heat of controversy. How would our second author respond to this claim? The second author, remember, writes in the concluding paragraph of Passage 2 that "no elaborate theories of intrigue and secret identity are necessary to explain the accomplishment of William Shakespeare." Surely author 2 would regard the **scenario** described in Passage 1 as just this kind of **unnecessary** theory, so (C) is the best guess for how author 2 would react.

As for choice (A), author 2 may or may not agree that the plays were **controversial** in their time, so (A) won't work. (B) gets the thrust of author 2's argument wrong. Author 2 denigrates the notion that Bacon wrote the plays *not* by arguing that Bacon wasn't a great scholar, but by arguing that it didn't require a great scholar to write the plays. (D) tries to turn author 1's argument on its head. A nice idea, perhaps, but author 2 shows no hint of doing anything of the kind. And (E) brings up the notion of Shakespeare's social *respectability,* which really isn't of much concern to author 2.

12 C—What would be author 1's reaction to author 2's skepticism that Bacon, the author of Latin treatises, could be the "premier stylist in the English language"? Well, author 1's repeated assertions of Bacon's scholarly genius and Shakespeare's lack of education are both reflected in choice (C), which makes it a good bet as the correct answer.

(A)'s mention of the **similarities between Latin and English** is enough to kill this choice, since author 1 mentions no such similarities in the passage. (B) is a true statement, perhaps, but it doesn't really address the issue. (D) is fairly nonsensical, since it would weaken author 1's entire theory about why Bacon hired Shakespeare. Finally, (E) makes a good point, but again, there is no hint of this sentiment in author 1's statements.

Step 1: Figure out your Verbal raw score. Refer to your answer sheet for the total number right and the total number wrong for all three Verbal sections in the practice test you're scoring. (If you haven't scored your results, do that now, using the answer key that follows the test.) You can use the chart below to figure out your Verbal raw score. As the chart shows, your Verbal raw score is equal to the total right in the three Verbal sections minus one-fourth of the number wrong in those sections. Round the result to the nearest whole number.

PRACTICE TEST A

	NUMBER RIGHT	NUMBER WRONG	RAW SCORE
SECTION 1:	☐ −	(.25 x ☐)	= ☐
SECTION 2:	☐ −	(.25 x ☐)	= ☐
SECTION 3:	☐ −	(.25 x ☐)	= ☐

VERBAL RAW SCORE = ☐
(ROUNDED)

PRACTICE TEST B

	NUMBER RIGHT	NUMBER WRONG	RAW SCORE
SECTION 1:	☐ −	(.25 x ☐)	= ☐
SECTION 2:	☐ −	(.25 x ☐)	= ☐
SECTION 3:	☐ −	(.25 x ☐)	= ☐

VERBAL RAW SCORE = ☐
(ROUNDED)

Step 2: Find your practice test score. Use the table below to find your practice test score based on your Verbal raw score.

FIND YOUR PRACTICE TEST SCORE

Raw	Scaled	Raw	Scaled	Raw	Scaled
−3 or		22	450	48	620
less	200	23	460	49	630
−2	230	24	470	50	640
−1	270	25	470	51	640
0	290	26	480	52	650
1	300	27	490	53	660
2	310	28	490	54	670
3	320	29	500	55	670
4	330	30	510	56	670
5	330	31	510	57	680
6	340	32	520	58	690
7	350	33	530	59	690
8	360	34	530	60	700
9	370	35	540	61	710
10	370	36	550	62	720
11	380	37	550	63	730
12	390	38	560	64	730
13	390	39	570	65	740
14	400	40	570	66	750
15	410	41	580	67	760
16	410	42	590	68	770
17	420	43	590	69	780
18	430	44	600	70	790
19	430	45	600	71 or	
20	440	46	610	more	800
21	450	47	610		

Don't take your practice test scores too literally. Practice test conditions cannot precisely mirror real test conditions. Your actual SAT Verbal score will almost certainly vary from your practice test scores. Your score on a practice test gives you a rough idea of your range on the actual exam.

If you don't like your score, it's not too late to do something about it. Work your way way through this book again, and turn to Kaplan's *SAT & PSAT*, our more comprehensive test prep guide, for even more help.

About

KAPLAN

Educational Centers

Kaplan Educational Centers is one of the nation's premier education companies, providing individuals with a full range of resources to achieve their educational and career goals. Kaplan, celebrating its 60th anniversary, is a wholly-owned subsidiary of The Washington Post Company.

TEST PREPARATION & ADMISSIONS

Kaplan's nationally-recognized test prep courses cover more than 20 standardized tests, including entrance exams for secondary school, college, and graduate school as well as foreign language and professional licensing exams. In addition, Kaplan offers private tutoring and comprehensive, one-to-one admissions and application advice for students applying to graduate school.

SCORE! EDUCATIONAL CENTERS

SCORE! after-school learning centers help students in grades K-8 build academic skills, confidence, and goal-setting skills in a motivating, sports-oriented environment. Kids use a cutting-edge, interactive curriculum that continually assesses and adapts to their academic needs and learning style. Enthusiastic Academic Coaches serve as positive role models, creating a high-energy atmosphere where learning is exciting and fun for kids. With nearly 40 centers today, SCORE! continues to open new centers nationwide.

KAPLAN LEARNING SERVICES

Kaplan Learning Services provides customized assessment, education, and training programs to K-12 schools, universities, and businesses to help students and employees reach their educational and career goals.

KAPLAN INTERNATIONAL

Kaplan serves international students and professionals in the U.S. through Access America, a series of intensive English language programs, and LCP International Institute, a leading provider of intensive English language programs at on-campus centers in California, Washington, and New York. Kaplan and LCP offer specialized services to sponsors including placement at top American universities, fellowship management, academic monitoring and reporting, and financial administration.

KAPLOAN

Students can get key information and advice about educational loans for college and graduate school through **KapLoan** (Kaplan Student Loan Information Program). Through an affiliation with one of the nation's largest student loan providers, **KapLoan** helps direct students and their families through the often bewildering financial aid process.

KAPLAN PUBLISHING

Kaplan Books, a joint imprint with Simon & Schuster, publishes books in test preparation, admissions, education, career development and life skills; Kaplan and *Newsweek* jointly publish the highly successful guides, **How to Get Into College** and **How to Choose a Career & Graduate School**. *SCORE!* and *Newsweek* have teamed up to publish **How to Help Your Child Suceed in School**.

Kaplan InterActive delivers award-winning, high quality educational products and services including Kaplan's best-selling **Higher Score** test-prep software and sites on the internet (**http://www.kaplan.com**) and America Online. Kaplan and Cendant Software are jointly developing, marketing and distributing educational software for the kindergarten through twelfth grade retail and school markets.

KAPLAN CAREER SERVICES

Kaplan helps students and graduates find jobs through Kaplan Career Services, the leading provider of career fairs in North America. The division includes **Crimson & Brown Associates**, the nation's leading diversity recruiting and publishing firm, and **The Lendman Group and Career Expo**, both of which help clients identify highly sought-after technical personnel and sales and marketing professionals.

COMMUNITY OUTREACH

Kaplan provides educational resources to thousands of financially disadvantaged students annually, working closely with educational institutions, not-for-profit groups, government agencies and other grass roots organizations on a variety of national and local support programs. Also, Kaplan centers enrich local communities by employing high school, college and graduate students, creating valuable work experiences for vast numbers of young people each year.

Want more information about our services, products, or the nearest Kaplan center?

Call our nationwide toll-free numbers:

1-800-KAP-TEST for information on our live courses, private tutoring and admissions consulting
1-800-KAP-ITEM for information on our products
1-888-KAP-LOAN* for information on student loans

Connect with us in cyberspace:

On AOL, keyword:"Kaplan"
On the World Wide Web, go to: http://www.kaplan.com
Via e-mail: info@kaplan.com

**Write to:**

Kaplan Educational Centers
888 Seventh Avenue
New York, NY 10106